S0-AHS-037

STAGING TOURISM

Jane C. Desmond

STAGING

THE UNIVERSITY OF CHICAGO PRESS
CHICAGO AND LONDON

TOURISM

Bodies on Display from Waikiki to Sea World

The University of Chicago Press, Chicago 60637
The University of Chicago Press, Ltd., London
© 1999 by The University of Chicago
All rights reserved. Published 1999

08 07 06 05 04   2 3 4 5

ISBN: 0-226-14375-9 (cloth)
ISBN: 0-226-14376-7 (paper)

Library of Congress Cataloging-in-Publication Data

Desmond, Jane.
    Staging tourism : bodies on display from Waikiki to Sea World /
Jane C. Desmond.
        p.   cm.
    Includes bibliographical references.
    ISBN 0-226-14375-9 (cloth : alk. paper). — ISBN 0-226-14376-7
(pbk. : alk paper)
    1. Tourism.   2. Culture—Semiotic models.   3. Symbolic
interactionism.   4. Heritage tourism.   5. Ecotourism.   I. Title.
G155.A1D4775   1999
338.4'791—dc21   99-18914
                                                                        CIP

Portions of the present work were previously published in slightly different versions: chapter
1, as "Invoking the 'Native': Body Politics in Contemporary Hawaiian Tourist Shows," appeared in *TDR: The Drama Review: The Journal of Performance Studies* 41:4 (winter 1997): 83–
109; chapter 2 appeared in *Positions: East Asia Cultures Critique;* chapter 9, in part, appeared
in *Cruising the Performative: Interventions into the Representation of Ethnicity, Nationality, and
Sexuality,* ed. Sue-Ellen Case, Philip Brett, and Susan Leigh Foster (Bloomington:
Indiana University Press, 1995), 217–36.

This book is printed on acid free paper.

Contents

List of Illustrations   vii

Acknowledgments   ix

Introduction: Touring the Essential   xiii

PART I   *Staging "The Cultural"*

INTRODUCTION
Cultural Bodies: Hawaiian Tourism and Performance   2

ONE
Let's Lū'au   10

TWO
*Picturing Hawai'i: The "Ideal" Native and the Origins
of Tourism, 1880–1915*   34

THREE
*Pictures Come to Life: Rendering "Hawai'i" in Early
Mainland Hula Performances*   60

FOUR
*Advertising, Racializing, and Performing Hawai'i on Site:
The Emergence of Cultural Tourism in the 1920s*   79

FIVE
Tourism and the Commodification of Culture, 1930–1940   98

SIX
*Surfers and "Beachboys": Euro-American Representations
of Native Hawaiian Men and Interracial Romance*   122

CONCLUSION
Up to the Present: Profiling Visitors   131

PART II   *Staging "The Natural"*

INTRODUCTION
*Looking at Animals: The Consumption of Radical
Bodily Difference*   144

SEVEN
The Industries of Species Tourism   153

EIGHT
In/Out-of/In-Fake-Situ: Three Case Studies   176

NINE
Performing Nature: Shamu at Sea World   217

CONCLUSION
Bodies and Tourism   251

Notes   267
References Cited   317
Index   331

Illustrations

following page 102

1. Advertisement, Sheraton Hotels, Hawai'i, 1996
2. Advertisement, Polynesian Review, 1995
3. Advertisement, Paradise Cove Luau, 1995
4. Germaine's Luau, 1995
5. Postcards featuring hula dancers, 1995
6. Hula, Germaine's Luau, 1995
7. Hula, Prince Lot Hula Festival, 1995
8. Postcards featuring Native Hawaiians, ca. early 1900s
9. Stereoscope photograph, pre-1900
10. Photograph of Native Hawaiian woman, pre-1900
11. Ioane Ukeke and his hula troupe, pre-1900
12. Dancers at King Kalākaua's birthday celebration, 1885
13. Postcard featuring Native Hawaiian men fishing, ca. 1909
14. Postcard featuring sailors and hula dancers, ca. 1910
15. Hawaiians "before" and "after" American influence, 1899
16. Illustration of racial types, 1880
17. Comparative illustration of "Polynesians" and "Negroes," 1880
18. Kanoa, Governor of Kaua'i, 1880
19. Sheet music illustration, 1916
20. Gilda Gray, 1925
21. "Haole Hula Girl," 1925
22. Bray troupe at the Royal Hawaiian Hotel, ca. 1930s
23. Pualani and Pi'ilani Mossman teaching hula, 1935
24. Tootsie Notley performing at the Kodak Hula Show, ca. 1941
25. Navy servicemen at a hula show, ca. 1941

26. Hawaiian show in Washington, D.C., 1946

27. Advertisement, *Travel Magazine,* 1916

28. Tourists at the Kodak Hula Show, 1962

29. Postcard featuring model with a hapa-haole look, ca. 1970

30. Dancers in the Frank Kawaikapuokalani Hewett lūʻau show, 1994

31. Merrie Monarch Hula Festival, 1996

following page 230

32. Elephant House, Budapest Zoo

33. Lion House, Lincoln Park Zoo

34. Lion's point of view, Lincoln Park Zoo

35. Viewing "nature," Lincoln Park Zoo

36. Lion Grotto, San Diego Zoo

37. Great Ape House, Lincoln Park Zoo

38. Worker building scenery, Lincoln Park Zoo

39. Snow Leopard, Lincoln Park Zoo

40. Gorilla Tropics, San Diego Zoo

41. Kelp Forest, Monterey Bay Aquarium

42. "Jellies," Monterey Bay Aquarium

43. Park ranger and visitors, Año Nuevo State Park

44. Elephant seals, Año Nuevo State Park

45. Kissing the killer whale, Marine World Africa

46. Bird show, Marine World Africa

47. Tiger show, Marine World Africa

48. Tourist souvenirs, Marine World Africa

49. Shamu photo spot, Sea World, San Diego

50. Shamu balancing trainer, Sea World, Orlando

51. Shamu launching trainer, Sea World, Orlando

Acknowledgments

What a pleasure it is to be able to say thank-you to the many people who have helped me with this work. Greatest thanks of all must go to Virginia R. Domínguez, who accompanied me on these journeys literally and metaphorically, traipsing through Marine World Africa in the freezing rain, stopping at every zoo wherever we were, and accompanying me with pleasure to innumerable hula shows, political rallies, and lūʻaus in Hawaiʻi. Not just her presence but her enthusiastic engagement with all there was to see and think about have significantly shaped this work, as has my engagement with her own intellectual work, especially its conceptual clarity in thinking about how groups come to be, come to see themselves as a group, and come to be seen by others. Above all she encouraged me to write the book I wanted to write, even when the centrifugal force of its disparate parts threatened to pull it apart.

The same must be said of Bryan Wolf and Jennifer Wicke, who, as dissertation advisors at Yale, had the flexible intellects and generosity to engage with early versions of these ideas even as the ideas got farther and farther from their own areas of work. This book is significantly different from that dissertation, built on new archival research and fieldwork in Hawaiʻi over the period 1993–96, and I hope they will take pleasure both in what has changed and what has remained the same as this work has undergone the crucial metamorphosis from dissertation to book.

There are other debts, too, less specific but just as important, and they have to do with my own transition from being a dancer and choreographer to being a scholar. For their stimulating presence and implicit support I thank my former colleagues at Duke University, who encour-

ix

aged me through the at-times schizophrenic artist/scholar double life when I was simultaneously a scholar-in-residence in dance on the faculty there and completing a Ph.D. at Yale: Jan Radway, Marianna Torgovnick, Barbara Dickinson, Jane Gaines, and Jean O'Barr all made more of a difference than they may have known. Similarly Bobby Allen, professor of American Studies and film at U.N.C.–Chapel Hill, who stimulated my early interest in film theory, which lead to my decision to become a scholar, has encouraged and prodded now and then at just the crucial times.

My parents, Dorothy Ann Garfield Desmond and Alton H. Desmond, never saw a split between artistic work and scholarly endeavor and encouraged both from the very beginning. Given the strict disciplinary divisions that divide the arts and scholarship in most other realms, that conviction from early on has proven essential to all I have tried to do. It was a remarkable and very unusual gift, for which I thank them.

I often get teased when people find out I work in Hawai'i—such a hardship, they say, with knowing envy. They are right, of course. While the interest in the work grew out of a single two-week "vacation" in 1990, every trip back since then has proven illuminating and challenging. I could not have taken on this work without the generosity of both intellect and spirit of many involved in the hula community in Honolulu. I am profoundly grateful to them for having the patience to answer my questions and for welcoming me as a serious student of hula. To master teacher, *kumu hula*, Noenoe Zuttermeister I owe a great debt of thanks for the privilege of studying beginning hula in a six-week intensive course during the summer of 1994 at the University of Hawai'i. Noe's depth of knowledge and extraordinary dancing were both a profound pleasure to be exposed to and a source of great delight to me as I returned to dancing every day after having retired as a modern dancer in 1986. Other members of Noe's classes, including Pat Couvillon, Noreen K. Hong, and Carol Yamaguchi, beautiful dancers and thoughtful commentators, helped me better understand contemporary hula practices and were patient and welcoming of my beginning efforts to learn.

Kumu hulas Vicky Holt Takamine, Manu Boyd, Earl Pa'Mai Tenn, and Kimo Alama Keaulana all consented to do formal interviews with me, and I am grateful for their time and willingness to share their knowledge and opinions. In addition, noted hula experts Pat Namaka Bacon and Adrienne Kaeppler helped me through their conversations, as did musicologist Rick Trimillos and former dancer Dovie Borges. Many other hula students and *kumu hulas*, including Frank Kawaikapuokalani Hewett and the students in Amy Ku'uleialoha Stillman's Hawaiian music class at the University of Hawai'i in the summer of 1994, spoke to me about hula in more casual conversations, and from them I learned much about what is important in the islands. To Amy Stillman I am especially grateful for allowing me to sit in on her music class, from which I learned a great deal. But, even more, I am thankful for a summer's worth of conversations about things Hawaiian and the complexities of learning about and writing about Hawaiian cultural practices. I am thankful too for the access the Sheraton Hotels gave me to their uncatalogued archive, allowing me to rummage through boxes of old publicity photos. My thanks also to B. J. Hughes, then director of public relations at the Sheraton Waikiki Hotel, and to Christina Kemmer, former president of the Waikiki Improvement Association, for granting me interviews and providing materials about the business community in Waikiki. These conversations, only some of which will find their way directly in attributed quotes into the body of the book, were essential to my understanding of hula and tourism. The opinions expressed here, unless directly attributed, represent my own interpretations.

A big debt for anyone doing historical research goes to archivists— and I send enthusiastic thanks to the staff of the Bishop Museum Hawaiian archives for their cheerful assistance—whether on site or with later long-distance requests. Thanks, too, for sharing their knowledge with me, especially to Stuart Ching and DeSoto Brown, as I tried to decipher dates and places from unmarked photographs and postcards.

Geoff White and Monty Lindstrom provided an invaluable opportunity by selecting me to participate in a 1993 National Endowment for the Humanities summer seminar for faculty on politics of the Pacific. From them and from the other participants, especially Vince Diaz and Tamar Gordon, I learned a lot. The grounding in wider issues of cultural politics of the Pacific region proved to be invaluable, as I threw out everything I had written earlier on Hawai'i as part of the dissertation and began completely anew. Geoff has continued to send clippings, videos, and much aloha through the mails and to provide important support, including office space at the East/West Center in Honolulu, during the summers of 1994 and 1995. To him and the former staff of the Program in Cultural Studies, my deepest thanks for facilitating this work.

Also in Honolulu, I thank Ken Redman, director of the Honolulu Zoo, for sharing his own materials with me and for taking time to do a formal interview as well. Similarly, I am grateful to John Spafford of Sea World in San Diego for his time in an interview and for letting me watch Sea World videotapes of early Shamu shows.

Institutional support—both time and money—has made a crucial difference. A University Dissertation Fellowship from Yale helped early on. A paid leave from the University of Iowa, accompanied by an appointment at the wonderful Obermann Center for Advanced Studies of the University of Iowa, made a significant difference. So did the work of several research assistants at Iowa, including Mike Lewis, Kevin Quirk, Jillian Duquaine, Hakan Dibbel, and above all the magnificent historical sleuthing of Florence Tonk, whose thoughts and enthusiasms for the project helped sustain my will to write when teaching and administrative responsibilities threatened to overwhelm the urge. Also from the University of Iowa came a significant research grant from the Central Investment Fund for Research, which funded six weeks of research in Honolulu during the summer of 1995. I thank them for not thinking Waikiki couldn't possibly be a legitimate research site and for recognizing that conducting work in "paradise" is expensive, as Honolulu residents know well.

Cathy Davidson, Richard Schechner, and members of the women's studies faculty at the University of Iowa (Susan Birrell, Florence Babb, Anne Donadey, Margery Wolf, Laura Donaldson, and Jael Silliman) all made helpful comments on an early draft of chapter 1, and Kathleen Newman and Ralph Cintron read the whole book in draft, offering generous helpings of two important gifts, encouragement and criticism. I thank them for their insights. I thank also the reviewers for the University of Chicago Press, especially Janice Radway, whose engagement with this work helped me to sharpen its arguments during the final stages of writing.

Few scholarly authors can get away with thanking their pets in a formal acknowledgments section, but I'm lucky that the subject of this book demands it. To my feline companions, Mocha and Pumpernickel, the extraordinary beings whose physical evidence covered every draft as they sat on me, the computer, and the manuscript, your presence and unconditional affection has encouraged me to cross the species barrier in this book.

Introduction: Touring the Essential

The genesis of this book came from a sense of shock: shock at how ubiquitous live performance and bodily display are in certain tourism industries and at how much money these industries generate. Many, many people are willing to pay a lot of money to see bodies which are different from their own, to purchase the right to look, and to believe that through that visual consumption they have come to know something that they didn't before. And indeed, certain types of knowledge are purveyed. But I argue in this book that the ultimate lesson we can take from these bodily geographies and the huge economies of which they form the lynchpin is that much more than the ethics of entertainment are at stake.

From Shamu the dancing whale at Sea World to Hawaiian lūʻau shows, this book analyzes issues of bodily display in a wide range of tourist venues. I argue that the public display of bodies and their materiality (how bodies look, what they do, where they do it, who watches, and under what conditions) are profoundly important in structuring identity categories and notions of subjectivity. And that, when commodified, these displays form the basis of hugely profitable tourism industries.

The origins of this visual and kinesthetic basis of codifying "difference," on which tourism relies, reach back to the late nineteenth century (with antecedents much earlier), when the nexus of visual representation, popular performance, anthropology, and bodily "sciences" like craniology came together to produce a popular, "scientific" ethnographic gaze. This mode of knowledge proposes that cultural difference is represented by and understandable through direct observation of "specimens." It is coupled with a conceptual system which maps species, peoples, and races into typologies based on bodily difference—type of hair, arms, or flippers, black or white "blood."

Despite a century of change, including the rise of academic anti-essentialist, social constructionist arguments (coincident with the development of anthropology and more recently with poststructuralism), I propose that these presumptions, sometimes in their most simplistic form, are still with us, as the following chapters will detail. This is true even though the forms such conceptual maps render may have changed somewhat. For instance, tourism has changed; the design of zoos has changed. Postcolonial politics have remapped the globe. Race talk has in some cases been transmuted into "ethnicity," and species collection has been renamed conservation and species preservation. "Identity" has replaced some earlier labels of affiliation, like race, but retains, at end, notions of biological bases that seem impervious to change, just as notions of species difference now seem (to the general public at least) not provisional taxonomies, but irrefutable statements of relationships between various types of beings.

What I have been most profoundly struck by in this work is the intractability of the notion of the "body" as that which is really "real," a repository of truth. I term this epistemological function "physical foundationalism." In common discourse, bodies function as the material signs for categories of social difference, including divisions of gender, race, cultural identity, and species. Bodies, seen as "natural," can naturalize these systems of thought in a tightly braided union which proposes the following: bodies are "natural," bodies are different from one another, typologies of difference are natural, and what is natural is necessarily right or "true."

Critical race theory has begun to articulate the intransigence of physical foundationalism in terms of the category "race." Feminist thought has long ago named this as a problem and continues to chip away at physical foundationalism relative to "gender." But my work purposely looks outside those spheres of classification: first, by analyzing the production of "cultural difference" (a category seemingly *not* based on physical difference) and, second, by crossing the species barrier to a realm where "race," "culture," and "gender" are not the acknowledged categories of difference. In doing so, I have been struck by how ubiquitous are the ways that bodies function implicitly as the final authenticators of identity categories. In numerous realms of thought, and not just the obvious ones, bodies are the epistemological equivalent of "the buck stops here."[1]

We remain tied to a late nineteenth-century idea/ideal of the "real," dependent on the body to anchor systems of knowledge that articulate social difference. Sometimes those conceptions of social difference form the bases for armed conflict—as in Bosnia, where in recent clashes Serbs battled Croats, or in Rwanda and Burundi, where Tutsis fought Hutus—but more often they operate in less obviously dramatic ways. This book examines bodily anchored differences as the bases for two huge moneymaking industries. I call these "animal tourism" and "people tourism."

Included in "animal tourism" are safaris, animal documentary films, zoos, animal theme parks, nature parks, and much of ecotourism. "People tourism" refers to "cultural tourism," leaving home (even if that just means going outside your own neighborhood) to encounter cultural practices different from whatever you conceive your own to be, done by (and this is the important link) people who are "different" from you. This type of presentation of difference, in the form of physical enactment, often takes the form of song-and-dance tourism, just as the newest theme parks and even the most modern zoos include animal "shows" where watchers can *see* the animals doing something. The nonverbal and basically non-narrative aspects of these shows underline the centrality of the performing body, binding notions of "facticity," presence, naturalism, and authenticity together under the sign of spectacular corporeality.

Live performers not only authenticate these packaged differences; they also offer the possibility of contact with them. The co-existence—in the same time and place—of the audience and the performers is essential to these industries. Unlike *National Geographic* or PBS nature shows, both of which support similar constructions of knowledge, in tourist shows, the "real" people, or in the case of the animal industries, "real" animals, are there to be seen, heard, met, and usually literally touched in some way. This might be in the moment of making a souvenir photograph of a tourist in the light embrace of a costumed dancer before a lūʻau, or through audience participation in Sea World shows. Boundaries are temporarily crossed but ultimately reconfirmed.

Such face-to-face encounters produce a safe sublime—a literal enactment of what is metaphorically a broader merging between past and present, here and there, "them" and "us." These shows stage the "them," the specificity of difference, whether that be the cultural specificity of particularly marked bodies in Waikiki (the presentation of "culture" as that which is always already "raced") or the physical mass and power of an orca whale splashing the audience on cue. Simultaneously, these shows stage the "us" in contradistinction to the "not-us" on display. A temporary collectivity among tourists unites strangers in the same space and time through a shared experience. In the cases considered in this book, that "us" is predominantly middle class Euro-Americans.

Through these techniques of staging the natural, the audience gets a show of (and is shown) the culture of the natural world (i.e., its distinctive, unique, and "essential" characteristics) in much the same way tourists attending folkloric shows see a performance of "traditional" (i.e., "naturally occurring") behaviors which celebrate the difference and particularity of the performing group. Spectacle—an emphasis on sights, sounds, and motion—replaces narrative, and with it the possibility of historical reflection. The social, political, and economic histories which brought performers and spectators together in the same space are either entirely absent, re-presented as nostalgia, or recoded as cultural or natural conservation.

Factors of force, domination, and hierarchy necessary to the divide between performers and audience are either naturalized or rendered invisible. The status quo is validated. Erased, too, is the social history of such displays over the last century, a history which once brought together flora, fauna, and humans from specific parts of the globe in world expositions of imperial might and which now has given rise to two separate spheres of tourism, one for animals and the other for people, still from specific parts of the globe and not others.

I am not proposing that all tourism or even all tourist shows conform to these models. Tourism travel by Euro-Americans to the big cities of Western Europe—Paris, London, Rome—may also evoke nostalgia, but it is not generally the Edenic naturalism associated with trips to Hawai'i. In the continental United States, some cultural tourism, like performances of clog dancing at Dollywood, Dolly Parton's mountain themed park in Tennessee, also present a slightly different ideology. The valoration of a simpler, more authentic life is parallel, as is perhaps a primitivizing discourse ("mountain folk"), but the whiteness of the audiences and the performers provides a potential bond of sameness rather than difference.[2] Each site, each audience base, each set of staging techniques and marketing campaigns must be closely analyzed on its own. In these analyses, increased attention to the centrality of the body in marketing, staging, and audience reception is necessary if we are to better understand the powerful attraction and huge ideological impact that these industries have.

SITUATING TOURISM RESEARCH

As is apparent from the preceding description, this book stands at the juncture of several scholarly approaches. It intersects with debates in cultural studies and performance studies focusing on bodies, performativity, and the generation of social meaning. It is also indebted to the new wave of humanities and social science scholarship focusing on tourism, reminding us, in Dean MacCannell's words, that "tourism is not just an aggregate of merely commercial activities; it is also an ideological framing of history, nature, and tradition; a framing that has the power to reshape culture and nature to its own needs."[3]

Scholarship on tourism takes on a new urgency when we realize that by 1984 international tourism was already the second largest item in world trade and that the U.S. Office of Consumer Affairs estimates that travel and tourism will be the largest industry in the United States by the year 2000.[4] Hawaiian tourism alone already generates $11 billion a year, and roughly 40 percent of U.S. adults go to zoos, aquariums, and wild animal parks each year—making "animal tourism" a huge industry as well. While no absolute aggregate figures are available, it is likely that the two tourist industries I consider in this book generate a combined income in the range of tens of billions of dollars.[5]

To approach a topic of this scope, I have united historical research with multisited ethnography and have taken the relatively unusual approach of working across tourism categories (cultural tourism, ecotourism) while retaining a focus on bodily display. I use the term "ethnography" primarily for its connotations of participant-observation as a methodology. In my work on Hawai'i, which forms the basis for part 1 of the book, research was conducted on site over a period of several years, with many stays of several months complemented by shorter trips for particular events. Observation, participation, and innumerable informal conversations and formal interviews of people involved in hula and/or tourism were supplemented by archival research.

Since I am not primarily writing an "ethnography" of hula (in a more traditional sense of a description of the community involved), but rather presenting an analysis of tourist performances with an emphasis on mainlander consumption, most of the conversations and observations are not reported explicitly. In some cases this choice has been made in deference to the complicated politics of the situation and in appreciation of those who spoke their opinions frankly to me without expectation of having those opinions made public. Such fieldwork, even in the attenuated way in which it is explicitly represented in the following chapters, has been crucial to my understanding of the current situation and has in turn deeply informed my framing of the historical analyses as well.

In terms of the animal research presented in part 2, rather than spend extended periods in one site, I made numerous visits to many sites throughout the country where animals were on display, thus replicating the common forms of consumption. At each site I participated in as many activities as were offered to tourists, including "behind-the-scenes" tours, film presentations, animal rides, and so on. These sites (in many different states and regions) included animal theme parks, large and small zoos, ecotourism boat rides, circuses, aquariums, and roadside attractions visited between 1992 and 1996. Video and still photography supplemented on-site notes about tourists' behavior, performers, and exhibit design. And formal interviews and informal conversations with zoo professionals and animal trainers provided additional information. Only a few of the sites receive extended analysis in the following chapters, but again, my thinking has been shaped by the full range of animal tourism that I have encountered.

Through these approaches, I try to specify the ways in which tourist experiences are actively constructed by the industries themselves—through specific strategies for advertisement, stagings, narrations, and choreography, for example—while simultaneously sketching the wider social contexts and ideological frameworks through which tourists negotiate the meanings of these experiences. I hope such an approach encourages further research on tourist industries as crucial arenas of public culture where embodied notions of identity are sold, enacted, debated, and occasionally contested.

For all its massive scope, tourism remains relatively undertheorized. In fields where ideological analysis is popular (among them, cultural studies, American studies, postcolonial studies, and literature), relatively few scholars have devoted themselves to tourism research. A majority of those writing about tourism come from the social sciences and take a more quantitatively oriented sociological approach, producing vast amounts of information about who travels where, work which appears in journals like the *Annals of Tourism Research*.

Among those producing qualitative research, few are concentrating on tourist shows. Anthropologists have often focused on negative impacts of contact between "hosts" and "guests," changes in arts production for the tourist market, or economic shifts in local communities. Literary scholars have concentrated mostly on travel literature, not the actual practice of tourism or its infrastructural bases. Social historians have more often analyzed immigration than the temporary population shifts of tourist travel. Also, little contemporary research on animal-based industries is being done, although increasingly humanities scholars are writing about historical relations between humans and animals.[6] There is, however, a vast literature on ethology, the study of animal behavior, mostly anchored in the hard sciences or the quantitative social sciences. Environmental writings with humanities-based perspectives more often concentrate on issues of land and landscape than on human-animal interactions. There are exceptions to all these generalities, but they amount to a relatively small number of works out of a vast array of research literature.[7]

In contrast, I have tried to combine analyses of the historical conditions which gave rise to the present situations, of the infrastructures of the industries, of the specific construction of the shows, and of ideological work done by the shows, all with attention to the common theme of bodily display. In this way, my work is most in conversation with that of theorists like Barbara Kirshenblatt-Gimblett, Dean MacCannell, David Whisnant, and John Urry, all of whom have offered ideological readings of certain aspects of tourism. Building on that work, I am proposing a more embodied conceptualization of tourism and of tourists and underlining the need for greater specificity in situating acts of tourist consumption within a wider frame of the historical relations between specific groups of consumers and the places and populations they visit.

MacCannell's breakthrough 1976 book, *The Tourist: A New Theory of the Leisure Class*, melding Marxist analysis with semiotics, offered very useful concepts of the sacralization of sites, the staging of "constructed authenticity," and the notion of noncommodifiability as a true marker of the authentic.[8] The shows and exhibits I discuss here all conform somewhat to MacCannell's model of "staged authenticity." Such an idea is operative, for example, at Marine World Africa animal theme park in California, where animal shows are framed as "extensions of natural behaviors." But, above all, I argue here, it is the physical presence of *some* bodies, not others, which functions as the ultimate grounding for these notions of the "authentic."

In zoos this means the display of "genetically pure" specimens. For example, in the late 1980s U.S. zoo directors found to their dismay that several lions they had been displaying and breeding as Asian lions were actually, genetically, Asian/African hybrids (246 out of 333 animals). Breeding was immediately stopped, so that "the hybrid species will be eradicated," and they will be "managed . . . to extinction through attrition" as old animals die.[9] In the lūʻau show it means casting dancers who, for mainlanders, fit a physical stereotype of the "Hawaiian native." The political and personal subjectivity of the performers (for instance, the lūʻau dancer who declares he is "100% Samoan and proud of it!") evaporates under the pressure of such "physical evidence." On display, MacCannell suggests, such bodies become both signs and signifiers of themselves.

Barbara Kirshenblatt-Gimblett, one of relatively few theorists to write about the staging of live performers in tourism, develops this last point in her discussion of folk dance, festivals, and the history of live "ethnographic" displays. "Live displays," she writes, "whether recreations of daily activities or staged as formal performances, also create the illusion that the activities one watches are being done rather than represented, a practice that creates the illusion of authenticity, or realness. The impression is one of unmediated encounter. Semiotically, live displays make the status of the performer problematic, for people become signs of themselves."[10]

We must clarify the equation to read: the performers become signs of what the tourist audience believes them to be. This is exactly what happens in big Hawaiian lūʻau shows, when performers become signs of Hawaiian "natives" whether or not they themselves have any Native Hawaiian ancestry. This belief, based, I will argue, on an unproblematized collapsing of "racial" categories into "cultural" ones, is underwritten by a whole variety of related discourses, including the long visual history of the development of the "hula girl" as a tourist icon. The big commercial shows do little to disrupt these preconceptions, a necessary component of which is the tourists' ignorance of the social and political history of the islands.[11]

A specific mode of looking characterizes these patterns of consumption, one John Urry calls the "tourist gaze." Although this looking varies somewhat in different historical periods, it is always performed in contradistinction to everyday looking—it looks at "difference," differently. As Jonathan Culler notes, the "tourist is interested in everything as a sign of itself."[12] Thus a tiger's body at the zoo becomes both a sign for a tiger ("Oh, look, there's a *tiger*!") and an example of one ("Look, there's a *real* tiger!").

While stressing the wide variety of potential objects of the tourist gaze (landscape, "townscape," an ethnic group, historical artifacts), Urry proposes that tourist gazes can be divided into two broad types: the romantic and the collective. The "romantic" form of the tourist gaze emphasizes "solitude, privacy and a personal, semi-spiritual relationship with the object of the gaze," often found in the contemplation of nature. The second mode of looking, the "collective" tourist gaze, "necessitates the presence of large numbers of other people," also engaged in tourism, so that the atmosphere takes on a sense of carnival, that "this is the place to be and that one should not be elsewhere."[13] What unites these two types of gazes and the vast variety of objects, locales, and activities which can make up their objects, argues Urry, is not just a search for something, anything, "authentic." "A crucial feature of tourism," writes Urry, is that "potential objects of the tourist gaze must be *different* in some way or other. They must be out of the ordinary. People must experience particularly distinct pleasures which involve different senses or are on a different scale from those typically encountered in everyday life."[14] Throughout these investigations, I try to uncover just what some of these distinct pleasures are and why ultimately they are so attractive to those who engage in them.

The tourist audiences sitting shoulder to shoulder on bleachers at Sea World in San Diego, or rubbing knees under the lūʻau table in Hawaiʻi, are for that moment collectively constituted as fun seekers, as learners, as participants, as witnesses to that which is outside their everyday routines.[15] The naturalizing discourse encompassing both the cultural shows and the animal shows unites the romantic gaze with the collective gaze, linking a more solitary rejuvenating contact with "the natural" through its collective celebration. In doing so, it facilitates the white, middle-class tourists' experience of themselves as a collective "other" from those whom they are watching. This is part of the pleasure being sold. To better understand this experience, we need a more fully embodied concept of the tourist, expanding the notion of the "tourist gaze" to include other embodied aspects of experience (movement, sound, touch, and so forth) both in the physical and imaginary realms.

For my formulations of these wider contexts, other writings on bodies and conceptions of culture have also proven useful: for example, Donna Haraway's unique work on bodies and biologism, as well as Emily Martin's writing in related areas have been influential. A new surge of performance studies writing that energizes dance criticism with questions of gender and race has also provided part of the context for these investigations, as has Foucault's discourse analysis of embodied histories like *The History of Sexuality*. Equally important has been the self-reflexive move in anthropology during the last fifteen years, which has brought poststructural concerns to the practice of ethnography with books like Clifford and Marcus's *Writing Culture: The Poetics and Politics of Ethnography* and the feminist critiques of that work which have extended it further. Other work on the deployment of "culture" in the service of social collectivities, such as Benedict Anderson's notion of "imagined communities," Hobsbawm and Ranger's work on the "invention of tradition," and critical studies of museum exhibition practices, have also proved relevant, as have theories of visual perception drawn from media studies and art history.[16]

Combining theoretical and methodological approaches from both the humanities and social sciences, I track the force of bodily essentialism in two realms, dividing the book into two parts. Part 1 analyzes the historical development of the tourist industry in Waikiki, with special attention to the importance of staging "Hawaiian culture." I argue that the female hula dancer, "iconicized" as the "hula girl," has emerged as the most ubiquitous symbol of Hawaiian culture, and that the purveyance of this symbol and the marketing of live performance are central to the Hawaiian tourist industry. Beginning with an examination of the earliest manifestations of organized tourism in the islands at the turn of the century, I demonstrate how performances of the hula girl became firmly entrenched as part of the tourist experience by the 1930s. And I analyze exactly what this image of a representative body came to look like and how she came to signify "Hawaiian-ness."

I unpack the assumptions about race and culture that engendered this symbol and its performative rendition "in the flesh" in the form of hula shows, both on the mainland and in the islands. I argue that the female hapa-haole (half-Caucasian) "look" emerged as a sign of the "ideal native," which simultaneously differentiated Hawai'i from other sites of imaginary "primitivism" and from racial divisions on the mainland between Caucasians and African Americans. I show too how hula for Native Hawaiian populations and for non-Native or part-Native "local" populations is both similar to and quite different from that promulgated by the tourist industry. Indeed, even within the tourist industry visual images and live performative renditions of Native Hawaiian culture sometimes exceed the dominant meanings.

By combining on-site participation, observation, interviews, analysis of public discourse, and performance analyses with archival research in the islands and on the mainland, I try to show two things: (a) how history is actively written out of the tourist industry representations and commodifications of Hawaiian culture and (b) how bodily representation and bodily presence function instead as the guarantors of historical authenticity, the claim to "authentic" difference on which cultural tourism is based.

The second half of the book crosses the species barrier. I wanted to see what would happen if I looked at issues of "identity" but in realms normally not included in such discourse: not race, not gender, not class, not ethnicity, not nationality, but species. Historically, animal tourism and cultural tourism are related. Zoos and certain types of cultural tourism both share historical origins in colonialism and in the concepts of natural history which undergirded colonialism. Difference, represented by bodily difference, became the basis of typologies of both animals and peoples. This intensified in the decades of the late nineteenth and early twentieth centuries. At the same time that stereoscope pictures were being sold in Europe and the United States in sets of world tours cataloguing "exotic" people and places, civic leaders were building zoos as part of constructing a "modern" public culture. Notions of a "natural" world and a "primitive" one were both placed on display as necessary counterpoint to the late nineteenth-century Euro-American sense of "modernity."[17]

Contemporary cultural tourism replaces talk of race with talk of culture but retains the earlier notions of particular races' giving rise to particular cultures. Race becomes the authenticating ground of cultural specificity, sold in cultural tourism through the live performance of real (fill in the blank: Hawaiian, Native American, Amazonian) "culture" by "real" (i.e., biologically "correct") inhabitants or, to use the most revealing name, specimens.

This is precisely the conceptual thinking that structures zoos today despite the significant shifts in design from the early barred cages to the elaborate habitat designs that strive to show species in relation to one another and to a wider ecological habitat. In the chapters on animal tourism, I examine the history of zoo design to track the implicit changing/unchanging conceptions of animal subjectivity that it reveals and to see how the visual encounter between animal bodies on display and human bodies as audience is staged. I look at some of the "big ticket" animals that almost all U.S. zoos need to succeed, like lions, tigers, and elephants, the remnants of European colonial "booty" from Africa and India. Then, just as I decided to look across the species boundary, I look outside these central mammalian displays—offering three case studies of fish bodies and sea mammals to better understand how bodily difference and its categorization into species hierarchies are elaborated and sold. I develop a framework of "in situ," "out-of-situ," and "in-fake-situ" ways of displaying animals and dissect what each implies about the corporeality of the animal on display. Finally, in the chapter which ends this section of the book, I look carefully at the choreography of the Shamu show, the killer whale performance at Sea World of San Diego, to see how the grafting of concepts of difference between humans and animals (the cultural and the natural) is enacted in the water and ultimately based on implicit assumptions about differences between groups of people.

In drawing comparisons between animal tourism and cultural tourism, I am not suggesting that viewing Hawaiian tourist performances is just like viewing animals in a zoo. I am not saying that complicated subjectivities are reducible to bodily evidence, although this is precisely what the epistemological structures of these industries imply. Nor am I saying that bodily differences are merely epistemological tropes to be overcome, that a jellyfish is really no different from a whale, that animals and humans are exactly the same. Nor am I saying that histories of genocide and animal annihilation are irrelevant predecessors to tourism, and we should just investigate the rhetorical structures of tourism that transpose such histories into nostalgia for a utopian past instead. My interest throughout is in understanding how bodily differences are marked, calibrated, measured, and mobilized politically to naturalize various social relations and how these operations are both constituent of and constituted by certain types of tourism.

To support my arguments, I have included many illustrations in this book. In doing so, one always runs the risk that they will be perceived as merely reinforcing the very operations of physical foundationalism that I am writing against. Nevertheless, I feel that such evidence provides an essential part of my argument and that we can understand the power of such images only by engaging with them. Many of the images were originally produced by the tourist industries—old postcards of hula dancers, travel brochures, photographs for magazines, and so on. Other photographs are contemporary, many taken by myself on site to indicate something of what the tourist sees standing in front of a zoo exhibit or walking down the street in Waikiki. As snapshots, they duplicate the tourist practice of archiving sights seen. I urge readers to note their own reactions to the illustrations. How do you encounter them? Do you scan the image for bodily clues of authenticity? If the image seems authentic or powerful, why? How do you react to the site of a leaping Shamu surrounded by thousands of clapping fans? Our own reactions are clues to the ways such images operate. I hope that the power of the text and the visual power of the pictures will collide in a way that illuminates both.

In the concluding section of the book, I consider the implications of my research for further work on tourism and try to imagine what alternative modes of tourist shows might look like. I suggest the need for a more embodied concept of tourism and of the tourist as consumer, and for greater specificity in analyzing how particular acts of touristic consumption contribute to a sense of social citizenship. Ultimately I hope that this study of tourism persuades readers that physical foundationalism is with us now as much as it was a century ago, that it still makes a lot of money for some people and not for others, and that as long as we are unaware of its force in shaping contemporary discourse, political configurations, and even our own anti- essentialist postmodernist artistic and scholarly interventions, we will remain in its grip even as we strive to envision new cultural and political forms for the twenty-first century.

Part I **STAGING**

"THE CULTURAL"

Cultural Bodies

Hawaiian Tourism and Performance

In the late nineteen fifties I was growing up outside Washington, D.C. Vividly, I remember dancing around in the living room one day until I crashed into a side table and left a dent in the wall. The song was "The Hukilau" ("Oh, we're going to the hukilau, hooki, hooki, hooki, hooki, hooki, hukilau . . ."), and the record was my parents'—hits from the radio show *Hawaii Calls*. I don't recall exactly what rendition of the hukilau I was attempting, but it was probably a seven-year-old's version of waving arms and wiggly hips. Already in my mind some vision of hula was associated with the islands. The dent in the wall is still there, and my involvement with hula has come full circle. When I made my first trip to Hawai'i in 1992, more than thirty years after the hukilau mishap, I was amazed at what I saw. Hula seemed to be everywhere, and somehow I knew so many of those songs, like "Little Grass Shack." I sat in the audience at the Don Ho show with the oddest sense of déjà vu, watching hula dancers and, like everyone else in the audience, singing along with "Tiny Bubbles." (Yes, he was still singing it thirty years later!) How, I wondered, did this indelible association of hula with Hawaiian tourism come to be? And why?

Returning from that first brief trip, I found myself thinking more and more about this question. What had been intended as a vacation became a passionate inquiry. It intruded itself into my other work, and soon took over. Many other trips followed during the next several years, some brief, to catch a specific festival, and several others many months long. As a former professional modern dancer, I was eager to begin the study of hula and was able to do so with a superb *kumu hula*, or master teacher. An unexpected bonus was the great joy I felt at being back in a dance studio again. Through an intensive six-week summer session of daily classes,

2

followed by weekly lessons whenever I was in Honolulu, I began to see something of what the dance meant to those involved in it. In Honolulu I talked to hula students, to professional dancers, to musicians, to *kumus*, and to managers in the tourist industry. I watched hula festivals, elite hula competitions, recreation center shows, rehearsals, first performances of kids on shopping mall stages, spontaneous hula renditions at local bars and at outdoor music concerts, at *hālau* (hula school) fund-raisers, at Hawaiian sovereignty rallies, on the local cable channel, and everywhere else I could find hula. Public lectures, chant demonstrations, and discussions by *kumu hula* sponsored by museums, universities, and the Office of Hawaiian Affairs helped me get a sense of some of the current debates within the hula community, as did the patient explanations that many experts and practitioners generously offered in private conversations.

I paired this participant-observation learning with historical research. At the Bishop Museum Archive in Honolulu I looked at every image in their hula file of photographs and postcards, paged through dancers' scrapbooks, and watched videos. The Sheraton Hotel, one of the largest chains in the islands, let me rummage through their boxes and boxes of uncatalogued memorabilia, looking for information on early guests and performances. In libraries in Honolulu and on the mainland I traced records of old performances and performers, tracking advertisements, oral histories, reviews, and journalistic articles to piece together a historical sense of multisited public discourse about Hawai'i and hula.

At the same time, I participated as fully as possible in the wide range of activities promoted for tourists. I collected brochures, read guidebooks and promotional material, took bus tours and lei-making classes. I visited souvenir shops to catalogue material representations of Hawaiiana, purchased "how-to-hula" videotapes, and danced along in free tourist lessons in shopping malls. And of course I watched many, many tourist shows, noting the audience and their behaviors as carefully as I did the events on the stage.

The complexity of hula practice, its vibrant, ubiquitous, multifaceted presence on the islands and its century-long rendering on the mainland, began to come into focus. The present and the past, the tourist and nontourist formulations, the mainland and the island renditions, took on a generative relationship, mutually informing, sometimes overlapping, at times contradicting. I began to look at the tourist industry's commodification of hula, its insertion into a cash economy of performances by insiders for outsiders, within this larger context of local relationships and of the social and political histories of relations between the islands and the U.S. mainland.

The centrality of performance and the importance of live (predominantly female) bodily presence in the success of the Hawaiian tourist industry stood out in relief and raised several important questions for me: Why is no other tourist destination so unequivocally associated with a dancing figure.[1] How has this bodily rendering, in both visual representations and live performance, been central to and enabling of the associations perpetuated by the tourist industry? What is its social history? How has it changed over the years? What is the "physical evidence" of the female hula dancer evidence of? What can an examination of hula and tourism in Hawai'i tell us about the commodification of cultural difference and how it is intimately linked with and articulated through notions of race, gender, and physicality? And, more generally, how has the performative display of "different" bodies been central to the rise of tourist industries in the twentieth century? The answers to these questions begin to take shape in the first three decades of the twentieth century, although their roots reach much farther back.

By the late 1920s, tourism had become an established industry in the islands. A formal system of tourist infrastructure—hotels, travel companies, a tourist service bureau, special tourist publications, new, vigorous advertising on the mainland, and so forth—had replaced the more haphazard services rendered to visitors during the nineteenth century. For the first time the islands aggressively sought visitors. Leading businessmen organized to lure them and to serve them on site. By the end of the second decade, tourism ranked third in the amount of income generated, after the pineapple and sugar industries.

By the 1930s, components of cultural tourism were fully integrated into the tourist experience, and live performances of hula were situated right in hotels. But before that happened, representations circulating on the mainland (visual, written, and song-and-dance renditions) generated particular notions of a Hawaiian "native." These early discourses shaped later public reception of live performances, which boomed on the mainland and then in the islands during the period from 1915 until World War II, as I will discuss in following chapters. By World War II, the ideological components of today's tourist industry were firmly in place. One of these components figures Native Hawaiians as "ideal" natives who are graciously welcoming to outsiders and who present visitors with a nonthreatening, alluring encounter with paradisical exoticism, a "soft primitivism," to borrow Bernard Smith's phrase.[2]

In the chapters that follow, I demonstrate how at the end of the nineteenth-century imperial expansion, "scientific" discourses of race, and visual representations combined to produce this notion of Native

Hawaiians as "ideal natives" and set the stage for the rise of tourism to the islands. Throughout these discussions I will use the term "Native Hawaiian" to refer to those of indigenous ancestry, and the term Hawaiian "native" to refer to the Euro-American imaginary about indigenous islanders. The social and political conditions for the emergence of this sign are the same as those for the emergence of tourism as an organized industry: imperial expansion combined with bourgeois desires for contact with the rejuvenating primitive.[3] But, despite a generalized Anglo-Saxon longing for primitives, not just any primitive would do. Hawaiians occupied a special position in this Caucasian imaginary at the end of the nineteenth century.

From the beginning, this enabling discourse of the ideal native was "raced" and "gendered" in particular ways: female, not male, and "brown," not "black," "yellow," or "red." Combined with ideologies of colonialism, these ideas can produce imaginaries that merge the feminine and the exotic. As Marianna Torgovnick notes, what is "typical indeed of Western thinking about the primitive [is] the circularity between the concepts of 'female' and 'primitive.'"[4] This looping and doubling is an essential component of capitalism, where, Judith Williamson argues, "the sphere which is supposedly most different from the capitalist system is crucial to it."[5] Women become a preserve of the natural and leisure arenas.

"Woman is an island," Williamson writes, because "she is . . . a place to take a holiday; but she is also an island within ideology . . . held intact as the 'Other' within a sea of sameness. . . . Femininity is . . . a package tour of the natural."[6] In the first years of the twentieth century, capitalism's commodification of feminized leisure in the form of tourism unites the "islands" of woman, "exotic primitivism," and Hawai'i in this package tour of the natural, held together under the sign of the "hula girl." This sign simultaneously symbolizes bodily presence ("native," "woman") and cultural enactment (Hawaiian-ness), and stands for the "destination image" of Hawai'i.

The destination image, as Kye-Sung Chon has noted, is that set of visuals and ideas associated in the tourist's mind with a particular locale, and it acts both as a lure for potential customers and as a framework for perception and evaluation of the tourist's experience once she or he is on site.[7] Destination images result not only from publicity materials but also from other circuits of representation, including news stories, pictures, songs, historical narratives, literary descriptions, cuisine, fashion, and so forth.

From the 1880s until the teens, Hawai'i's destination image was shaped mainly by visual and verbal representations. Live performances outside the islands were rare.[8] Postcards, photographs, and stereoscope cards contributed to the circuit of images, as did sketches in advertisements. Further visual representations of Hawaiians adorned everyday commodities like canned goods, playing cards, and serving trays. Educational articles and documentary and scientific reports also circulated in public discourse, contributing to the generation of the destination image, the outlines of which had been laid out during the preceding century by European explorers' reports, missionary diatribes, and writers' encomiums, like those of Robert Louis Stevenson and Mark Twain. Both of these writers visited Hawai'i and popularized visions of the islands through mainland newspaper reports and numerous stories. Twain, looking nostalgically back upon his 1866 visit, wrote in 1889: "No other land could so longingly and so beseechingly haunt me, sleeping and walking, through half a lifetime, as that one has done."[9] Counterdiscourses generated among Hawaiians and others in the islands sometimes contested these romanticized nineteenth-century representations, but they rarely circulated on the mainland.

Each historical period over the last century has figured the otherness of Hawai'i slightly differently, especially in relation to mainland discourses of race and nation. Even so, the contemporary tourist industry still bears the traces of this originary period at the turn of the century despite the rise of mass tourism since the 1960s, the Native Hawaiian "cultural renaissance" of the 1970s and 1980s, and the strong anticolonialist sentiments of some branches of today's Native Hawaiian sovereignty movement. Hawaii, as a tourist site, is still represented as the home of ideal natives, who are still represented ubiquitously by the figure of the dancing hula girl.

Key developments during the period 1900–1930 demonstrate the emergence of this raced and gendered figure in tourism discourse. In the earliest period of the fledgling tourist industry, natural features of the islands, like volcanoes, were most heavily promoted. The place, not the people, predominated. However, the figure of the hula girl first appeared in advertising in the teens, and, by the twenties, images of Native Hawaiians and specifically hula iconography had become an integral part of tourist promotions. The use of these images would increase in later decades.

A second key development was an increase in live performances as a part of the tourist experience.[10] Native Hawaiian culture becomes commodified and enacted through dance shows as a way of authenticating the destination image. Hula shows join a set repertoire of tourist activities (including auto tours, golf, surfing, and lū'aus) promoted by advertising, guidebooks, and hotel management. By the late 1920s hula performances were brought right into the hotels and contracted by management, a practice that expanded in the 1930s. The physical, visible presence of Native Hawaiians was, from these early decades, a constitutive part of tourism discourse. Hawai'i, once promoted as a lush tropical site full of marvelous scenic wonders, now became promoted as a lush tropical site that was the home of Hawaiians.

This early move toward cultural tourism was crucial, as it set up the possibility of distinguishing Hawai'i from other potential tropical tourist sites (i.e., a way of providing product distinctiveness in the industry). Culture, embodied in the physical presence of natives, can be used to distinguish one surf-and-sand destination from another. The embodied aspect was important. Racial discourses of the period provided crucial linkages of body (race) and culture, which was conceived of not only as a set of social practices but also as a marker of moral, intellectual, and ethical development for a whole people. Both body types and the cultures associated with them were arranged in complex hierarchical typologies in contemporary racial discourse. Unfailingly, Caucasians/Europeans appeared at the apex of such systems. In these hierarchies produced by Caucasians, the Native Hawaiians were judged intellectually, morally, and physically superior to most other non-European groups.

Construction of this ideal native stereotype grew out of a specific nexus of U.S. colonial expansion, racial discourses of the time, and conceptions of U.S. nationhood. Hawaiians emerged in these discourses as brown (not black, not Asian), and as primitive (but delightfully so), not modern. These racial concerns were linked to assertions of nationalism—how and in what ways Hawai'i, taken over by the United States in 1893, was just the same as the rest of the United States, and how and in what ways it was different. Nationalism, figured as white, troubled by blackness, grappled with the challenges of encoding Hawai'i's racial polemics and complexity within a model of nationalism that could barely contain them.

During the first three decades of the twentieth century, tourist advertisements, postcards, and popular journalism articulated these pressures in particularly striking ways. They ignored almost completely the complexity of Hawai'i's demographics. The last half of the nineteenth century and the beginning of the twentieth saw huge waves of immigration to the islands as the plantation systems expanded. Large numbers of Chinese, Portuguese, Japanese, and Filipinos immigrated and sometimes intermarried with Hawaiians and European-Americans. Yet tourist advertisements portrayed Hawai'i as an Edenic playground for urbane Caucasians, a playground inhabited solely by Native Hawaiians. Non-Hawaiians, non-northern Europeans, and those of mixed descent remained invisible even though they formed the largest segment of the population by that time.[11]

Hawai'i, peopled by Native Hawaiians, thus emerges as a site of white Edenic regeneration. A concerted effort was made to represent Hawaiians as living in the past, as romantic savages who co-existed with the contemporary sophistication and modernity of the visitors and their accommodations in Honolulu. The presence of the Native Hawaiians, who along with nature, were conceived of as timeless and unchanging, was a necessary counterpoint to the modernity of the tourists' lives; indeed such modernity was represented by their difference from it. As an analysis of popular discourses will show, active processes of denying the contemporaneous presence of Natives are necessary to produce this divide between Native Hawaiians and mainlanders. For example, photos of Hawaiians from the past (in grass houses, bare-breasted hula dancers) were often used to represent Native Hawaiian life in the present even though the accompanying written text denied that such scenes still existed.

Women hold a special relation to this configuration of modernity, as Torgovnick and Williamson have argued. In the case of Hawai'i, implicit parallels between Caucasian and native women occur in songs, on the stage, and in advertisements. This nativized the white women, "whitened" the Hawaiian, and, in general, feminized Hawai'i as a destination site. By the 1915–30 period a vision of the "hapa haole" (a person of half-white, half-Hawaiian descent), epitomized by the half-white hula girl, emerges as the ideal, literally embodying the fantasy of the nativizing trope, melding the two bodies into one. In today's biggest contemporary commercial lūʻau shows, this look still predominates.

Underpinning these analyses is my contention that the interplay between specifically marked bodies (perceived as always already marked in terms of sex, of race) and their enactment of marked behaviors (i.e., behaviors denoting affiliation with a particular group) fuels the process of social categorization and that this process of social categorization is necessary to and commodified by Hawai'i's tourist industry. The tourist industry sells Hawai'i tautologically: Hawai'i is a place where Hawaiians live and do Hawaiian things, like hula. Such determinations only become meaningful by taking a racialized, bodily concept of identity as the starting point for calculating the meaning of performative actions.

In the tourist arena, the complex dialectic between bodies and their actions is usually, but not always, weighted toward physical determinism. Bodily identity is seen to precede and determine the meanings of performative actions. In the next chapter I discuss these operations in terms of the body politics of contemporary tourist shows. I then look back a hundred years to trace historical developments on the mainland and in the islands to show how this linkage of cultural commodification with bodily display came to be, arguing that by the eve of World War II, the prime ideological components of today's tourist industry were already well in place.

ONE

Let's Lū'au

ong before they disembark from the plane, Hawai'i's visitors have encountered the image of the "hula girl."[1] She is predominant in advertising, along with images of sea, sun, surf, and sand, and the unique topographical outline of Diamond Head etched against a moonlit sky framed with tropical palms. Through a century of visual representations on or in everything from canned goods to Hollywood films, her body has come to signify a complex of associations with the "soft primitivism" inseparable from today's Hawaiian islands.[2]

Take, for example, the 1993 glossy brochure produced by the Hawaiian Visitors Bureau which invites you to "COME TO LIFE IN HAWAI'I." A map of the Hawaiian islands is studded with photos of natural beauty, such as mountain landscapes, deserted beaches, and the smiling woman on the cover holding a flower lei and wearing a huge red hibiscus behind her ear. She stands in front of a profusion of green leaves, midriff and shoulders bare, as if just emerging from the tropical rain forest to receive us and to help us "come to life" in Hawai'i. On the back of the brochure is a similar image of a woman dancing the hula in a ti-leaf, or "grass," skirt. The text invites us to "experience the beauty of nature . . . the sights and scents of tropical flowers . . . tradewinds [that] enhance the romantic, natural setting."

The final paragraph clinches the associations of hula and Hawai'i as it proclaims: "The image that is most associated with Hawai'i is of a beautiful woman clad in a hula skirt. She offers a lei, plays the ukulele or dances the hula. The hula expresses what words often cannot through the poetry of movement. It remains that sunshine gesture of olden days and its traditions are still thriving in today's performers." Native Hawaiian scholar and dancer Momi Kamehele critiques this "little brown gal" stereotype: "Images of brown-skinned women with soft, dark eyes, teasing smiles and supple hips, stimulated within the tourist the sexual attraction of the female Hawaiʻi. This image has become the definition of Hawaiian women in general, and of Hawaiian hula dancers in particular."[3]

Embedded for the U.S. mainlander in a web of vague associations with the South Pacific (even though Hawaiʻi isn't in the south), the European-derived cultural imaginary of Polynesia subtends the hula girl symbol and reaches back two hundred years to the first encounters of European voyagers and islanders. Over those two centuries a rich European and Euro-American cultural imaginary has fed upon and produced a variety of manifestations by non-Hawaiians: explorers' reports and sailors' sketches, missionary denunciations, anthropologists' descriptions, novels, plays, fashion designs, wallpaper images, Aloha shirts, and mass media images like films, the television show *Hawaii Five-O,* and *Hawaii Calls,* the internationally broadcast radio show that reached into millions of homes in its heyday in the 1950s.[4]

Such European and Euro-American discourses of primitivism are, as Marianna Torgovnick has argued, infinitely malleable and respond to the sociopolitical needs of the societies that produce them, not to those they purport to describe.[5] From the 1700s on, notions of primitives as noble or savage permeate literature and historical accounts about the Pacific, serving either as an ideal model for a lost Edenic past or as a fearful vision of human nature run amok without the constraints of (European) "civilization." Bernard Smith's term "soft primitivism" describes the former category, connoting such attributes as: childlike, libidinous, free, and natural as opposed to violent, dangerous, irrational, and out of control.[6] With the exception of some missionary denigrations, Hawaiʻi and Hawaiians have emerged during the two hundred years since contact with whites as exemplars of European soft primitivism's imaginary of an Edenic ideal. While there are some shifts in this image historically, the more remarkable thing is its durability.

As Torgovnick notes, "Sooner or later those familiar tropes for primitives become the tropes conventionally used for women."[7] Native Hawaiian scholar and activist Haunani-Kay Trask specifies these links between imperialist visions of soft primitivism and gender: "Hawaiʻi— the word, the vision, the sound in the mind—is the fragrance and feel of soft kindness. Above all, Hawaiʻi is 'she,' the Western image of the Native 'female' in her magical allure. And if luck prevails, some of 'her' will rub off on you, the visitor."[8] Trask's "soft kindness" is key. The hula girl is sexy, yes, but never aggressively so. The innocence associated with the Edenic trope prohibits knowing, aggressive deployment of sexual allure, making the hula girl nonthreatening to men and women alike and associating her more with sensuous heterosexual romance than with sex per se. With her dark hair, bare skin, grass skirt, beckoning smile, and graceful gestures over swaying hips, the hula girl image evokes the feminized lushness of the tropics: accessible, hospitable, beautiful, exotic, and natural.

It is this broader web of associations with Hawai'i that the tourist industry builds upon in its advertising campaigns. A destination image, as they say in the tourist business, is the sum of all of these popular associations with a place.[9] Advertising, like television ads or the above brochure, focuses and particularizes the destination image, activating a desire to visit the islands.[10] Analyzing the Hawaiian Visitors Bureau advertising campaigns from 1972–92, John Goss summarizes the constellation of ascribed attributes as: alterity, paradise, marginality, liminality, femininity, and aloha. This is what is being sold.[11]

The figure of the barefooted, grass-skirted hula dancer encapsulates all of these qualities and ties them to cultural distinctiveness. This cultural distinctiveness is what distinguishes Hawai'i from competing vacation beach sites closer to the mainland, such as Puerto Rico or Jamaica, or on the mainland, like California and Florida. And most importantly it does so through the repeated iconographic linkage of a specific physicality (the body of a Native Hawaiian woman) with specific cultural practices (hula) and traits (aloha). In this discourse of alterity, bodily difference parallels and functions as authenticating evidence of *cultural* difference.

For the Caucasian mainlander tourist, who forms the bulk of the industry, there is an important racialized subtext to this embodiment of difference. Hawaiians are portrayed as neither black nor white. The significance of this presumed racialization in the visitors' imaginary is that it helps to manufacture and "authenticate" at the bodily level a sense of "exotic" difference while escaping from the tendentiousness of the black/white dichotomy that most powerfully frames racial discourse and fuels discord on the mainland.[12] The resulting soft primitivism proffers a gentle, sensuous encounter with difference, different enough to be presented as "alluring" but not threatening, of which the hula girl's body is metonymic.

This racial subtext is important because by far the dominant category of Hawaiian tourist is the Caucasian U.S. mainlander.[13] The white mainlander may be upper class or working class, but the mass tourist industry caters to the vast middle class that forms its core. The second most populous tourist group in Hawaiʻi is from Japan, with Japanese visitors accounting for slightly less than two million of the six million visitors annually. Owing to language differences, Japanese tourists often travel in large tour groups, stay in Japanese-owned hotels, eat at Japanese restaurants, and are catered to by Japanese-speaking tour services. They stay largely inside a Japanese bubble in Waikiki and are not visible in large numbers at the commercial lūʻaus that will form the core of this discussion, although some dinner shows do put on special performances catering to Japanese visitors. Given cultural differences in bodily perceptions and the Japanese consumption of Hawaiʻi as "American," my remarks here cannot be presumed to apply equally to the Japanese tourist.[14] Unless otherwise noted, it is the experiences of Euro-American middle-class tourists that I will analyze in this chapter. Other populations, including small numbers of African-American and Asian-American tourists, may also have significantly different experiences.

PRODUCING THE DESTINATION IMAGE ON SITE

The destination image described above successfully lures six million visitors a year to the islands and is crucial to the islands' economic survival.[15] The tourist industry is the leading source of income for the state, generating $11 billion a year in revenue, representing a quarter of Hawaii's gross state product and employing nearly a third of all workers.[16] As such, tourism's economic indicators, like room occupancy rate, number of visitors per month, length of stay, per-capita expenditures while in the islands, and so forth, are a leading topic of discussion in daily newspapers and in business and governmental offices. At the heart of the industry lies Waikiki, that segment of Honolulu on the island of Oahu where most visitors stay, perhaps leaving only for a bus trip to the World War II *Arizona* Memorial at Pearl Harbor Naval Base or a trip to a lūʻau staged out of town.

A tourist "ghetto," Waikiki is a rectangular strip of highly developed land geographically bounded by the ocean on one side, the Ala Wai canal on the other. Its ends are indicated by the huge green expanse of Kapiolani Park on the east and the forty-five degree angle made by the Ala Wai canal near the massive site of the Hilton Hawaiian Village hotel complex on the west. Traffic is concentrated on two main one-way streets, Kalakaua Avenue, which runs right by the ocean, and Kuhio Avenue, one big block further *mauka*, or toward the inland mountains. On the beach are the most expensive hotels, the Halekulani, the Royal Hawaiian, and the Sheraton Moana Surfrider, along with the Sheraton Waikiki, the Outrigger Reef, and Hilton Hawaiian Village, and several others. Prices go down as the accommodations move inland, which range from large complexes like the Hawaiian Regent to tiny walk-ups on side streets. Traffic is jammed, as tour buses navigate the streets crowded with strolling tourists shopping for bargains and vacationers celebrating their freedom on shiny red mopeds. High-rise hotels block the horizon, and tee-shirt vendors and handbill hawkers clog the corners.

This is a far cry from the pristine beaches and romantic privacy for lounging couples that many advertisements imply.[17] Andrew Ross has argued that this tension is constitutive of tourist sites promising both "modern" living and "ethnographic" actuality. A highly developed infrastructure provides the luxury, while a "primitivist superstructure" freezes and spectacularizes cultural difference.[18] While Ross is writing about "Third World" tourism in general, the situation is more complicated in Honolulu. As a major cosmopolitan city of nearly three-quarters of a million inhabitants, including a significant number of "Fourth World/First Nations" people, and as part of the United States, Honolulu is not easily reduced to the status of Third World. However, the dependence of the tourist industry on invocations of rural Native Hawaiian past life, and its primitivizing of contemporary inhabitants, demand extra ideological work in managing this tension. Rural peacefulness must be recreated within the tourist bubble in the form of shows, while the urban crowded scene is rewritten and sold as "excitement"—the excitement of lavish lobbies in the big hotels, of nighttime glitter in restaurants and nightclubs, and daytime activity—shopping, diving, snorkeling, surfing, submarining, hang gliding, or sightseeing.[19]

The tension between the urban setting of Waikiki and the invocation of a nonurban "paradise" that subtends most visions of Hawai'i is further modulated by the selling of Hawaiiana. Markers of Hawaiian-ness customize the urban "touristscape" in large and small ways. The performative symbol of the hula girl encapsulates the destination image and sits at the center of what might be conceptualized as a series of concentric circles opening out to less specific and less tangible representations of Hawaiian-ness. These circles of consumption are most concentrated in the commercial lū'au, which presents live dancers, and will be discussed in detail in the next section. Other circles expand to include free renditions of Hawaiian music and dance in public spaces like shopping malls, as well as the iconography of hotel decoration, and employee uniforms and interactions.

For tour groups flying in from the mainland, tour company personnel, usually young, attractive "local" men and women dressed in tropical print uniforms, wait with a skein of orchid or carnation leis draped on their forearms, ready to welcome each visitor in the promised traditional lei greeting.[20] In the upscale hotel lobbies, dramatic six-foot-high flower arrangements of torch ginger and birds-of-paradise remind the visitor that she is in a tropical paradise. Palms blow in the cooling breezes of the trade winds, and hotel personnel wear aloha shirts (patterned cotton shirts in floral designs) or similar dresses. "Tropical" drinks function as tiny doses of "exotica," festooned with pineapple wedges and paper umbrellas and mixed with coconut milk. Open-air architectural styling blends the indoors and outdoors on the street-level approaches of hotels, and rattan furniture and koa-wood decor enhance the sense of tropicalness in many hotel designs.

Public areas are decorated with statues and pictures of Hawaiians, like portraits of the past monarchy hanging in the Royal Hawaiian Hotel or photographer Kim Taylor Reece's sepia-toned images of bare-breasted but lei-bedecked hula dancers, ti-leaf skirts swinging and hair blowing in seascape winds, which decorate the Sans Souci dining room at the Kai'mana Beach Hotel. Hotel menus feature island specialties like poi pancakes, papaya chicken salad, and seared opakapaka, along with teriyaki chicken and kalua pig. Sound systems pipe in island music, or live musicians serenade guests at late afternoon happy hours in poolside bars and cafes.

"Hawai'i" is encoded in the service staff clothing, visual decor, breezes, brilliant flowers, and the smells, tastes, and sights of the hotel industry. Dean McCannell calls this process "reconstructed ethnicity," that is, "the maintenance and preservation of ethnic forms for the persuasion or entertainment not of specific others . . . but of a 'generalized other' within a white cultural frame."[21] In the tourism industry these reconstructions are packaged in large and small containers—from the paper umbrella on a mai tai to the megashows and performance installations at the Polynesian Cultural Center.

This creation of "Hawai'i" is a conscious effort, as signaled by the advent of the "Keep It Hawai'i" campaign sponsored recently by the Hawaiian Visitors Bureau (HVB).[22] Such a campaign reveals the anxiety about "losing" Hawaiian-ness, which is defined as a complex of place, people, behaviors, and beliefs, especially the aloha spirit, associated with a rural, precontact past but persisting in the present and yielding "a magic that eludes other islands." As a promotional brochure for the campaign puts it: "As Hawai'i continues to blossom in an ever-expanding tourist industry, it's quite possible that these attributes could get lost in a maze of high-rise towers and souvenir shops. If that happens, Hawai'i becomes just another island chain in the sun. And if we're the same as other resorts that are closer and less expensive, why would anyone come here?"[23] In 1997, the HVB Keep It Hawai'i "best of show" award went to American Hawai'i Cruises for their Aloha Festivals/ Hawaiian Heritage theme cruises, cited for "making the most significant contribution to the preservation of Hawaii's culture." These interisland cruise packages feature instruction and demonstration of Hawaiian dance and music by some of the leading proponents in the islands.[24]

Increasingly hotels are offering doses of Hawaiian culture as part of their hotel services, but this is not a new strategy. The opening of the lavish Royal Hawaiian Hotel in 1927 featured a staged pageant representing and commemorating the landing of Hawaiian King Kamehameha I at the same beach nearly 100 years earlier.[25] Staged by Princess Abigail Kawananakoa, it featured a large cast of warriors, hula dancers, and standard bearers and was decreed a great success, a "colorful and semibarbaric pageant" suitable for such an auspicious opening. At the Royal, hula lessons were made available to wealthy guests from all over the world, and the Royal Hawaiian Girls Glee Club serenaded guests on the lawn at dinnertime and provided hula dancing shows as well.

Today, to keep the destination image sharply delineated, hoteliers are adopting a number of different strategies to foreground Hawaiian culture. The Japanese-owned, U.S.-managed Sheraton Waikiki, for example, offers free historical "timewalks" tours to its guests, provides Hawaiian-theme activities for kids, arranges for craftspersons to sell their wares on the entrance patio, and even has brought educational exhibits like "Ka Lei" (The Lei), developed by the Bishop Museum, right into its lobby, complete with display cases, captions, and placards. The Sheraton has also "adopted" (their word) a local hula hālau (troop)— providing a guaranteed number of paid performances per year. They even bus local children to the hotel to perform. All totaled, the Sheraton Waikiki spends nearly a million dollars a year on hotel entertainment and has more than seventy performers on the payroll.[26]

The venerable Ala Moana Hotel recently introduced a new program designed "to offer guests a chance to learn about the Islands' unique culture through a variety of displays and demonstrations." On Fridays and Sundays the Moana's neocolonial style lobby is turned over to demonstrations of lau hala weaving and displays of leis, hula implements, and malos (loincloths). The hotel has developed an ongoing relationship with Kamealoha Hula O Ka Pu'uwai Hula Hālau O Mapuana. And on Maui, the well-respected and very popular kumu hula and singer Keali'i Reichel was invited in 1995 to use the Maui Intercontinental Hotel as a rehearsal site for his dancers, so that "live" culture would be integrated into the physical space of the tourist sphere.[27]

Live cultural shows provide the most concentrated dose of Hawaiiana. Tourist shows depend on unstated racializing discourses to produce their single-note concepts of cultural difference, and the bodily presence of certain live dancers (and not others) serves as a guarantor of the authenticity of this cultural difference. Such performances are the perfect vehicle for cultural tourism both in Hawaiʻi and elsewhere. They literally "show" culture to the audience, a process that depends on a conceptual linkage of notions of "*Kultur*" as the arts with "culture" as a way of life. As cultural artifacts, songs and dances are believed to be representative of and, since expressive, to be specially revealing of, a culture or a people (both of which are conceived of as unitary things). They are portable and can be brought to the audience, unlike other cultural practices which are less easily detached from their broader social and physical contexts. Music and dance, already familiar to mainlanders both as art forms and as a popular type of entertainment, are easily accessible to an audience. Their commodification and consumption are easy, expected, and accepted. A "culture," "a people," "a song," "a dance," all become interchangeable, commodified signs.

In addition, shows provide a sanctioned public arena for this type of consumption, for looking, for staring, with pleasure. Their spectacular aspects—sound, movement, colorful costumes, lighting, stage design—all appear to provide access to some sort of cultural knowledge without requiring special preparation or verbal comprehension on the part of the audience. In a sense tourists are already constituted as audience even before they embark for the islands; they are ready to "see" Hawaiʻi. Once there, they literalize that act of seeing by becoming part of an audience. That exchange between performers and audience provides a special lived experience, a safe encounter with a different culture, one of limited duration and with pre-set boundaries for interaction. (In Waikiki, shows are an industry unto themselves, contributing an estimated $50 million a year to Hawaiʻi's economy.)[28]

The lūʻau is paradigmatic of these shows. As early as the turn of the century a guidebook for tourists noted a commercially available lūʻau. By the 1930s such "cultural" aspects of tourism were fully integrated into the tourist experience. Today, commercial lūʻaus are big business.

MAPPING PERFORMANCES

There are two main commercial lūʻau companies in Honolulu: the Paradise Cove Luau and Germaine's Luau, which offer dinner shows seating hundreds every night of the week. There are also smaller operations, including a weekly lūʻau at the Hilton, and twice a week at the Hale Koa, a military hotel in Waikiki. According to my rough calculations, the two largest operators might average, say, 350 people per night, seven nights a week at Germaine's, and at least 500 per night, seven nights a week at Paradise Cove. That puts the combined total at nearly 6,000 visitors, spending an average of $45 per adult, yielding approximately $270,000 per week, before expenses. On a yearly basis, the take might be $13.5 million, with 300,000 visitors participating. Still, this is a small portion of the roughly six million visitors per year, only about 5 percent of all visitors.[29]

But the lūʻau itself is only one instance of the multiple Hawaiian performance viewing opportunities, actively sought or casually encountered, that are presented to the tourist. Additional Hawaiian shows include the ever-popular and free Kodak Hula Show on Tuesday and Thursday mornings in Kapiolani Park, the Brothers Cazimero show, formerly at the Royal Hawaiian Hotel and more recently the Bishop Museum, and numerous Polynesian shows that include a lot of hula along with other forms of dancing, such as the Sheraton Princess Kaiulani Hotel's Polynesian Spectacular, the Don Ho Show, and the Magic of Polynesia (which combines spectacular magic acts with Polynesian-style entertainment). In addition, the Polynesian Cultural Center, an hour or so outside of Honolulu, draws millions of visitors a year to its theme park–like recreation of Polynesian villages.[30]

All of these shows, with the exception of the free Kodak Hula Show, are expensive. With prices running around $35 for a show and one watery mai tai, much more if dinner is included, the shows represent a (hopefully memorable) night out on the town during a vacation. These shows remain very popular, often booked by tour-group operators, even though they must now compete with non-Hawaiian theme nightclub shows like the female impersonator spectacular "Boylesque" or "Legends in Concert," a Las Vegas–style show with impersonators of famous stars, like Elvis and Madonna.

Even if the tourist chooses not to fork out a lot of money to attend one of the Hawaiian or Polynesian shows, she or he stands a good chance of running into Hawaiian music and dance for free. In the gigantic Royal Hawaiian Shopping Mall on the main street in Waikiki, the Polynesian Cultural Center offers daily "miniconcerts" of music and dance, and the tourist can also find free hula lessons by the well-respected *hā lau* Hula O Maiki, along with lessons in lei making or ukulele playing. On weekends, a torchlighting ceremony and hula performances may be presented free for tourists at the Queen's Surf Beach at the eastern end of

Waikiki's main drag. For the dinner-cruise set, hula and Hawaiian music are often featured on board.

Hotels like the Sheraton Waikiki feature free poolside entertainment—various hula *hālaus* and musical groups—as the sun goes down, hoping to draw hotel guests back to their premises to spend money on dinner and evening entertainment. Bars and restaurants also feature Hawaiian music and often dancers as well. For the price of an (expensive) beer, a tourist might hear the popular group Kapena play at the Hawaiian Regent Hotel or see hula on the veranda at the Moana Surfrider Hotel. Wherever there is contemporary Hawaiian music, dance is likely to follow, if not by contracted performers, then by local residents in the audience, professional or not, who might be enticed to perform.

Part of the industry's reason for supplying top-notch Hawaiian entertainment in these settings is to bring local residents down to Waikiki. One of Waikiki's business relations professionals notes that residents add to the "authenticity" of the show and of the tourist's experience.[31] The group targeted here is "locals," the umbrella term most often used in the islands to indicate local residents of Native Hawaiian, Japanese, Chinese, Filipino, and Portuguese descent, in any of the complicated hereditary combinations that are extant in the islands. Most often "haoles," Euro-American residents who are not genetically mixed with any of the above groups, are not included in this label.[32] The business community's desire to bring locals to Waikiki can thus be seen in terms of providing a visual, physical backdrop of difference for the white mainlander which supposedly enhances his or her experience of exotica.

Even if the visitor somehow manages never to see any performing renditions of Hawaiiana, the outer circle of surrounding iconography will reinforce the association of hula performance and Hawaiian-ness. Artistic sepia-toned photographs decorate hotels with windblown Hawaiian maidens dancing by the sea, gift shops feature hula girl postcards and notecards, and a line of "Island Girls" calendars provides a "soft-porn" version. Even the smiling locals employed as service personnel in the hotel will reinforce to some extent for mainlanders the melding of physical difference and Hawaiian-style aloha that is associated with the hula girl image.

When all of these possibilities for encounter with the performance of Hawaiiana are taken into account, the probability is that most visitors to Waikiki will experience this enactment of Hawaiian-ness framed by the touristic discourse of soft primitivism and feminized sensuality. The literal consumption of Hawaiiana is laid bare most dramatically in the large commercial lū'au, the centerpiece of which is the dancing hula girl.

Germaine's Luau

Lū'au is not a tourist-only activity.[33] People living in Hawai'i have lū'aus, simple or fancy, for special occasions—to celebrate a wedding or a child's first birthday. But unlike the social occasions and social networks that ground local lū'aus, the tourist version revolves around consumption: of foods, sights, sounds, and a lot to drink. Both of the main lū'au companies claim to be authentic lū'aus. The companies gather patrons at hotels all over Waikiki and then drive them thirty miles to the west, past suburbs and industrial parks to a beautiful beach site, where a stage and platoons of long tables have been set up. Entertainment— singing, joking and, above all, dancing—is at the heart of the experience. But before the on-site entertainment begins, the tourists are "warmed up" by the bus driver and host or hostess on the hour-long bus ride from the city. The continual patter also has the effect of distracting tourists from the view of suburban tract housing, industrial sites, and multilane freeways that are inimicable to the tourist experience of Edenic Hawai'i. The bus becomes an extension of the tourist bubble of Waikiki until the tourists can safely be deposited at the beach site owned by the lū'au company.

The first two lū'aus I attended, I drove myself. It was only when I took the bus out to Germaine's in the summer of 1995 that I realized how much this "captive time" was a part of the experience for the vast majority of lū'au attendees. "Captain Bob" somehow managed to drive the huge bus through multilane highway traffic while cracking (bad) jokes and gesturing nonstop. The key theme was: "hang loose" and enjoy yourself. The organizing subtext was sex. For instance, while instructing the bus of adults in how to make the Hawaiian "hang loose" hand sign (pinky and thumb up, rest of fingers folded in), Bob cautions, "If you do it wrong, ladies, you'll have five big Hawaiian guys following you around all night . . . and, men, if you do it, you too will have five big Hawaiian men following you around!" Bob tells us that this is a "home-style backyard lū'au" that we are going to, a "real touchy-feely show," and the touching and feeling starts right after we get on the bus. Bob instructs us to raise our right hands and put them on the shoulders of the strangers sitting in front of us and give them a little back rub, then "look them deep in the eyes and tell that cousin your name and where you are from."

The instructions in enforced intimacy with strangers and the permission given to indulge ourselves in freedoms rarely taken will be themes that are stressed throughout the night. So too will the fake sense of *ohana,* or family ("Can you say the word *ohana?*" asks Bob, and of course we all repeat it back in the school-kid style of call and response), that structures the rest of the show. In this spirit of *ohana* we will be collectively addressed as "family" and "cousins" by the master of ceremonies (MC) at the show all night.

As soon as we arrive at the beach cove, the subtext of heterosexual sex and romance as the essence of the islands is staged. We line up to have our pictures taken (available for purchase after the show). But, first, we have to give a (complimentary) lei to our companion, along with the traditional kiss on the cheek. Only a man and woman can participate in this ritual, apparently, so the man from the couple in front of me is drafted to kiss both me and my female companion as he presents us with leis. This is only the first kiss from a stranger that I will receive tonight.

After the commemorative photos, people drift toward the bar or they stand in line to have their picture taken with a man or woman from the show, dressed in a costume associated with one of the Polynesian islands. Plastered smiles are repeated again and again by the performers as one tourist after another jumps into their embrace and cameras click. Photos mark the encounter with "the exotic," here made tangible in "native" bodies, and reproduce it as evidence and remembrance in the form of a souvenir.

A half-hour show before dinner continues the hang-loose warm-up that started on the bus. Tahitian drums explode in a cascade of sound as the handsome MC shouts, "It's party time! Aloooooooha!" He looks a little like an Elvis impersonator, in his mid to late twenties, with a dark pompadour hairstyle and long sideburns, dressed in a red-and-yellow aloha shirt and dark pants. Greeting the five hundred people there that night, he introduces himself as "Keikilani," although given the distortion of the sound system my hearing of his name may not be accurate. He runs us through a series of exercises to "get us more comfortable" now that we are in the "hang loose capital of the world." For the next half-hour, under the pretext of developing *ohana* and aloha, hundreds of men and women, from teen through grandparent, but predominantly twenties through forties, will kiss one another, cheer, shout, laugh, and in some cases make fools of themselves on stage.

Touching and kissing strangers come to the fore again. "Ladies," says Keikilani, "do you want to feel loved, wanted, appreciated, and respected tonight?" The key is for men to give the "*honi-honi,*" built on "*ha,*" the breath of the spirit. Demonstrating on a female volunteer (Christine, from San Francisco), he tells the men to approach each woman very gently, inhale, "*ha,*" and kiss her on the cheek. Now, "share a *honi-honi* with every woman at your table, no nibbling!" And, remarkably, everyone in the audience does this. There is absolutely no way, short of direct rudeness, for either a man or woman to refuse. For the second time that evening, I am kissed by two more strange men.

Following a brief hula lesson, where fifty female volunteers from the audience follow along (badly) to the still popular *hukilau* song, it is time to extend this *honi-honi* concept into the "world-famous kissing line." Male audience members line the sides of the stage, each receiving a kiss from the fifty women, one by one. Another hula-by-amateurs segment follows this gargantuan enactment of heterosexuality, but this time it is more directly played for laughs. Three male volunteers are stripped of their shirts, don coconut-shell bras and fake grass skirts, and improvise a hula, competing for the prize, a Germaine's Luau tee-shirt. "Ever do this dance before?" asks the MC. "Ever do it again?"

Almost all tourist shows incorporate some version of this teaching-the-tourist-to-dance motif, usually playing on the awkwardness of the neophyte and the embarrassment that is supposed to accompany shaking your hips (badly) in public. For example, later in the show, a sole male volunteer dances in close proximity to a sparsely clad female, who demonstrates rapid lateral Tahitian hip shakes. The guest is instructed to think of each hip being a "pineapple" or "coconut" and to bump them dramatically from side to side to make fruit salad. The exuberant but incompetent male is warned not to bump his "papaya" (penis) to the front while making fruit salad with the female dancer facing him. The motif unfailingly points up the sensuousness of the hula dancer (female dancers always demonstrate in these events) and the awkward, unsensuality of the white mainlander, thus enacting one of the tropes of Hawai'i as a paradise for romance peopled by "primitives" who, being closer to nature (knowing how to hang loose), are "naturally" more comfortable with their sexuality and hence can release that sexuality in others. Advertising promotes this theme, as the 1993 HVB "Come to Life in Hawai'i" campaign cited earlier makes clear.

Following a trip through the buffet line with compartmentalized styrofoam trays, a dinner of *kalua* pig, *poi,* and *haupia* pudding is consumed, along with more "free" alcoholic drinks. The after-dinner show is built on the theme of a trip among the Polynesian islands, thus allowing for a variety of costume, music, and dance styles and the inclusion of some of the more spectacular dances of the Maoris of New Zealand (Au Tearoa), Samoa, and Tahiti. A pop-style band with electric bass, guitar, and a set of trap drums is spelled by a small group of drummers for some of the numbers, especially the Tahitian, as this pan-Polynesian spectacle unfolds.

There are six female dancers and five male dancers. The young women are extremely slender, all with long dark hair flowing down their backs. Most look "hapa haole," or part Caucasian, while two appear to be Filipino. None looks primarily Chinese, Japanese, or Caucasian, and none appears to be primarily of Polynesian heritage. No female dancer possesses the larger body size often found among both male and female Polynesians and locals living in Honolulu.

The men are also young, and usually appear bare-chested, making their muscular bodies easy to see. Most are slender, but there is one who is somewhat chubby, something rarely seen among professional female hula dancers in these commercial lū'aus. Among the men, the hapa-haole look does not predominate, although it is represented prominently by MC Keikilani, who occupies the stage more than any other performer. Interestingly, the range of looks among the men seems to require some explanation by the female co-host, who plays a very secondary role in the show. She introduces the men as examples of the fact that "Hawai'i is the melting pot of the Pacific." The irony in using the mainland term "melting pot," which implies assimilation, to describe the population of a country that was taken over by the U.S. government 100 years ago with the deposing of Queen Lili'uokalani, is lost on this audience.

Each of the five men introduces himself by his first name, but that is hard to catch as he speeds through his speaking part. The first and last men both introduce themselves as "100% Samoan, and proud of it!" The tension between Samoans and locals is both glossed over and pointed up in this brief assertion. The third man describes himself as Micronesian, the fourth as Filipino-Hawaiian, and the fifth as Hawaiian-Italian-Chinese. These last two introductions are common ways of situating oneself in the "locals" population and indicate the complexity of the results of waves of immigration associated with the missionaries and the plantations up through the first decades of the twentieth century.

In every other tourist show I've seen there is no such labeling—instead, the audience is left to believe that the performers are "Hawaiian." And at Germaine's, the visible differences are recoded as Hawaiian by virtue of the melting pot, a reassuring trope of difference for mainlanders. Given that most in the audience probably do not know the difference between Polynesia and Micronesia or where Samoa is, these performers may be perceived mostly as nonblack and nonwhite natives, especially given their costuming in lavalavas (loincloths) or grass skirts and bare chests, brandishing spears or clubs in some of the dances.

Importantly, the women are not introduced by name or by ethnicity or by country of origin. They remain unindividuated examples of the Hawaiian hula girl. This image is so compulsory that to disrupt it with details of genealogical specificity that might deny the Hawaiian tautology (hula is done by people who live in Hawai'i, who are Hawaiian) would be too disruptive. The look for the women is more uniform, with the hapa-haole look predominating, not only in this show but in several others available in Waikiki. Although this is certainly not always the case, less now than in the past during the 1970s, for instance, it remains a dominant look.[34] A dusky, slightly Polynesian, Sophia Loren look is very popular. Rare indeed is a dancer with anything but black hair and brown eyes. Also rare is what in the islands is termed an "Oriental" look—that is, straight rather than slightly wavy hair, a very flat bridge of the nose, wide flat cheekbones, and pronounced eye folds. An emphatically Caucasian look of blonde hair and blue eyes would be impossible. Neither can the dancer appear to be "black" to a mainlander white audience. Melanesian dancers, from Fiji for example, are rarely seen in professional shows, because their complexion and hair might be interpreted as African-American. Given the complexities of genealogical history in the islands, many of the dancers may actually have little if any Native Hawaiian ancestry. They may be predominantly Filipino, or Portuguese-Chinese, for example. But it is important that when seen through the racialized lens of the white mainlander's perception, they appear to be Hawaiian.[35]

The rest of the Germaine's Luau show opened out from the Hawaiian dances to a tour of Polynesia that included a New Zealand poi balls dance, a male Samoan slapping dance, a spectacular Samoan fire-knife dance by a male soloist twirling two blazing batons, female Tahitian dancing, and several Hawaiian implement dances, where the women shake rattles (uli uli) or gesture with gourds (ipu) at an unbelievably frenetic pace to the strains of a pop music chant. Overall, the dancing was not particularly good. It lacked the precision in technical execution and in group unison that is expected at the big hula competitions and in many hālaus. The emphasis throughout was on male strength, female gracefulness, rapid movement, and spectacle. Costumes often bared arms, thighs, and backs, accenting them with day-glow orange grass skirts or loincloths, tall feather headdresses, and fake flower leis.

While the dance smorgasbord has some parallel in a growing pan-Polynesian political awareness in many of the islands, its purpose here was to provide an excuse for as much variety of visual "native" spectacle as possible. Most of the Samoan, Maori, and Tahitian styles in the shows are showier than Hawaiian hula, often faster, and for the males, more aggressive, even warlike with some dances including mock fighting.

Tahitian-style hula, which has been popular in Hawaiʻi for more than three decades now, and the Samoan fire dance form the highlight of every contemporary Polynesian show. Tahitian dancing emphasizes graceful arms that frame the torso as hips make rapid, isolated, percussive movements or slow grinds. It is dramatic and sexualized in the tourist shows, swinging suggestively between frenzy and languor, and highlights female dancers. By contrast the solo fire-knife dancer is always male, emphasizing virility, danger, expertise, and even painful endurance, as the flame is deliberately brushed over bare skin or the batons are balanced on the soles of the feet in a prone position. In these two showstoppers, male and female sexualities are diametrically opposed. The presentational emphasis is on spectacle more than skill, ultimately reinforcing two mainlander stereotypes of the "South Pacific": the graceful, sexy maiden, and the whooping, drum-driven, "savage" clad in loincloth. While framed in this wider Polynesian context, the hula and Hawaiʻi remain at the heart of the show, underscored by the setting, food, and narration.

WHAT'S LEFT OUT

By comparing the practice of hula in the tourist context with the practice outside the tourist arena, we can see key differences and similarities emerge. The tourist shows are not simply cheap imitations of the real thing, which exists elsewhere, nor are they solely their own genre of tourist art. Rather, a continuum exists, with a strong overlap. Many of the same dances, songs, costumes, and performers are found in both arenas. But there are also practices and people that do not appear in both contexts. For instance, coconut-bra tops would never appear outside a tourist show, except perhaps for comic effect, and certain of the oldest dances, associated with pre-European-contact religious rituals, would not be shown in the lighthearted context of a tourist show. A key difference of course is the audiences. Few long-time island residents, who might bring a more nuanced familiarity with Hawaiian history and culture, attend the big commercial lūʻaus. And few mainlanders, whose knowledge of Hawaiʻi is most often limited to the paradisical mythologies of the Euro-American imaginary uncountered by any exposure to the history of the islands, bring other than the dominant stereotypes of Hawaiiana to their encounter with the experience. The staging of the biggest commercial lū'aus does little to disrupt these presumptions even as they present them in continually updated forms.

The active construction of a notion of a "Hawaiian native" by this segment of the tourist industry also masks one of the most striking paradoxes of hula, that is, that the art form most strongly associated with Native Hawaiians is studied and performed throughout the islands at all levels of expertise by people of widely varied (and often non-native) genealogical backgrounds.

Tremendously popular in the islands, especially since the cultural renaissance of the 1970s, hula is now studied and danced by both men and women of all social classes, from tiny tots to those in their eighties. Hula is an ongoing part of daily island life—a visible part of public culture danced in bars, at parties, at weddings, on the stage and in the aisles at pop music concerts, on television, and even in aerobics videos. Important competitions like the annual Merrie Monarch Festival draw thousands of spectators, sell out months in advance, and are broadcast for days in a row throughout the islands. The competition results are front-page news. Such competitions, as Stillman has noted, "provide venues of high visibility and prestige for hula performance."[36]

Hula is taught in city recreation departments, in some public schools, on college campuses, in community centers, and in innumerable hālaus (hula schools or studios). The most respected hālaus are headed by kumu hulas, highly trained master teachers who have studied for years under another kumu until they graduate in a formal ceremony, after which they may form their own hūlaus. Most hālaus teach both 'auana and kahiko style. Although many 'auana, or modern-style, hulas are danced gracefully to the soft melodious music of steel guitars, other hulas in the kahiko, or ancient, style, which have grown in popularity since the renaissance, stride through space. Dancers squat, punch, and spin to the strong throaty chants of kumu hulas accompanied by powerful, rhythmic drumming, emphatically overturning any mainland images of sweetly smiling hula girls.

The leadership of the hula community, as evidenced in who is chosen to judge prestigious competitions and who heads the winning hālaus, is self-identified as Native Hawaiian. Yet, simultaneously, this group both acknowledges (through names like Cazimero, Zuttermeister, Holt Takamine, Chang, McKenzie, Silva, Namaka Bacon, Hewett, and Ching) and phenotypically embodies the social complexities of Hawaiian history, which include waves of immigration and extensive intermarriage among various groups. For instance, some of the leading *kumu hulas* may, on the mainland, be perceived as Caucasian.

The same histories are arranged on the competition stages, for example, where featured dancers might have blond hair (as did two of Kealiʻi Reichel's male dancers).[37] Blondes would never be hired in the big commercial shows because they wouldn't look Hawaiian. At *hoʻikes* (recitals), fund-raisers for *hālaus*, and in celebrations like the Prince Lot Hula Festival, dancers might be hefty or slender, young or even retirement age, local or Oriental looking, white, black, part-Caucasian, Hawaiian, or any mixture of the above.[38]

While there may be a tendency for *kumu hulas* to transmit their most closely held knowledge to those of Native Hawaiian ancestry, thus enabling them eventually to join the ranks of *kumu hulas* themselves, this is not always the case. And, indeed, the vast majority of hula practitioners and students never reach or aspire to this level of expertise and its attendant responsibilities. In most *hālaus*, access to knowledge at most student levels appears to be earned through diligence, humility, seriousness. and talent. As Stillman notes, "Basically, anyone who demonstrates a commitment to delving into the tradition is able to find a willing teacher."[39] While "blood" may be noted, and while some *hālaus* may be more closed or open than others, hula, the social practice most strongly and most visibly identified with Native Hawaiians, is, paradoxically, performed by Hawaiian residents of all backgrounds.[40]

The meanings of such performance may be different for those who identify themselves most strongly as Native Hawaiian and those who consider themselves local, or Japanese, or haole, and so forth, but this does not produce exclusionary groupings. So, while for some *kumu* and some of their students, hula "will continue to express political resistance in the context of [Native Hawaiian] cultural nationalism," few propose that others should not study or perform hula.[41] (And, indeed, hula is a worldwide phenomenon, with *hālaus* in Mexico, Finland, the Netherlands, Japan, and Indonesia).[42] There is no one "right" body, phenotypically, in terms of bodily looks, or genotypically, in terms of genetic heritage, in hula *hālaus*.

This point was brought home to me the day after I attended Germaine's Luau. At a beautiful beach site less than a mile away from the lūʻau stage, *kumu hula* Māpuana de Silva staged her annual recital and fund-raiser. The scene was a sharp contrast to the night before. Haoles, locals, and Orientals were all present in the audience and dancing on the hula mound as classes ranging from tots to middle-aged women performed to the live music of Kawai Cockett's Hawaiian-language songs. The parking lot held Volvos, Chevys, and pickup trucks, and tee shirts proclaimed the wearer's support for everything from ecology to Hawaiian nationalism.

Although geographically next door to Germaine's, the fund-raiser was another world. The tourists at Germaine's, watered by mai tais, warmed up by sophomoric jokes about newlyweds, encouraged by required sexualized contact with strangers, had consumed more than *kalua* pig and a little song and dance. They encountered the symbol of their destination image writ large in the bodies of sexualized natives costumed in feathers and shells, their contemporaneity suspended in time in the pulse of a strobe-lit stage. In this "marketing of heritage," the complexities of who and what are Hawaiian are lost.[43] Hula as an enactment of attachment to the islands, or as an act of resistance to assimilation and decimation, is invisible in this lū'au show.[44] The performers become what Barbara Kirshenblatt-Gimblet terms "living signs of themselves" or, more precisely, of what the audience imagines them to be.[45]

Thus, in the symbolic economy of tourism, Hawai'i becomes a place where Hawaiians (natives) live and do Hawaiian things, like hula. History cannot coexist with the mythologizing processes of primitivizing. Hawaiians are nativized in the sense of being situated outside contemporary time in a double ideological move that claims that the past (as historical change) never existed and the past (as an eternal present) has never changed.[46]

The complex histories of immigration, colonialism, and cultural change, involving early Polynesian voyagers, European traders, European and Euro-American missionaries and businessmen, Chinese, Japanese, Filipino, and Portuguese plantation workers, U.S. servicemen, as well as more recent arrivals from Samoa, Tonga, and the U.S. mainland, are mostly left out of this symbolic economy, as are the contentious dimensions of current political debate.

Alternative Tourist Shows

The most commercial lū'au shows and the nontourist hula events, like the festivals and fund-raisers discussed above, may seem diametrically opposed in many ways, especially in their conceptions of who and what are Hawaiian. However, as Elizabeth Buck has noted, hula is an "intertext where Hawai'i, the West, and the social context of the present continuously interact to construct, deconstruct, and reconstruct the myths of Hawai'i."[47] Such processes are always in motion, and the current political context has given rise to some small commercial shows that actively contest the dominant tourist industry trope of the Hawaiian native and incorporate some of the complexities generally found in the nontourist realm.

On the island of Kauaʻi, Frank Kawaikapuokalani Hewett's lūʻau at the Coconut Beach Hotel keeps many of the same components of the big lūʻaus—tourist hula lesson, Hawaiian wedding songs, and cellophane skirts—but decisively reframes these through introductory voice-overs that situate these images as part of a history of tourism and Hollywood visions. In addition, his costumes are, overall, less revealing, and there is no Tahitian dancing or Samoan fire-knife dancer. This lūʻau recently won the 1993 HVB "Keep It Hawaiʻi" award, indicating that even within commodified tourism it is possible to rewrite such images from the inside.[48] Similarly, the Cazimero Brothers, Robert and Roland, are as popular with local residents as with tourists, and their small-scale audiences are treated to a soaring sampler of contemporary music, hula, and social commentary that makes it impossible even for the most uninformed tourist to fall back on simplistic stereotypes of Hollywood natives.

Whether these small, innovative shows will force a shift in the formula used by the big commercial lūʻaus remains to be seen and ultimately will depend on the power of Native Hawaiians to determine which representations will predominate. Currently these shows serve a much smaller group of visitors each night than Germaine's or Paradise Cove lūʻau and appeal mostly to visitors who are sophisticated, repeat tourists. They are not included in the big Waikiki tour packages, although their costs are no higher. The Cazimero show recently completed a long run at the Bishop Museum, a fifteen-minute car ride outside Waikiki, its setting alone connoting a more middle-to-upper-class appeal.[49] Prior to that, they played for many years in the Monarch Room of the Royal Hawaiian Hotel, an upper-class venue. Hewett's shows, while situated in more middle-class hotel sites, require a trip to neighboring islands.

In both cases, these shows open up the representation of who and what are Hawaiian. In the Cazimero show, young, slender male and female dancers are complemented by the expressive expertise of award-winning *kumu hula* Leināʻala Kalama Heine, a large woman of middle age, as well known and well respected in the nontourist hula world as are the Cazimeros. Hewett's dancers in the Kauaʻi show generally fall within the Paradise Cove bodily type, unlike the large-bodied featured dancers in his own *hālau*, who perform with him in concert settings for nontourists. However, in the Hewett lūʻau the meanings of what his dancers do are historicized and presented as a mainlander imaginary of

Hawai'i, a sort of Brechtian device that satisfies tourist lū'au expectations while simultaneously undermining them.

Even in Waikiki itself there are departures from the commercial lū'au experiences. At the huge Sheraton Waikiki, for instance, a free, informal, early evening poolside show, meant to draw guests back to the hotel for nighttime spending, offers a range of local *hālaus* on a rotating basis. These *hālaus* include the full range of hula practitioners, sometimes even featuring young children and older women, breaking the stereotype of the hapa-haole hula girl.

A related site also works somewhat against the grain. At the Royal Hawaiian Shopping Center, right next to the Sheraton, members of the highly respected Hula Halau O Maiki give tourists free hula lessons twice a week. While at first glance this may seem like just an extension of the lū'au teach-the-tourist-to-dance segments, there are no jokes about tourist sexual incompetence dressed up in talk of pineapples, coconuts, and mixing fruit salad, as there are at Germaine's. Instead, the lessons are really lessons, and twenty (mainly middle-aged, Caucasian) women, many of whom return on each visit to Hawai'i, line up for a half-hour drill to learn a complete song. Some purchase a recording so they can teach their children back home. The youngish female instructors are friendly but demanding. Hula, while fun, is not to be taken lightly. The sexualized hula girl image, still perhaps persisting in the hapa-haole songs and the graceful figures of the attractive instructors, is counterbalanced by a discourse of education and personal interaction that somewhat uncouples the flattening of culture into race that undergirds the big lū'aus.

All of these alternatives to the big commercial lū'aus remain limited in their appeal because of location, a casual presentation style that militates against engaged viewing (the poolside show), or by their upper-middle-class address, yet they indicate something of the dialogic relationship between the tourist and nontourist hula practices, where some personnel and some specific dances migrate between both settings. They also indicate the variety of potential audiences, with a segment of the tourist population seeking out the smaller shows which do not match the destination image precisely. In these shows the image of Hawai'i gets rewritten. The bodily image of the "hula girl" as Hawai'i's icon is undermined by the proliferation of bodies of different sizes, ages, and looks.

The cultural image of Hawai'i as paradisical home to happy Hawaiians is also rewritten. In both Hewett's and the Cazimeros' shows issues of history come center stage and are connected with the current political situation. Even the shows at the Sheraton sometimes include a reference to sovereignty. Embodiment and enactment—being, acting, and looking Hawaiian—are in dynamic relationship in these alternative shows, just as they are in the hālaus and in the public discourse of sovereignty debates where several dozen organizations present competing visions of who and what are Hawaiian.[50]

One reason this may be so, at least in the case of shows involving Hewett, Heine, and the Cazimero brothers, is that they are among the relatively few kumu hulas who publicly participate in political events such as the 1993 'Onipa'a (Stand fast) commemoration, observing the hundredth anniversary of the overthrow of Hawai'i's Queen Lili'uokalani, or sovereignty teach-ins, or more direct actions like sit-ins on public lands.[51] However, there are some indications that this may be changing. In 1997, several kumu hulas and their supporters formed a coalition called 'Illio'ulaokalani (Red dog of the sky) and, staging a dramatic overnight vigil of chanting and drumming at the state capitol, successfully protested a proposed piece of legislation which would have required Native Hawaiians to register their cultural practices or lose protection for them under the law. As kumu hula Sonny Ching stated in 1998: "The kumu hula are standing up and taking their place in the sovereignty movement. . . . We no longer have that luxury of sitting back . . . of staying in our hālau and doing our own thing, because our existence [the existence of Native Hawaiian cultural practices and people] is being threatened."[52]

Whatever their personal political views may be on sovereignty, the majority of the kumu hulas do not include direct references to such issues in the choreographies they present in tourist shows or at important festivals, such as the Merrie Monarch and King Kamehameha hula competitions or the Prince Lot Hula Festival. However, some dances do include indirect references to the contemporary situation by stressing themes of justice and the perpetuation of Native Hawaiian values.[53] For example, at the 1995 Merrie Monarch competition, kumu hula Leimomi Ho's hālau presented a kahiko style hula danced to "He Mele No Ku'u Pua" (A song for my beloved flower). The program notes, necessary for the majority of the 5,000 spectators who did not speak Hawaiian, described the meaning of the hula: "The truth of our Hawaiian values bestowed upon us by our ancestors will flourish and thrive through the strength and innocence of our children." On the next night, kumu Chinky Mahoe presented his hālau in "Ke Alaula." Program notes described this hula 'auana (modern style) as "an ethereal message that awakens one's spirit to understanding the mysteries of life. It invokes a

sense of unity, and an appeal to keep life sacred. It is also a compassion-
ate plea to renew and set right the promise made by the first generations
of this land." Also, it should be remembered that a good number of both
kahiko and *'auana* hulas invoke the time of Queen Lili'uokalani or King
Kalākaua, the "Merrie Monarch" who in the late 1800s revived the hula
after missionary repression, thus implicitly providing a cultural frame
of reference for sovereignty claims which focused on U.S. colonial actions at the end of the last century.

Still, the move from implicit cultural celebration to explicit cultural
nationalism is rarely made. At a large July 1995 gathering of *kumu hula*
and hula students sponsored by the Office of Hawaiian Affairs, the political issues surrounding Native Hawaiian claims to justice were spoken of only briefly by three participants, and then toward the very end of
an intensive two days of discussion about contemporary hula practices.

It is ultimately the political power of such claims for justice which
will force any fundamental change in the tourist industry. The movement for sovereignty for Native Hawaiians has gathered speed rapidly
in the last few years and now is a highly visible and ongoing part of public and governmental debate across the islands. Positions range from a
call for the secession of the islands from the United States to calls for a
test of cultural knowledge as the basis for citizenship. One of the most
visible groups, Ka Lāhui Hawai'i, demands the restoration to Native
Hawaiians of millions of acres of land ceded to the government. While
not all Native Hawaiians support the sovereignty movement, and not all
supporters of sovereignty are Native Hawaiian, a majority of Native
Hawaiians favor some form of restitution for the taking of Native lands
by U.S. interests and some form of Native government.[54] Already the
visibility of the debate has prompted the Hawai'i Visitors Bureau to issue a statement acknowledging the illegal overthrow of the Hawaiian
monarchy 100 years ago and to prepare press packets on centennial ob-
servances for major national and international media, including the
New York Times.[55] And recently the HVB established a new Culture and
the Arts Committee to see how the tourist industry can contribute to
"preserving the culture and . . . establishing a joint partnership that can
be of mutual benefit."[56] The extent to which such mutual benefit will
truly benefit Native Hawaiians and not just turn into another marketing
tool for the destination image will depend on the political power they
and their supporters can generate.

It will depend also on the knowledge base of the mainland tourist/
consumer. President Clinton's apology to the Native Hawaiian people
(Public Law 103-150), issued officially on behalf of the U.S. govern-

ment in 1993, has contributed to a growing mainlander awareness of the current situation. In it Congress acknowledged that "without the active support and intervention by the United States . . . the indigenous Hawaiian people never [would have] directly relinquished their claims to their inherent sovereignty as a people or over their national lands," and "whereas the long-range economic and social changes in Hawaii over the nineteenth and early twentieth centuries have been devastating to the population" and "whereas the Native Hawaiian people are determined to preserve, develop and transmit to future generations their ancestral territory, and their cultural identity in accordance with their own spiritual and traditional beliefs, customs, practices, language, and social institutions," the Congress "apologizes to Native Hawaiians on behalf of the people of the United States for the overthrow of the Kingdom of Hawaii on January 17, 1893 and [acknowledges] the ramifications of the overthrow."[57] Such an acknowledgment of "ramifications" sets the stage for reparations claims. If major economic reparations are made, as they have been in Australia to Aboriginal populations, for example, it is not inconceivable that some structural shift in the economy of the state and hence in the tourist industry could occur.

The ultimate influence of the growing political power of Native Hawaiians on the tourist industry remains to be seen, as does the capacity of the tourist industry to recognize fully the complexity of the islands' populations, which far exceeds the stereotype of Hawai'i as home only to Native Hawaiians happy to play host to visiting whites. Meanwhile, at Germaine's Luau and others like it, these histories and politics, present and past, are masked and reduced to the embodiment of a naturalized difference, staged as song and dance, and sold as the concept of aloha. And it seems to be working—for the tourist industry, that is. A recent research report on visitor satisfaction reveals that lū'au attendees are significantly more likely to rate their Hawaiian vacation "excellent" than nonattendees. Perhaps even more significantly, substantially more lū'au attendees than nonattendees rated their Hawaiian vacation "far superior" to vacations they had taken elsewhere, revealing the importance of bringing the destination image (literally) to life through these staged encounters.[58] To understand the source of this satisfaction, we have to look back nearly a hundred years, to the beginnings of the Hawaiian tourist industry.

TWO

Picturing Hawai'i

The "Ideal" Native and the Origins of Tourism,
1880–1915

In April 1995, I was flying from Honolulu to Hilo, Hawai'i, to watch the Merrie Monarch Hula Festival, the leading hula competition. The plane was filled with excited participants and spectators, and the in-flight magazine, *Pacific Connections*, featured the festival on its cover: a contemporary sepia-toned photo of a female dancer, Ku'uleialoha Rivera.[1] The background is airbrushed out, accenting the lines of the figure, a young woman with arms extended, gaze directed upward, costumed in a profusion of greenery covering an apparently bare torso. At her waist is a very short skirt, loose strips of bark cloth parted to reveal a bare thigh. The intensity of her gaze, the controlled angle of the arms, the precision with which her fingertips are folded together into a flower shape all indicate a serious, highly trainer performer. But this is a highly ambiguous image.

This nostalgic evocation of the past, used to promote an event of key significance to Native Hawaiians and others involved in hula, is also an unsettling reminder of another era, one that turns up just a few pages later. A good-sized advertisement for a Hilo gallery selling vintage Hawaiian photography features two other sepia-toned photos of bare-breasted hula dancers in ti-leaf skirts. Pictured in photographers' studios around the turn of the century, these dancers lacked the breast-covering leis of the magazine photo. Their near nudity constructed a different version of Hawaiian women. If the cover photo was meant to celebrate a pre-European-contact past, before the missionaries covered breasts, brought cloth skirts, and drove the hula underground, these photographs did likewise, but with very different intent. The title of the gallery advertisement, "Buying and Selling," unwittingly prompts the question, buying and selling what to whom? The answer is found in the

34

nexus of visual representation, "primitivism," and the feminine that the old photographs promoted. They are early icons of an emerging tourist industry.

BEGINNINGS OF ORGANIZED TOURISM

Euro-Americans had visited Hawai'i on pleasure trips before the turn of the century, of course. But the development of organized tourism as a concerted commercial venture was new and coincided with the end of the Hawaiian monarchy's rule in 1893. American-backed businessmen, many of whom were plantation owners and descendants of missionaries, overthrew the Hawaiian monarchy headed by Queen Lili'uokalani in 1893. Hawaii was annexed to the United States in 1898, despite protests by Native Hawaiians, and in 1900 became a territory of the United States.[2] The intervention in Hawai'i echoes that in Guam, Cuba, the Philippines, and Puerto Rico and was part of the same expansionist policy that fed the Spanish-American War in 1898 and established the new U.S. "imperial archipelago." After the war, public discourse would situate Hawai'i both in relation to these other new colonies and in relation to mainland populations, as part of a renegotiated imaginary of the U.S. nation.

The overthrow was possible because U.S. interests were already firmly established. Missionaries had arrived in the 1820s, and much of the population, including the ruling elite, had quickly converted to Christianity. Caucasians took high posts in the chiefly government, and some intermarried with the Hawaiian ruling class. Missionaries and businessmen pressed for conditions favorable to the development of a capitalist economy, including the privatization of land holdings.[3] In 1876, a special reciprocity treaty admitted Hawaiian-grown sugar duty free into the United States, and the following year rights to a naval base at Pearl Harbor were established. By the turn of the century, Hawai'i was clearly positioned as a strategic outpost, as an important supplier of foodstuffs for the mainland, and as home to important American businessmen.

After the overthrow of the queen, however, the commercial prospects of U.S. tourism seemed to offer new opportunities for business expansion. In 1901 the Merchants Association in Honolulu began discussing tourism possibilities, and by 1903 the Hawaiian Promotion Committee was created.[4] Wrote one enthusiastic businessman: "The tourist travel to these Islands is capable of an almost indefinite expansion. It might yield an income of several millions a year."[5]

While some hotels and restaurants had served visitors before this time, this marked the inauguration of what would become an elaborate infrastructure to advertise the islands, transport tourists there, and cater to them on-site.

Immediately, advertisements were placed in mainland publications like *Life* magazine, inviting readers to "Hear of Hawaii." A souvenir book, "full of interesting photographs and information," was available upon request.[6] Advertisements promised "Sunny Shores," "Unrivalled in Equable Climate, Unequalled in Variety of Scenic Resort," and "Unexcelled Tourists' Accommodations."[7] A sketch of the distinctive profile of Diamond Head and the palm-fringed arc of Waikiki beach adorned the advertising text, anticipating what would soon become, along with hula dancers, the iconic representation of the islands.

Advertisements also linked Hawai'i to "the glorious orient." It was sold as a stop on tours to Japan and China and as part of Pacific Ocean cruises to Samoa, New Zealand, Australia, and Tahiti.[8] These latter ads, by the Oceanic Steamship Co., featured pictures of languorous native women of unspecified nationality, framed by palm fronds. The distinctive iconography of the hula girl had not yet appeared in these advertisements, but the association of alluring native women with the sites was clear.[9] Honolulu was thus positioned in tourist advertising just as it was in geopolitical discourse, as both an extension of the U.S. West and a gateway to the "Orient."[10]

The construction of the Moana Hotel typifies this union of geopolitics and business. In 1901 the Matson Steamship Co. bought a beautiful site on Waikiki Beach and built the elegant Moana Hotel. While there were already a few hotels available, the Moana signaled a new era of luxury and began Waikiki's contemporary development as a tourist area. It became the first formal resort hotel on the beach and is still one of the most luxurious. The first visitors were mainly wealthy elites who came and stayed for long periods, vacationing for a month or more after making the four-and-a-half-day ocean crossing. A graceful neoclassical style, elegant verandas, and an imposing porte cochere drive testified to the substantial wealth and status of these patrons and their colonial positioning. The opening of the hotel was greeted enthusiastically in Honolulu by businessmen whose "clinking of champagne glasses betokened the fact that Honolulu had at last become metropolitan indeed."[11]

We can assume that Hawaiian-language newspapers, if they discussed the event, did so with less wholehearted endorsement.[12] Memories of Queen Lili'uokalani's overthrow in 1893 and a brief attempted 1895 armed revolt by royalists who wanted to restore her to the throne were only a few years old. Few of these newspapers have been translated as yet. However, research on Hawaiian songs composed during the 1890s and printed in Hawaiian-language newspapers clearly indicates the strong attachment to place and to a growing Hawaiian nationalism that surely stood in opposition to expanding haole-owned businesses like the Moana. In her analysis of the 1895 *Buke Mele Lahui* (Book of national songs), Amy Ku'uleialoha Stillman translates these texts and notes both their evocative power and clear articulation of a growing Hawaiian nationalist sentiment. As one such song states: "The message travels, and America hears,/ Here is Hawaii in turmoil,/ There above at Diamond Head,/ Those who love the land gather. . . . "[13] The Moana, built on land formerly used by Hawaiian royalty, and sited with a beautiful view of Diamond Head, stood as a monument to the failure of the royalists' restoration dream.

The hotel was described as a "magnificent hostelry . . . dedicated as a resting place for the tourists of the wide, wide world who visit the Paradise of the Pacific."[14] The latest conveniences, such as individual phones in each room, were combined with "stately outlines of the old colonial period," so that the new building "rivalled even the finest hotels . . . in the most metropolitan cities on the mainland or on the continent." The union of business, "modernity," and U.S. colonialism was underlined by the ending number of the opening evening's musical program, "The Stars and Stripes Forever."

SOCIAL DARWINISM, THE ETHNOGRAPHIC GAZE, AND TOURISM

The organized development of tourism in Hawai'i was part of a larger European and Euro-American fascination with things "exotic," an aestheticization of imperialist expansion. At the heart of this aestheticization was the "ethnographic" gaze, a gaze which constructed "modernity" by picturing the "primitive" as its defining other.[15] The nascent sciences of anthropology, sociology, and psychiatry, which arose in the late nineteenth century,[16] saw the development of a related ethnographic gaze, aided by the new technologies of photographic reproduction which could picture "specimens" with precision.[17] Tourism, as aestheticized ethnographic travel, brought these discourses (of modernity, primitivism, visualism, anthropology) together with the commodification of new colonial possessions as pleasure zones.

It is also significant that the rise of the discipline of anthropology and the beginnings of tourism as an organized industry coincide, with each a different dimension of the ethnographic gaze. Both practices emerged within, and supported, the mutually constitutive ideologies of modernism and primitivism. As Johannes Fabian has argued, in its early years as a discipline, anthropology created its object of study by denying the coevalness of populations deemed appropriate subjects for investigation by Europeans and Euro-Americans.[18] Those who lived elsewhere were often seen as existing in an earlier time, retarded in their "progress."

This notion of modernity and primitivism gained support from Social Darwinism. As George Stocking Jr. notes, social evolution was conceived of as pyramidal. It denoted "a process by which a multiplicity of human groups developed along lines which moved in general toward the social and cultural forms of western Europe. Along the way, different groups had diverged and regressed, stood still, or even died out, as they coped with various environmental situations within the limits of their peculiar racial capacities, which their environmental histories had in fact created. The progress of the 'lower races' had been retarded or even stopped, but the general level had always advanced as the cultural innovations of the 'superior' or 'progressive' races were diffused through much of the world."[19] Within such a paradigm lies the rationale for colonial expansion—the need to civilize those judged uncivilized.

During this period, biological and social theories shaded into each other in a whole variety of debates about bodies and social practices and organizations, or about race and culture. Of the ideas circulating in these scientific circles, some were holdovers from earlier periods, others newly emerging. Races were conceived of as having separate origins and developments (polygenicist thinking), or as having essences, or souls, like individuals, a holdover from earlier romantic conceptions. Debates about race amalgamation (Was race mixing good or bad, and for whom?) and assimilation (How would "lower" races be "lifted up"?) abounded. The effects of climate had earlier been thought to determine cultural proclivities, and these ideas lingered. In one theory, learned knowledge was thought to be inherited, so that a race developed through the same stages as a child, from youth to adult. While only a close study of these various strands of thought can do justice to this complex period, in general, notions of race as a system of bodily based cultural classification dominated European and Euro-American thought at the turn of the century. Not surprisingly, Caucasians were ranked at the top of these typologies.

For Victorian evolutionists, "only the large-brained, white-skinned races had in fact ascended to the top of the pyramid."[20] Other groups were seen as exhibiting earlier stages in Caucasian cultural development, hence their "primitivism." Aspects of these earlier stages could be seen as good or bad, since such calculations were made by Europeans and European-Americans in the context of their own current evaluations of their own societies. Hawaiians, as we shall see, emerged on the good side of the scale. Tourism commodified this good.

Emergent "cultural tourism" provided the wealthy vacationer with a dose of anthropological contact with selected primitives—just enough to reinvigorate through contact with the "authentic" and "natural" those suffering from ennui because of the deadening pressures of modern, urban life.[21] T. J. Jackson Lears calls this longing for an antidote to modernity "antimodernism," a pervasive desire for authentic experience.[22] Hawai'i—with its promise of a healthful climate, scenic beauty, breathtaking volcanoes (the power of nature on display), and singing and dancing natives—emerges as an Edenic site for white regeneration. By 1899 it was already being dubbed "The Paradise of the Pacific."[23]

This specific formulation of reinvigoration through contact with "authentic primitives" emerges in tourist advertisements from the 1920s, which assure the reader that in Hawai'i "you'll find life now much as it was a century ago," and a "vacation this summer among such laughing, gentle folk will wipe out mental cobwebs and ennui."[24] But earlier advertisements, with their promotion of healthful climes and sunny shores, foreshadowed this promise and responded to what George Beard had dubbed "American Nervousness" in his popular 1884 book of the same name. In it he described a particular brand of neurasthenia that supposedly attacked upper-and middle-class (Anglo-Saxon) Americans who struggled to maintain "civilization" in the face of rising class factionalism, increasing urbanization and immigration, and the pressures of technological expansion into everyday life. As Beard wrote: "All our civilization hangs by a thread; the activity and force of the very few make us what we are as a nation; and if, through degeneracy, the descendants of these few revert to the condition of their not very remote ancestors, all our haughty civilization will be wiped away."[25]

The doctrine of Social Darwinism that underwrote anthropological visions at the time also bolstered this hierarchical view of increasing U.S. social stratification. In this "survival of the fittest," upper-class Anglo-Saxons saw themselves as representatives of civilization, which was under threat. They sought refuge from the different ethnicities of lower classes, moving out to the suburbs from crowded urban centers, and seeking the vigorous outdoor life advocated by Teddy Roosevelt. In contrast to the burgeoning immigrant classes, who were seen as threatening, "natives" in far off Hawai'i were not. While equally distant on the Darwinian scale from the rich visitors who visited Waikiki, Native Hawaiians represented a pre-urban, pre-industrial, pastoral vision of harmony with nature. Those whose wealth was built through the labor of urban working classes could escape them, and their increasingly fractious labor demands, by vacationing on the healthful beaches of Waikiki.[26] Here the welcoming natives and the unspoiled lush terrain alike assured the tourists of their "civilized" distance from such seeming simplicity while restoring them with its balm of pleasures. This ideology of restoration, however, depended upon specific representational strategies.

REPRESENTATIONAL STRATEGIES

For most mainlander visitors at the turn of the century, what little they knew about Hawaiians would have come through visual and verbal representations (including tourist advertisements), as few Native Hawaiians had visited the United States. Exceptions included some miners during the Gold Rush, the hula dancers from King Kalākaua's court who performed at the 1893 World's Columbian Exposition in Chicago, and very occasional visits by Hawaiian royalty. Most people encountered Hawaiian natives through stereoscope pictures, postcards, photographs, and even pornography. As an examination of these representations reveals, they actively constructed an image of Native Hawaiians as primitives living in the past. A variety of visual and verbal techniques, including shot and subject selection, the staging of images, and the circulation of old images as if they were new, all contributed to this creation of "the primitive."

A specific decontemporizing representational tactic emerged at this time and continued up through the thirties. Written texts describing contemporary Native Hawaiian life were paired with visual representation of a practice (a way of dressing, an activity) said no longer to exist. Such a strategy lays bare the process of constructing the primitive as the necessary complement to modernity by denying the coevalness of the viewer and the viewed. In fact, the Native Hawaiian population (especially the elite class) was, in some ways, almost too "modern" to sustain the dichotomy. They were highly literate, often part-Caucasian, overwhelmingly Christian. Thus, decontemporizing became, for Euro-Americans, a necessary way of "nativizing" the Native Hawaiian population.[27]

This disjuncture between image and text was widespread, occurring not only on postcards and stereoscopes but also in journalistic articles and books. In each of these cases, the two truth regimes of verbal and photographic representation are in contradiction. I want to suggest, however, that the visual evidence, supported by new codes of photographic realism, overpowered the verbal claims. As half-tone techniques for the reproduction of photographs were perfected in the late nineteenth century, photographic images became increasingly associated with newspapers, documentary exposés, and travel stories, enhancing the public's perception of their ability to capture "real" life. The photograph supposedly presented a less mediated representation of "the real" than authorial description, thus providing more dependable evidence.[28] One of the most widespread forms of such evidence was the stereograph.

In the latter half of the nineteenth century stereoscopic photographs were remarkably popular.[29] They brought what were regarded as realistic pictures of faraway peoples and sites into middle-and upper-class parlors, libraries, and schools of the United States, providing entertainment and spectacle under the guise of education.[30] The mounted cards of double photographs, viewed through a special lens holder, provided three-dimensional views which combined with the presumed evidentiary nature of the photograph to set a new standard in the aesthetics of realism. As Oliver Wendell Holmes wrote when he first proposed the name "stereograph" for such pictures: "By this instrument that effect [of three-dimensional solidity] is so heightened as to produce an appearance of reality which cheats the senses with its seeming truth. . . . The very things which an artist would leave out, or render imperfectly, the photograph takes infinite care with, and so makes its illusions perfect."[31] Although these images were complemented by long captions on the backs of the cards, the processes of viewing and reading were necessarily separate: the mini-essays could easily be ignored while the images were consumed, with only a title as anchor.

One example, titled "A Hula Dancing Girl," was released some time before 1900.[32] Sold as part of the Keystone "South Sea Islands and Hawaii" set, this stereocard features an oval photo of a young, slender woman in raffia skirt, posed bare-breasted on the beach, right in front of Diamond Head's profile. Palms etch the distant horizon. Her hair is pinned up loosely, and she stands, hands on hips, left foot extended—a position apparently made up by the photographer to indicate "dance" while still meeting the static requirements of photomaking. This appears to be a studio shot against a painted canvas backdrop. Its caption is worth quoting at length:

Dancing is one of the favorite amusements of the people, and the hula-hula is the national dance. It is a love dance and with it goes a sad and doleful music on gourds, tom-toms, flutes, guitars or ukeleles. It is not now much practiced, and the dress and nature of the dance have been much changed.

This picture shows the girl in the original costume. It was a skirt made of grass, with garlands of flowers for a waist. Her hair was also trimmed with flowers. The brightest colors were chosen for those garlands, and leaves were often used with them. This native costume is now seldom worn.

The clanging of gourds, a half a dozen of them first being tossed into the air and then beaten with the palms of the hands, produced the desired effect upon the dancers. Their hands and feet moved faster and faster. The dancing was done quite as much with the body as with the limbs. There were convulsions of the chest and the entire body. The gymnastic contortions would do credit to some of the old dervishes. No matter how much such a scene was enjoyed by the natives, it was too intense to prove anything but disappointing to civilized people.[33]

Although the dance is "not now much practiced" and "this native costume is now seldom worn" (we should especially note that Native Hawaiian women had covered their breasts in response to missionary urging decades earlier), the long caption describes both the dance movements and the dress style in great detail. The image is brought vividly alive, animated in the present, despite the past-tense verb forms. Further, by emphasizing the embodied aspect of the natives' behavior, the text further separates them from the presumably more civilized viewer who would find such "convulsions" vulgar (but no doubt titil-lating). Contemporary Native Hawaiians were thus twice decontempo-rized—represented in the present through an illustration of their own past, which is simultaneously a past that Euro-American viewers had supposedly long ago left behind in their social evolution.

A second, later image, probably from the early 1900s, repeats the vi-sual elements of women, dancing, palm trees, and grass skirts along with a nearly verbatim repetition of the verbal text, including the phrase "disappointment to civilized people" and the assertion that both the dress and the dance are now much changed.[34] As with the earlier image, the accompanying text reinforces, while denying, the primitivizing subtext. The hula dancer is pulled into the past even while she faces her audience of contemporaries.

But there is a key difference between the views. The earlier one shows the dancer posed against a natural landscape—static, bare breasted, and staring straight at the camera/viewer. The latter shows several dancers performing on a stage, wearing ti-leaf skirts and sleeveless hula blouses, in a pose from the dance's conclusion (arms together, out, and one foot forward). This view is shot over the hatted heads of several Caucasian-looking women, placing the viewer not in direct contact with the performers but situated behind a tourist audience. If the first view positions us both as armchair travelers and as imagined face-to-face voyeurs, the latter positions us on-site as tourists watching the staged, embodied, performance of "Hawaiiana." It thus records the beginnings of commodified cultural tourism, the material realization of the fantasy that the first stereocard represents. It also foreshadows the increasing ubiquity of images of Native Hawaiian women, especially hula dancers, who become the visual icon of the ideal native during the first decades of the twentieth century.

POSTCARDS AND PHOTOGRAPHS

Picture postcards helped circulate those images while promoting tourism. Like stereoscope cards, they were astonishingly popular during the early twentieth century.[35] The two decades between 1898 and 1918, considered a golden age for postcards, coincide with the emergence of the Hawaiian tourist industry. The plain cards of the previous, government-issue era were replaced by colorful commercial picture cards, and changes in postal regulations made postcards widely available and affordable. A postcard craze exploded, with billions in circulation, and collecting clubs were organized in Europe and the United States. Postcard albums were displayed in middle-class homes, so a single postcard would ultimately be viewed by guests as well as its recipient. Postcards thus formed an important social circuit of visual imagery during the period before film (and later television) regularly brought exotic images of faraway places into U.S. communities.[36]

As Susan Stewart has noted, postcards serve as a sort of bona fide: generally only available on-site, they guarantee that the sender is really there, seeing the sights represented. They thus authenticate the acts of travel and of witnessing and then in turn position the recipient as witness to the sender's experience. In this way, a public act (seeing a sight) is transformed into a private history (what I saw) with social meaning (look at what I saw). Of course, a postcard is also a souvenir or, as Stewart terms it, "both a specimen and a trophy."[37]

To function as such, images must be distinctive, that is, recognizable, and synecdochic—standing for the place they reference. In the first years of the century, picture postcards of Hawai'i focused not only on scenic sites, on dramatic flora, and on fancy homes of wealthy Euro-American residents but also on the images of hula dancers. Gradually, the increasingly popular image of the hula dancer came to stand for the distinctiveness of Native Hawaiian culture and thus of Hawai'i. Through the possession of the postcard, sender and recipient shared specimen and trophy—the miniaturized body of the Hawaiian female, "appropriated within the privatized view of the individual."[38]

A range of poses and presentations of hula girl portraits can be seen in the postcards and photos that have survived from the turn of the century through the teens. In the first decade of the twentieth century, hand-tinted postcards with captions like "Hawaiian Beauties, Hawaiian Islands" often featured portraits of light-skinned lei-bedecked women with Polynesian features and flowers in their hair.[39] These women looked at the camera with expressions of what reads now as self-contained dignity or gentle sadness. These earliest "Hawaiian Beauties" were not dancing, but other postcards did feature raffia skirts and some stiffly posed limbs to indicate hula.

One such card, postmarked in 1913, features four Polynesian-looking dancers, each with left foot extended forward and left arm stiffly out to the side in a sort of chorus line effect. An indistinct backdrop erases social context and emphasizes the iconographic linkage: woman-hula-native-body. The brief message sent from "WM in Honolulu" to Dave Pearson in Ontario, Canada, hints at the heterosexual allure already associated with hula dancers: "You see I am in the Pacific ocean near Japan their [sic] liable to land me in Panama Cuba or Frisco—they got big jobs here . . . tell Marie that I am with the Hula Hulas every day."

Postcard manufacturing provides another example of the decontemporizing representational practices that continually, implicitly situated Hawaiians in the past. Photos from the 1880s often circulated as postcards twenty years later with their original date unmarked.[40] One such photo from the 1880s shows three women wearing what appear to be raffia skirts with cloth underskirts and blouses, their hair elegantly swept up and adorned with leis. They are posed in a triangular seating composition, the central figure elevated and playing guitar, the other two strumming ukuleles, against a painted backdrop of plush ferns and a rushing stream—these are "natives" in "nature." These same women, thought to be dancers at King Kalākaua's court, appear in a lithographed color version of the same photo, on a postcard mailed in 1909 to Miss Victoria Miller of Buffalo, and reproduced yet again as a slightly modified black-and-white postcard in the teens. Their status as elite dancers of the court is never indicated; the generic caption on the front of the card merely reads: "Hawaiian Hula Dancers."[41]

The somber self-possession of this pose is repeated, but with less self-assurance, in other studio photos that feature young, bare-breasted women. While sexually commodifying the woman's body, such portraits also underlined the supposed decontemporaneity between the woman or girl in the picture (the "romantic savage") and those (fully clothed and "civilized") who viewed her.[42] Importantly, this type of photo circulated simultaneously in three different discourses: pornographic, educational/scientific, and commercial/touristic. Each realm reinforced the others. Sometimes the same photo could be seen on a postcard and in an educational publication, for example. Such pictures developed a distinctive iconography that depended on the hula dancer motif as a framing device which called for short raffia skirts, long and loose hair, and a thin lei of maile leaves across the chest, leaving the breasts exposed. Hula implements are also common: in one photo a dancer even sits on a *pahu* drum, the type used to accompany the oldest chants and usually handled with great respect. Clearly these women were posed by the photographers, very few of whom were of Native Hawaiian descent. Sometimes the edge of the backdrop is visible, quietly citing the act of construction of the native that these poses represent.

In certain cases the tension between the backdrop and the posing woman is very strong. One unattributed (ca. 1880–1900) sepia-toned photograph features a painted backdrop of an elegant bookcase. An unidentified Hawaiian woman sits facing slightly off center, with her breasts exposed, ti-leaf skirt split over the knees to show as much bare leg as possible, and long hair flowing to her waist. Her hands are posed awkwardly on her hips, giving her body a stolidity that betrays the vulnerability of the pose. Importantly, the model is not reading—no half-opened book rests in her hand to indicate the civilizing influence of Euro-American culture. Rather, the photo evokes a contrast between the markers of literate civilization and the iconicity of the (primitive) embodied native, clad only in forest ferns, rendered mute, exposed.

A similar hand-tinted postcard, one of a series shot with a different model around 1905, circulated as late as 1941, when it was sent from Hawai'i's U.S. Army Schofield barracks to Pennsylvania. This last provides an extreme example of the time-lag practice in representing Native Hawaiians. As primitive people were supposedly without history and hence unchanging, these iconographic representations could cir-

culate among Euro-Americans, unquestioned, as documentation, perpetuating images a century out of date.

Sometimes bare-breasted pictures circulated as part of educational
or scientific discourse, but they may also have been part of what was apparently an early market for pornographic pictures of Native Hawaiian
women.[43] Sailors and visiting male tourists were likely consumers. Although little information is available about these pictures, at least one
Honolulu photographer, Joseph W. King, was run out of town in 1870
for making obscene photographs of hula dancers.[44] Since photography
entered a boom period in Hawai'i at the end of the nineteenth century,
King was probably not the only photographer taking such pictures,
which contributed to the circuit of images about Hawai'i, and no doubt
found their way back to the mainland.

But the images described above were not the only photographs taken
around the turn of the century. By 1890, some sixty photographers were
working in the islands, with at least twenty based in Honolulu. While
the earliest photographers had been mainly Caucasian, by the end of the
century many were of Chinese and Japanese descent. Few, though, were
Native Hawaiian. Consumers represented the full demographic range
of the islands, however. Native Hawaiians and missionaries, royalty and
laborers on plantations, all flocked to photo studios to have their portraits taken.[45] These photographs, mainly family portraits given to
loved ones, offer a counterdiscourse to that of the tourist industry. However, for the most part these did not turn up on postcards or circulate on
the mainland as part of the tourist trade. The only exception might
be portraits of the royal family. Photos of famous people were popular
collectors items, and tourists as well as residents may have purchased
pictures of Hawaiian royalty in commercial photo galleries.[46]

Other photographs provide further evidence of a counterdiscourse.
For example, in the late 1800s the well-known chanter and hula master
Ioane Ukeke and his hula troupe posed for a photo in front of a fake rock
and a painted backdrop of coconut palms by the shore. Four largish
women wearing leather shoes, cotton leggings, cotton dresses, and leis
sit on bales of hay, staring out at the camera while Ukeke stands behind
them in suit coat, top hat, lei, and with a cigar.

Ukeke, who had picked up the nickname "Dandy," wears the tall hat
slightly at an angle. He looks serious, assured, and slightly cocky—not
the standard image of Hawaiian men (mainly half-naked fishermen)
circulating in photos and postcards of the time. The substantial women
also have serious faces. Legs are crossed at the ankle, extending out in
front or, in one case, solidly apart to support the body. Dresses fall below

the knees, and lace-up leather boots complete the outfits. Neither posed gestures nor costumes and props indicate dancing. And these women are not all young. Their hair is upswept, carefully dressed and adorned with flowers, not flowing freely, that is, naturally. This photo documents a troupe whose status would have been well known among elite Native Hawaiians and others associated with the court. There was no need for them to reproduce the hula girl iconography of stiff gestures— they were known to be dancers.[47]

Ukeke's troupe appeared during King Kalākaua's 1883 coronation ceremonies, and photographers also caught dancers at Kalākaua's November 1886 jubilee, thus documenting hula's return to favor despite missionary efforts to ban or regulate it. To my knowledge, these photos, which provide a glimpse into pre–twentieth century hula practices as a counterdiscourse to that of the nascent tourist industry, never turned up on postcards, however.[48]

Ioane Ukeke's photo is unusual in other ways when compared with tourist representations. An image of an obviously successful Native Hawaiian male was a rarity. In fact, the majority of postcards of Hawai'i during this early period, as since, feature women only. Native Hawaiian males were rarely pictured, and when they were, almost never with Hawaiian women, only alone or perhaps fishing with other men; they usually are pictured wearing only *malo*s, or loincloths, thus perpetuating a stereotype of the primitive native. In the visual iconography of the late nineteenth and early twentieth centuries, the absence of Native Hawaiian men is constitutive. It makes the emerging tourist iconography of the hula dancer = beautiful female = Native = Hawai'i stand out in full relief and leaves the pictured women available for visual consumption by white males.

Most often this visual consumption depended on a portrayal of Polynesian women as "brown," not "black," a point I will develop later in this chapter. But during the early teens, some evidence of a different, competing racializing perception emerges. Two postcards in Honolulu's Bishop Museum archive provide an example. They show cartoonlike drawings of large, dark-skinned "hula girls," barefooted, smiling, dressed only in leis and hula skirts. One card features a vignette involving two women with two Caucasian sailors. One couple makes hula gestures at each other, and the other walks arm-in-arm by the shore under a huge fern umbrella. They gaze happily at each other, a view of Diamond Head in the background. The caption in large print on the front says: "The Girls in These South Sea Islands Dress Mostly in Black—I Saw a Great Deal of Them," suggesting a perception of the women's skin

as black. The permission given to such interracial sexual liaisons or
even dating is striking during this time period.[49]

The second postcard, sent from Hilo to Eric Olson, of Brooklyn, New
York, and postmarked 1913, is also a colored, cartoonlike drawing. A
similarly large, dark-skinned woman is pictured in front of a grass
house, surrounded by a thick forest of palms. A verse on the front, titled
"The Captivating Hula," goes:

> If you never saw the hula, I'll show it now to you:
> I give a little wiggle and a little twist or two,
> An undulating motion with my body and my hand;
> That's how we dance the hula in Fair Hawaii land!

The hula girl in grass skirt by her grass shack is clearly sexualized and
primitivized. However, these two examples of "black" natives are
rare.[50] Dominant representations of this time featured a "brown," Polynesian look, denoted explicitly as such on some stereoscopic views, for
example.[51]

Hula girl images on postcards and in photographs during this period
thus ran the gamut from beautiful to alluring, to sexual, to pornographic. But they all presented a gendered and sexualized image of the
native.[52] Posed against either a backdrop of nature or an indeterminate
background, bodies are decontexualized, subjects are decontempo-
rized. The Polynesian-looking "hula girl" emerges during this period
as the dominant signifier of Hawai'i—a feminized site of nature and
romance. Alluring, entertaining, sensual, graceful, and natural, this
representation implicitly presents Hawai'i as an ideal vacation spot inhabited by ideal native hosts. This look will change somewhat over the
next several decades as a hapa-haole, or half-white, half-Polynesian,
look emerges as a dominant image of Hawaiian female beauty; but the
fundamental linkages of visual perception, embodied primitivism, and
cultural performance, implied here in the hula poses, will not change.
Such images will only become more and more popular, reinforced by
links between tourist and educational/scientific discourses.

HIERARCHIES OF "NATIVES" IN EDUCATIONAL
AND SCIENTIFIC DISCOURSES

Visual representations promoted by the tourist industry constitute one
realm in which specific Euro-American notions of Hawaiians were de-
ployed. Two other realms of discourse which had an important, and I

suggest lasting, effect on outsiders' perceptions of Native Hawaiians are the educational and scientific writings of the day, which promoted ideas of race and of presumed linkages between race and culture. Therein lie the precursors to the implicit linking of bodies and culture that persists in today's popular tourist performances like the big commercial lū'aus discussed in the previous chapter. These discourses, when combined with the circuit of tourist images discussed above, helped create the notion of Native Hawaiians as ideal primitives, an idea which was to prove crucial to the development of the tourist industry.

Following the Spanish-American War, there was a boom in photo-illustrated books devoted to depicting the newly annexed territories and possessions forming part of what Lanny Thompson Womacks has termed the "imperial archipelago." Utilizing the newly available half-tone process for reproducing photographs directly onto the same paper used for printed text, these heavily illustrated compendiums, linking Cuba, the Philippines, Puerto Rico, and Hawai'i, were very popular. For example, the two-volume *Our Islands and Their People, as Seen with Camera and Pencil* sold 400,000 copies within three years of its publication in 1899. The importance of the photographic record is stressed in the editor's opening statements: "In the exquisite photographs of actual scenes embodied in this work there is no room for the inaccuracies of chance or the uncertain fancies of the artist's imagination. The camera cannot be otherwise than candid and truthful."[53] In such an assertion, the photographic renderings of the places and their inhabitants are presented as a factual record, faithfully recorded without mediation. *Our Islands* is illustrated with 1,200 black-and-white photographs, nineteen color photos, and a variety of maps. In conjunction with this visual evidence, the narratives also promote a sense of objectivity, drawing on eyewitness accounts and the experience of colonial administrators to present an inventory of the resources and people newly available to the United States

Other books of this genre published around this time include Trumbull White's 1898 *Our New Possessions* (Boston: Adams); Murat Halstead's edited volume, *Pictorial History of America's New Possessions* (Chicago: Dominion, 1899); Mast, Crowell, and Kirkpatrick's *Picturesque Cuba, Porto Rico, Hawaii and the Philippines* (n.p.: 1899); editor G. Waldo Browne's eight-volume *The New America and the Far East* (Boston: Marshall Jones, 1901); and William Boyce's *United States Colonies and Dependencies*, published in 1914 by Rand McNally. Their common denominator, as Womacks has noted, is the feminization of these possessions. By utilizing a female figure as a metaphor for "the people," these books represent these sites as in need of the masculine dynamism of U.S. colonial administration. In most cases, the educable female is also a metaphor for the raising up of what were deemed primitive societies to a more civilized rung on the ladder of societies.[54]

But despite the commonalities of feminized representation, specific islands are differently represented. Womacks notes that the Cuban female, for example, was depicted as attractive and coquettish but unfortunately living under the vigilant eye of her male protectors. The Puerto Rican female was shown as an attractive mulatta. The Hawaiian women, however, were portrayed as incomparable: "Eve in paradise, under missionary influence."[55] Photographs of Hawaiian women fall into two groups. Many showed partially nude women, while others demonstrated the adoption of European dress, but adorned with flower leis.[56] Womacks concludes that this double discourse results in a merged representation: the Hawaiian woman can be civilized without losing her eroticism. By way of contrast, the Filipina was characterized as attractive but ultimately the least desirable owing to her hatred of white invaders.

Representative of this "civilized exoticism" is Princess Kaiulani, of Scots-Hawaiian ancestry, touted for her beauty and highly educated both in Hawai'i and in England. Following the overthrow of Queen Lili'uokalani in 1893, the eighteen-year-old Kaiulani, who had been heir to the throne, journeyed to Washington, D.C., to plead the cause of the monarchy with President Cleveland, who appointed a commissioner to investigate. Elegant in sumptuous European-style dress, adorned with jewels, the young princess epitomized a hapa-haole style of beauty that captured the imagination of the American public.[57] The princess and the monarchy as a whole presented a dignified, quasi-European rendition of Hawaiian-ness. Counterposed to that of the primitive native, this version simultaneously retained the mantle of exoticism, the sophisticated, noble counterpart of the primitive Hawaiian commoners.

Publications like *Our Islands and Their People* helped situate Hawai'i as a subjected colony in public discourse and focused attention on Hawaiian women as beautiful, desirable natives, precisely the soft primitivism that would come to dominate later tourist advertisements. As Womacks notes, in these compendiums of the people of the imperial archipelago, classifications based on concepts of race were an important part of the evaluations of the relative merits and potentials for civilized development that each site received. Nonwhites were distinguished in these publications through comparisons and contrasts of physical and cultural traits.

The rigid distinctions between "white" and "black" and "Indian" which structured racial discourse in the turn-of-the-century United States were now inadequate to the new tasks of description. For instance, the category "mixed race" was applied to a majority of Cubans, with all its connotations of the time of "mongrel." For Puerto Rico, the complexities of white, black, and mulatto seemed to call for civilizing through a "whitening" under the domination of the United States.[58]

In the case of Cuba and Puerto Rico, the upper classes, associated with the greater racial "purity" of Spanish descent, were deemed the more attractive and respectable. Although photo captions did admit that some "brown-skinned maidens are quite pretty, with large, languishing black eyes and teeth of pearly whiteness," a description of Puerto Rican girls at work on a coffee plantation, "the [lighter-skinned] women of the artistocratic class of Puerto Rico represent the higher and better civilization of Spain as it existed a hundred years ago."[59] Social class, especially when it correlated with Caucasian ancestry, was a qualifying factor in the mainland assessments of new colonies.

But unlike Cuba and Puerto Rico, where legacies of slavery yielded populations of mixed European and African genealogies, Hawai'i was not part of this black-white dichotomy and its (for the United States) troubling mixtures.[60] Hawaiians were not black or white or mulatto. This was extremely important in figuring the Hawaiian native as an ideal type.

On Not Being Indian

The "new colonies" books may have situated Native Hawaiians in relation to the populations of other colonies, and to black and white inhabitants of the mainland, but a shadow comparison with America's internal colonies, Indian tribes, was implied as well. Just as it was important that Native Hawaiians were not black, it was essential that they not be seen as Indians either. As one photo caption for an image of "lei sellers" in Waldo Browne's book declared, "Their complexion is neither yellow like the Malay nor red like the American Indian, but a kind of olive and sometimes reddish brown. . . . They belong to a branch of the Polynesian race, which was undoubtedly of Aryan stock."[61] Thus, although not European, the Hawaiians could be brought into the fold of American-ness relatively easily. Such was emphatically not the case with Native American tribal populations, where a great ambivalence about various tribes emerged.

White governmental policy toward Native Americans during the period 1880–1900 had shifted from one of extermination or reconcentration on reservations to one of assimilation, resulting in a profound ambivalence. As Leah Dilworth has noted, two strands of representations competed in the national imagination and circulated in dime novels, magazines, books, photographs, and postcards: the older vision of the "wild savage" and the newer one of the idealized "first Americans." The conclusion of U.S. government wars against Indian tribes like the Apache left images of warlike savages, finally tamed, fresh in the national imagination. At the same time, other tribes, especially those living in the Southwest Pueblos, were depicted as harmonious, industrious, peaceful (if primitive) craftsmen, ultimately assimilable into the nation, if not on equal terms with whites.[62] These latter tribes, like the Hopi, were promoted by the railroad companies as tourist attractions in the emerging cultural tourism business.

In some ways tourism to the Southwest set the stage for the development of tourism to Hawai'i. Organizations like the Fred Harvey Company, working in concert with the expanding railroad lines, promoted travel to the area by featuring "encounters" with Native Americans, hiring Indian craftspeople to produce goods on company property, and ubiquitously using images of Native Americans in their promotional materials. The active promotion of such cultural tourism seems to have preceded similar developments in Hawai'i by a few years, perhaps in part owing to the heavy investment of large national institutions like the Smithsonian Institution in promoting ethnographic studies of Native Americans, studies which were widely disseminated to the public through world's fairs and expositions.

Most important, however, were the differences drawn between Native Americans and Native Hawaiians. Compare the pictures of hula dancers with the two dominant pictorial representations of Indians in Southwest tourism during this period. Women were most often featured as water bearers or potters. While maidens in squash blossom hairdos and potters shaping beautiful works of clay may have had an allure, it was never the highly sensualized allure of the hula dancer. Indian men were most often depicted in the Hopi Snake Dance, called the "most popular photographic subject in North America," until the Hopi outlawed photography at their ceremonies in 1915.[63] One of the dancers' most striking actions involves holding live snakes in their teeth. For the many camera-toting white outsiders who inundated these ceremonies, this sacred ritual represented a surviving "wild" exoticism that countered the docile allure of the maidens. There is no comparable representation of Native Hawaiian men (mostly depicted as fishermen) during this period. In short, depictions of Native Hawaiians were more positive and never had the bad stereotype of "wild savage" to overcome.[64] As we shall see, scientific discourse, like that in educational books and pictorial depictions, also reinforced the ideal native stereotype of Native Hawaiians.

Scientific Racism

The perceived necessity to locate populations in a mapping of "stock" by tracing chains of "development," separation, and interrelatedness was one of the driving concerns of the fledgling social sciences of the day. Alexander Winchell, professor of paleontology at the University of Michigan, published his book *Preadamites; or, A Demonstration of the Existence of Men before Adam, together with a Study of Their Condition, Antiquity, Racial Affinities, and Progressive Dispersion over the Earth* in 1880. Arguing that Adam was not the first human, but rather the man from whom the white race ultimately developed, he proposed black races as the pre-Adamites, followed by the brown races, including Mongoloid and Dravidian races, and finally the white race (Mediterranean, or "blushing," race.)

Relying not only on color distinctions but also on linguistic and cultural difference, Winchell presents a typology that places Hawaiians in a favored position relative to other, supposedly inferior peoples. This book is remarkable for its solipsistic ethnocentrism. Systems of measurement are based on European standards and then applied elsewhere to provide scientific evidence of others' inferiority. One such measurement was cranial capacity, which included size, shape, proportion, and weight of brains as meaningful indications of intelligence. Other measurements marked differences among populations in skull thickness, the angle of projection of the jaw (prognathism), and the ratio of arm length to body height (reporting that the arm is "shortest in Whites, longest in Negroes [hence more like an ape], and intermediate in mulattoes").[65]

Not surprisingly, in most cases the hierarchy of white, brown, and black was "proven" by these measurements, which were seen to correlate with intelligence, morality, and cultural achievement.[66] In cases where one measurement seemed out of line with the others—for instance in the case of Estonians and Lapps, who had higher cephalic indexes (90.39 and 85.07, respectively) than North Americans (79.25) or South Germans (83.00)—the angle of the jaw or presumed differences in development of regions of the brain could be counted on to produce the desired conclusion.[67]

If more evidence was needed, it was found in the judgment of relative "psychic" profiles, since "races differ widely and ineradicably in the relative strength and influence of the various powers of the soul," such as religious emotions, intellectual conceptions, indolence of body and

mind, and so forth.[68] For example, "proof" of the "Negro's" mental indolence was offered in the form of her or his supposed lack of achievement in poetry, sculpture, painting, mathematics, philosophy, or
letters. Exceptions—individuals who had achieved incontrovertible
results measured by European standards, such as Phyllis Wheatley in
her published poetry—were attributed to the influence of white blood
in their veins.[69]

Within these hierarchies, which placed blackness on the bottom of
every measurement, "brown" people fared somewhat better. The Polynesians were believed to be brown "Maylays." Certain other Pacific inhabitants, like the Papua New Guineans, Melanesians, were linked to
the more primitive, darker-skinned "Papuan Race." Winchell argued
that the Fijians were superior to the New Guineans, but lesser than the
Maoris, Tahitians, and the Kanaks (Hawaiians). Indeed, he writes,
"Some of the full-blooded Kanaks express a truly Aryan intelligence."
Kanoa, the governor of Kaua'i, is singled out as an exemplar, his dignified head and face deemed suitable for praise.[70]

Phrenologist Samuel R. Wells, in his 1883 *New Physiognomy; or,
Signs of Character, as Manifested through Temperament and External
Forms, and especially in "The Human Face Divine,"* is also complimentary to the Hawaiians, placing them in terms of mental and physical
beauty just below the Tahitians.[71] He notes the debates in determining
the proper racial location for Hawaiians (as Malay or Maylayo-Polyne-
sian) but argues that the cranial shape of Hawaiians hardly justifies such
a placement. The Hawaiian skull, he argues, is more like the Caucasian
type than the Malay.[72]

Not surprisingly, the beauty of Hawaiian women is singled out in the
brief section of his text on Polynesia, where he notes that "some of the
women are very beautiful and elegantly formed. Their features are often
regular; their noses long and straight or aquiline; and their lips full and
handsomely curved. Their hair is black and often curly or bushy, but
sometimes smooth and straight." Complexions, he notes, are tawny
and tend toward either white or brown. Class differences seem readily
apparent in stature, features, and complexion, "the privileged order being much fairer and taller than the common people, and having better-
shaped heads and more regular features." With some ambivalence he
concludes: "Some of the latter can hardly be distinguished from Europeans, and perhaps are not naturally inferior to them."[73] The accompanying engravings depict "A Sandwich Island Man," dressed in royal
feather cloak, and the "Queen of the Sandwich Islands," in European
clothing, a before-and-after vision of the civilizing process.

To be sure, Caucasian scientists were not the only ones aware of racial typologies. While social classification among Native Hawaiians before European contact was intense, it was drawn along lines of class and genealogy, with the *ali'i*, or ruling class, at the top. There was no systematic categorization based on physical looks or skin color. But as Virginia Domínguez has argued, Euro-American concepts of racial classification were imported into the Hawaiian Islands. Native Hawaiians became aware of concepts of race and its connection to slavery in the southern United States in the 1850s and 1860s.[74] And sometimes, as historian Momi Kamahele has noted, they felt these connections firsthand: while King Kamehameha V (who ruled from 1863 to 1872) and his brother Liholiho were traveling in the United States, they were referred to as "niggers."[75]

A similar "blackening," or linkage of Hawaiians with African Americans, occurs in public political discourse around the time of the 1898 annexation. In contradistinction to the scientific works at the time, which were obsessively cataloguing and ranking differences among nonwhite populations, political cartoons sometimes collapsed these distinctions. For example, one political cartoon from the Spanish-American War caricatures Native Hawaiians, like the inhabitants of Cuba, the Philippines, and Puerto Rico, as black-skinned pigmies with kinky hair and big lips, balanced like circus performers on ringmaster Uncle Sam's outstretched arms, comic children in need of direction.[76] This depiction coincided with the institutionalization of racial concepts immediately after the war in 1900, Domínguez argues, when the U.S. census began gathering population data about race in Hawaii.[77]

Still, despite this flattening of categories in the political and popular arena, the tourist and scientific discourses of the time did not promote the negative perception of Native Hawaiians as black. Quite the contrary. For example, in the four-volume work *The Great Races of Mankind: An Account of the Ethnic Origin, Primitive Estate, Early Migrations, Social Evolution, and Present Conditions and Promise of the Principal Families of Men* (1893), Dr. John Clark Ridpath speaks glowingly of the Hawaiians, and of Polynesians in general: "The Polynesian islands furnish an admirable station from which to study mankind in the process of natural development."[78] He provides examples of what he terms the evolution of civil government and of property rights, dependent on use rather than ownership, and controlled by the chiefs in the name of the whole "tribe." Women are seen as being well off: "Hardly any barbarians or half-barbarians hold their women in better estate than do the Polynesians, where women may be queens, princesses, and even chief."[79] The Polynesians in particular, and especially the Hawaiians, thus are seen to represent an earlier, sometimes idyllic, stage of civilization through which Europeans have already passed. One of their uses for the colonizing powers is to serve as an example, a living experiment in the evolutionary paradigm of civilization. "They" are living the Europeans' past. But, however praiseworthy, it is implicit that they will never "catch up," or be seen as contemporaries, since presumably the white societies will also continue to evolve to ever-higher states.

While European and Euro-American societies are generally presumed to be the most highly evolved, some of their members pose a danger to the "innocent native." Ridpath blames European vices for the precipitous decline in the Native Hawaiian population to what he estimates is fewer than fifty thousand: "Until the Christian states can control their own emissaries and keep back the importation of vice and crime, the cargoes of alcohol and opium, and the dreadful infection of criminal diseases, it were far better that the innocent, though barbarous, outlying races of mankind would be left to themselves, to the simple pleasures and activities of which they are capable under the laws of their own nature, rather than that they should be corrupted, defiled and destroyed by the insidious poisons of civilizations."[80]

In Ridpath's book, we find once again that the Hawaiians, decimated but not corrupted by such vices, are rated as "physically . . . the best race of the Pacific—excepting, perhaps, the Tahitians." At one with nature, they delight in water sports, "tumbling and rejoicing like porpoises in the freedom of the sea." Even more importantly, "Their intellectual faculties are sufficiently acute. They learn readily, and apply themselves industriously to mental as well as physical tasks. They have adapted themselves to civilized conditions . . . and yielded in large measure to the dominion of reason." The monarchy appears just and efficient, and the Hawaiian government is recognized in Europe and America: "Its representatives are seen in many of the most important cities in the world." Still, underneath this approval is the almost-but-not-quiteness of the ever-subordinate: "Titles of nobility [are] arranged and graded with as much nicety as if they signified something!" The native may aspire to but never attain the status of authentic monarchical government, always aping his betters.[81]

An Ideal Type

The tone of approval firmly sets the boundaries: attractive, nearly Aryan in some ways, existing simply in a beneficent climate but not succumbing to indolence, industrious enough, intelligent enough, freed now from non-Christian superstitions, the Hawaiian native comes to represent an ideal type in the Euro-American imaginary—oscillating between the noble and the romantic savage. The elite Hawaiian classes seem to represent more fully the "noble savage," although now lifted up to European ways, while the rural commoners, housed in grass huts, frolicking like porpoises, represent the strain of romanticism. The one promises movement toward modernity, while the other, pulling nostalgically backward while the monarchy roams the civilized capitals of Europe, remains the image of a romantic ideal. The hula dancer becomes a prototype for this rural romantic vision, in contrast to queens and kings in European formal dress in neoclassical Iolani Palace.

A hula dancer was singled out for commendation in the book *The New America and the Far East*. A photo caption asserts: "With her profusion of raven hair, tied with a gay bandelet of feathers and ohia blossoms, softly expressive dark eyes, pleasant countenance, erect figure, graceful and steady carriage, she commands the admiration of the beholder. The young waihine [sic] woman, a dazzling vision of sparkling eyes, pearly teeth, bright flowers, and bare legs . . . startles the timid stranger with her boldness of address, her voluptuous bust rounding in graceful curves."[82] The tension between ideas of the potentially civilized ("graceful" and "steady") and the exoticized primitive in this description encapsulates the frisson of difference, sensuousness sliding to sexuality and back again in one sentence.

The feminized status of the Native Hawaiian also guaranteed an apparent tractability, so important to the imperial mission. For example, while all colonial subjects supposedly exhibited a desire to acquire knowledge once under American influence, "in Hawaii we found a population already educated even above our own high standard, for there are scarcely any of the natives of those islands who cannot read and write; and yet even there we perceive the same earnestness of desire to advance to the higher planes of knowledge."[83] Thus, the potentially unsettling high rate of literacy, which exceeded that of the mainland, is recuperated into evidence of tractability, of a desire to learn more civilized ways. Eminently civilizable yet fundamentally different, from the Euro-American point of view the Hawaiian fit perfectly what Bhabha has referred to as mimicry, the almost-but-never-quiteness of the native who learns and reproduces colonial ways.[84] Native Hawaiians, especially perhaps the women, could be enjoyed but never posed a real threat to the sovereignty of the ruling whites because, as Bryan asserts, "the ruling and influential class in Hawaii is of course American, and it will remain so."[85]

While Native Hawaiians were seen by mainland whites as tractable, the other populations of the islands posed different problems for Euro-American scholars, politicians, and tourist promoters. Around the turn of the century, tens of thousands of immigrants from China, Japan, and the Philippines were brought in to work on the expanding plantation system. They soon outnumbered both whites and Native Hawaiians.[86] Tourist promoters and scholars or educational writers dealt with this fact differently. By the former these other populations were rendered all but invisible, while for the latter, the new immigrants were acknowledged but were ranked below Native Hawaiians in desirability.

Without exception, the imperial archipelago books concur that Native Hawaiians were to be placed at the top of the nonwhite hierarchy, above the Chinese, Japanese, and Filipinos and the North American Indian, as well. The Chinese, largely shut out of U.S. immigration by the 1882 Chinese Exclusion Act, were not regarded as desirable, and the Japanese, already at 30 percent of the island population, presented a possible threat in the form of a rival civilization and potential political power in the Pacific, regardless of their lower status. The Filipinos were always relegated to the most primitive rung of the civilization hierarchy in part because of sensational stories about wild "headhunter" tribes inhabiting remote islands in their home country.

Of the entire imperial archipelago, only the Hawaiian Islands had been colonized through the immigration of a sizable population of U.S. whites, thus situating the territory as a new westward frontier and raising the question of the islands' ultimate incorporability as part of the nation. In order for the islands to be conceived of as a part of the United States, the presence of Chinese, Japanese, and Filipino residents had to be downplayed. Instead, U.S. nationals and the admired Native Hawaiians were emphasized—one ready to rule and the other presented as eager to learn. In touristic publications this masking of other populations is carried to an extreme.

All in all, Hawaiians, especially Native Hawaiian women, emerge in these mental maps of imperialist designs as erotic/exotic, nonthreatening, nonblack, non-Asiatic, civilizable, desirable natives, precisely the trope developed by the emerging tourist industry over the next several decades. In contrast, the Chinese, Japanese, Filipino, and Portuguese populations were invisible because they could not be represented as desirable, at least not in terms of the emergent U.S. nationalist discourse that had to encompass Hawai'i as a part of itself. Hawai'i would seem to consist only of whites (visiting or happily resident) and Native Hawaiians (vanishing, but still there).

Indeed, their vanishing status—Native Hawaiians were already in the minority in 1898—engendered the nostalgia that doubled the de-contemporaneity effect. From the Euro-American perspective, it was the past (the innocent past of European peoples, the "childhood of the race"), not the present populace, that was in danger of vanishing forever. This nostalgia, an obsession to document living remnants of the past before it forever slid from view, linked superbly with photography as a technology of nostalgia. The moment photographed is always already past, and the picture becomes, in some senses, a relic. Roland Barthes's term for this sense of a lost moment is the "punctum." For Euro-American viewers, the stereoscopes, photographs, and picture postcards of the turn-of-the-century period melded punctum and icon into desire for the perfect colonial subject and touristic hostess, and set the stage for of the emerging tourist industry.[87]

Obviously, the view from the islands was much different. The dignified hula performances at King Kalākaua's coronation, the popular Hawaiian-language newspapers, and the many photographic portraits Hawaiians and immigrant groups had taken as family mementos all provided different renditions of what it meant to be Native Hawaiian during this period.[88] But these counterdiscourses, with the exception of some photographs of Native Hawaiian royalty, and of newspaper reports of Hawaiian protests to annexation, rarely circulated on the mainland.[89] They were no challenge to the powerful educational, scientific, and visual depictions reinforcing one another on the mainland. Soon those images would come to life. A boom in hula dancing exploded on the mainland following the appearance of Hawaiian performers at the San Francisco Panama-Pacific Exposition of 1915. Millions of Americans would encounter hula in tent shows, vaudeville houses, on Broadway, in supper clubs, and ultimately in Waikiki hotels, as the following chapters detail.

THREE

Pictures Come to Life

Rendering "Hawai'i" in Early Mainland Hula Performances

The decades surrounding the turn of the twentieth century set the stage for an outsider's view of Hawai'i as romantic, feminized, and delightfully, ideally "primitive," a view that combined a hierarchized racial demarcation of the world's populations with a growing U.S. imperialism abroad. As I have demonstrated, visual and verbal representations in pictures, postcards, stereoscopes, advertisements, and scientific discourses during this period rendered a vision of Native Hawaiians as "ideal natives," and set the stage for the development of tourism. But these two-dimensional representations were not the only ones available. Mainlanders did not have to wait until they got to Hawai'i to encounter "live culture." Hawaiians and non-Hawaiians alike provided renditions of island song and dance in mainland venues ranging from tent shows to Broadway.

These performers brought the pictures to life, representing Native Hawaiian looks and cultural practices in embodied form. In many instances these performances turned out to be mere caricatures of what was going on in the islands. At times, they provided the inspiration for new forms of music and dance, such as hapa-haole music, which in turn became part of Hawaiian music back home in the islands.[1] Whether regarded as hybrid, authentic, exploitative, or educational, all of these singing and dancing versions of Hawaiiana eventually contributed to the mythology of Hawai'i and its destination image and became something for the Hawaiian tourist industry to draw on, defend itself against, or recirculate. Thus, mainland performances both created an appetite for tourist performances in the islands and became a counterpoint to them. This chapter examines the vision of Native Hawaiians that mainland performances provided and argues that such performances ultimately contributed to an ideal of a white native or nativized white woman which gave an embodied presence to the Euro-American imaginary of "Hawai'i."

MAINLAND PERFORMANCES

Mainland performances would boom following the appearance of Hawaiian musicians at the Panama-Pacific Exposition, but some Hawaiian performers (and their impersonators) had appeared in the latter half of the nineteenth century. As early as the 1850s hula dancers were performing in California, responding to the emergent entertainment business for gold rush miners, many of whom were Native Hawaiians and haoles (Caucasians) who had come over from Hawai'i. A surviving poster from that period advertises as the "Greatest Attraction of the Season" "KANAKA DANCING GIRLS" in the "Celebrated Sandwich Island HULA! HULA! Ladies Prohibited."[2] Here the exclusion of women from the audience clearly situates the performers as spectacle for males.

The poster includes a detailed listing of the dances on the program with titles in Hawaiian and translations in English, and lists the names of performers: "Wahines or Dancing Girls Hoo-kie-kie and Keo-ho-hina" and "Kanaka Drummers and Chanters Ka-na-au, Kua-mo-ku, Na-o-ni-hi-ni-hi, Ne-wa, and Ka-i-li." Five male chanters and drummers support the two female dancers who are presented as the main draw. Part one opens with a Pule ia Laka (Prayer to Laka, goddess of hula) and includes several hulas, including an implement dance with *pu'ili,* or bamboo poles, chants, and dancing puppets (*hula ki'i*). The specific listing of named dances, dancers, and chanters is juxtaposed with the largest print, KANAKA DANCING GIRLS, indicating that the targeted audience probably included both Hawaiian and non-Hawaiian males. The inclusion of the Hawaiian language not only addresses Hawaiian male patrons directly but also provides a sense of authenticity and makes it seem that the program will be chock-full of interesting, exotic attractions (i.e., "real Hawaiians"), well worth the fifty-cent admission.

As the programming indicates (Prayer to Laka), hula had been connected to Native Hawaiian religious practices, as well as existing in more secular forms. Before contact with Europeans, hula had played an important social role, with special chants and dances produced in honor of royalty or to commemorate important events. Dancers and musicians underwent years of instruction, observing explicit training rituals and taboos. However, missionaries arriving in the first half of the nineteenth century regarded the hula as lascivious, and circumscribed it heavily. The hula nonetheless continued, in part underground. Native Hawaiians themselves were divided in their attitudes toward its practice, some who were Christian decrying it along with the missionaries, others supporting its importance.[3] For instance, Z. M. Kauhi, writing in the weekly Hawaiian-language newspaper *Ka Nupepe Kuokoa* on March 27, 1880, remarks: "There are many people of our race who flow like running water to this worthless occupation, the hula, from boys and girls of ten to adults of fifty or more. Hearken, O parents, do not allow your children to indulge in such a worthless practice lest it become a nest of prostitution."[4] A key turning point for the return to importance and respectability of the hula came in the administration of King David Kalākaua. He refused the missionary denigration of hula and prominently featured hula dancers and chanters at both his 1883 coronation ceremonies and his 1886 jubilee celebration.

One of the first important documented performances of dancers from Hawai'i on the mainland occurred soon after and took place at the Chicago World's Fair in 1893, when former court dancer Jennie Wilson, along with several others, performed on the Midway Plaisance for six months.[5] Wilson's mother was Hawaiian, and her father was from Ireland. She typified a hapa-haole look that would become popular during the teens in mainland shows.

Wilson was situated across from the Java Village and next to the Samoans at the fair, in an exhibit space devoted to "South Sea Islanders."[6] Linked thus with what came to be called "belly dancing" in the nearby Egyptian pavilion, the hula was positioned as part of the "hootch" dance, a style attributed to non-European women which carried mild to explicit connotations of sexuality and lasciviousness, just as the "Kanaka Girls" advertisement ("ladies prohibited") implied forty years earlier.

In an interview in 1961, at the age of eighty-nine, Wilson's memories of the Midway were still strong.[7] The Midway was packed with people, and Wilson stood on a table to do the "ballyhoo," the verbal advertisement for the show, singing: "Where the 'naughty' girls from Honolulu do the naughty hula dance. . . . On the midway, the midway, the midway plaisance." One had to do something like that to attract the crowd, she recalled. After a crowd had gathered, she ran inside to dance, after which the crowd was ushered out the back, and the whole sequence began again with a fresh crop of viewers. If the dancers hadn't succeeded in attracting viewers, she said, the act would have been canceled. Photographs of the hula dancers in the local papers helped ensure their popularity, as perhaps did the details of her performance style. Wilson recalls that the actual hulas they performed were in the old style, but "they pepped it up a little" sometimes, and she played to the most elderly men in the audience, making eye contact and winking.

Wilson's reminiscences indicate how the mainland perceptions of hula and Hawaiian women as sexualized and exotic shaped to some extent not only the audience's perceptions but perhaps the performances themselves (pepped up, "wiggles" added), although it should be remembered that secular hulas in Hawaiian island performance contexts could also have a flirtatious, sometimes comic, dimension. But in the new context of the Midway these interactions carried a differently freighted meaning, linking "exotic" physicality with sexuality and female spectacle. These linkages were underlined by the exact location of the South Seas exhibit.

The physical placement of the Hawaiian dancers was not accidental. As Robert Rydell has noted, the various populations on display were mapped according to a racial hierarchy of civilized to savage, with the German and Irish villages nearest the official, modern White City of the main exposition grounds, and the furthest sites occupied by those considered least civilized: Africans and Native Americans. As the *Chicago Tribune* put it: "What an opportunity was here afforded to the scientific mind to descend the spiral of evolution tracing humanity in its highest phases down almost to its animalistic origins."[8] So-called brown people were placed in the middle of the Plaisance, where the Hawaiians were. Such groups were presented as primitive, perhaps, but charming and ultimately civilizable, precisely the evaluation necessary for annexation, as discussed in the previous chapter.

Chicago wasn't Wilson's only appearance on the mainland. She also danced at the Trans-Mississippi and International Exposition in Omaha in 1898 and at Buffalo's Pan American Exposition in 1901, before touring Europe.[9] Such fairs were wildly successful and contributed significantly to mainlanders' perceptions of Hawaiians and other non-Caucasian populations. The Chicago 1893 exposition alone drew twenty-seven million visitors to its visions of white cultural "progress" underwritten by an emerging discourse of anthropology and Social Darwinism.

Despite her status as an accomplished court dancer for King Kalākaua, Wilson was shunned when she returned home to Hawai'i, and she stopped dancing. Some Native Hawaiians thought she had participated in immoral hootch presentations, disgracing Hawai'i and Hawaiians by dancing a dirty hula abroad. People made fun of her on the street. Sixty years later, Wilson still recalled the stinging disapprobation, remembering how boys ran up to her on the street, touched her, asking her to dance; she hit one of them in return. Three older women in Honolulu pestered her, running her off the sidewalk into the gutter when they passed on the street. But Wilson had the last word. Years later her husband, John Wilson, became mayor of Honolulu, and Jennie Wilson finally danced again in public at a party, receiving the approbation of all, including those same three women. The status of hula was no longer under the shadow of missionary disapprobation, as it had been in the nineteenth century. Wilson's experiences reveal both the sexualized reception of hula on the mainland at the turn of the century as well as the tensions over hula's respectability in the islands at that time.

Jennie Wilson was not the only hula dancer appearing on the mainland in the 1890s. Although little is known about other performers, the *Annals of the New York Stage* yield an intriguing glimpse into the framing of hula during that period. "Hawaiian Hula-Hula Girls" were featured at Doris's Museum on Eighth Avenue in New York City in the 1893–94 season. They appeared for a full month, performing in the curio halls of this dime museum on a bill with a legless gymnast, a tattooed man, a midget, the albino Martin Sisters, and Mackenzie's Kiowa Indians. Each week the other "freak inducements" changed, at times including a two-headed cow, George the turtle boy, Polly the talking seal, Zamassa the Zulu chief, and Esquimos [sic], as well as plays by a resident stock company of actors and vaudeville acts like the Elliot Sisters ("tough girls from Mulberry Street"). Reporting on a "truly rural sensation—the Kilkenny Milkmaids, ten young ladies in a butter-making contest," a reporter couldn't help joking, "No wonder that this was the last week of the Hawaiian dancers—domesticity came to the fore!"[10] Embedded in this remark is the assumed opposition between the sexualized dancers and the attractive, domesticated innocence of the rural milkmaid.

We can assume from the longevity of the hula act, compared with the one-week engagements of the others, that it was a popular draw with audiences. Situated in the curio hall, the dancers were (literally) framed as something between a vaudeville act and a talking seal, a living curio, not quite fully human because not civilized, just like the "esquimo" and Zulu and Kiowa Indians. However, neither the Zulu chief nor the Eskimos were so explicitly sexualized. Reports do not reveal whether these dancers were Hawaiian or not, or whether they had ever actually studied hula. What is important, however, is that they were probably perceived as Hawaiians performing hula and were presented as part of the same visual spectacle of exotica that had framed Jennie Wilson's performance at the World's Fair.

A more sedate version of Hawaiian music and dance became one of the biggest moneymakers of its era. Premiering on Broadway in 1912, the dramatic play "Bird of Paradise," a story of a Hawaiian woman and two white men, was to have a long life through its several incarnations over the next forty years. Running for 112 performances on Broadway in 1912, the play was then restaged by Rogers and Hammerstein as the musical comedy "Luana" in 1930, reappeared as a 1932 film, *Bird of Paradise*, directed by King Vidor and starring Delores Del Rio and Joel McCrea, and was remade yet again under the same name in 1951 by director Delmer Daves, starring Debra Paget. Finally, as a sort of coda to these remakes, a short-lived network television show about a white man living in Honolulu, *The Byrds of Paradise*, came and went in one season in the mid-1990s. The multiple remakings indicate both the enduring power of the imaginary it presented and its malleability as presentations shifted through various historical moments.

While the involvement of Native Hawaiian music and dance experts varied with these different stage and film incarnations, the basic story line remains the same throughout the remakes, as does the practice of casting a Caucasian female lead as the Native Hawaiian woman around whom the story revolves. The impact of the original 1912 version was considerable. After the show played on Broadway, several road companies were formed, and it toured the United States and Europe, contributing to the visual and ideological framing for the post-1915 Hawaiian music fad which was soon to ignite.[11]

The narrative is one of sloth and redemption, downfall, "going native," and returning to civilization. A white American woman, Diana, and a native woman, Luana—played by Caucasian New Yorker Laurette Taylor, who rode to fame on this role—serve as the centers for the life trajectories of two men.[12] Diana, a visiting writer, saves the dissolute American, Dean the beachcomber, from his "degradation" through the "stimulating influence of her inspiring faith in the better side of his nature." While he is raised up, another white American, physician Paul Wilson, who has gone to Hawai'i to help treat lepers, falls under the spell of beautiful Luana, a Native Hawaiian of royal lineage. He "grows languid under the effects of the woman's charms, and the native viands, and liquors, and climate," ultimately becoming Luana's mate and "living a lazy life in a grass hut." Dean returns to America with Diana, triumphs professionally, even discovering the "leprosy germ," which was Paul's dream. Meanwhile, Paul sinks into the native life, casting his ambitions aside. The ultimate sacrifice in this melodramatic tale is Luana, who casts herself into the boiling cauldron of a volcano, a human sacrifice to the god Pele. As the *New York Times* put it, "For all her insistence that she is now American and not Hawaiian," she is "unable to shake off her superstition."[13]

The allure of the native woman, her ultimate difference from whites (unable to become truly "civilized," remaining "superstitious"), and her siren-like danger and appeal for white American men become the hub around which the story revolves. By contrast, the uplifting function of the white woman, leading to the ultimate betterment of humankind (inspiring scientific discovery and professional accomplishment in white men), is counterposed to the native woman's allure.[14]

Although most critical attention was focused on the dramatic narrative, the reviewer for the *New York Times* saluted the "weirdly sensuous music," performed by five Hawaiian musicians. Hulas were also performed, and a few minor roles were played by Hawaiians, according to the cast listing. Exactly what these stagings yielded must remain open to speculation, but one reviewer questioned whether "a native Hawaiian would not find much of it as strange to him as it is to us." However, questions of authenticity were of little consequence to the ultimate success of the vehicle, which rested upon notions of the dangerous allure of native women and the exoticism of Hawai'i. As one reviewer put it: "The sense of superstition in the Hawaiians is so graphically conveyed in their speech, their dances and ceremonials that even the least intelligent entity of the theatre audience will be able to grasp its ultimate significance."[15] Just as important, the play underwrote a vision of whitened native female beauty by casting a Caucasian in the leading Native Hawaiian role—a practice which would expand in the next few years.[16]

While these early performances by Jennie Wilson and others paved the way for a mainland interest in Hawaiian music and dance and began to popularize a hapa-haole look, the real explosion began after musicians and dancers appeared at the 1915 Panama-Pacific Exposition in San Francisco, which celebrated the opening of the Panama Canal and continued the themes of the 1893 exposition: progress, expansionism, and Social Darwinism. The Territory of Hawai'i legislature, with an eye toward promoting its products and itself as a tourist destination, appropriated $100,000 to build a Hawaiian Pavilion. It was a huge hit, with hula dance and music shows running several times a day. All together, nearly nineteen million people attended the seven-month run of the exposition.[17] Thousands of people heard Hawaiian music for the first time, and the popularity stimulated a rush of Tin Pan Alley compositions. The results were dramatic. A full-scale national fad was underway. In 1916 Hawaiian-style music sold more records on the mainland than any other type of popular music.[18]

This music fad was accompanied by an explosion of hula-style dancing throughout the country. From the most elite theaters on Broadway to tent shows and chautauquas in small towns, "hula girls" proliferated. The dancers were almost always female, often Caucasian, and rarely highly trained in hula. From the mid-teens through the 1920s these performances reached mainland populations of all social classes and helped codify a vision of Hawai'i as feminized, embodied, sensual, and hapa haole. These renditions of a Hawai'i imaginary contributed to the growth of a tourist destination image and prepared the way for substantial growth in tourism in the 1920s and 1930s.

Dancers like Toots Paka exemplified this trend. Paka, reputedly of Native American and Caucasian ancestry, married July Paka, a musician and a favorite of Queen Lili'uokalani, while he was on tour in San Francisco. Although she had never been to Hawai'i, she designed glamorous costumes that exposed her ankles, learned a few hulas and a few words of Hawaiian, and packaged herself as a Hawaiian dancer. She toured with several musicians as "Toots Paka's Hawaiians" and was instantly successful, attracting the services of Pat Casey, the most exclusive agent in New York City at the time. As one of the most famous touring Hawaiian troupes on the mainland during the first quarter of this century, they played to big crowds in Chicago, Baltimore, Boston, and San Francisco, paving the way for other performers.

They played the Orpheum circuit and on Broadway, as a "class" act. For a performance at the Bell Opera House in Chicago, their act was promoted as: "It's among the classics; go where society goes." In 1916 they had a full thirty-minute slot in Madison Square Garden on the same program with Ethel Barrymore, Lionel Barrymore, and Charles Dana Gibson.[19] Their big success helped publicize a non-Hawaiian, half-Caucasian look as the prototype of the hula dancer.

In the teens, hula dancers' popularity was driven in part by a burgeoning entertainment market for non-WASP representations and, sometimes, nonwhite performers. The staging of "exotic primitives" of all sorts, including renditions of African-American, Native American, and Egyptian performances, whether presented as alluring or frightening, whether denigrated or celebrated, was a key component of both popular and more elite entertainment during the latter part of the nineteenth century and into the first decades of the twentieth. It coincided with both imperial expansion abroad and increasing social segmentation at home as shifts in urban populations resulted from waves of im-

migration from southern and eastern Europe as well as migration to urban centers by African Americans. As Eric Lott and Amy Koritz have respectively shown in their studies of mid-nineteenth-century U.S.
minstrelsy and British fascinations with Salome dancers in the late
1800s, such popular representations functioned as complex stagings
of desire and disgust, with implicit nativist, nationalist, and gendered
ideological meanings.[20]

Although white appetites for entertainments based on racialized exotica were wide-ranging during this time, Hawaiian manifestations of
this desire had the added allure of being outside time, memory, and important mainland historical events, such as slavery and its aftermath.
They escaped the legacies of fear and potentially violent hatred which lay
submerged in the black-white mainland interactions, even when those
were commercialized and sold as desire, as they were in the white treks to
Harlem during the twenties. So even though Hawaiian female performative representations must be considered part of this generalized production of a primitivist Other, its specificity must also be distinguished.

As Nicholas Thomas has argued with respect to the history of colonialism, all instances of colonialism are unique, although they may
share certain characteristics.[21] Similarly, in terms of representations of
nonwhite populations and their perceptions by whites, each population carries a specific historical charge based in part on historical relations between the representers and represented. I have argued that the
brown-not-black formulation, the feminine-not-masculine embodiment, and the imaginary of the South Seas as a romantic paradise are all
key ideological frames that shape the cultural meanings of these Hawaiian performances.

These aspects differ from the predominantly male African-American
representations of nineteenth-century minstrelsy as well as the popularity of African-American shows with urban white audiences during
the twenties. These shows usually featured light-skinned females, reflecting the Caucasian standard of beauty melded with a frisson of alluring difference, the supposed hypersexuality of the black female, as
Linda Mizejewski has noted.[22] While a similar mixing of (white) beauty
category and assumed (nonwhite) sexiness may have been going on in
the hulas of performers like Doraldina and Gilda Gray, the sexuality ascribed to Hawaiian women was different from that ascribed in the popular white imagination to African-American women.[23] The hula girl
retained a sense of innocence as part of the imaginary of soft primitivism, shading this sexuality toward a nonaggressive sensuality rather
than the hyperbolic sexuality sometimes ascribed to African-American

women. Visual representations on postcards, calendars, and sheet music covers bear this out.

Such performative renditions of Others also served to consolidate a vision of a national identity which was white, as white as the All-American Girl. In her complex discussion of the Ziegfeld showgirl as icon, Mizejewski points out that "whiteness [was] produced by the Ziegfeld enterprise through its constant need to distinguish, to define, and to allude to the Otherness by which an American Girl can be determined."[24] In the case of the Ziegfeld girl, this whiteness also had an upper-class dimension, excluding other populations doubly, first on the basis of racial category, and second as lower class. Ironically, the production of such whiteness was dependent upon the alluring representation of that which it was not.

However, as Amy Koritz has argued with regard to English nationalism at the turn of the century, nationhood is also a gendered concept. The association with Orientalized others through the dances of white women on the concert stage had a double function. It simultaneously Orientalized the white female, indicating her linkage with other females, and thus her ultimate exclusion from English nationhood, which was defined as masculine, while also signaling Englishness by representing others who were not and could never really be English.[25]

In terms of this function of uniting race with notions of a national identity, the situation regarding Hawai'i was somewhat different. Popular U.S. entertainments that referenced Africa and African Americans remained melded with a specific U.S. legacy of slavery, a position not associated with Hawaiians. And Hawai'i was by that time already situated as a playground for white mainlanders, both a safe part of the United States and apart from it. These "natives" were "ours," as turn-of-the century books shouted, celebrating the annexation of new lands with titles like Our Islands and Their People. Ultimately, Hawaiians were seen as more civilizable than African Americans, more potentially assimilable into the nation. The "brownness" that placed Jennie Wilson in the middle of the 1893 Midway rather than on the end with the "real savages," also made later Broadway incarnations more suitable as an advertisement for pleasurable tourism. The hapa-haole look came to symbolize this attractive native presence, as the Hawaiian craze swept through theaters, cabarets, and summer resorts in the mid-teens. But the ultimate ambivalence about assimilation of nonwhites seeped through in discourses of primitivism. While not as primitive as Africans, Hawaiians still apparently needed some refinement in order to succeed on Broadway.

Doraldina, one of the best known hula specialists during this period, exemplified this look and this process of refinement. Like Toots Paka, she was not of Hawaiian descent. Conflicting reports place her birthplace in Barcelona or Chicago, and her parents are described as Indian and Spanish. The *New York Sun* touted her "extraordinary skin and complexion."[26] Her look was not Polynesian, but rather closer to the look of combined Polynesian and Caucasian descent that would become dominant in island tourist shows later. She also anticipated the dark-haired Caucasian "native" look made popular by Hollywood stars in hits like "Waikiki Wedding" during the 1930s.

Just as popular social dances of the period were being adapted from African-American styles and repackaged, "whitened," for middle-and upper-class white consumption by dance instructors like Vernon and Irene Castle, so too did Doraldina supposedly "improve" on the source. A 1916 review of her dancing in the *New York Sun* describes this process while saluting her hula dances in the Lew Fields revue "Step This Way" at the Schubert Theater as "something new under the sun in stage dancing." What was new, apparently, was not hula but the quality of this rendition. The reviewer notes: "The Hula dance, though not new either in name or imitation, had yet to be presented in such a manner that its sensuous gracefulness and its exotic originality would be preserved and at the same time so that the sensitiveness of Western audiences would not be outraged by the native Hula in all its primitiveness."[27]

Doraldina's artistry, for this reviewer, resides in her ability to modify the original dance so that "she neither offends by the least vulgarity nor disillusions by spoiling its originality by too great an application of Western refinement." Such a statement recalls the combination of desire and disgust spelled out on the back of the pre-1900 stereoscope card cited earlier: "No matter how much such a [hula] scene was enjoyed by the natives, it was too intense to prove anything but disappointing to civilized people." Doraldina contends she accomplished this conversion by immersing herself in the study of hula and folklore in Hawai'i.

But questions of authenticity were hardly the point for these audiences. A more germane clue to Doraldina's appeal can be found in her insurance policies, which insured her legs for $125,000.[28] The stock hula girl costume was perfect for presenting her "respectable" version of sexuality. As Erenberg has noted in his discussion of new leisure activities for heterosexual couples: "The ideal chorus girl [had to] combine a sensuality with niceness, and this showed up in the clothing she wore. . . . The approach to dressing was a peek-a-boo style, with neither customers nor performers having to admit the full sexual, and hence dangerous, potential of the women." Hula skirts, with their peek-a-boo grass skirts, were perfect for this effect, and as Erenberg notes, "Soon after the Hawaiian craze, chorus girls donned grass skirts as a staple of their costuming and performed hulas as a regular part of their act."[29]

Doraldina's performances were not limited to New York supper clubs like the Montmartre and Reisenwebers and Broadway shows like the 1916 *Step This Way*. Like many performers of the time, she also toured her most popular dances on the Keith Vaudeville circuit and worked in early silent films, playing a South Sea Islander in the 1918 Pathé release, *The Naulahka*, and Metro's 1921 *The Passion Fruit*.[30] This wide range of venues visited by Doraldina and the many other "ethnic" dancers that she influenced helped saturate the U.S. public with these hapa-haole hula images.[31]

Among these was Gilda Gray, born Marianne Michalski and one of the few non-WASP types to work for Ziegfeld.[32] She became known for her hula dances on Broadway in the late 1920s and was even touted as a more beautiful Hawaiian than the Hawaiians by columnist Karl Kitchen, who, upon seeing hula in Hawai'i, denigrated the performers as "too fat." Describing these "tropical babes of the South Seas," he says, "there never was a South Sea Islander who could shake a hip in competition with Gilda Gray."[33] This remark, and the performances of Gray, Doraldina, and Paka, all contribute to the popularization of a "whitened" ideal of the Hawaiian hula girl, a hapa-haole look that would dominate the Hollywood screen during the thirties and forties.

It also indicates a process of sexualizing Caucasian performers through their associations with natives, a linkage that would emerge in Hawai'i tourist advertising, on calendars, and on sheet-music covers in the teens and later, when Caucasian hula maids were portrayed or Caucasian women were shown in tandem with Hawaiian women. I call this process "nativizing," a kind of temporary imaginary racial crossing signaled by visual and performative cues. It is akin to the concept of "going native" but retains a brief temporality, caught in "vacation" mode.

SONGS AND DANCES

A mixing of Caucasian and non-Caucasian stylings took place not only in bodily presentation but also in the emergence of hapa-haole music, and at the level of the choreography too. The Broadway craze of the teens was fueled by an explosion of interest in Hawaiian music and the rise of hapa-haole songs (meaning part-white, or foreign). Sung in English rather than Hawaiian, and invariably accompanied by the ukulele,[34] these songs adapted *hula ku'i* (nineteenth-century chant) melodies to current mainland musical styles.[35]

The images of Hawai'i created by these Tin Pan Alley stylists are still familiar to us today. As musicologist Elizabeth Tatar notes, the "lyrics, often comical and risqué for that early period, invariably conveyed images of Waikiki—sand, surf, coconut trees, and girls (preferably dancing the hula)."[36] One typical and successful song, published in 1916, was called "Oh, How She Could Yacki Hacki Wicki Wacki Woo: (That's Love in Honolu)." The sheet music features a drawing of a coyly smiling hula dancer on the cover and includes such immortal lines as "She had a hula hula hicki boola boola in her walk,/ She had a ukulele wicki wicki waili in her talk. . . ."[37] Although some of these words are Hawaiian (*wiki-wiki* means "to hurry," e.g.), the comedic, nonsensical implications come strongly through, placing the Hawaiians and the hula girls firmly in the realm of the cutely inarticulate, hence primitive or childlike.

Tin Pan Alley marketers distributed music every way possible to reach the widest audience, and records, sheet music, radio, stage productions, vaudeville, and piano rolls all spun out their songs. Hawaiian music became spectacularly successful. Hawai'i was re-created through these songs as an arena of sensuous play for white mainlanders, a place of mental escape which seized the national imagination.

The staged choreography to these songs also mixed Hawaiian motifs with non-Hawaiian dance steps. For example, prolific stage director and choreographer Ned Wayburn, working on Broadway and in vaudeville circuits during the first two decades of this century, devised hundreds of solo specialty dances which could be easily inserted into musical revues. His hulas, vaguely described as Hawaiian, Polynesian, Javanese, or South Seas in origin, were popular from the mid-teens to early 1920s and are described by theater historian Barbara Stratyner as basically "a shimmy with waving arms." Most of these solo numbers were performed in the eccentric mode (an exaggerated movement of hips and limbs) and used Wayburn's codified techniques of musical comedy dance, tap, acrobatics, and modern, Americanized ballet.[38]

Three of these pieces were "I Left Her on the Beach at Honolulu," a ragtime number performed in the *Ziegfeld Follies of 1916*; "Luana Lou," in both *Ned Wayburn's Girlie Gambols* and the *Ziegfeld Midnight Frolics,* both of 1916; and "'Neath the South Sea Moon," from the *Ziegfeld Follies of 1922*. As Stratyner reveals, each of these numbers included a song and dance inserted into the revue, featuring a nostalgic male singer remembering his past romance with a Hawaiian dancer. Palm trees formed the setting for both "Beach" and "Moon," and both numbers featured a chorus of twenty-four women performing a barefoot hula. "Moon" also featured extensive dialogue, the characters of a male and a female tourist, and vocalist John Steele singing to "mainlander" Ina Claire while Gilda Gray danced the hula. Such stagings brought to life similar scenes depicted on sheet-music covers and in tourism advertising, where Caucasians find love through the sexualizing presence of the hula dancer. This intertexuality linked entertainment and tourism, reinforcing the talismanic iconicity of the hula dancer and her centrality to the destination image of Hawai'i.[39]

Given that Weyburn's shows often included parodies of straight renditions of both elite forms like Anna Pavlova's ballet performances and his popular "Arabian" numbers, it is possible that parodies of hula co-existed on the same stage, too.[40] Such a co-existence of a simulation and its potential parody would lighten the import of the dance further, emphasizing its playful, unthreatening quality of otherness. In the same mode of play, Caucasian women could experiment with exotic styles noted in magazines, trying them on as one might a dress, shading themselves with a dose of the primitive for a limited time, provocative yet protected from any real danger for their difference. This play with nativizing continues to form one of the subtexts of Hawaiian vacation advertising, as the next section will discuss.

As consumers of dance routines, women were given the chance to act out this motif. Home-study courses in dance were popular at the time, and Weyburn produced manuals and dance instructions of all sorts. Gilda Gray's "South Sea Dance," for example, was notated by a student of Wayburn's and published in *Dance Lovers Magazine* in 1924. As Stratyner has noted, this dance was "in strict routine format, with all the identifiable elements of Wayburn's musical comedy choreography, including the repetition of steps, the emphasis on oblique angles, and the use of step turns."[41] Picture shimmying hips and waving arms pasted on top of these lunges, and you have an image of Gilda Gray's hula.

Following Gilda Gray's instructions from *Dance Lovers Magazine*, I tried to reconstruct this dance in my own living room.[42] It proved to be a challenge for which my previous hula training was of absolutely no help. It is clear from the choreography and the framing of her instructions that fidelity to any original or authentic hula was immaterial. The real frames of reference were the stage-dancing conventions of the day, combined with a generalized Orientalism (which for Gray included far more than East Asia).[43] Various models of non-European-derived styles provided narrative and ideological framings which facilitated a certain type of female body display. These cross-racial or cross-cultural representations, which I call "facilitating fictions," required hip and pelvis movement, sensuous framing of the body with the arms, the shuddering of shoulders, breasts, and hands, and quite a bit of bared skin on the legs, arms, and torso.[44]

Gray discusses this facilitating fiction when she traces the relationship between the shimmy and the "South Sea Island Dance": "You see the 'shimmy' was popular for a while, but then the blue law vogue came in, and it was one of the very first things picked on. I had to think of something new to do. Then I decided to enlarge the 'shimmy'—instead of just the shoulder shaking I used the whole body. Well, of course this could get me even further in wrong with the censors if I wore every-day clothes. So I decided to wear a 'Hula-Hula' costume, as the dance was really suitable for that—and didn't I get away with it? Even the old cranks think it is perfectly all right for a 'Hula-Hula' to shake, so that costume squared everything."[45] The grass skirt anchored this rendition of the shimmy in the South Seas.

Gray gives instructions for making this costume. A grass skirt is best made out of green raffia sewed on a wide canvas belt that will ride on the hips. For a top, she suggests covering a brassiere with red silk. Artificial flowers (poppies are good) are worn around the waistband, as a headband, and at the ankles, unless one prefers feathers attached to the toes. Still more adornment is needed: "You will want as many necklaces as you can beg, borrow or steal. Beads of every color and shells are the best. Also wear lots of bracelets, both wrist ones and those for the upper arms," she advises. The popularity of Gilda Gray and her costumes is indicated in the article by the final illustration, a photograph of "Baby Jeannette Sauer," two-year-old imitator of Gilda Gray, decked out just as advised above, in a costume combining a flapper aesthetic of headbands, bangles, and beads with a baring of skin.[46]

The ideological relation of the South Seas to other mythic, non-European locales and populations is indicated in the opening instructions for the dance. Gray states: "When you do a 'South Sea Dance,' a 'Hula-Hula' dance, a 'Voodoo dance,' or any kind of an Oriental dance, one of the most important things for you to remember is that you are not Mary Smith or Jones or whatever your name may be. While you work you have another personality, you have left commonplace America behind and you are out on the white sands of a desert island. . . . You are this girl, Hawaiian, Indian, or whatever she may be."[47]

The genericism of this Orientalia is indicated in the instructions about music: "For this dance . . . I would suggest something like 'Dance Orientale,' 'Three African Dances,' or 'Tunisienne.' Of course the music will require cutting and arranging as these steps are not worked out especially for any of those selections."[48] Thus, although in one sense the hula is situated in this amorphous "Orient" that includes Africa (as in the lumping together of "the 'Hula-Hula' dance, a 'Voodoo Dance,' or any kind of an Oriental dance"), it is simultaneously specified as South Seas and thus carries all the positive associations of the "good" (brown, not black) native that I have argued earlier is essential to Hawai'i's success as a tourist destination.

What exactly did she *do* in this dance, once the beads and fake flowers and grass skirt were donned? Above all, the dancer is advised to keep the movements as smooth as possible and to use the hips. Various segments in phrases of eight, sixteen, or thirty-two counts structure the piece. Begin with arms curved overhead and one leg forward, knee bent and ball of the foot touching the floor. Sway your hips for eight counts. Follow this with a series of "Oriental turns," which consist of pivoting on one foot in place while using the other to paddle yourself around. Bend the standing knee in a pumping action on each beat, and don't forget to shimmy your hips as you go. (This, she notes, may be too much for the beginner. If so, add the hip shimmy after you have mastered the turn.)

Next follows a series of steps to the front which seems to resemble the Charleston. The dance finishes with a series of lunges in big circles traveling around the stage, more "Oriental" turns, ending in the opening position with arms above the head. Then, starting at the knees, the dancer sends a shimmy up the body, adding hips, shoulders, and hands until the whole body is shimmying, finishing it off with a quick turn and lunge to the side.

Building from the stationary hip sways of the beginning, the dance first elaborates the swaying hips with added arm movement and torso bends, displaying the body in all directions, front, back and side, and climaxes with a full shimmy rolling up the whole body. Opening out into space, the dancer then circles the stage only to end back at center with another climactic shimmy, a shuddering built over sixteen counts, to be capped at the end with a quick turn and lunge. The structure posits an increasing drama of expanding space and speeding shimmy with a climax of closure.

While the implied sexual dynamics of arousal and climax may be clear, the relation of the choreography to hula traditions is completely imaginary. Big circles through space, shaking shoulders, lunges in all directions, bent torsos, and arm movement limited to swinging and fluttering would have produced a rendition of hula unrecognizable in the islands. There, many styles valued a portly carriage of the spine, relatively stationary footwork, with little traveling through space, and, above all, hand-and-arm gestures that were figurative representations of the words to songs or chants.[49]

This "misrepresentation" may have been important to some island residents, but it was not a prime determinant of the meanings these hulas held for their mainland audiences or for the women who pieced the dance together from such instructions and hoped to be, as Gray put it, "one of . . . my rival[s] on Broadway!"[50] The Gilda Gray version signified a South Seas beauty, and the centrality of the shimmy provides a key to understanding just what that stood for.

The shimmy, which Gilda Gray claimed to have invented after it just came to her "naturally," actually had its origins in African-American social dances, many of which were whitened and re-presented by Caucasian theatrical performers.[51] It thus signaled a link to the "dusky belles" who populated African-American musicals of the period. These musicals attracted large white audiences as well as black audiences or, in the "black and tan" clubs of 1920s Harlem, mixed audiences. Linda Mizejewski has argued that the black musicals and white musicals of the period were intimately linked both in particular elements of performance style (revues of leggy chorus girls, e.g.) and in the occasional crossover of performers (black performers in predominantly white musicals, or white performers donning "cafe au lait" makeup to reproduce the light-skinned African-American showgirl look of the twenties).

Most important though, she suggests that such renditions framed the white, northern European–style beauty as fundamentally American during a period of rising immigration, Jim Crow laws, race riots, and eugenicist arguments against so-called miscegenation during the first decades of the twentieth century.[52] By donning the darker makeup, Mizejewski suggests, the "white" white (not Italian, not Jewish) American showgirl both identified with the allure of her counterpart on the "darker" end of Broadway (e.g., the all-black hit musical *Shuffle Along*, of 1921) and simultaneously established her distinctness from her. Similar moves had been going on in the emergent modern dance world since the turn of the century, as Amy Koritz and I have argued.[53] In all of these renderings the difference between acting or looking like, and being, was crucial to the cultural work of the representation.[54]

This linkage of sexuality, race, and nation plays out in the hula girl discourse in a way which is at once the same as and different from the "dusky belle" type of beauty. These light-skinned African-American showgirls combined blackness with Caucasianesque features in a creole look that is similar to the hapa-haole look that Toots Paka had popularized in the previous decade. Both looks validate a standard of beauty based on Western European bodies while simultaneously undercutting its pre-eminence.

But, as Mizejewski notes, all nonwhites were not equally situated on the stage or in the hierarchy of "true" Americans. African Americans were on the bottom as the least assimilable, southern Europeans and Jews in the middle, and northern Europeans ("native" Americans) at the top—the most authentically "American" Americans. Zeigfeld's elaborate construction of 1920s "female pulchritude" was part of just such a public discourse articulating a nativist vision of America. "The circulated images of white women were dependent, for their value, on the presence and performance of other racial and ethnic identities," argues Mizejewski.[55]

Recall Gilda Gray's instructions to those who would learn her dance: "One of the most important things for you to remember [while dancing] is that you are not Mary Smith or Jones or whatever your name may be. While you work you have another personality, you have left commonplace America behind."[56] The invocation of Anglophone names (Smith, Jones, Mary) and "commonplace America" is telling. These explicit instructions for the nativizing performative process are targeted at and simultaneously construct a (particular kind of) white America which it is possible, temporarily, to "leave behind."

Marianne Michalski, a Polish immigrant who had settled in Milwaukee, had changed her Eastern European name to the more English-sounding Gray and added the gilding of "Gilda."[57] Thus repositioned as "really" American, and "really" white, she could become the leading hula dancer in New York, safely nativizing herself while positioned at the center of a nativist (i.e., Anglo-American) discourse. This imaginary process of nativizing thus cut both ways, articulating in one act both senses of the word "native": "going native" and being native born to the United States. Only the latter could do the former. While the transformative process of nativizing was usually rendered publicly through performance, advertisements, and sheet music covers, it now also became available to women in the privacy of their homes as they practiced Gilda Gray's dance, literally rehearsing an embodiment of difference.

I would suggest that the tremendous popularity of the hula craze on the stage during the teens and twenties is due to its complexity as one strand of these intertwining racial, sexual, and national discourses. Following the 1898 imperial moves by the United States, Hawai'i had emerged as the "best" of the new colonies. Hawaiian women were judged the most beautiful, the population was deemed intelligent enough to be assimilable, and the stereotype of the soft (ideal) primitive was confirmed, as I argued at the close of the preceding chapter. Thousands of miles away, yet part of the United States, Hawaiians were perfect imaginary Others, nonthreatening, lacking a history of substantial conflict with mainlanders (at least as the story was known on the mainland), and colorful (literally) enough to be exotic without being (dangerously) black. When (Eastern European) Marianne Michalski did the (African-American) shimmy as a (South Seas) hula to the (Far Eastern) music of "Danse Oriental," she staged in all their complexity the imaginary geographies of desire, fear, and competing visions of America that female bodies on the stage could be made to bear.

These wildly popular mainland performances—from Broadway to tent shows to world expositions, on records and in supper clubs—exposed millions to an embodied vision of an imaginary Hawai'i. They prepared the ground for the development of a Hawaiian tourist industry based on cultural tourism and created an appetite for Hawaiian music and dance among tourists that would eventually bring performers right into the hotels as a constituent part of the tourist experience in the 1920s. The gap between visiting Broadway for a night of Hawai'i and spending a week on a boat to get there was bridged by a new wave of advertising that developed following World War I. The next chapter examines the relationship between such advertising, scientific discourse, and island performances during the 1920s.

FOUR

Advertising, Racializing, and Performing Hawai'i on Site

The Emergence of Cultural Tourism in the 1920s

By the end of the 1920s, tourism ranked as the third largest industry in the islands, behind sugar and pineapple plantation agriculture. The earliest turn-of-the-century advertisements of "Sunny Shores" and "Unrivalled Climate" would be replaced by images of hula dancers, who came to stand in for Native Hawaiian culture as a whole. The institutionalization of cultural tourism, aided by the proliferation of mainland performances previously discussed, had begun. This chapter examines the intricate linkages between advertising, on-site performances, and contemporary racial discourse that were the enabling conditions of the emergence of such an embodied, performative vision of Hawai'i in the 1920s.

ADVERTISING HAWAI'I

Following World War I, tourism was fueled by an increase in advertising by steamship companies and the Hawaiian Tourist Bureau. Honolulu was increasingly portrayed as a refuge from the demands of work for the urban elite, as a safe, American, holiday destination, exotic yet comfortingly familiar, unspoiled, yet with all the modern conveniences one might need. It was a playground for whites, who often visually dominate the advertisements.

Yet the native presence is always just below the surface, even when not visually represented. It is evoked by ad copy references to "flower-scented breezes . . . Languorous charm . . . Seductive native music and song . . . ," all of which implicitly feminize, naturalize, and nativize the island destination, portraying it as a place where languorous, nonworking natives indulge their every sense of pleasure.[1] Tourists, the ads imply, can recover such lost innocence for themselves.

An early precursor to the 1995 "Come to Life in Hawai'i" ad makes this promise explicit. In 1926 *Life* magazine ran a Hawaii Tourist Bureau advertisement headed by the slogan "Take a South Sea Honeymoon this autumn—Grow young again in Hawaii."[2] A Caucasian couple in sport clothes encounters two seated smiling Native Hawaiian women stringing leis, against a backdrop of mountains and palm trees by the shore. One woman offers a lei to the man. Below, the text invites you on that honeymoon: "Even if it's a few years past due—no matter! Shake off the clutches of the workaday world! Come where the islands of Hawaii sun themselves in the blue Pacific. . . . Where *you*, growing staid in business, will live the dreams that should never have been put away." Presumably, these dreams include a sexual rejuvenation—a second honeymoon. (Weddings, honeymoons, and anniversaries remain a big portion of the Hawaiian tourism market, underlining the continuing linkage of heterosexual romance with the islands.) The "hula girl" becomes the symbol through which this transformation happens.

All this is sold as "inexpensive," but this transformation was really only available to the very elite. A trip of "four or five weeks [which] gives you a comfortable round trip, with time for golf, tennis, interisland cruising, hiking, swimming and outrigger canoeing at Waikiki to your heart's content—days of *resting*!" is packaged at $400–$500 for all steamer fares, hotels, sightseeing, the volcano trip to Hawai'i National Park, with ample accommodations throughout. And, indeed, it may have seemed inexpensive for some. During the nineteen twenties, although many workers on the mainland did improve their standard of living, the disparity between rich and poor grew as well. The richest 5 percent of the population came to control a third of the country's wealth, with the top 1 percent controlling 19 percent of all income.[3] Estimates of the required income to maintain an acceptable standard of living for a family during that period ranged from $2,000 to $2,400 a year, the same amount a wealthy family might spend on their Honolulu vacation.

Although the lei sellers in the advertisement noted above are in dresses, not grass skirts, they wear flower wreaths in their hair, linking them to the hula girl iconography. The hula girl does appear in ads by the Los Angeles Steamship Co. toward the end of the 1920s, but not yet (at least as far as I have found) in Hawaiian Tourist Bureau ads. In the steamship ads, the hula girl dances or sings, strumming a ukulele, and is spotlighted by a giant moon or a steamship lamp, which reduces her to a silhouetted icon.

One such 1928 ad, by the Los Angeles Steamship Co., recalls the nativizing function discussed earlier in terms of mainland stage shows.[4] It shows a secluded beach scene with Diamond Head in the background. A native hula maiden wearing only a strategically placed lei and grass skirt leans against a palm, strumming a ukulele. Angled toward her, sitting on the beach, is a Caucasian woman in a bathing suit, light hair bobbed, gazing out at the sea. Their gazes do not intersect, yet they appear to live in parallel worlds, each caught in her own dreams. The ad text invites us to "Hanamalea!"—to enjoy the very essence of perfect relaxation in the native Hawaiian "spirit-of-taking-life-easy." Soon we will reach *hanamelea*, the state of relaxation to the point of indolence sublime.

This ad foregrounds the feminization of Hawai'i and the transposition of the white and native women. This iconographic pairing of white and native women will occur in later advertisements as well, but this is one of the earliest renditions. Presumably such a pairing addresses both male and female viewers—males who might want their rest from work to include female indolence, and Caucasian women who might want to experience the same, for themselves or as nativized objects of Caucasian male desire.

Similar nativized renditions of Caucasian women were featured on calendars and on posters for Mid-Pacific Honolulu Carnival festivals in the teens and twenties. Surviving examples of calendar illustrations feature numerous versions of grass-skirted Euro-American beauties with light or dark brown hair. White limbs are warmed in the glow of sunshine or moonlight, while the obliging skirt falls open to reveal expanses of creamy skin. Sometimes topless, with a ukulele or lei partially covering the bare breasts, and sometimes more modestly covered in a colorful bandeau top, the hula girl smiles dreamily, surrounded by lush foliage: woman as nature/native.

On sheet-music covers she may be accompanied by a handsome white suitor. For example, the 1922 sheet-music cover for "Moonlight, Hawaii, and You" foregrounds a Caucasian couple on the beach at Diamond Head in formal clothes, he in a camel-colored suit, she in a strapless sheath. Moonlight kisses the waves and highlights their skin. The woman strums the ukulele while the man gazes contemplatively down the beach. In all of these visual renditions, it is the Caucasian woman who is nativized, takes on the look, accessories, and presumably the alluring sexuality of the native hula girl, while the man, if present in the image or if, in the case of pin-ups, situated as the viewer of the image, does not become nativized. His pleasure comes from his contact with the nativized woman.[5]

This nativizing transformation is made explicit in a postcard circulating in 1925, captioned "A Haole Hula Girl." The photo, by Jerome
Baker, poses a white grass-skirted Canadian named Rose Heather
against an unpainted backdrop. Adorned with leis and wearing a sleeveless hula blouse, she laughs out at us while playing the ukulele.[6]
Presumably the postcard serves as evidence that once in Hawai'i, Caucasian women can happily and easily "go native."

Like the steamship advertisements, the Hawaiian Tourist Bureau advertisements also included drawings of Native Hawaiians at this time,
but none uses the explicit iconography of the ukulele-playing, grass-
skirted hula girl yet. Aeko Sereno has argued that the HTB wanted to
rescue the image of the hula girl from its mainland misrepresentations
as elite tourism began to boom, and this may indeed be the reason. It's
true that "hootch dancing" in tent shows and burlesque houses hardly
presented a good image, and these renditions persisted even as late as
the 1940s in circus sideshows, continuing the midway associations begun by Jennie Wilson fifty years earlier.[7] A 1925 guidebook defensively
remarks: "Many bands of Hawaiian troubadours are forever abroad, de-
lighting the people of far places with the plaintive music of Aloha-land,
though there are numerous organizations wrongly calling themselves
Hawaiian, and not a few—Hawaiians and make-believe Hawaiian—
that 'jazz' Hawaiian music out of all resemblance to the real. The genuine 'hula' dance of Hawaii is a charming exhibition, though mercenary
exploiters frequently seek to substitute sensation for art."[8]

As I have noted earlier, however, the representation of hula on the
mainland was a complicated one. While hootch dancing was one perceived strand, with lower-class associations, another more elite strand
co-existed on Broadway and in supper clubs. These renditions may not
have borne much relation to hula in the islands, but they did not merely
offer a debased version of something authentic. Rather, they seem to
have offered an iconic image of feminized exotica that ran the gamut
from the sensual to the frankly sexual and involved both Hawaiian and
non-Hawaiian performers. Surely the elite guests had already encountered some of the more refined versions of hula on the mainland, like
Doraldina's or Gilda Gray's performances. The dominance of the hula
image on the mainland doubtlessly bled over into tourists' perceptions
of images of native women, such as the lei sellers in the advertisement
discussed above.

In some ads of this period, men and boys are also shown, most often
surfing or paddling a canoe, hence relatively unclad, yet nimble, strong,
unaggressive. But, strikingly, Native men and women are never shown

together in these ads. Such an omission accomplishes several things. It allows the image of the hula girl to seem available to the viewer, unrestricted by Native male sexuality. In a similar, though less obviously emphasized, way it does the same for the male figures. And, in addition, the omission destroys any parallelism with the white couples portrayed. Native Hawaiians are apparently not sexual with one another and do not have full family units in these pictures. They are unencumbered by domesticity, precisely one-half of the work/domestic life dyad that vacationing elite are trying to escape.[9]

They are also, apparently, unencumbered by work, living simply on the bountiful Edenic land. The only work images are of flower stringing or palm weaving. Surfing with tourists is portrayed as play rather than the money-earning work it is, and the full-blown plantation economy is almost without exception invisible. Natives seem only to play, sing, dance, and frolic. For example, one 1927 advertisement features a young boy climbing a coconut tree to retrieve nuts.[10] (Such demonstrations were part of hotel entertainment; hence the ad actually shows a young man working, represented as playful gymnastics.) Inviting us to "Skim Blue Seas to an Island Eden," this Hawaiian Tourist Bureau ad asks, "Have you ever seen a lithe bronze-skinned boy walking up a cocoanut palm? Hawaiians singing at a luau (native feast) on the beach in the moonlight? . . . A volcano so friendly that you can motor to its edge and peer down into its smoking depths—so awe-inspiring that you half believe the native legends of the goddess Pele who lives inside? Then imagine yourself on these cool, enchanted islands in the South Seas this summer—with two thousand miles of dreamy ocean between you and the humdrum of home and business!" Temporarily, the tourist, too, can become like the carefree natives.

Here the emphasis on nature tourism in the earliest ads is melding with more explicit references to Native Hawaiian culture. It is important that these natives are bronze skinned (not black, not white) and friendly, ready to extend hospitality. This is especially important during a period when race riots were erupting on the mainland following the post–World War I migrations of thousands of African Americans to northern urban centers.[11] Two years later, a full-page color ad in *Life* magazine foregrounds the "natives are friendly" theme in visuals and text.[12] A Diamond Head scene is dominated by a handsome Caucasian couple strolling on the beach, where they encounter the figure of a young Native Hawaiian weaving a palm-frond hat. The text says, "Where friendly beach-boys weave native hats or conquer racing waves, erect on charging surfboards . . . " (Beach "boys," hired by the hotels to serve as ocean escorts for tourists, were rarely boys, but rather young and not-so-young men.) In the advertisements, male Native Hawaiians are either reduced to the status of boys, a familiar denigrating term used to refer to African-American men as well, or they retain an adult "manliness" but turn this into service to whites—paddling canoes or giving surfboard rides.

In the above advertisement, the seated male figure looks only at his weaving, providing entertainment for the white tourist couple, described in the ad as "sophisticates enticed by the bizarre" who "know the miracle of a moon of molten silver . . . dancing waters . . . the haunting harmony of sobbing steel-guitars and plaintive voices . . . fragrant breezes . . . [in] a land of enchantment . . . [where] idle days may be dreamed away in tropic bowers still primitive and unspoiled." Lest we worry about how primitive, the fine print at the bottom assures us that we "do not have to bother with passports or other formalities. Hawaii is an integral part of the United States—as much so as your own State." The Native Hawaiians, of course, are not citizens, although "an integral part of the United States."

No other populations are shown in these advertisements, with the exception of one which shows a woman in Japanese dress working in a pineapple field, but her face is hidden, and the ad touts "Nature's summer ambrosia . . . salad of the gods!"[13] Here the silhouette of the woman stands in for island hospitality, not the modern plantation agriculture system and the problematic potentially unassimilable non-Hawaiian populations of Japanese, Chinese, Filipinos, and others it has brought to the islands.

Hawai'i may be "an integral part of the United States," but its twentieth-century tourism has always depended on its positioning as a part of, yet apart from, the mainland. Hawai'i is safe, secure, yet exotic, and the ads emphasize its essence as a slice of the past, reassuring visitors that here, if nowhere else, "Old Hawaii Still Lives," and "Time treads lightly on these isles." In Hawai'i "you'll find life now much as it was a century ago," and a "vacation this summer among such laughing, gentle folk will wipe out mental cobwebs and ennui."[14]

The erasure of history emerges emphatically in these assertions that the past lives on unchanged. In fact, life was nothing like it was a century ago before the arrival of missionaries, the banning of Hawaiian language in the schools (making English-speaking tourists all the more at home), the overthrow of Native Hawaiian Queen Lili'uokalani, the annexation to the United States, the rise of plantation agriculture and the population shifts it caused, and the development of tourism. All of these events are absent from tourist representations, as are all non-Native populations except visiting Caucasians. Also absent are facts about Native Hawaiians which do not fit the tourist native image: their extraordinarily high literacy rate during the nineteenth century for instance, or the fact that they actively participated in government before the overthrow, or of their diminishing populations since white contact. The tourist industry must actively reconstruct a past vision in the present to particularize the destination image of Hawai'i as a place where (only) Native Hawaiians live and whites play.

RACIAL FANTASIES: MIXED AND UNMIXED

Some of these tensions emerged in nontourist, educational publications, just as they did in the stereoscope cards decades earlier. *National Geographic* devoted a full issue to Hawai'i in February of 1924.[15] Gilbert Grosvenor, president of the National Geographic Society, offers the magazine-length report "The Hawaiian Islands: America's Strongest Outpost of Defense—The Volcanic and Floral Wonderland of the World," following an eight-week sojourn in the islands. Although a scientific tone is adopted rather than that of a travelogue, the majority of the text is given over to detailing the strategic importance of the islands and the volcanic wonders that await the intrepid traveler.[16] The essay opens with reference to the Hawaiian people: "When discovered, the Islands were already inhabited by a handsome semicivilized race, a happy and kindly people, fond of music and of the beauties of Nature. . . . The Hawaiians were sufficiently removed from the Tropics to be compelled to work for a living, and thus became intellectually and physically more alert and vigorous than the islanders of the South Pacific. Life in the sea, from which much of their food was obtained, developed superb and agile figures, making them the most daring and powerful swimmers in the world."[17]

Here is repeated the trope of the soft primitive, happy, healthy, attractive, living with the abundance of nature, but not slothful. In short, a type of ideal, except for a misguided un-Christian religion. But beyond these opening remarks and a few references to the elegant table manners of the "early Hawaiians," little is said of Native Hawaiians. The difficulty in conceiving of the Hawaiian population as contemporaries is revealed most sharply in the photographs. At least two-thirds of the photographs are of geologic fixtures, like Kilauea volcano, mountains, valleys, or huge trees. While Caucasians are pictured as Lilliputian hikers amid gigantic ferns or as plantation experts, the photographs of

Hawaiians show "natives" in grass huts, grass skirts, fishing in brief loincloths, or, in the case of three children, lying naked on the beach. What is most interesting is the tension between the text, which describes contemporary Hawai'i, and the photos and the captions, several of which explain that what is shown in the photograph is no longer seen in contemporary Hawai'i.

While reporting the demise of the primitive, National Geographic perpetuates its image. For instance, a large photograph of a grass house accompanies the segment discussing ancient Hawaiian religion. Men pound poi outside, bare chested but wearing trousers. The grass house, surrounded by foliage and tall palms, dominates. The caption says, "An old-time grass house in Hawaii, 1890: The only grass house to be found in the Islands to-day is carefully preserved in the Bishop Museum, and the only hula-hula girls to be seen are those in burlesque shows."[18] Sure enough, a few pages later, a picture accompanying the discussion of the first missionaries in 1819 shows a barely pubescent bare-chested girl with long hair, dressed in raffia skirt, bare legged, and holding a ukulele. She is posed in a studio photograph sitting on a stool, against a floral backdrop. The caption reads "A pure-blooded Hawaiian Girl Wearing the Costume of Past Generations," but the visual impact has been made, reproducing the native stereotype.

Similar double messages come from a portrait of a lone fisherman wearing a malo and holding a long spear, set against a horizon of majestic clouds. Titled "A Hawaiian Landscape: In the Hawaiian Islands to-day only fishermen when in action wear this abbreviated costume."[19] As with the required cancer warning on cigarette advertisements, who is going to read the fine print? The visual power of the photos continually asserts the presence of the past while the words invoke the present. Ten pages later a full-page photograph of three naked children lying on the sand is captioned "Clothed in Nothing But Sunshine." With only bare bodies and sand and sea, and the beach devoid of any marks of built structures, these children seem set in a timeless nature, lacking even the cultural marker of clothing.[20]

The narrative asserts the cosmopolitan sensibility of Honolulu, but nowhere is it seen in the illustrations: "Nor does the visitor, however well prepared by reading and by conversation with Hawaiian advertisers, escape amazement at the great enterprising metropolis of Honolulu which greets him in these lonely islands in mid-Pacific—vociferous taxi-men, flivvers and luxurious limousines, spacious hotels, many miles of suburban concrete roads, morning and afternoon newspapers that publish long press dispatches from the mainland and even give the

daily quotations of the New York stock markets and the big league baseball scores; large department stores thronged with buyers and displaying the latest New York, London, and Paris fashions, a great university
plant and fine public school buildings; a superb country club. . . ."[21]
These marvels are not pictured because they presumably serve mainly
the white business community or tourists, not fit subjects for ethnology.
That any persons of Native descent might use the same facilities, even
attend the university and read the newspapers, is inconceivable within
this narrative.

But race is a fit subject for ethnology, and discussion of it is prominent in the article. Unlike the tourist discourse, which leads us to believe that only Caucasians and Native Hawaiians inhabit Hawai'i, the
article marvels at the number of "races" and their intermixing in
Hawai'i. This is countered by a submerged fear of the Japanese, who, it
is reported, intermix less but are very industrious and now a majority, so
that, as much as annexation is termed "a boon both to the United States
and Hawaii," it brings fear also. Quoting from a 1919 survey under the
direction of the U.S. Commissioner of Education, the article notes ner-
vously the "racial qualities inherent in the Japanese . . . [are] patience,
persistence, thrift, initiative, endurance, ambition, group solidarity,
coupled with acumen and astuteness. This group will soon have a majority of voters of the Islands."[22]

But even more striking is the "Amazing Mixture of Races," as one
subhead proclaims. A full-page photograph illustrates the phenomenon, captioned "Thirty-two Girls, Each of a Different Race or Racial
Combination, All Attending Kawaiahao Seminary, Honolulu: A Striking Illustration of the Mixture of Races that is Taking Place in Hawaii."
The girls, some dressed in plain white dresses, stockings, and shoes,
others posed in Korean dress, Japanese kimonos, and so forth, are all
marked with a number which corresponds to a list, each a specimen of
the mixing: (1) Hawaiian, (2) Ehu Hawaiian, (3) Japanese, (4) Chinese,
(5) Korean, (6) Russian, (7) Filipino, (8) Portuguese, (9) Polish-Rus-
sian, (10) Hawaiian-German, (11) Hawaiian-Chinese, (12) Hawaiian-
Russian, (13) Hawaiian-American, (14) Hawaiian-French, (15) Hawai-
ian-Portuguese, (16) Hawaiian-Filipino-Chinese (17) Hawaiian-
Indian-American, (18) Hawaiian-Japanese-Portuguese, (19) Hawaiian-
Portuguese-American, (20) Hawaiian-Spanish-American, (21) Hawai-
ian-German-Irish, (22) Hawaiian-Spanish-German, (23) Hawaiian-
Chinese-American, (24) Hawaiian-Portuguese-Irish, (25) Hawaiian-
Japanese-Indian, (26) Hawaiian-Portuguese-Chinese-English, (27)
Hawaiian-Chinese-German-Norwegian-Irish, (28) South Sea (Nauru)-

Norwegian, (29) African-French-Irish, (30) Spanish-Porto Rican, (31) Guam-Mexican-French, (32) Samoan-Tahitian. The numbers do not correspond to the positions in the row-by-row placement on the steps of the school, but seem to run along some continuum from "pure" to "mixed" to "very mixed," reaching a high of five claimed ancestries with number 27, and then declining slightly. Once again, female bodies serve as the evidence of racial "essence." Today, people often specify just such complex ancestry patterns in identifying themselves in Hawai'i, and in public mainland discourse a related idea of Hawai'i as a"multicultural paradise" indicates, if not mixing, then harmony among races.

Throughout this extended essay, an increase in future tourism is taken for granted. Hawai'i is presented as a marvel of nature. Unique races and unique geological features combine with nationalism in this narrative of the pleasures and fears involved in being at home, abroad, in the United States and the Pacific. The tourist industry discourse masks these discussions of "racial mixing" and of present cosmopolitanism to produce the trope of the "pure" Native. National Geographic, while acknowledging some complexity in its written text, actually reproduces the tourist images, with their erasure of history, in most of its illustrations. A similar time lag occurred in the stereoscopic pictures discussed in the preceding chapter. The dominance of the visual combines with the evidentiary power of the photograph and the evidence of bodily representation to authenticate and naturalize Hawai'i as a living past.

PERFORMING HAWAI'I ON SITE

Unlike the mainland American West, where the image of the noble savage in the form of the male Indian came to stand for a vanishing way of life and covered over the bloody expansions of Euro-American settlement, in Hawai'i it is the image of the female dancer that stands for a paradisical past, unspoiled by modernity yet willing to be its entertaining hostess. The opulent opening of the Royal Hotel in 1927 sets this contrast and its constitutive role in defining Hawaiian tourism in bold relief.

In the late 1920s, the Matson Navigation Co. decided to expand its Honolulu-based shipping business by building luxury liners to carry visitors from the West Coast to Honolulu, and to house, feed, and entertain them while they were there. To this end, and with the backing of one of the "Big Five " plantation companies, Castle and Cooke, they built the costly Royal Hawaiian Hotel in 1927 on a fifteen-acre parcel on Waikiki Beach. Despite the objections of many Native Hawaiians in the area, the land was purchased from the Bernice Pauahi Bishop estate (owner of most Waikiki land following the controversial privatization of land in the nineteenth century).[23] Just a few years earlier, the Ala Wai canal had been cut through the Waikiki area, draining its mosquito-infested wetland and preparing the way for expanded resort development. Built in two years, at a cost of $4 million, the pink stucco palace was lavishly landscaped and opulently designed in what would then be the largest building project in the Pacific Islands.[24] Banking on success, Matson hired an advertising agency to sell the hotel even before construction started, and all of the hotel's 360 rooms and suites were booked to capacity within six weeks of its opening day on February 1, 1927.[25]

The Spanish-Moorish architecture of the hotel reflected the influence of popular Rudolph Valentino movies of the period, as well as a hint of California Mission style in its cupolas, visual reminders of the West Coast of the United States, of which Hawai'i represented something of a continuation, a pushing of the frontier of the United States beyond the continental boundaries.

The generalized Orientalism of the hotel's architecture was continued in the outdoor dining room, "The Persian Room," in the decorative images of barges floating down the Nile which adorned the original theater/ballroom, and in the massive patterned rugs imported from Tunisia. Reminiscent of the generalized Orientalism of the stage shows discussed earlier, this staging of exotica for the wealthy extended to the service staff as well. Waitresses on the veranda dressed in kimonos to serve tea (their costumes were discontinued during World War II), and eight Chinese men were hired as baggage handlers and dressed in "Chinese"-style uniforms of rounded hats, cropped pants, black slippers, and high-necked jackets with frog closures down the front. The first bellboys, of various local ethnic heritages, were dressed in white shoes, white gloves, white pants with side stripe trim, and jackets, recalling British colonial servant garb.[26]

This splash of an opening at the grandest hotel in Waikiki indicates several things: the luxury market for early tourism which would continue right through the Depression, the generalized Orientalism that pervaded, and, as we shall see, the importance of placing Hawaiian culture right *in* the hotel as a part of the tourist's experience. The phrase "colorful and semibarbaric," which was used to describe the opening night's pageant, also echoes an ambivalent attitude of desire and dismissal, which framed Native Hawaiians as both necessary and expendable to this enterprise.

The grand opening was a massive event, previewed with an eighty-page supplement in the local newspaper, the *Honolulu Star-Bulletin,* which carried advertisements by all the companies involved in building the hotel, as well as any organizations wishing to publicize themselves by printing congratulatory messages. Twenty-two thousand copies were printed of this special souvenir edition. This massive publicity effort, melding business interests, tourism, and high society, used fifteen tons of paper, six hundred pounds of ink, and required the outlay of enough paper to stretch 159 ¾ miles, or the distance from Honolulu Harbor on the island of Oahu to Kona on the neighboring big island of Hawai'i, or so declared page one of the special edition.[27] The hoopla was about more than just the opening of a big hotel. It provided an occasion for the celebration and promotion of tourism as one of the leading industries in Hawai'i; it laid claim to the future; "progress" was in the air.

Already, as noted in the earlier discussion of ads, there was a nostalgia for the past that coexisted with a celebration of the present modernity. In this romanticized vision, the progression from primitive Hawai'i to modern Hawai'i was embodied in the successive waves of migration, culminating in the dominance of the Caucasian "captains of industry." One of the editorial statements in the special addition details it in big type: "What a succession of men and events has moulded Hawaii—up from the obscurity of a primitive people, to the civilization of today, with its conveniences, its luxuries, its achievements! In that misty past . . . brown men in long canoes voyaged afar . . . and peopled ancient Hawaii. Following them came an unending succession of strangers . . . other men—other races: the Spaniard . . . the bold and intrepid explorers . . . the trader . . . the missionary, bringing the Christian religion to take the place of paganism . . . the whaler . . . the merchant . . . the agriculturalist, seeing here the immense possibilities of sugar and pineapples; the laborer, his humble energies bent to making fruitful the soil; the manufacturer; the captain of industry; the builder of great transportation lines [surely an implicit salute to Matson lines]."[28]

But the present wave of newcomers is different: "They come not for business but for vacation. They are men and women seeking recreation, amusement, entertainment. They come for the superb and restful climate, the scenery of a second Eden, picturesque entertainment, island sports. They come to find here that romance and glamour which still remain from the far-gone days of kingdoms and tribal principalities." Encapsulated in this one statement is the tourist industry's vision of their prototypical client as well as the role Hawai'i and Hawaiians are expected to play.

The tourist industry aggressively sought this wave of newcomers during the 1920s. The Hawaiian Tourist Bureau placed advertisements in publications like *National Geographic,* the *Literary Digest, Travel Magazine,* and *National Business,* among others. They kept an index-card file of every likely prospect who wrote for information and checked the boat passenger lists to see what percentage actually arrived.[29] The aggressive approach was working. By 1927, the tourist industry was regarded as Hawai'i's third largest industry (after sugar and pineapples) in income generated.

Tourist travel to Hawai'i doubled between 1922 and 1927, resulting in nearly $18 million in revenues during that period. To get this yield, the Hawaiian Tourist Bureau spent $127,000 in 1926, the year 16,762 passengers came, or an average of under eight dollars per visitor. On the eve of the Royal Hotel's opening, two new Matson steamers, the *Malolo* and the *City of Honolulu,* were set to join the fleet. Their combined capacities would mean up to 9,000 additional visitors in the next year—a 50 percent increase.[30]

At the time Hawai'i's total population was reported to be 328,000, with the city of Honolulu having the majority, 104,000. The tourist population already represented 15 percent of the resident population, and nearly one-half of the so-called European population. Of the total population, 36,000 were of European ("not Spanish, not Portuguese") descent, Hawaiians were 21,000, Caucasian-Hawaiians 15,000, the largest group were of Japanese descent, 75,000 citizens, and there were 54,000 alien residents.[31]

The opening-night affair at the Royal Hawaiian made clear whom this new era was for. With the exception of Princess Abigail Kawananakoa of the former royal family, who staged the pageant and was honored by being the first guest to sign the register, and a few other Native Hawaiians, all the rest of the invited guests were Caucasian.[32]

The local non-Caucasian populations were cast in service and entertainment roles that night, positions some groups would continue to hold for much of the rest of the century. Sometimes these roles demanded overt direction, even when the "performance" was off the stage. For example, two days before the Royal Hawaiian was set to open, the police rounded up fifty "diving boys" on the wharfs and brought them into district court. The local boys and young men earned their livings by diving from the piers to retrieve money thrown into the water by tourists. They also earned tips carrying passengers' baggage. But these endeavors had apparently gotten out of hand, according to the steamship companies, which had lodged complaints with the police that "their rowdy actions could be tolerated no longer."

After a "heart-to-heart talk" with Sheriff David Desha, the group of young men agreed that "henceforth their conversation and ejaculations will be untinged with the taint of vulgarity. They will not knock passengers down in a rush to carry their baggage. They will not wander the streets and wharves clad only in tights. They will confine their perambulations on shipboard to those decks which are not used by passengers. They will not sass the ship's officers." They will, in short, be "diving gentlemen."[33]

These local inhabitants had clearly crossed the line between being "picturesque" and being threatening to the class privilege of the arrivals. Their interactions, at least as reported in this story, laid bare some of the most fundamental exchanges involved in this tourism—picturesque difference, performed (diving) and visibly embodied (lightly clad), in a service role, for money. Indeed, here the diving retrieval of money *was* the performance.

But during the grand opening celebration, a more complicated representation of Hawaiian-ness served as the highlight of the evening—a "colorful and semi-barbaric," pageant as one reporter described it, reenacting the landing of King Kamehameha at that very spot more than one hundred years earlier.[34] Before this event, the 1,200 dinner guests, representing government, military, and business elites, were greeted upon their entrance to the glittering hotel by "a bevy of pretty Hawaiian girls, bare of foot and wearing attractive hula costumes," who draped important shoulders with maile leis. Dressed in tuxedos or swathed in beaded chiffon, the guests sat down to a multicourse Europhilic feast, followed by an orchestra concert. Then they made their way toward the beach area, where they were joined by several hundred more spectators for the highlight of the evening.

Here the sounds changed dramatically as faint tones of chanting wafted across the water from a flotilla of fifteen Hawaiian single and double outrigger canoes. Torches dotted the sea with orange lights, and "for awhile the curtain of time was drawn back and there was revealed in resplendent color and splendid semi-barbarism a living picture of ancient Hawaii. Once again Kamehameha, the stalwart, trod the sands of Waikiki. Once again the thrilling meles of victory were chanted."[35]

King Kamehameha I, subduing rival leaders on neighboring islands, is credited with unifying Hawai'i into one kingdom. The site of the Royal Hawaiian is reputed to be where he and his warriors landed to fight on Oahu. Accompanied by a large cast of warriors, *kahili* (feather standards of royalty) bearers, and oarsmen, the king landed, and mounted to a throne to be saluted with a program of chants, songs, and hula dancing staged by the Princess Abigail Kawananakoa.[36]

Little was reported (at least in English-language newspapers) about the specifics of the performances, but a large photo featured the king and his retinue, clad in *malos* (loincloths) and long feathered capes, and flanked by twenty sword-bearing men, their bare chests and shoulders capped by short capes. Twenty women in cloth-wrap skirts and, over the shoulder, toga-style tops also participated, captioned in a large photo as "The Hawaiian girls, who composed one of the most beautiful features of the pageant."[37] Five local women had been chosen as "island princesses," each representing one of the Hawaiian islands. Characterized in the newspaper as "attractive," these women all had European names (Gladys Brandt, Zena Schuman, Josephine Hopkins, etc.) indicating most probably a European or Euro-Hawaiian background or association through birth or marriage. Their featured status indicates that "attractive" in this case probably referred to a European or hapa-haole look.[38]

The complexity of this representation lies in its being promoted and reviewed as the highlight of the evening, its nod of respect to Native Hawaiian history and royalty, and yet its restrictive encapsulation as a nostalgic reminder of a past evoked only for its romantic fragrance, to put the "royal" into Royal Hawaiian hotel. The vision of the present and future acted out that night clearly belonged to those in the audience, not those on stage.

As the paper reported, a curtain had risen on the past, and then "the curtain dropped back into place. From somewhere in the distance came the strains of a foxtrot," leading the guests back into the present. The pageant staged the past, with Hawaiians serving as a foil for the pleasure of those fully swept up in their self-reflexive sense of themselves as "modern." The only presentness of Hawaiians was represented by the token appearance of Princess Kawananakoa and the local servers in bow ties and waiters' suits. Don Blanding, a local writer, waxed poetic about the princess: "How delightfully she makes the royal gesture. I wish that she might be ruler of one of those gay mythical kingdoms of Graustark which the novelists love. There would be pomp and pageantry and the vivid ritual of olden days which we, democratic and commercial as we may be, remember fondly from our early reading of romantic historical tales."[39] Linking the guests' childhoods ("our early reading") with a past supposedly composed of picturesque yet primitive predemocracies clearly states the way many elite Caucasians, and certainly the HTB, positioned Hawai'i and Hawaiians: picturesque relics of a previous stage of European development now long lost in the shrouds of myth.[40]

The staging of the pageant proved to be a harbinger of the importance of performance. Hawaiian entertainment was planned as an integral part of the hotel's recreational offerings right from the beginning.[41] And Hawaiian music was performed at least once a day at the Royal, sometimes twice.[42] Over the next few decades, the Royal would become a performing home for some of Hawai'i's most talented and highly regarded musicians and dancers, including those associated with the Royal Hawaiian Girls' Glee Club, the Hawaiian Serenaders, and Harry Owen's band. Clara Inter ("Hilo Hattie"), Iolane Luahine, and Henry Pa were just a few of the greats who would perform there.

At the same time the guests at the Royal Hawaiian were being entertained by Hawaiian song and dance, so were happy patrons in San Francisco's Capitol Theater, home to "large and boisterously enthusiastic audiences at every performance" of Charles King's opera "The Prince of Hawaii," presented by an all-Hawaiian cast. Although the dialogue was in English, many songs were in Hawaiian. The sextet of hula dancers was one of the highlights of the show.[43] Perhaps some of the steamship passengers saw this show before departing San Francisco for the islands. Even if visitors had never seen any type of live hula before they arrived, they would meet a hula girl even before setting foot on the islands.

MEETING "HULA GIRLS"

For visitors to the Royal and Moana, their encounter with a "hula girl" was the first thing that happened when they docked. She represented the destination image in the flesh, literally welcoming them with open arms. That moment of physical contact staged the meeting of the wealthy "sophisticate" and the "primitive," a meeting that was broadcast around the world in society photos.

The Matson line employed greeters, a custom continued today by tour companies, which send attractive, young local people to greet arriving tourists as they step off the plane in Honolulu and to drape leis around their necks. These moments of arrival were extensively documented in a stock way. Prominent travelers, most often couples, were photographed smiling at the camera as a hula girl in grass skirt placed leis around their necks. Sometimes dancing saluted the ship's arrival, but, even if it did not, the women employed as greeters brought alive the image of the hula girl.

In the majority of these photographs, the woman faces away from the camera, her hair, bare arms and legs, blouse, head lei, neck lei, and ti-leaf skirt captured in the picture, but rarely more than a glimpse of her face. This iconography of native in grass skirt and sharply contrasting Caucasian visitors in suits and dresses being welcomed with the spirit of aloha was reproduced thousands of times during the days of ship travel. And unlike today, when such a photo serves mainly as a personal memento, those pictures were reprinted throughout the U.S. mainland and even abroad, extending the circulation of this image of hula girl as Hawai'i synecdoche. Captions on the back of surviving photographs in the Sheraton Hotel archives reveal that they were sent to city editors of the travelers' home cities for the society pages.

Occasionally the greeter was also featured in the photo. For example, the March 9, 1929, photo of W. T. P. Hollingsworth features a man posing with his arm around a woman who appears to be of Hawaiian-Chinese descent. Her hair is bobbed (unlike the other greeters pictured in this series), and she wears a print cotton top and knee-length ti-leaf skirt over bare legs. The caption sent to the photo editor of the *Chicago Tribune* in Paris and the editor of the *New York Tribune* states: "W. T. P. Hollingsworth, President of Neon Lights company of America. Snapped in the coconut grove of the Royal Hawaiian Hotel with a typical Hawaiian Hula Girl."[44] The greeter is unnamed. This reference indicates that the term "hula girl," rather than Hawaiian native or hula dancer, was well established.

The "snapped in" references a sense of casual encounter rather than staged photo, as if Hawaiians in 1929 strolled in grass skirts past the hotel, where this encounter with a "typical" native just happened to take place. That the woman was working, and in costume, is obscured in the rhetoric of the photograph. This same "snapped with" documentation of visitor and native continues to be a reenacted theme staged at various sites in Waikiki, most especially the Kodak Hula Show, but also at commercial lū'aus.

The linkage of notions of arrival with meeting hula girls was structured into the advertising of the time. A 1920s travel poster for the Matson line, for example, features a steamship cruising on tranquil seas, with a volcano in the background. In the foreground, a Polynesian-looking woman with flowing black hair and festooned with flowers strums a guitar, her figure larger than the ship.[45] This is slightly unusual, in her Polynesian features and in the cloth rather than ti-leaf skirt portrayed, but it clearly links the arriving ship with serenading hula girl under arching palm and the "natural wonder" of the volcano.

A very similar iconography appears in a 1915 advertisement for a February Mid-Pacific Carnival celebration.[46] Here, rather than the

spouting volcano, we have a view of Diamond Head rising in the background, Waikiki swimmers in the middle ground enjoying the beach,
and a prototypical hula girl figure dominating the foreground, framed
by large banana palm fronds as she overlooks Caucasian bathers on the
beach from her secret spot. With long brown hair, and Caucasianesque
facial features, she is clad only in a strategically placed lei on her chest,
a head lei worn like a flapper's head piece, and a straw skirt, as she smil-
ingly sprinkles colorful flowers toward the beach. This image of a Native Hawaiian, or nativized woman, surrounded by foliage set as a part
of, rather than apart from, the lush natural landscape, wearing a grass
skirt and little else, and smiling toward visitors is an iconography repeated ad infinitum in advertisements since and continuing today.
Once they arrived, the early tourists immediately enacted this part of
the destination image, encountering the hula girl. She was there to greet
them as they stepped off the ship and to entertain them in the hotel.

For some visitors, the hula shows made a lasting impression. A photo
sent to the *New York Times* on October 30, 1929, featured "The Ma-
haraja of Kapurthala, India," who stopped over in Hawai'i on his way
from the mainland to an audience with the emperor of Japan. An excep-
tionally long, hand-written caption reads: "Snapped with hula dancer
("Princess" Keanini) on the grounds of the Royal Hawaiian Hotel. His
Highness spent much of his time in the surf at Waikiki and was especially delighted with the native hula dancers. So eager was he to see the
Hawaiian hula that he radioed ahead from the S/S *President Monroe*, on
which he traveled from San Francisco, in order that preparations might
be made for him and the best dancers secured."[47]

These loops of publicity simultaneously highlighted the individual
lives and careers of the elites by publicizing their travels, publicized the
shipping lines and the hotels where they were pictured, and promoted a
particular vision of Hawai'i and Hawaiian culture centered on the figure
of the hula girl, song, and dance, along with nature, sea, and sand, and
warm welcoming aloha service. The reputations of such wealthy and famous visitors during those early days of the tourist boom of the first
decades of the century also added an aura of respectability to the image
of the hula girl and hence to the islands as nonthreatening exotica, a
controllable sublime along Edenic lines, different yet knowable, approachable, even literally touchable, as these encounters in publicity
photos documented.

These webs of live mainland performance in vaudeville, elite theaters, tent shows, world's fairs, dime museums, and supper clubs intertwined with the visual and aural representations of hapa-haole songs,

steamship advertisements, publicity photographs, and hotel performances to produce an image of soft primitivism based on the display of Native female bodies. No matter how substantial or complex the meanings of hula performances were for Native Hawaiians, the Caucasian tourist encountered them already framed by powerful discourses of racial hierarchies, hierarchies that neatly mapped onto cultural and moral scales which sustained imperial expansion during this period. As "good" natives, Hawaiians were positioned as alluring soft primitives, the perfect hosts for elite tourists' escape from modernity's workaday ennui. By the end of the 1920s the hula and the image of the hula girl had replaced the allure of natural wonders as the primary signifier of Hawai'i. As the next decade unrolled, tourism would continue to grow, spurred by Hollywood's new fascination with the islands. Tourist performances in the islands would proliferate, becoming an important part of the industry infrastructure as performances moved right into the hotels, providing ever-greater opportunities for the tourist to encounter performative renditions of Hawai'i.

FIVE

Tourism and the Commodification of Culture, 1930–1940

The stock market crash of 1929 did not put an end to elite tourism in Hawai'i. Ironically, it ushered in a period of massive growth following on the successes of the 1920s, during which tourist visits had nearly tripled, adding roughly $75 million to the Hawaiian economy for that decade.[1] Although tourism income dropped by half between 1929 and 1932, it quickly recovered, aided by somewhat lowered prices and the introduction in 1936 of the first regular commercial flights from the West Coast, drastically reducing the travel time to the islands from four days by boat to less than one day in the air. Increased advertising and mass media coverage kept the islands visible on the mainland and contributed to this surge.

For example, in 1931 a special travel issue of *Life* magazine featured a cover drawing of a curvaceous hula girl, arms raised overhead, eyes closed, head lolling languorously, swaying grass skirt slung low, revealing belly and a long line of thigh, breasts nearly escaping a brief bandeau top. Looking on admiringly is a middle-aged white male tourist, cigar in mouth, camera and tourist brochures at the ready while his wife, a plain, stout woman—the presumably asexual, antifeminine "battleaxe" stereotype—looks on disapprovingly. The iconicized sexual allure of the fantasy is encoded in the opposition between the languorous self-pleasure of the dancer and the uptight, buttoned-up couple, making the reason for travel plain.[2]

A few months later in the same magazine, a similar but more toned-down version of this scenario emerges in a full-page advertisement by the Hawaiian Tourist Bureau.[3] In this hand-drawn color sketch, a spotlighted hula dancer (a more modest sleeveless blouse replacing bandeau) sways beneath a full moon on a hotel's seaside terrace. The disapproving "battleaxe" is replaced by happy, attractive, heterosexual couples gazing on. Ad copy invites readers to feel the "soft thrill of tropic nights" and emphasizes that a trip to Hawaii need not be expensive—less than $350, all-inclusive.[4] An elite class survived the crash even if they lost money, and lowered prices offered a feeling of wise spending combined with the pursuit of luxury. When they arrived, these travelers knew what to expect: the thrill of tropical nights filled with Hawaiian entertainment.

During the 1930s, Hawaiian cultural practices become increasingly commodified, and the tourist industry consolidates its reliance on live performance. Selected cultural practices which once circulated mainly in noncommercial social contexts now enter the cash economy, marketed for outsiders. This commodification is aided by an emerging anthropological discourse of culture which links notions of distinctive practices and products to specific population groups.

HAWAIIAN ENTERTAINMENT AS AN INDUSTRY

As more and more visitors came searching for Hawaiiana, a variety of live performances were developed to entertain them. These performances commodified certain cultural practices only—like songs, dances, coconut tree climbing, and so forth, which could be presented as aestheticized spectacle—and pulled them into the cash economy.[5] As mentioned in the preceding chapter, performances were now moved right into the hotels like the Royal Hawaiian, but there were also other sites available, including one of the first "living museum" type of exhibits in the islands, Lalani Village. In addition, lūʻaus, dance performances on the beach, nightclub shows, private parties, and tourist hula lessons were available. This explosion of entertainment meant more jobs for local performers and helped to fuel a resurgence of the public performance of hula outside the tourist sphere. Thousands of residents flocked to free performances sponsored by the Honolulu Parks and Recreation Department as hula enjoyed a new (but not undebated) public respectability.[6] In addition, performances on the mainland proliferated too as fancy hotels opened "Hawaiian Rooms" in New York and other cities. Hula was everywhere, and guidebooks in the 1930s assumed that visitors would be looking for it when they came and told them where to go.

These types of cultural performances had been commercially available to tourists on a smaller scale at least two decades earlier. While the emphasis in earlier tourist promotion seems to have been on climate, scenery, and natural wonders, there is some evidence that tourists attended commercial lūʻaus and hula performances in the early years of the century. A surviving photo postcard of a lūʻau attended by Queen Liliʻuokalani (who is unidentified) was used as an advertising device around 1910. An announcement on the back reads: "VISITORS: Apply to Hawaii Tours Co., 76 Merchant near post office for tickets and transportation to the big luau and hula Saturday, Dec. 4, at the Kaneohe Coral Gardens." Kaneohe is a long drive over the mountains from Honolulu, so this was a major excursion, indicating something of the event's allure.

This same photograph had appeared earlier in a 1895 tourist guide, then in its second edition (*The Tourists' Guide through the Hawaiian Islands Descriptive of their Scenes and Scenery,* by Henry M. Whitney).[7] While most of the guide's 200 pages detail scenic beauties of the islands, lūʻaus and hula dancing are briefly mentioned, although there is no indication of commercial availability. However, a magazine article of the same year, predicting a rise in tourism should Hawaiʻi be annexed, notes that "strange cultures will attract the visitor. . . . He will be made welcome by the people if he shows himself the least bit friendly. A luau will be made in his honor. . . . "[8] Earliest tourists were thus aware of lūʻaus and related hula entertainment.

Clearly, though, the commodified display of culture was at the turn of the century only an emerging part of the industry. Elinor Langton, writing in the Honolulu-based and Euro-American dominated *Paradise of the Pacific* in 1905, makes an impassioned plea for the development of such attractions, noting their lack of availability: "A lady residing in Portland, Oregon, who made a short stay at the Alexander Young Hotel last January, told the writer that it would give her the greatest pleasure to see the aborigines in their native haunts. . . . A large number of tourists have the same desires as this lady, but, unfortunately, they find the opportunities of gratifying them lacking. While they know that barbarism in the islands is practically eclipsed by civilization they look for a few relics of the life of the early Hawaiians. Native color (. . . surfboard or canoe riding . . . the luau or the hula . . .) is what the pleasure seeker likes to have imbued in his entertainment."[9]

In other words, what was missing, in her view, was the opportunity for Caucasian visitors to see natives "in situ" enacting distinctive cultural practices—"something never seen in California or any other part of the mainland," as she put it. These practices were seen as residual relics of a distinctive, authentic precivilized past. She suggests that the Hawaii Promotion Committee would "not find the presentation of old Hawaiian customs and sports entirely out of bounds of its course." Indeed, apparently an idea for a sort of in-situ village for tourists had already been discussed a year or so previously: "The expense, which would involve the keeping of several native families and a superintendent to look after the exhibit, might or might not be warranted by the undertaking. [But it] would engage deeper attention on the part of foreign spectators than any like assemblage of Hawaiians at a world's fair." Here a clear link between the imperialist displays of the world's fairs and the rise of tourist spectacles is drawn, and the economic underpinning (an expense which might or might not be warranted) is highlighted. The commodification of Native Hawaiian cultural practices would start to play a major role in tourism two decades later.

That proposed village attraction never came to pass, but a simpler solution was at hand: lūʻaus with hula shows. "Too much importance cannot be attached to the luau as a means of imparting strength to Hawaii's general attractiveness," wrote Langton. When the traveler "sits down among a company of laughing natives, the poi bowl within easy access of every one, he is enthused with the sociability of the assemblage even if he does not know the language." Langton had specific recommendations: "Give the luau more publicity and let the bill include everything land and sea provide in the way of edibles. . . . The hula is generally part second of the luau. Eliminate some of its varieties and it is a Hawaiian dance worth preserving. It should be rejuvenated by those who take an interest in perpetuating old customs. . . . It needs young blood. Most of the women who today execute its figure are as old as baseball, but there is a grace and rhythm in their movements accompanying the tum, tum, tum of the ukulele that might be envied by many girls in their teens. The fame of this Hawaiian dance has spread to the ends of the earth and left the impression in some places that the people of these Islands find little else to do but trip the hula through the livelong day. Newcomers demand it and it ought to be shown to them [along with] plenty of native music."[10]

After the surge of mainland hula during the teens and twenties, the demand that Langton spoke of twenty-five years earlier was even greater. In the 1930s, the tourist industry organized to meet these demands, its development aided by concomitant growth in the advertising industry and in the mass media, both of which expanded in the 1930s and helped spread the destination image of Hawaiʻi and images of hula dancers as never before. By the end of the decade, every aspect of Langton's prescription came to pass: a living village, young hula dancers, commercial lūʻaus, and a lot of easily accessible music and dance.

Oral histories of dancers like "Tootsie" Notley Steer, who worked in Waikiki in the thirties, provide insight into the structure of the tourist industry at that time, its labor conditions, and the relations between performers and tourists, who, like those of Langton's 1905 article, retained a nostalgic appetite for the "natural native."

Performance as Labor — Staging "The Natural"

Doveline "Tootsie" Notley Steer, born in 1915 in Honolulu, became one of the featured dancers in tourist performances of the thirties. She performed at the Royal Hawaiian Hotel, worked as a lei greeter for the Pan American Clipper in 1936 (one of the early tourist flights), and was a featured dancer in the original Kodak Hula Show when it began in 1937. In addition, she was chosen as the "Matson Girl," her face and physique representing the popular Matson Cruise Line in advertisements for three years, starting in 1939. Her recollections of the Matson publicity work are especially revealing of the construction of the hula girl image—an image I call the "natural native in Nature," an active process of decontextualizing, iconicizing, and decontemporizing. Among the photographers she worked with was Edward Steichen, whose prize-winning photos of her were highly regarded and widely displayed.

Steichen wanted a "natural" look and went to great lengths to create it both by directing Steer's bodily presentation and through elaborate staging techniques. He told Steer to stop trimming her hair, to cut off her long fingernails, and to stop using fingernail polish. (She had regarded manicures and pedicures as necessary to her professionalism as a dancer but stopped during the months of picture shooting.) Steichen posed Steer against dramatic natural features like waterfalls. "He used to hunt," recalls Steer in a 1985 oral history interview. "He used to look for the beautiful, natural places to take pictures. That was how intense he was about his work."[11]

Steichen worked his model just as hard as himself, preparing photos to send to Condé Nast publications. "He knew what he wanted," said Steer. "It was getting it out of you, that's another thing, see. Tell a model to do something. See if she can do it. It just didn't look natural and that isn't what he wanted. So, he used to work me to death. Sometimes we work for eight hours to get what he wanted." Steer recalls one shoot up on the roof of the Royal Hawaiian Hotel: "It was just [gravel] on the top of the roof. And I had to run with a dozen of those torch gingers [flowers]. . . . Well, why didn't he tell me he wanted me to look tired? But there was a certain look he wanted. And I ran, and I ran. And finally he said, 'I got it.' I said, 'Why didn't you tell me?' He said, 'Oh, no.' He says,

1. A hula dancer beckons tourists in this full-color, full-page advertisement for Sheraton Hotels, Hawaiʻi. *Travel and Leisure*, April 1996.

SHERATON PRINCESS KAIULANI'S
SPECTACULAR
Polynesian Revue

Fire and fury. Pulsating
tropical rhythms.
Seductive maidens.
Ferocious warriors.
Take a tour of the
South Pacific that
explodes in a blaze of
color, dance and songs.
And travel to the past
in a moving tribute
to Hawaii's Monarchy.

Two dinner and cocktail
shows nightly.

2. A 1995 brochure advertising the Sheraton Princess Kaiulani Hotel's night-time Polynesian Review in Honolulu.

3. "Enjoy Hawaii's warmest welcome." A 1995 brochure advertising the Paradise Cove Luau.

4. The author's companion poses with performers during the photo session at Germaine's Luau, 1995. Photo: J. Desmond.

5. Images of hula dancers—some topless, all sepia toned—are featured among these postcards for sale in 1995 in Waikiki. Photo: J. Desmond.

6. A hula number from the pre-dinner show at Germaine's Luau, 1995.
Photo: J. Desmond.

7. A hula troupe performs for a predominantly nontourist audience at the
1995 Prince Lot Hula Festival in Honolulu. Photo: J. Desmond.

8. Two hand-tinted postcards, early 1900s, models unknown. *Top:* A contemporary reproduction of an original in the Bishop Museum collection. *Bottom:* "Hawaiian Hula-Hula Dancers," collection of the author.

9. Stereoscope photograph, pre-1900, model unknown. Photo: Frank Davey. Courtesy of the Bishop Museum.

10. Pre-1900 photograph of a Native Hawaiian woman posed beside the markers of European "civilization." Model and photographer unknown. Courtesy of the Bishop Museum.

11. Ioane Ukeke and his hula troupe pose in this pre-1900 photograph. Left to right, the seated women are identified as sister of Ukeke's wife, wife of Ukeke, Anne Kapule, and Mary Kapule. Courtesy of the Bishop Museum.

12. Dancers at King Kalākaua's birthday celebration, November 1885. Courtesy of the Bishop Museum.

13. A typical postcard of Native Hawaiian men, fishing, ca. 1909. Courtesy of the Bishop Museum.

The Girls in These South Sea
Islands Dress Mostly in Black
I Saw a Great Deal of Them

14. A colored postcard of sailors and hula dancers, ca. 1910. Courtesy of the Bishop Museum.

15. "Before and after," from Murat Halstead's *Pictorial History of America's New Possessions*, 1899. Models and photographers unattributed.

16. Frontispiece from Alexander Winchell's *Preadamites*, 1880, showing racial types.

Between the form of the upper lip of the Negro and that of the Polynesian, a very perceptible and charac-

Fig. 20. Outline of the muzzle of the Polynesian.

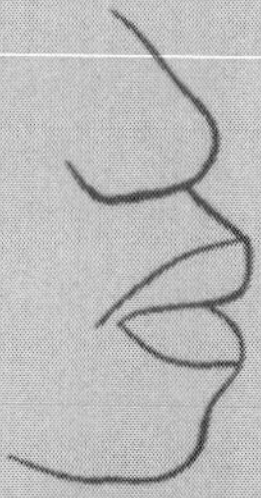

Fig. 21. Outline of the muzzle of the Negro. Compare also the Hottentot, Fig. 46.

teristic contrast exists, to which my attention has been called by Rev. S. E. Bishop, of Honolulu. In the Hawaiian, the skin of the upper lip seems a little too short, and the lip is consequently lifted up from the lower into a semi-horizontal position; and this retroversion extends well toward the angles of the mouth.

17. Comparison of bodily differences between "Polynesians" and "Negros" in Winchell's *Preadamites*, 1880.

18. An engraved portrait of Kanoa, Governor of Kaua'i, singled out for praise as "nearly Aryan" in Winchell's *Preadamites*, 1880.

19. An example of the Hawaiian music craze in the 'teens, this 1916 sheet music cover for Cobb and Edwards's song, "I Lost My Heart in Honolulu," features a hula dancer with bobbed hair and bangles. Collection of the author.

20. Gilda Gray in her South Seas Island Dance, 1925. Photographer unknown. Billy Rose Theatre Collection; The New York Library for the Performing Arts; Astor, Lenox, and Tilden Foundation.

A Haole Hula Girl
PHOTO BY BAKER HONOLULU

21. Postcard of "A Haole Hula Girl," 1925. Rose Heather, photographed by
Baker. Courtesy of the Bishop Museum.

22. A hand-colored postcard from the 1930s featuring the Bray troupe dancing at the Royal Hawaiian Hotel. Odeta Bray and Kahala Bray are on the far left and right, respectively. Courtesy of the Bishop Museum.

23. Pualani and Pi'ilani Mossman teaching hula in 1935 at Lalani Hawaiian Village, Honolulu. Courtesy of the Bishop Museum.

24. Postcard of Tootsie Notley performing in the Kodak Hula Show in Honolulu, ca. 1941. Courtesy of the Bishop Museum.

25. Navy servicemen enjoy a hula show at the Roof Garden of the Alexander Young Hotel in Honolulu, ca. 1941. Photo: Tai Sing Loo. Courtesy of the Bishop Museum.

26. Hawaiian shows proliferate on the mainland. This 1946 Associated Press photograph features Ray Kinney's orchestra and dancers at the Congressional Club's Hawaiian Room in Washington, D.C. Among the dancers is Pualani Mossman Avon, far right. Courtesy of the Bishop Museum.

27. Surfing, a popular depiction of Native Hawaiian men. Advertisement from *Travel Magazine*, 1916.

28. Tourists photographing dancers at the Kodak Hula Show, Honolulu, 1962. Photo: Laurence Hata. Courtesy of the Bishop Museum.

29. A 1970s postcard featuring a model with a slender, hapa-haole look, captioned "Tropical Beauty." Courtesy of the Bishop Museum.

30. Dancers in Frank Kawaikapuokalani Hewett's lūʻau show at the Coconut Beach Resort on the island of Kauaʻi, 1994. Photo: J. Desmond.

31. The 1996 Merrie Monarch Hula Festival in Hilo, Hawaiʻi. The festival attracts 5,000 spectators each year. Judges sit right in front of the stage while competing *hālaus* occupy the bleachers behind. Photo: J. Desmond.

'You would have to put it on. I didn't want that.' So that was his whole point in that whole campaign. He wanted to be natural."[12] Steichen assumed that while he as (modern) artist could successfully stage the "natural," his (native) model could not knowingly do the same.

Steer's labor in production of the natural was never made visible in these evocative photos of course. The natural only works when it can be seen as naturally occurring. Steer recalls with humor how Steichen coaxed her into a romantic-looking pose: "He says, 'I don't want you to look like you're going to fall asleep,' because that's exactly what I was doing . . . you worked how many hours. I think I was so tired." Steichen directed her: "What I want you to look like is you're waiting for your boyfriend." I said, 'forget it. I'm married.' (laughter) He told me, 'that's the trouble.' (laughter) So, that was the look . . . but he couldn't get that look until he put me through this process. Yes, I really worked hard." Photography like Steichen's reveals the work involved in staging the natural, tying it to sexual allure and availability and quickening it with flushed immediacy.[13]

The dramatic presentation in these photos also reveals Steichen's past as a fashion and celebrity photographer. He reveled in what he called the quality of "aliveness," a quickening of emotional response ideal for advertising's effectiveness.[14] A signed sample of his work appeared in one of the first Matson Cruise Line advertisements to use photography, a full-page spread in *National Geographic* in 1934. A scenario of arrival demonstrates this quality. A young Caucasian woman stands on deck in jaunty white hat and jacket, crowned by a profusion of leis. She smiles directly at the camera as a brown-skinned, Polynesian-looking woman in ti-leaf skirt and sleeveless blouse puts one more lei over her head. The women are quite similar, the same height and proportions, both with bobbed hair. The greeter stands slightly behind and beside the new arrival, her smiling face turned toward the visitor and somewhat hidden in shadow. Her left hand rests on the white model's shoulder, and the visitor seems to burst with pleasure at the moment— the staging of the ritualized moment of arrival and not coincidentally a moment of literal touch by the local woman, in many ways her physical double, who is the proximate source of this "enlivening."[15]

As this advertisement reveals, in the 1930s the marketing concept for "natural Hawai'i" sometimes meant using a model who was Native Hawaiian or part–Native Hawaiian. This happens just as photography began to replace sketches in Hawaiian advertisements.[16] The increased realism quotient may have required a more deliberate presentation of physical difference than the hapa-haole look (nativized whites and whitened natives) that had dominated posters and calendars earlier. Steer, who describes herself as "full-blooded Hawaiian," notes this as a new marketing trend: "Well, they were so excited about those pictures because it's the first time they've had someone that's so Hawaiian. But I guess they were in gear for that kind of composition at that time, Hawaiian. Heretofore, they liked the Oriental; they liked the others. They liked the hapa Haoles at one time. But they were all geared for the Hawaiian, man, that whole thing. So, that's the way it went."[17]

This shifting depiction of hula dancers emerges in the work of other artists as well. The lavishly illustrated menus of the Matson Line, designed by commissioned artists in the 1930s and 1940s and taken home by more than a hundred thousand tourists as collectors' items, featured both the more hapa-haole look in its Frank MacIntosh light-skinned hula girl images of the 1930s and a more Polynesian-looking, darker-skinned depiction in the murals and menus of Eugene Savage in the late 1930s and 1940s. MacIntosh drew highly stylized figures in bright colors, and his Hawaiian females were depicted with skin tones decidedly lighter than Hawaiian males. Savage's work featured complex group scenes of Hawaiian life, including dancing and fishing. While his drawings depict Hawaiians with darker skin than MacIntosh's, the facial features of those portrayed often have a somewhat European rather than Polynesian bone structure. A still different portrayal by artist Marguerite Blasingame graced the foyer of the Waikiki Theater in 1936. Her hula dancers have medium skin tones and more Polynesian features, including a flatter bridge of the nose and fuller lips, than those of Savage and MacIntosh. The December 1935 issue of *Paradise of the Pacific* magazine (a holiday issue, which circulated on the mainland as well) featured a similar looking female on its cover. These visual images indicate the range of depictions circulating in the 1930s to 1940s, a range which included the hapa-haole look but also embraced a less European and more Polynesian style of beauty.[18]

This emerging Polynesian commercial look was not without detractors, however, and never replaced the hapa-haole look. For example, photographer Toni Frisel, who had worked with Steer briefly in 1938, rejected Steer's Native Hawaiian looks. "She liked the girls with the little Oriental [look]. You [may] think I was Oriental, but she didn't," Steer chuckles. "She didn't think I made a good model." While many of the leading performers of the 1930s, like Pualani Mossman and Meymo Holt (both of whom performed in New York), were hapa haole in their looks, Steer's new popularity was clearly an opening up of the tourist iconography, one that was facilitated by photography.

Photography's importance in creating and extending the image of the islands is revealed not only in Steer's work with Steichen but also in other aspects of her career. Right before she became the "Matson Girl," she was selected by an agent for N. W. Ayer and Sons, a leading advertising and modeling agency located in New Jersey, as the first official greeter for the Pan American Clippers. These flights marked the beginning of commercial air travel to the islands and came in several times a week. Each arrival was met by photographers from the *Honolulu Advertiser* or the *Honolulu Star-Bulletin,* as well as by the local Japanese-language papers. "And for years . . . sometimes four times a week, I'd be in the newspaper," Steer recalls. "But they're always nice shots, though. . . . they knew they either had to make 'em good, or the people who [received] the picture are going to grumble. They knocked themselves out. . . . Oh, sometimes, they like me to come with just the brassiere and a hula skirt. I looked all right. Or sometimes, they like the tops. Or sometimes they like the cellophane [skirts, associated with nightclubs]. But I said, 'cellophane is out for this.' I said, "You don't go meet planes in a cellophane. That's out.' And so that's that." To some extent then, Steer was able to exert control over the construction of her image, but the standard iconography of the hula girl remained intact: grass skirt, bare arms and legs, slender figure, a smiling youthful beauty bedecked in flowers.[19]

The linkage of performance, photography, tourism, and the production of the iconic image occurred even more explicitly in the Kodak Hula Show, which began in 1937 and continues today, still free to tourists. Steer was one of the earliest performers in what has become the longest-running Hawaiian cultural show in the islands. Started by the Kodak photography company in concert with the Matson Line, the show gave tourists a chance to photograph the hula dancers, a possibility unavailable during the dimly lit night-time shows. Besides, reasoned Kodak Vice-President Fritz Herman, who founded the show, the dancers wore cellophane skirts and paper leis at night. He wanted to supply dancers in ti-leaf skirts (a costume the show's dancers have been wearing since), posed against a natural background of palms, sun, and sand, a more iconic representation of the hula girl, a suitable souvenir.

The whole show is built around photo opportunities, including the showcase number, "My Sweetie Pie," where female dancers in ti-leaf skirts hold up big red and yellow letters that spell out Hawai'i, literally inscribing the name of the destination on their bodies; at this moment Hawai'i and hula girl are one. They pose in front of each section of the bleachers while tourists snap away. In addition, performers pose with tourists after the show and at intermission. An estimated 60 million photographs of the show have been taken to date, extending the circuit of visual images and acting as word-of-mouth advertising when tourists go back home and share these images with friends.[20] Recalling the early days, Steer notes the show's raison d'être: "All you did was buy film. That was the idea," says Steer.[21]

Steer's busy career is indicative of the burgeoning entertainment business and the demand for Hawaiian entertainment and hula dancers in elite circles. There was a lot of work. "I was very busy and all I did was entertain," notes Steer. She performed all over town, both on her own and with the Royal Hawaiian Girls' Glee Club, appearing at the Royal Hawaiian Hotel, the Moana Hotel, and the Young Men's Christian Association.[22] She danced at elite parties and weddings and entertained visiting royalty like the Prince of Wales and the Emperor of Japan, as well as the U.S. business and political elite. In addition, the dancers entertained often for private parties given by local sugar industry magnates like the Cookes and Castles. "They always hired the top performers. That's why people came, for the entertainment," recalls Steer.[23]

The pay scale for hula dancers indicates the importance employers placed on their presence.[24] "When I started, you were doing good if you earned $25 for a performance," recalls Steer. "That's about what featured dancers were paid." These were excellent wages in Hawaii in the decade of the Depression, where women earned an average minimum wage of only $1.05 per day in agriculture. Women's wages were somewhat higher in tourist-related industries like restaurants and hotels, but racial differentials persisted, as did gender inequities. For example, Filipino workers were confined to kitchen and cleaning tasks, averaging $50 per month; Japanese women were permitted to work as hotel maids, averaging $56 a month. In comparison, Caucasian men working in posts with high tourist contact, like hotel desk clerks, earned $102 a month.[25] Good wages for hula dancers indicated that the hotels considered them an important part of what they provided to the tourist, an expense of running the hotel that would presumably be well recouped in hotel profits.

But the best-paying hula jobs came from unlikely places: private parties given by illegal madams for their prostitutes. Most of the guests at these affairs were females, the only men being in the band. "What I made for one performance I'd have to work three months to get at the Royal," said Steer.[26] Most audiences were more socially respectable, however, and drawn from the upper classes: "At that time we didn't get the scrub tourist. Even if you got the middle class, you always got the nice middle-class people," said Steer.

Leila Reiplinger, a contemporary of Steer's, also enjoyed this work and the audiences.[27] In an oral history recorded in 1985, she recalls the audiences before World War II: "[Those audiences] were good. They were people that were quite affluent, very wealthy people that came down then in those days. No package deals like we have today." She characterizes their attitudes toward the local performers as "lovely. Of course, they were inquisitive like everybody else, but they didn't bother us. I mean, it wasn't like other places we may go to visit and people say, 'Oh, well, she's a dancer and she's a singer' [meaning, not worthy of respect]. No, they treated us very nicely. Well, most of them were so educated, and they had . . . money."[28]

Reiplinger's experience reveals something of the construction of the tourist repertory in relation to the wider range of hula practiced at that time. She learned the old temple dances (*hula pahu*), the 'auana, or modern, style (then called *hula ku'i*), and *kahiko,* or ancient, style (then called *ōlapa*) of dances, picking up different modes of chant and movement styling from her various teachers. Some of this repertoire, like the *hula mai* (chants celebrating the procreative powers of members of the chiefly class), were never performed in Waikiki. "To us, it was sacrilege to have other people see what was written for a personality," said Reiplinger. These were reserved for descendants of the *ali'i* for whom they were originally written. "We did common dances for the visitors that were well known. But personal things were not put out for the eyes of the public."[29]

At the Royal Hawaiian Hotel, Reiplinger recalls, performances took place on a big dance floor outside by the ocean. These shows featured a band and three or four hula dancers performing unison dances in a line. This was followed by a series of solo hula numbers. Although it is hard to know exactly what tourists thought of these shows, one travel book writer describes his own reactions explicitly: "The lawn shows of Waikiki," writes Sydney Clark in 1939, "are avowedly commercial and touristy, but I think you will be most happily surprised at the quality of them. The hotels put them on at frequent intervals as visitor-attractions, without charge, and one might expect the entertainment to be a little too obvious for pleasure, something to be yawned at and escaped. [But] dance, song, and chant were splendidly done, without undue self-consciousness or that bane of many shows, 'giving 'em what they want.' The [Hawaiian Girls' Glee Club] troupe has, as a matter of fact, won considerable fame both on the islands and on the mainland."[30]

As these remarks suggest, the shows at the Royal and the Halekulani Hotels, as well as other nightspots such as Don the Beachcomber's, featured some of Hawai'i's very best dancers and musicians. Tourists, at

least those of the upper-class majority, were exposed to a range of repertory that may have featured lighthearted hapa-haole songs like "My
Little Grass Shack," with English lyrics that tourists could understand,
but also included dancing to older chants in the Hawaiian language.[31]
These latter dances were surely harder for the mainlander audience to
perceive simply as lighthearted sensual entertainment, although the
drumming and chanting may well have carried connotations of primitivism to uninformed viewers. Face-to-face contact with performers,
who often mingled with tourists after these shows, may have mediated
the primitivizing by working against the decontemporaneity necessary
to sustain it.[32]

Still, the mainlander myths of natives in grass shacks and grass skirts
persisted, as Reiplinger's experience at the end of that decade indicates.
While a junior in high school, Reiplinger traveled to New York City
in 1940 to dance at the Hotel Lexington with Lani McIntire. With
her mother as chaperone to a group of four young female dancers,
Reiplinger performed nights and went to school days. Although the
hula dancers got along with the mainlander kids, the latter were in for a
surprise: "Their impression of [seeing a Hawaiian] was that they didn't
expect us to be so modern. I mean, we didn't look like cannibals. We are
from the South Pacific, right, or the Pacific Ocean. And we wore clothing, same thing they did. We used forks and knives the same way they
did. We ate the same food they did." And that surprised them, "because,
well, they think of people that are foreign and not heard of you know.
. . . We had people, let's say, our history teacher. She thought, well, we
were still the Sandwich Islands, which we corrected her at the time and
said, 'No, we're the territory of Hawai'i.' It's funny. We laughed. (laughs)
And she was embarrassed. So, after they got to know us, talking, we had
a lot of great friends. . . . You know, social wise, the way we lived and the
way they lived, no difference."[33]

These myths of grass shacks and natives in grass skirts persisted long
after World War II, as the experiences of one former professional dancer
who worked in the tourist industry in the 1970s reveals. A very attractive, slender woman with hapa-haole looks, dark hair, and dark eyes,
she toured with travel agents to the eastern half of the mainland, giving
presentations to potential tour groups. She would dance, talk about a
tour package, discuss the islands, and show a clip of the Don Ho Show.
After seeing pictures of Honolulu, mainlanders would often remark to
her how surprised they were to see a real city, because they thought
Hawaiians still lived in grass shacks. This was more than a decade after
Hawai'i had become the fiftieth state![34]

The tourists' appalling ignorance is testimony both to the persistence of the ideal native stereotype (grass huts as Edenic) and the power of the ideology of primitivism, of which the hula girl image had, by the 1970s, been a key signifier for nearly a century in Euro-American discourse. Tourists' encounters with this extremely articulate dancer in the 1970s must have at the very least temporarily unsettled those linkages. However, her hapa-haole looks simultaneously confirmed the dominant practice in tourist industry hiring: hiring dancers who satisfy the aesthetic requirements for a "safe" exoticism—not black, not too white, and not too Polynesian or Oriental.[35] In the 1930s the film industry did its part to propagate this image.

Hawai'i on Film in the 1930s

In the 1930s, an increasingly complex web of Hawaiian representations and performance practices emerges, as the discussion of Tootsie Notley Steer's career indicates. Commercial advertisements, ship and airplane greeters, tourist shows, and souvenir snapshots are only part of the picture of a period in which both live performances and mass-media images proliferate. Commercial films with Hawaiian themes, travelogues, newsreels, mainland dance shows, radio broadcasts, and even fashion designs and canned food advertisements reproduce variations on the "hula girl" image at an unprecedented rate. Sometimes these representations are subtle and complex, like the mix of hapa-haole songs and traditional chant in the Royal Hawaiian Hotel show, reproducing, undercutting, and extending the mainland hula girl signifier. At other times, although semiotically complex, they render a simplistic image of Native Hawaiian culture—like Minnie Mouse's version of the hula in Disney's 1935 animated film, *Hawaiian Holiday.*

Like advertising, the film industry expanded in the Depression, and films with Hawaiian themes were produced by most of the main studios: RKO, Warner Brothers, Paramount, Twentieth Century Fox, MGM, and Universal. Between 1920 and 1939 more than fifty feature films were made in or about Hawai'i. A genre of South Seas island romance was particularly popular, often featuring interracial romance between native women and Caucasian men (businessmen, shipwreck victims) visiting the islands.[36] The casts typically featured white mainland actors as stars and island locals in minor roles only. Polynesian roles were usually played by non-Polynesians, especially Latin American women such as Mexican Dolores Del Rio and Argentinian Mona Maris, or by Euro-Americans like Betty Compton.[37] These casting practices, like the roles Gilda Gray and Doraldina played in live performances and earlier films, reinforced the "tanned exotic" hapa-haole look and the association of the islands and hula dancers with alluring and sometimes illicit sexuality.[38]

For example, Del Rio's performance in King Vidor's 1932 *Bird of Paradise,* a remake of the popular 1912 play, was praised by a *Variety* reviewer as the film's "greatest asset." Her hula was dubbed a "stimulating South Seas calisthentics [sic] [that] will be the subject of much talk hither and yon." Native Hawaiians clearly were positioned as spectacle, performing "tribal dances which are emphatically oo-la-la in the wild abandon of the hula girls and the not less eloquent wriggles of the men Kanakas. . . . with Miss Del Rio, an eyeful of undraped symmetry, occupying the center of the picture."[39] While the Hawaiian setting and the imaginary associated with the South Seas enabled the deployment of mass spectacles of sexualized displays, narratives also reinforced the appeal of the forbidden. In the 1931 *Aloha,* for example, a beautiful part-native woman played by Raquel Torres marries a young American businessman, who is then disowned by his outraged father. Distraught, she sacrifices herself to the goddess Pele, leaping into a volcano.

Following Robert Sklar's contention that film producers cast Europeans to depict emotions unacceptable for Euro-Americans, Aeko Sereno proposes that the casting of Latin Americans in these Hawaiian films performs a similar function.[40] But the casting of Euro-Americans like Betty Compton ("Betty will shock you with her hula," shouted advertisements) complicates matters, as does the fact that Native Hawaiians were so rarely cast in featured roles. The association of sexuality with darker-skinned women has a long history in European and Euro-American literature, painting, and theater. But, as I argued in earlier chapters, despite a trend toward a generalized otherness, there is also a specific limit to that generalization. Note that Latin American and not African-American or Asian-Americans were cast. Latin Americans, like Native Hawaiians, were placed in a category of "near white." But they claimed a European background which elevated their star potential, a potential denied Native Hawaiian women in the casting process. Native Hawaiians could be played by Latin Americans or by Euro-Americans, but they could not in turn play either, nor could they portray themselves. A "star" was a thoroughly modern persona, something that the Hollywood conception of native women militated against. Betty Compton could "go native" in Hollywood, but Native Hawaiian dancers could not "go white," in the sense of becoming stars.[41]

Audiences were well aware of the conventions of the South Seas romance genre and kept some ironic distance toward these portrayals, as the 1937 *New York Times* review of Bing Crosby's *Waikiki Wedding* suggests. Noting that dance director LeRoy Prinz had his own "sub-realistic" ideas about the "hula-hula," critic Frank Nugent describes the scores of studio chorines as "a straw-skirted chorus . . . all over the place, caroling blithely along the beach, undulating around the tribal campfires." In fact, the dancers included island professionals Kahala Bray and Pualani Mossman, along with several other well-known Honolulu performers, but their skills were lost in the staging frenzy. Nugent suggests that "it might have been better all around had Mr. Prinz's brigade been called upon less: there's nothing quite so synthetic as a synthetic Hawaiian dance."[42]

Reviews in the islands were even more acidic, the *Honolulu Advertiser* pronouncing it "the purest hokum," a "pseudo-Hawaiian narrative," with costumes reminiscent of "Indian headdresses" and "Roman togas."[43] Still, the film was popular, its hit song "Sweet Leilani" winning the Oscar for best song in a soundtrack that also included "Blue Hawaii" and "In a Little Hula Heaven."

As a way of publicizing the islands during the Depression, the Hawaiian Tourist Bureau began to produce its own films in the 1930s, both to build upon and counter some of the mainland film images of Hawaii. In 1934 it funded several short promotional films and a feature, which were shown in thousands of theaters on the mainland and on ships bound for Hawai'i. These films thus acted as a tourist lure and once the tourists were on their way, served as a sort of guidebook or instruction manual preparing them for what they should/would see on their visit.

Four of these films are ten-minute shorts, featuring hotel scenes and scenic beauty on different islands.[44] But if these shorts are travelogues with a sort of documentary feel, the opposite is true of the HTB-produced feature *Song of the Islands,* a promotional film also released in 1934.[45] Here the emphasis is on romance and fantasy, and hula and Native Hawaiians are the main focus. Completely framed by the tourist experience, the narrative opens with shots Honolulu visitors might encounter, including lei sellers, beaches, surfing, and dancing to the Harry Owens Orchestra from the Royal Hawaiian Hotel. But most of the narrative unfolds as the story of a Hawaiian legend told by a white male visitor to his white female companion as they sail away from Waikiki. He relays the story of "Princes Pualani," played by Pualani Mossman, who typifies the dark-haired hapa-haole style of beauty. The rest of the film depicts the story of this Hawaiian princess forced to marry another of royal lineage instead of the commoner she loves. This narrative slightly rewrites the South Seas Hollywood genre, with its interracial plot, but retains the idea of Hawai'i as a romantic site, with natives as the spark to romance for visiting whites.

The story functions as an excuse to display all the common markers of Hawaiiana, from a *hukilau,* to a huge lū'au for the wedding feast, boys climbing trees for coconuts, torchlight fishing at night, and grass houses. In the end, the princess sails off to another island with her new husband, and tosses her lei back toward the shore as a token of her desire to return to her lover. "And so," ends the narrator as the shot returns to the couple on the steamer, "that's why we toss leis into the sea today, in hopes that we too will return." Nostalgic strains of "Aloha Oe," ironically written by Queen Lili'uokalani a few years before her overthrow, bring the picture to a close. This film is a rather remarkable demonstration of the harnessing of Native Hawaiiana (and its manufacture) in the service of the tourist industry. The entire depiction of Native life is framed as a story told by the tourist for other tourists.

But the history of the filming reveals a more complicated relationship between the tourist industry and cultural depictions by insiders and outsiders. *Song of the Islands* was shot by a Hollywood production company at Lalani Village and featured many members of Pualani Mossman's family.[46] In 1931 Mossman's father, George, had started Lalani Village in Honolulu as a way of preserving and teaching what he termed "Hawaiian lore that is fast vanishing."[47] A "village" of eight grass houses was erected on one acre, and a program of classes (in Hawaiian language, hula, music, food preparation, surfing, and fishing), along with lū'aus and performances led by members of the Mossman family, was offered.

Lalani Village and Hula Lessons

The Mossmans lived at the village and engaged Palea Kuluwaimaka, the last living chanter from King Kalākaua's court, to perform and give instruction. Additional hula experts, such as Akoni Mika from Hilo, were engaged for shorter periods of performing and instruction. Young women such as Annie Au and Louise Kahanu also worked at the village, chosen from among a large group of applicants. Job requirements included a pleasant personality for public contact and the ability to sing, dance, speak Hawaiian, cook Hawaiian food, and explain Hawaiian life. The village was thus conceived of as living museum, archive, school, and tourist entertainment center.

For two dollars, Pualani Mossman recalled, the visitor received a one-hour lecture on village life by her mother, followed by a lū'au and a show. Some sense of tourists' response is indicated in an article in

Harper's magazine in 1938. Writer Sigmund Spaeth notes: "You will be struck by the entertainers' catholicity of taste. When the Hawaiian musicians are putting on a show they make no distinctions as to periods or materials. At one moment you may be watching an ancient ritual dance, with the performers sitting on the ground, some beating on drums or gourds . . . the next number may be a modern song of the Tin Pan alley type, by Harry Owens or Johnny Noble . . . you may hear samples from every style, from an ancient mele [chant] to the veriest jazz or swing."[48]

As both "living exhibits" and knowledgeable guides, the performers at Lalani Village offered a representation of Hawaiians as both traditional and modern (from chant to swing), a more complex representation than that found in film or advertising. They presented themselves as historically aware, contemporary actors portraying a past usually rendered in the Caucasian imaginary as without history. They embodied the seemingly oxymoronic notion of a "modern native," the Euro-American blind spot which had so stymied the editors of the 1924 *National Geographic* issue on contemporary Hawai'i, illustrated only with pictures of Hawaiians in settings that no longer existed.

Both tourists and local residents came to Lalani Village to learn hula. Looking back in 1995, Pualani Mossman recalled that ten dollars purchased thirty lessons and ten different dances, including "My Little Grass Shack," implement dances with bamboo sticks or gourds, three hulas with chant accompaniment, and even comic hulas. While some studied only for a week, those who stuck with the whole program were graduated, received a diploma and a Hawaiian name, and danced at the lū'au in front of guests.[49]

The lessons were part of a hula resurgence that was taking place on many fronts at once, as the presence of locals and visitors together indicates. Tourist shows boomed, hula studios catered to female visitors wanting instruction, and numerous island dancers dispersed throughout the U.S. mainland, performing in a variety of venues. In addition, hula became more visible in the public sphere in the islands, featured in both elite and popular settings. For example, a county-wide contest sponsored by the recreation division drew 170 dancers and 4,000 spectators to Honolulu's Kapiolani Park in June of 1939 and was so successful that it became an annual event. A month later the Academy of Arts sponsored a program of eighteen sacred and secular dances. In the preceding year, 500 young women had entered a "Queen of Hula" competition sponsored by Consolidated Amusement company and Metro-Goldwyn-Mayer, the winner being promised a screen test.[50] The tourist and nontourist activities intertwined, although they did not overlap fully, with differences in repertory, costume, performance style, and reception depending on the makeup of the audience.

The reasons for this resurgence are many, including the sponsorship of classes by the Mormon Mutual Improvement Association, which encouraged the practice of traditional dance among its many Native Hawaiian church members, and a growing sense of public acceptance of hula.[51] Hula studios saw an influx of local students as well as visitors. Teacher Dorothy Campbell, of the Betty Lei hula studio, noted the increase in the early thirties: "Tourists do not make up all my pupils by any means. A great many Honoluluans are learning the dance. I have classes nearly every afternoon, with students ranging from age two to adults."[52] The growing demand for dancers in the tourist industry, and the appetite for things Hawaiian on the mainland fed by the spate of films featuring hula mentioned above, also contributed to this boom.

Female tourists flocked to hula studios, hoping to take a hula dance home as a living souvenir of their visit, enacting for their friends exactly the same type of "nativizing" transposition promised on the sheet-music covers and advertisements discussed earlier. A 1927 poem called "Priscilla Poses" indicates the popularity of posing as a hula girl and learning hula:

> Full many a gentle tourist dons
> A hula skirt of hay,
> To pose before the camera
> For snaps to send away.
> Here Miss Priscilla Plentynice,
> Of Providence, Rhode Isle,
> Is all equipped, from top to toe,
> To hula half a mile.—
> "Please teach us how to hula-dance,"
> Her friends will cry with glee,
> When Miss Priscilla Plentynice
> Goes home from Waikiki.[53]

Apparently the social cachet was a boon. In an article announcing the opening of her hula studio in Waikiki, dancer Ruth Lani Lane, who also taught hula in the Royal Hawaiian Hotel, noted that "feminine visitors to Hawaii who return to the coast find that if they can give these dances gracefully, they are decided additions in social gatherings."[54] The demand was so great that one Waikiki teacher was quoted as saying that, if she had any more tourist business, it would be the death of her.[55] If hula shows commodified the performance of Hawaiiana, hula lessons commodified its enactment through the nativizing process I discussed earlier. Caucasian bodies acquired a patina, like a "cultural tan," of the hula girl allure. White bodies were sexualized by performing actions associated with exotic females.[56]

MAINLAND SHOWS

The desire for these classes was doubtlessly fed by a new wave of Hawaiian performers being featured in urban mainland shows during the 1930s. Unlike Doraldina and Toots Paka of the teens and twenties, these women, many of whom were of combined Caucasian and Native Hawaiian ancestry, came from the islands. Contemporary discourse in the islands refers to them as "Hawai'i's goodwill emissaries" sent to "strategic centers such as San Francisco, New Orleans, Chicago and New York" and replacing the "synthetic shimmies of yesterday" with "real Hawaiian hula." The dancers also performed in Minneapolis, Detroit, Cincinnati, and Hartford and in Colorado, indicating that the phenomenon was not limited to a few cities.[57]

Railing against perceived mainlander misperceptions of hula, one 1939 island article opened this way: "Ten years ago, Mr. and Mrs. America's idea of the hula and Hawaii could be summed up in a very small nut shell. To them the hula was a strange dance, announced by a circus barker, executed in the privacy of a Barnum and Bailey sideshow. The hula consisted of erratic hip movements, fast jazz music, [and] a thin bronzed girl, probably from the Bronx, who sported heavy beaded armlets and anklets and a yellow grass skirt [in front of] a grinning mob of country hicks [who] thought vaguely that they had at last seen a South Sea island siren."[58]

This characterization is revealing for several reasons. It indicates the widespread allure of hula dancers, reaching out into rural populations, the whiteness of the performers, and the tensions between hula as sleazy sex (tent-show barkers) and as exotic entertainment suitable for the leisure of couples (Mr. and Mrs. America). As I have argued previously, this "hootch" aspect was only one part of a complicated representation of Hawaiian women in the mainland shows, but it appears that Hawaiian residents feared that this vision, which was seen as degrading, would predominate.

The new dancers presented a different image. Honolulu newspapers described the "envoys" as young, attractive, poised women who handled both public performing and publicity demands with "class," and provided "splendid advertis[ing] for Hawaii." These "flesh and blood representatives" (i.e., "authentic" Hawaiians) immediately "erase any memories of the cheap sideshows." The popularity of hula at the time is indicated by the opening of Hawaiian Rooms at both the Lexington and St. Regis Hotels in New York. Surrounded by giant tree ferns, a Waikiki beach scene, and stars twinkling above in a painted sky, patrons could dine, dance, and be entertained by a musical floor show. Dancers made from $75 to $100 dollars a week for three shows a night, six nights a week, and made additional money singing for recordings, posing for advertising, and teaching hula to patrons. Hula was so popular that some dancers, like Pualani Mossman, Meymo Holt, and sisters Leimomi (Lillian) and Jennie Wood squeezed in a fourth performance each night, dashing from the Lexington at Times Square to the Winter Garden Theater for a hula number in the Broadway comedy *Helzapoppin*.

The local press went wild, extending the images to a wider public than the upper-class patrons of the shows. New York papers ran an eight-column strip of Meymo Holt's dancing hands in action, Bradshaw Crandall drew her for *Cosmopolitan*, and Walter Winchell wrote about her in the *Daily Mirror*. (Holt's hapa-haole style of beauty, already popular on the mainland, may have contributed to the amount of publicity she received while reinforcing that image.)[59] The commercial success of all this marketing of Hawaiiana is indicated by the following figures about the Lexington Hotel Hawaiian Room. In just two years (1937–39), the room grossed revenues of $1,017,393.56, an increase of 20 percent over the preceding two years, when it was called the Silver Grill and featured non-Hawaiian bands. More than half a million guests were entertained, consuming 46,000 coconuts (used to serve Oke punch and taken home as souvenirs) and 5,000 miles of crepe paper leis.[60]

The success of the Lexington was not isolated. There were similar Hawaiian rooms not only at the St. Regis but also at the Roosevelt Hotels in Chicago and New Orleans, at the St. Francis in San Francisco, and the Statler in Buffalo, and even at the New Japan Hotel in Tokyo and the Mayfair in London. In addition, supper clubs with Hawaiian themes proliferated, including the Lord Baltimore in Baltimore, the Mayfair Casino in Cleveland, and the Pago Pago Room at Leon and Eddie's in New York.[61]

The passion for Hawaiian music and dance had been fanned by the beginning of what was to become the most widely known Hawaiian radio music program in the world, *Hawaii Calls*, first broadcast from under a banyan tree in the courtyard of the Moana Hotel in 1935 and running for forty years. Recognized from the beginning as a way of promoting Hawai'i as a tourist destination, the program was sustained by public funds appropriated by the state legislature from 1936 on. The program's popularity peaked in 1952, when millions all over the world listened to weekly broadcasts of "Hawaiian music played by Hawaiians from Hawai'i." Seven hundred and fifty stations in the United States, Canada, Japan, Korea, Europe, Latin America, Australia, South Africa, and New Zealand carried the show. The most popular songs, like "Lovely Hula Hands" and "Sweet Leilani," were indelibly associated with hula dancing.[62]

The expanding popularity of Hawaiian cultural products in mainland entertainment fed the tourist industry just as the tourist industry helped to create a demand for such products through its advertising campaigns and through the appetites of returning tourists. Throughout this linkage of production and consumption, performative renditions of Hawaiian-ness, most especially hula dance and music, came to bear the signifying weight of "Hawai'i." Hawaiian and part-Hawaiian performers on the mainland, along with film, advertising images, and radio, generated an interest that was met upon arrival by the greeters, dancers, and musicians that tourists encountered in Honolulu. The performance of culture, specifically as embodied by the female dancer, whose image was now widened to include the Polynesian looks of Tootsie Steer as well as the hapa-haole-style beauty of the Brays and Mossmans, and the faux-Hawaiian exotic hapa-haole allure of Delores Del Rio, had firmly established itself as both the lure and the guarantor of the specificity of Hawai'i as a destination.

By the end of the 1930s, the process of cultural commodification had become central to a booming tourist industry that earlier had relied on the selling of Hawai'i's scenery as a primitive paradise. But this process of commodification was not just one more instance of a growing consumer culture fed by the expansion of the advertising and tourist industries and watered by similar expansion in film, radio, and entertainment industries. It was enabled as well by mainland racial concepts and the emergence of a discourse of culture, a linkage I explore next.

THE CULTURES OF RACE

Mainlanders' racialist perceptions of Hawaiians were an amalgamation of presumptions about physical type and cultural practices. They were shaped not only by ideologies of primitivism and exoticism but also by contemporary racial theories and race relations, especially, but not exclusively, the relations between African Americans and European Americans.

As Peggy Pascoe has noted, these discourses were in the throes of change during the first three decades of the century. Pascoe argues that "during the 1920s, American racialism was challenged by several emerging ideologies, all of which depended on the modern split between concepts of biology and culture."[63] The influence of social scientists like cultural anthropologist Franz Boas and, later, Ruth Benedict challenged the previously widespread understanding of race as "an indivisible essence that included not only biology but also culture, morality, and intelligence," precisely the formulation manifest in the "races of mankind" type of books popular in the latter half of the nineteenth century and cited in chapter 2.[64]

For Boas and his followers, this constellation of attributes (morality, character, social organization, etc.) was precisely that which fell under the rubric of "culture," learned not inherited, practices not essences. Still, notions of biological difference lingered, although for the new culturalists they were of relatively little significance. Pascoe identifies a paradoxical split in positions. Some argued that "race" made no biological sense and pointed to the proliferation of races and current racial classification systems and their discrepancies as symptomatic of the fact that race was biologically indeterminable.[65] Others argued that races might be facts, that is, physical differences that could be catalogued systematically, but that these divisions were irrelevant to discussions of language, psychology, character, and morality.

These changes of thought in the scientific community coexisted in public discourse with residual popular notions from earlier decades. For example, a 1922 *Mid-Pacific* magazine article, "The Native Hawaiian," does not detail the bodily aspects of Hawaiian physiques as some earlier writing did, but it opens with a full-page photograph of a young Native Hawaiian girl, perhaps ten or twelve years old. The caption reads: "The native Hawaiian is almost perfectly formed and the children are often beautiful to look upon, both as to face and figure. There are about 48,000 Hawaiians and part Hawaiians living today."[66]

In the text that follows, the author details the generally positive traits he ascribes to Native Hawaiians, though in a paternalistic tone: "With all his limitations and defects, however, the Hawaiian is essentially a manly fellow, with many excellent qualities and a good deal of the natural gentleman about him. He is naturally brave, generous, hospitable, good tempered, and courteous. He is susceptible to good influences, capable of high and noble aspirations. . . . Neither is the native as lazy as is often asserted and very generally believed." Moreover, "the Hawaiians have considerable natural taste and artistic instinct. . . . Their good taste shows itself, for one thing, in their fondness for, and free use of, natural flowers as a material for personal adornment . . . there is none of that fancy for cheap jewelry and tawdry ornamentation which is such a pronounced characteristic of the negroes, Indians, and some others of the dark-skinned races."[67]

This last sentence cements the implicit biological underpinnings of the social and moral judgments articulated above. Dark-skinned races have "tawdry" taste, from which the somewhat lighter-skinned Hawaiian escapes. Lest the reader assume too much, however, the writer reminds us that despite a surprising "superficial but ready adaptability" that allows the better-educated Natives to combine European and Native Hawaiian living styles and dress, "both sexes still retain their aboriginal fondness for squatting on the ground or the floor in preference to sitting on chairs."[68] The text vacillates between concepts of cultural practices as learned (learning to sit on chairs, not squatting) and culture as inborn tendencies ("aboriginal fondness," pleasing aesthetic tastes).

Twenty years later, such linkages still persisted, as arguments against such assumptions reveal. In a 1942 article, "Eyes of the Pacific," Dr. William Krauss examines differences in eyefold formation among "East Asiatics," "Mongoloid," and "European" eyes. He closes with the assertion that: "Especially in the mid-Pacific Hawaiian Islands, where all groups of the population understand and speak the English language, we [can see] that these exterior differences in eye form are unessential as far as the qualities of the soul are concerned. For in these islands we find all groups, regardless of their differences in eye form, making honest and valuable contributions to their present homeland, American Hawaii."[69]

Gradually, however, the public stances of these new social scientists wedged their way into public awareness, influencing many areas of social life, including public policy. For example, the Indian Reorganization Act of 1934, which restored some measure of independence to Native American tribal groups, also promoted the "study of Indian civilization" and the preservation and development of "the special cultural contributions and achievements of such civilization, including Indian arts, crafts, skills and traditions."[70] A few years later Ruth Benedict and Gene Weltfish published a pamphlet aimed at the general public, called *The Races of Mankind,* in which they argued that racial differences were limited to "nonessentials such as texture of head hair, amount of body hair, shape of the nose or head, or color of the eyes and the skin."[71] However, the establishment of the culturalist argument as hegemonic, as common sense, took several decades and even now remains intertwined with presumptions about racial categorization, as current public discourse about multiculturalism reveals, recasting in the language of culture precisely the same population divisions previously named as races, as Virginia Domínguez has argued.[72]

What the gradual emergence of concepts of culture into popular discourse did though, through the middle decades of the twentieth century, was to promote public awareness of culture as a thing, and as a thing which could be commodified, sold, and experienced. This understanding facilitated the consumption of cultural experiences as part of one strand of tourism. This was especially true in contexts where that being sold could be posed as authentic or traditional (handcrafted, homemade) as opposed to ersatz, mass-produced products.

Notions of culture as a shared way of life and of culture as artistic product sometimes merged and sometimes clashed in this period. While anthropologists generally embraced the former, wealthy liberals as well as conservatives sometimes embraced the latter, merging the notion of elite art object and folk tradition into the category of folk art. In both cases, art or folk art, an opposition to burgeoning mass culture was proposed.[73] A 1939 performance of hula in the Honolulu Academy of Art is an example of this merging.

The 1930s saw a rise in protest about mass consumption and its perceived potential for cheapening taste, the rejuvenation and reinvention of traditional practices in the form of folk schools, and the patronage of Native American arts and crafts.[74] Members of elite classes were involved as academics, promoters, consumers, and instructors in this search for a new authenticity, which found other outlets also in the "common man and woman" idealizations of the New Deal murals.[75] Ironically, these anti-mass-production strains ultimately contributed to the commodification of those practices associated with the preindustrial past they idealized.

In Hawai'i, performances of songs and dances, the artistic/social products which came to stand for whole complexes of culture, were uniquely suited to this commodification. They offered elite tourists an experience, proximity to and a chance to see (visible evidence) live natives enacting their culture. The bodily presence, as I argued earlier, ultimately guarantees authenticity (real natives doing real native things). This guarantee results from the intertwining of concepts of culture as biologically based and that of culture as socially based. Despite the emergence of a concept of culture as socially produced, it remained and still does remain implicitly tethered to the presumed biological specificity of its producers, even when this notion of biology is recoded as national origin or linguistic group.

I am proposing that the paradigmatic structure of tourist performances presumes this linkage in the minds of the mainland audience and that this transposition of culture as race and race as culture provides the primary frame through which such performances were and are still viewed. Throughout this chapter I've demonstrated how a dynamic nexus among three concurrent trends took place, uniting the rise of tourism as an organized industry with the popularization of racialized concepts of culture and the increasing commodification of leisure-time activities (i.e., the packaging and selling for cash of activities that in the past were engaged in outside a cash economy). In the 1930s the commodified performance of Hawaiiana (practices marked as uniquely Hawaiian) by Hawaiians (and those perceived as natives) for outsiders assumed its central role in the tourist industry.

SIX

Surfers and "Beachboys"

Euro-American Representations of Native
Hawaiian Men and Interracial Romance

In songs, postcards, and guidebooks, on the stage, and in film, the image of the "hula girl" did and still does predominate. Caucasian representations of Native Hawaiian men in the early decades of this century were limited to the occasional "ethnographic" photograph in *National Geographic* or a postcard of men fishing or pounding poi or, even more rarely, of a Hawaiian family together in a domestic scene. The sole exception was depictions of surfing. By the latter half of the 1920s, surfing was an established part of tourist iconography and tourist itineraries, and by the end of the 1930s Native Hawaiian "beachboys," hired by hotels to provide surfing lessons and outrigger canoe rides, were established workers in the tourist industry.[1]

Two aspects of this practice and its representation are striking: first, the admiring, sometimes gushing, tone in which both male and female writers from the mainland describe the surfing Hawaiian male, and, second, the access to wealthy Caucasian females that beachboys had, at a time when potentially intimate interactions between white women and nonwhite men were still under strict censure, and when interracial marriage was still illegal in several states.

REASSERTING "RACE"

New social scientists may have been countering racialist models of human difference with culturalist ones, but the intensified codification of race laws in the 1920s underlines the continuing persistence of "race" in legal and popular discourse. Post-Reconstruction migrations of African Americans northward and heavy immigration from southern and eastern Europe during the late nineteenth and early twentieth centuries posed challenges to white (Anglo-Saxon nativist) supremacy. Exacerbated racial tensions resulted not only in race riots and lynchings (primarily of African-American men) but also in new legislation. In the 1920s and 1930s new immigration laws limited Asian and southern and eastern European access, and many states passed new antimiscegenation laws.[2]

While the primary target of these laws was the prohibition of marriage and the guardianship of white property rights, roughly half also explicitly prohibited interracial sex. Buttressed by the power of the eugenics movement, which promoted the breeding of "better" families, more than a dozen states passed expanded laws in the 1920s and 1930s which prohibited marriage between Caucasians and American Indians, Asian Americans, and "Malays," "Mongols," or "Hindus." Oregon specifically prohibited "Kanakas" (Native Hawaiians) from marrying whites.[3]

Most previous antimiscegenation laws had only targeted Caucasian and African-American unions. The expansion of categories in the 1920s and 1930s was accompanied by a tightening of the definition of who was what. For example, Virginia's 1924 "Act to Preserve Racial Integrity," tightened the legal definition of "Negro" from the previous "one-sixteenth" of "Negro blood" to any Negro blood at all, and redefined whiteness as having absolutely no admixture. This put into effect the "one-drop" rule—anyone with any African ancestry was legally Negro.[4]

In these legal mappings of racial conceptualizations, little was explicitly said about Hawaiians. Some may have regarded Native Hawaiians as "Asiatics," "Mongols," or "Malays," but those terms seem to have been used more frequently to refer to populations of Chinese, Japanese, Korean, and Filipino origin. While the lack of explicit reference to Hawaiians (with the exception of Oregon) may have been due to the small number of Native Hawaiians living on the mainland, it may also have indicated something of the ideal native status I delineated in chapter 2. "Interracial" sex, love, and romance between Native Hawaiian women and Caucasian men had been a staple of the South Seas romance genre in plays, books, and films, which had plotted its allure, delights, and, at times, social costs. But rarely had these portrayals been as charged with racial enmity as black-white relations. The "offshore" location of these romances may have made them more acceptable than similar depictions of black-white romance, but the different status of the Native Hawaiian in a white imaginary was also important. Although most of these narratives had combined white male privilege with fantasies of native women as a source of sensual rejuvenation, in the 1930s something new happens. A newly visible discourse of romance between Caucasian women and Native Hawaiian men, surfers and beachboys, emerges. It is centered on depictions of male Native Hawaiian bodies and their enactment of culturally specific behaviors—the linkage of race and culture.

SURFING

Surfing, a Native Hawaiian sport, had been driven out of favor owing to missionary censure of it as frivolous play that promoted nudity and took time away from work. As late as 1892 ethnologist Nathaniel Emerson wrote: "Today it is hard to find a surfboard outside our museums and private collections."[5] However, surfing made a comeback starting at the turn of the century, and its popularity grew right along with Hawai'i's tourist industry, aided by mainland attitudes advocating outdoor sports as part of healthy living for both men and women, and idealizing a tanned physique shaped by athletics.[6]

The beachboys, most of whom were Native Hawaiian or part-Native Hawaiian, taught swimming and surfing, and gave outrigger canoe rides; they took guests sightseeing, kept an eye on visitors' children, supplied lomi lomi (traditional Hawaiian-style) massages, handed out towels, set up beach chairs, applied suntan lotion, clowned around with jokes and skits, played music in the afternoons, and, out on the pier at night, occasionally even did a hula. Most were consummate watermen, with a serious knowledge of the sea and excellent abilities on and in water. Some developed longstanding friendships with Hollywood stars like Cary Grant, millionaires like Doris Duke, and various industrial leaders.[7] Many of the leading beachboys of that period, like Chick Daniels, "Turkey" Love, "Steamboat" Mokuahi, "Panama" Dave Baptiste, Harry Robello, and "Rabbit" Kekai continued to work at the Royal through the 1950s, but after the war, with the rise of mass tourism, the linkage of beachboys with elite romance declined.

As early as 1906 the Moana Hotel had promoted surfing and canoeing as exciting sport opportunities for the tourist, and by the 1920s surfing had entered the tourist iconography through postcards and advertisements. While advertisements often depicted the beachboys in the service of wealthy white patrons, paddling them across breaking waves, sometimes they were pictured alone, "bronze athletes" standing tall on surfboards, rocketing through the water. Even in the service pictures they are shown to be strong, competent, completely in control of the situation, as grinning tourists, male and female, hold on for the exhilarating ride.

Hawaiian Tourist Bureau ads from the 1920s set up an explicit connection between white women and Native Hawaiian men. For example, in a 1929 HTB advertisement a trim, light-skinned young woman balances artfully on a speeding board while right next to her another white woman is paddled over the breaking wave in an outrigger canoe manned by several Natives.

The ad copy enthuses: "The water is a place to *play* . . . where bronze-skinned Hawaiians will teach you how to balance on speeding surfboards. Native outrigger canoes ride the breakers at toboggan-speed. There's a thrill even in watching them from the smart *lanai* of your beach hotel."[8] Presumably the "you" in the ad text addresses the female consumer who can picture herself on the surfboard, and her trim, graceful figure serves as enticement for male readers, who might like to surround themselves with such bathing beauties.

Travel books and tourist itineraries of the late twenties through late thirties promoted surfing (along with lūʻaus) as a must-do for visitors.[9] The consistently celebratory tone regarding male bodies is striking. J. Walker McSpadden, in his 1939 travel book *Beautiful Hawaii*, fairly gushes about the beachboys riding the surf: "At a distance they remind you of flying-fishes. . . . Clad only in the briefest of trunks, their fine bodies gleam like polished bronze. Their physical set up is wellnigh perfect. Why shouldn't it be, when wind and sea and sky give them the finest outdoor gym in the world! These fellows—it is interesting to note—are the descendants of the native Hawaiian, the stock that is running out all too soon. . . . There were many such in the islands of old, it is said. Looking at these god-like gymnasts one can well believe it." This is a tone of celebratory primitivism—bronzed skin, near nudity, the nostalgia of a vanishing race, the authenticating link to the "islands of old," intimations of natural (native) physical prowess, the surfer at one with the forces of nature—a version of the "natural native in Nature" that is akin to the hula girl.

In tourist discourse there were rarely any competing representations of Native Hawaiian men, no Natives in suits, no Natives working, or working at anything recognizable by visitors as work. But of course the beachboys *were* working. Beachboys were not salaried but made their money from charging by the hour for surfing lessons and canoe rides. Tips made up a large part of their incomes, too, incomes which were above the norm for that period. Three dollars per half-hour for canoe rides compared very favorably with men's wages in other service industries like restaurant work, where the going rate was twenty- three cents an hour. "Aloha" may have been freely given, but it was also the basis of incomes.[10]

The relatively high rate of pay, like that of the hula dancers in the 1930s, indicates the value tourists and the tourist industry placed on the services beachboys provided, especially in their role as conduits of distinctive Native Hawaiian cultural practices like surfing which contributed to the destination image. The lessons and rides, like the hula shows, provided tourists with a commodified version of such cultural practices, one that allowed the visitors directly to purchase the experience of such things for themselves, to "go native" in a limited way.

For women especially, this going native often involved close physical proximity to Native Hawaiian men, sometimes even romance and physical intimacy. Clifford Gessler's 1937 travel book, *Isles of Enchantment,* describes the scene at the Royal Hawaiian Hotel: "Here an eastern lady of fashion lies prone beneath the sun while a smiling Hawaiian youth anoints her back and legs with coconut oil to encourage protective and ornamental tan. Near-by, another bronze boy kneels over another fair visitor, kneading and manipulating the muscles in the soothing and relaxing Hawaiian massage."[11] Like the enlivening touch of the hula girl in Steichen's photograph, physical contact with a "genuine" native enables the tourist literally to come to her senses, to regain contact with her own (natural) self.

Reports vary regarding the romances between beachboys and mainland female visitors, but at the very least the potential for intimate contact was there, as implied in the visual representations of promotional shots. For example, a 1938 cover photo for *Vogue* magazine featured a light-skinned female tourist surfing across the froth of a cresting wave. She is balanced on her hands and knees with a similarly posed deeply tanned beachboy right behind her on the board. Surfing's kinesthetic thrill of speed and danger finds an echo in subtextual fantasies of interracial romance with their similarly thrilling combination of dangers risked and freedoms taken.[12]

For some female tourists, these sports encounters in the public privacy of the water clearly facilitated what might have otherwise been unallowable physical pleasures. As one beachboy recalled: "A lady once told me, 'When I was nineteen, you took me tandem [two people on a surfboard]. Can you imagine what it was like for me, going to a Catholic school on the mainland, to have a man take me surfing? To sit on top of me, on the back of my legs. The thrill I had. Skin to skin. In the water."[13]

Sometimes beachboys managed these maneuvers to maximize sexual stimulation. Melvin Paoa recalled certain beachboy techniques from the early days: "Like when you paddle tandem, your chest is always rubbing up against the wahine's *okole* [woman's buttocks]. Let's say you lift up your chest little bit, so your *da kine* [thing] is on their *okole*. They might like that. And when you sit back on the board, sit way back, so the board tilts up and they slide back over you. Then you go *lomi lomi* their legs or their shoulders. They could lose their bathing suit just by you rubbing them."[14]

Certainly not all beachboys and not all female tourists sought amorous encounters, and some have very different memories. One California woman remembered "The beachboys were gentlemen," echoing well-known beachboy Harry Robello's statement: "The beachboys had to be straight-line. Well mannered. Women were safe with the beachboys."[15] But the potential for such intimacies was noted in travel books and was part of the allure in tourist advertisements. Soft primitivism was central to this appeal; Native Hawaiian males were unfailingly portrayed as easygoing, playful, and happy-go-lucky. Their sensuality as graceful bronzed gods parallels that of the hula dancer image—always softened, never aggressively sexual or threatening.

Racial classification was also a key to this appeal and to the freedoms accorded interactions between white women and Native men. Travel writing stressed the bronze, not black, classification of Native Hawaiians. Sydney Clark writes: "Hawaiians are exceedingly dark of skin, next door to black, but there is nothing negroid about their features or their glossy hair, nor are they looked upon by any haole as black people. They are Polynesians and as such are held in high respect. . . . They are accepted socially by the haoles and even marriage with them is not necessarily frowned on, provided they are of good 'stock' (preferably with a trace of royalty) and with skins not *too* dark, in other words *hapa*-Hawaiian, *hapa* meaning half or part . . . the emphasis being definitely placed on the white half."[16]

Still, there were class and racial boundaries to these encounters. Robello recalled strict guidelines from the Matson company, which owned both the Royal Hawaiian and Moana hotels, where beachboys worked. As employees, beachboys were not allowed above the lobby floor except as invited guests (although this rule could be circumvented with a tip to a bellboy), and, while a beachboy might meet a female guest at a nightspot after hours, he wouldn't ask her out on a date. "She tell her parents, her parents tell the hotel, you out," said Robello. Beachboys were aware that any sexual advances might be reported to the management.

Racial difference also made interactions subject to censure. Many of the beachboys looked Polynesian and were of predominantly Hawaiian ancestry, but others, like Robello, who was part-Portuguese, were of European and Hawaiian heritage, and looked hapa haole. Robello remembered: "You a brown boy, get little bit dark skin, you stay away."[17] Although Caucasian-Hawaiian relations seem more freely accepted than black-white relationships on the mainland, these comments reveal the tensions between a potential for physical intimacy and the limits of those interactions based on a race hierarchies and class relations.[18]

Despite these hierarchies, relations between beachboys and tourists were inflected with a variety of power dynamics which sometimes enforced and sometimes countered the expected hierarchies of race and class. Beachboys were at once at the service of some of the world's wealthiest people and knowledgeable insiders on whose know-how visitors depended not only to learn about the sea but also to have a good time in Honolulu, joining the beachboys for singing and dancing in bars and clubs like the Tropics.[19]

In this capacity as gatekeeper to island pleasures, beachboys facilitated not only the romantic fantasies of female visitors but also the transformation of males. Some developed long-term friendships, even flying to the mainland to join wealthy men for parties. However, white men were rarely pictured surfing in tandem with Native men, as was so common for white females taking lessons.[20] Instead, beachboys represented a fantasized utopian vision, an antidote to the stress of jobs in a post-1929 decade, when the presumed equation of hard work with prosperity came under intense scrutiny, an emphasis on consumption challenged that on production, and the most popular self-improvement manuals were, as Lawrence Levine has noted, Edmund Jacobson's *You Must Relax* and Dorothea Brande's *Wake Up and Live!* Americans, these books proposed, needed to learn how to live, to stop deferring pleasure.[21] Native Hawaiians, at least according to the tourist promotions, travel books, and shows, seemed to know how to do just that, as their depictions as happy, pre-industrial, singing, dancing, surfers proclaimed.

A 1936 article in the *Saturday Evening Post* describes the process by which white businessmen from the mainland turn into "seven-day natives": "You come from the mainland, all full of business, politics and other troubles, and the first thing you know you are singing a lot of words like 'Wiki Wiki' and playing ukuleles and dancing the hula. At first you are startled when you see Judge Futzbutz from New England carrying a ukulele on the beach and wearing a carnation lei. . . . Next week you will meet him at a luau, eating poi with his fingers and dancing a hula. . . . Judge Futzbutz is not the only one who goes native—that is, turns human—out here. Businessmen forget about their business or lack of it, housewives their servant problems—I even met a Hollywood actor who didn't talk about the studio."

The opposition between the mainland and the islands is clearly drawn: "Imagine a country like [Hawaii] belonging to our United States. And then try to imagine us letting such a Never-Never Land become just another state where we're told we should be glad to work hard at a job we don't like in order to make money we can't save, to put it where we can't get it back, so we will have it when we are too old to enjoy it." The author cautions against the "snake in the grass" of "so-called Progress," which threatens to infect the islands.[22] In these reveries, Hawai'i becomes not the plantation economy beset by labor disputes that it was, but an idealized fantasy posed against the pitfalls of "progress."

A Modern Paradise

However, as I've suggested above, the attraction of Hawai'i was not just as an escape for mainlanders from the pressures of the Depression decade. As Lawrence Levine has argued, the idea that Depression-era populations sought escape is inadequate—we must account for the specifics of which cultural products were so popular.[23] The expansion of tourism to Hawai'i in the 1930s depended on a specific white imaginary of the islands and the ways it was counterposed to the mainland situation. The uncertain modernity of the 1930s, when nostalgia for a pre-industrial past emerged in WPA murals and in distrust of the corporation, of big business, was counterposed to the Edenic Hawai'i sold in tourist brochures and commodified in performances. The authenticity of the paradisical Hawaiian, who knew how to relax, how to live in gracious harmony with the environment, who seemed to have an abundance of pleasure in a time of scarcity, offered an alternative model. At home "abroad," in Hawai'i, elite white mainlanders could experience this alternative vision. Honolulu became a vision of a modern paradise where hula and skyscrapers could co-exist in what Robert Rydell terms a "coloniale moderne."[24] In this vision of the future, with all of the benefits and none of the perceived costs of modernity, Caucasians on vacation could imagine a more authentic life, they could "Come to life in Hawai'i."

By the 1930s, the hula girl and beachboy had become prototypical icons of the tourist industry's version of this utopian vision. Their bronzed (brown, not black, not white) bodies were cast as transformative talismans whose magic for whites was activated through a specific repertoire of commodified performative practices—hula and surfing. This union of racialized bodies, cultural practices, and commodification formed the heart of mainland representations of Hawai'i and would continue to do so for the next sixty years, despite the changes that took place.

Up to the Present

Profiling Visitors

Full social histories of tourism and of hula during the postwar period remain to be written, but those tasks exceed the limits of this project, whose emphasis is on the ways that embodied concepts of culture have functioned. As I have argued, the key components of cultural tourism, and its reliance on bodily display, were institutionalized by the end of the 1930s. In the most fundamental sense, this has not radically changed in the last sixty years. Yet, as the industry has developed, cultural tourism has become more elaborated, serving and attracting a much wider socioeconomic class of visitors. In this coda, I briefly sketch the expansion of Hawaiian tourism from World War II to the present and offer a consideration of today's tourist demographics. Finally, I analyze what is at stake for these tourists in their travel to Hawai'i, and how those "stakes" are linked to the embodied representations and practices I've discussed throughout part 1 of this book.

WARTIME WAIKIKI

By the early forties, patriotism overtook tourism as the war in the Pacific drew the United States into battle. Barbed wire replaced beach umbrellas, and the Royal Hawaiian Hotel was transformed from a playground for the rich to an R&R layover for soldiers. If anything, the exposure of mainland populations to hula increased during this time despite the suspension of the tourist industry. Many soldiers had already seen hula dancing in popular 1930s movies like Bing Crosby's hit, *Waikiki Wedding*, and some arrived expecting those Hollywood fantasies to come to life. "I expected to find grass huts," stated one soldier stationed in Hon-

olulu. "I expected it to be . . . a village and hula girls running around and
. . . to be primitive," confessed an Army sergeant.[1]

If soldiers were looking for "hula girls," they found them. Professional hula dancers performed at numerous USO shows, where, one
dancer reported, soldiers "whistle like demons when a group of lovely
Hawaiian girls come out swaying like palm trees in the wind. They do
not recognize its beauty and subtlety; they only see hips in movement."[2] Excited soldiers may not have been able to embrace the performers on stage, but they enacted this fantasy in countless souvenir
photos sent back home. Photo shops charged seventy-five cents for a
soldier to pose with a hula girl in front of a painted backdrop of
Waikiki.[3] This practice was so popular that Life magazine even ran a
story on it in 1942, reporting that these studios were among the most
bustling businesses in downtown Honolulu. Servicemen also collected
more risqué photos, probably sold "under the table," and saved them in
photo albums.[4] By 1944, Life could report that "interest in Hawaiian
customs and culture has tripled" since Pearl Harbor and that "un-
counted acres of grass skirts have been mailed home to girl friends by
servicemen." For those women, Life featured a "how to hula" photo
spread of a curvaceous brunette, Kay Toth (described as "an American
Girl"), interpreting an ancient hula chant. This representation reinforced the ideal of a hapa-haole look and invited wartime sweethearts to
participate in the nativizing fantasy, dancing hula in their living rooms
back home.[5]

While the popularity of hula provided more jobs for entertainers, not
all dancers were happy with the result. The highly regarded Nona
Beamer, member of one of the most prestigious families of musicians
and dancers in the islands, stated in 1948: "Just thinking about [how
hula is performed today] is enough to ruin my disposition. It's on a very
low level, comparable—I hate to say it—to the hootch. . . . And the sad-
dest thing of all about it [is that] it's what the modern public seems to
like. It's what appeals to the nightclub set."[6] Attempting to counter this
image, Beamer toured the mainland with her own troupe of musicians
and dancers, playing Carnegie Recital Hall and numerous theaters and
university campuses and performing more traditional offerings.

Part of what Beamer wanted to counter was the image of Hawai'i
propagated by Hollywood. As I've discussed earlier, there were film portrayals of Hawai'i before this time, but during the war and after there was
an upsurge of popular Hollywood musicals set in Hawai'i and the South
Pacific. During the 1940s, sixteen feature films were made in or about
Hawai'i, and during the next decade this number more than doubled to

thirty-eight. Among the most popular were the 1942 version of *Song of the Islands*, starring a vigorously hula-ing Betty Grable; an updated 1951 *Bird of Paradise*, starring Debra Paget, with choreography by highly respected *kumu hula* Iolani Luahine, and, in 1956, *The Revolt of Mamie Stover*, featuring Jane Russell in song and dance routines. Other films, like the Oscar-winning *From Here to Eternity* (1953), also featured beautiful shots of island landscapes and figured Hawai'i as a site of romance.[7]

Despite many inaccuracies in presenting island culture, all of these films served as advertising, and tourism climbed steadily following the war, increasing the market for on-site tourist performances. Good dancers were in such demand that they often performed in several spots in one night. As Leiana Long Woodside remembers: "In those days you . . . might start at the cocktail hour at the Moana Hotel, go to a nine o'clock floor show at the Royal Hawaiian, then go to the eleven o'clock show at Don the Beachcomber's. In the end we had to change in the car as we drove to each place. When you arrived at the hotel you just grabbed your things and ran from the car onto the stage just in time [for] the musical fanfare."[8]

In the 1950s, mainland debates about statehood (granted in 1959) kept Hawai'i firmly in the public eye, and the social class of tourists began to expand from the very elite to include those of the middle classes. Once promoted as a playground for the rich, the islands were now characterized in advertisements as nearby and affordable: "Tropic Isles of Romance . . . so exquisite . . . so easy to reach . . . at a cost *amazingly low*."[9] A passion for pan-Polynesiana, fed by the popularity of movies such as *South Pacific* (1958), with its generic Pacific locale, resulted in a change in tourist shows—with the addition of Tahiti and Samoan dance styles, they become more spectacular. "Tahiti Torso Twisters Take Over Waikiki" shouts the headline of a November 1955 issue of the *Waikiki Beach Press*, indicating the popularity of Tahitian's rapid-fire hip oscillations.[10] Likewise, the male Samoan fire dance becomes a "must see" novelty piece. Floor shows at the Waikiki Sands Nightclub (four times nightly, "a must for every tourist visiting in the islands"), the Club Jetty ("A Night in Tahiti"), and Don the Beachcomber's ("Tahitian Show") highlighted this new craze. Touring the mainland, performers like Ray Kinney and his Royal Hawaiian Hotel Review (featuring "Five Exotic Hula Maids, the Tahitian Dancers, Tafili the Samoan Flame Dancer) fed the Polynesian fad. Of course, during this time Hawaiian hula remained a core part of such shows, and many of the islands' most knowledgeable hula performers appeared on hotel stages, including the esteemed Iolani Luahine. But these performers and the more traditional style of dance and music that they offered had to compete for tourist attention with the more spectacular floor shows, which were gaining in popularity.[11]

In the 1960s the development of commercial jet travel suddenly made flying to Hawai'i quick and affordable, beginning the era of mass tourism. The tourist population, which had been rising steadily, now jumped dramatically. Waikiki exploded. Statistics tell the story: the number of visitors from the U.S. mainland increased one-hundred-fold from 54,000 in 1952 to 567,000 in 1965. Just three years later, the visitor tally topped one million and doubled again by 1973.

Not surprisingly, dancers were in high demand in the 1970s, and a certain look was required for commercial success. Dancers had to be "pencil slim," around 115 pounds, and roughly five feet, six inches tall to fit in the hula line. As one dancer recalled: "For a perfect show, you wanted the height, you wanted the hapa haole [look], you wanted the beauty, you wanted the size 7 girl." As another performer asserted, the actual genealogical backgrounds of the dancers mattered less than how they looked, since mainland tourists "think all Polynesians and Japanese are Hawaiian anyway." There were sharp limits to the appropriate look. Those with darker skin or more explicitly Polynesian looks found it hard to get cast, as did some dancers who looked "too haole." One dancer recalled: "Maybe their hair was a little too fuzzy, or their skin was a little too dark, or nose a little bit too wide, or their lips a little too thick. . . . That look was really important, it really was. You couldn't be blonde, or have straight black hair [too "Oriental"]. Hapa haole, that was it. Tan." There were some exceptions and some differences among the shows. For example, one Polynesian show, touting "the best dancers in Waikiki," included both Hawaiians and Caucasian blue-eyed blondes at one time, but the blondes wore dark-haired wigs for the hula numbers, thus approximating the hapa look.

After the war, hula costuming had been evolving toward what one dancer termed a "more alluring," more contemporary style: lower-cut mu'umu'us, off-the-shoulder blouses, and so on. By the 1970s, she recalled, things were more eclectic, and some shows were downright "cheese-cakey." A performance of "The Sophisticated Hula," might be followed by a soft-shoe number in a white fringed bikini, and then a jazz number in white Afro wigs. Ti-leaf skirts were often shorn way above the knee, in miniskirt style.

While Afros, bikinis, and hula mixed on the commercial stage, something quite different was happening off the stage, reasserting the primacy of Native Hawaiian music and dance. The late 1960s and early

1970s marked the beginning of what is now known as the Hawaiian Renaissance, an explosion of interest in Hawaiian music, dance, language, and cultural practices, nurtured by the rise of "ethnic pride" movements on the mainland.[12] A resurgence in male dancing began, and more training in *kahiko* (ancient-style) hula became widely available. Pageants and competitions, like the Merrie Monarch Hula Festival, the King Kamehameha Hula Competition, and the Prince Lot Hula Festival (all started in the 1970s and continuing today), heightened the non-tourist public presence of hula. So did numerous programs and workshops sponsored by state and local organizations, including the Kalihi-Palama Culture and Arts Society, which sponsored training workshops for hula teachers.

A feedback loop developed between the Waikiki shows and those at the big hula competitions. Although not all dancers or dance styles crossed from one realm to the other, and costumes often differed, other influences were noticeable. The complex staging of the Waikiki shows eventually showed up in more complicated entrances and exits for the competition dances, and the extreme precision of group dancing demanded in the competitions was reflected in the big shows.[13]

By the mid-1980s, the count of mainland visitors had doubled again from two million to four million per year, reaching the range current in the late 1990s.[14] These tallies tell a story of phenomenal growth over the last fifty years, mainly in the shift from an elite socioeconomic class to one that included the middle classes and eventually the working classes too. Despite these changing demographics, the importance of live performance, consolidated and commodified during the 1930s, has remained central to the industry's success.

Today, although the hapa-haole look continues to predominate in the big commercial lū'aus, some shows are also hiring more recent arrivals from the Philippines, and some advertising campaigns or postcards also now feature a more Polynesian or a more Filipino look.[15] But the basics remain the same: representations always require young (non-Caucasian) females with long wavy hair and slender, curvaceous figures, dancing hula. My reading of these somewhat different casting choices and images is not that the white U.S. mainland public is now somehow more open to a wider range of "beauty," which may look more "foreign" than the earlier hapa-haole look. Rather I think the constitution of difference, which is always both indicative and constitutive of a relationship between populations, has shifting representations at different times.[16] Despite some variety, all such representations communicate the notion of "Hawai'i" as different from the United States, and make those notions explicit through embodied signifiers. And certain characteristics remain constant throughout the century—commercial dancers must have long, dark hair (no contemporary cuts), no blonde hair, no blue eyes, no large body size, no strictly "Oriental" (Japanese) looks, and no Melanesian looks.[17] Hawai'i, as a product of the U.S. imaginary, remains not black, not white, not Asian, decontemporized, and feminized.

WHAT IS AT STAKE: DEMOGRAPHICS AND THE CULTURAL WORK OF CULTURAL TOURISM

What is at stake for all of these visitors? In chapter 1, "Let's Lū'au," I suggested that Hawai'i beckons white mainlanders because of its union of beautiful landscape, temperate weather, and "American-ness" (which guarantees a safe encounter with exotica) and because it is perceived, even today, as solely the home of welcoming natives (in the dehistoricized sense) whose cultural distinctiveness is what distinguishes Hawai'i from competing beach destinations and from the mainland. I described this difference as a set of feminized pleasures (sensuality and a nonthreatening soft primitivism key among them), represented in embodied fashion by female dancers. But why are *these* tourists so eager to buy *these* particular pleasures? What is ultimately at stake?

To answer this question, we must look more closely at some of the demographics of this population. Who are they, and what are their visits like? According to the Hawai'i Visitors Bureau, nearly half of tourists travel as couples (not as singles or family groups), staying for an average of nine to ten days. Most come to Oahu, and visit only that one island, staying in Waikiki. A majority (66.7%) are repeat visitors, indicating that they liked what they found and want more of it. Males and females are equally represented. The age range of thirty to fifty accounts for the largest proportion of tourists (50% total), with significant clusters (approximately 15%) for each of the twenty to twenty-nine, fifty to fifty-nine, and sixty or older groupings. Only 2.2% are under nineteen years.

But these statistics tell only part of the story. Three key identity categories offer clues to what is ultimately at stake for these guests: race, social class, and heterosexuality. Of these, only social class has changed since the early years of pre–World War II tourism. As I've noted, while the elite classes still come, they are joined now by members of the middle and working classes. Hotel pricing provides a rough guide to class breakdown. On Oahu, 35% of hotel units cater to the budget minded (up to $100 per night); 50% draw the middle classes (range of $101 to

$250 per night), and 14% cater to the upper classes ($251–$500 per night). Just 1% of hotel units cater to the truly wealthy, at over $500 per night.[18]

Visitors' occupations refine our profile further: 33% define their occupations as management or professional, while those in the clerical, technical/trade, labor, or military occupations account for 24%. Another 13% are retired (no previous occupations noted), and small numbers are students or self-employed.[19] But such measurements still only offer a rough indication of socioeconomic status.[20] A better indication would be level of education and a profile of what Pierre Bourdieu calls "cultural capital." The Hawai'i Visitors Bureau offers a version of that analysis in their "Lifestyle" profiles, developed from extensive survey data. All mainland visitors fall into four distinct marketing categories: "salt of the earth," "nest builders," "achievers," and "attainers."

The variables used in this analysis go far beyond income and occupation to include: which credit cards the respondent holds, level of education, age, lodgings chosen, the use of tour packages or independent travel, and whether the respondent travels alone, in a couple, or with a family. In addition, extensive "psychographic" data detail life-style traits for each group, such as whether they belong to a frequent-flyer club, sew, own a computer, garden, go fishing, work on their cars, like science, politics, or church, and ski, swim, or go jogging.

Four Group Profiles: "Salt of the Earth," "Nest Builders," "Achievers," and "Attainers"

The first group is called the "Salt of the Earth." This designation attempts to give dignity to a cluster that is clearly not the most desirable to the HVB. They spend the least per capita per day ($100) and are described as the "blue collar trade or vocational worker who has lived life with the traditional Protestant work ethic. . . . They have scrimped and saved and this first trip to Hawai'i was likely the culmination of a life-long dream. . . ."[21]

This group is often at or near retirement age, on a fixed income, and wants no surprises in their travel. They will look for bargains and come to Hawai'i on a package tour, from which they will choose their activities: "They may occasionally be spotted in Hawaii wearing black knee socks and sandals, or when in couples perhaps matching Hawaiian outfits." They come from urban environments overall, with a household income of less than $35,000 a year, and have completed high school. Unfortunately, the survey provides no breakdown on the percentage of mainland visitors who fall into this category or any of the other three clusters.

In the HVB report, categories are listed in ascending order of life-style complexity, implying a sort of peak at the end. Within this schema, the second group, who spends $126 per capita per day, is called the "Nest Builders," younger singles or newlyweds who have reached "middle income" status ($40,000–$70,000 annual household income). They often travel on group tours not for the social conformity and safety chosen by cluster one, but for economy. They come from all environments (rural, urban, suburban), may have attended college, might be honeymooning or celebrating an anniversary, and come on their first trip. In age, they range from twenty to forty-years-old, and while in Hawaii "they are likely candidates for night life activities, booze or inexpensive dinner cruises, and perhaps a lūʻau."

The third rung on the scale belongs to the "achievers," who are the biggest spenders, averaging $285 per person per day. They are often on their second or third return trip and come from suburban environments. Their household income tops $100,000, but they are not used to having a lot of money. The report characterizes them as "hedonistic, indulging themselves close to the limit of their means, and stereotypically behav[ing] like nouveau-riche." They tend to travel in couples and range in age from twenty to forty. Often employed in middle or senior management, they "crave credible acceptance and status."[22] They feel themselves growing more sophisticated, most likely have a college degree, and while in Hawaiʻi they might go whale watching, to a celebrity dinner show, to fancy restaurants, and attend a time-sharing presentation.

What this group of "nouveau riches" desires to achieve, the final group, the "Attainers," has already found. They are the group highest in cultural capital and may be professionally employed as lawyers, doctors, brokers, and so on. They often have postgraduate education and tend to live in urban areas. This is probably their third or fourth trip to Hawaii. In the forty to sixty age range, they "have reached a level of success that allows them to enjoy life on their own terms."

More experienced in their travel than the achievers, "attainers" are more difficult to please. They will spend lavishly if they wish, but only if they are sure they will get excellent value in return. Their household income may top $200,000 per year, but there is also a group of highly educated professionals with a $30,000 to $45,000 yearly income in this cluster, no doubt working in nonprofit endeavors by choice, as their high cultural capital would indicate. Although they spend less per day than the "achievers" (only $200 per person per day), they are valuable repeat visitors.

So, we can deduce from the above that the "typical" Hawaiian mainlander tourists can come from any part of the country. They range in age
from children to retirees, although those in middle age predominate.
They may be machinists, surgeons, waitresses or financial tycoons,
drive an RV or a Mercedes, spend a lot or a little, come casually or for a
once in a lifetime trip. Some come alone, some in a group, with family or
friends, but most arrive in couples. They may be looking for luxury or
bargains, adventure or predictable difference from home, quiet or excitement. Most striking of all is the appeal of Hawai'i to such a wide
range of the population, and the islands' ability to provide what might
be seen as mutually exclusive attractions, such as peacefulness and
activity, luxury or bargains.

For all four groups, the image of the safe, beautiful, natural paradise
dominates; "scenery," "beaches," "weather," and "cleanliness" receive
some of the highest marks in the survey's "ratings of visit components."
The sense of place is one that all visitors consume, as opposed to the
more particularized activities or services, like nightclubs, restaurants,
fishing, or sightseeing tours. This particularity of place, I have argued,
is marketed through the promotion of Hawaiian culture, and all of the
positive signifiers attached to it. This is essential whether or not particular culturally marked activities, like a lūʻau, are purchased by the consumer. Hawaiian-ness is dispersed throughout the vacation experience
in Hawaii, as I noted in chapter 1, and is denoted through architecture,
music, staff uniforms, drinks, and so on. To fully understand the allure
of Hawaiian-ness, we must know more than the HVB report can tell us.
We must turn to a key demographic component that is surprisingly un-
reported: race.

Race, Nation, Sexuality

The one thing that all four clusters of tourists have in common is their
"whiteness." Statistics on tourists from the United States are not broken
down by race, but my observations indicate that they are overwhelmingly white. Without more detailed information, including self-reporting about racial identification, it is difficult to give a more detailed
profile of the group, but the following are some speculations.

African Americans appear to be underrepresented among Waikiki
tourists, as are those with Spanish surnames, especially relative to their
populations in the West Coast areas, which provide a high percentage of
visitors. There are also few Japanese Americans. There might be many
reasons for such a profile. African Americans may be aware of the
antiblack attitudes that surface among some members of the local pop-

ulations.[23] Many Japanese Americans traveling to Hawai'i may have relatives in the islands. If so, they might be staying with family and less involved in tourist activities in Waikiki. And although I have seen one tourist guide written in Spanish available among the free guides on every street corner, it is clearly addressed to Spanish speakers from outside the United States.

My speculation about the relative absence of U.S. minority populations in the mix of tourists is not simply that minority populations correlate overall with lower per-capita income and thus less disposable income for vacations. (In fact, that is not the case with the Asian-American population and certainly not with all segments of minority populations by any means. And I have demonstrated that people from all economic groups participate.) Rather, I suspect that the particular allure of the islands lies in its imaginary as a Polynesian paradise, an imaginary which is most resonant for Euro-Americans, arising as it has out of a history of European and Euro-American explorers and missionary encounters.

In addition, I propose that the not–African American, not-Hispanic, not–American Indian, "Polynesian" figure is one of attractive exoticism for many Caucasian visitors precisely because it represents a difference perceived to be free of the domestic tensions and fears that diversity can raise for some whites. On the mainland, discourses of diversity and multiculturalism (defined in racial terms but named in cultural ones) usually refer explicitly or implicitly to African-American, Native American, Spanish surnamed–American (or Hispanic), and Asian-American populations. The first three of those groups appear, to the tourist, to be absent in Hawai'i.[24] And even if some mainlanders perceive local residents (of mixed ancestry) as "Asian American" (a category only recently and only rarely invoked by island residents), the stereotype of Asian Americans as a "model minority" means that their presence would not be regarded as threatening. Indeed, most visitors, unaware of the history of settlement and intermarriage in the islands, probably assume that most of the local population is simply Hawaiian, a supposition supported by tourist advertising.

Add to this sense of escape from domestic U.S. tensions a feeling of still being in the United States (English predominates, no passport required for U.S. citizens, U.S. currency, U.S. brand names in hotels and products, etc.), and Hawai'i provides a truly safe exoticism for white mainlanders. This experience reinforces their sense of still being the "core" of the American nation. How does this sense of nation emerge?

With every tourist show and sightseeing tour, the tourist is asked,

"Where are you from?" And tourists shout out: Florida, Chicago, Washington, California, and so on. They come from all over and are aware that their fellow tourists also hail from throughout the mainland and are mostly white. In these collective moments, tourists seem to share a sense of cultural identity that is more similar to one another's than to the Hawaiian culture they are learning about by eating poi, failing miserably in the "teaching the tourist to dance" segment of a lūʻau, or donning a fake grass skirt to have a souvenir photo made.

Hawaiʻi, as a part of the United States, but clearly apart from it, serves as a foil, defining through Edenic contrast what the "real" America is all about. This is true whether the tourist is a blue-collar worker from Detroit savoring his or her first lūʻau at Germaine's, or a member of the professional/managerial class from San Francisco attending the "Authentic Luau" advertised by the exclusive Mauna Kea Beach Hotel on the "Big Island," Hawaiʻi. While one may feature styrofoam trays and long buffet lines, and the other individual service with polished koa-wood bowls, the message is ultimately the same: this is not who you are, although it is who you might like to imagine yourself being for the moment. Additional comparative research on the perceptions of minority visitors would sharpen our understanding of this process of identity construction and illuminate the complex ways in which they see themselves as participating or not in this implied paradigm of "the American."[25]

Complicit with and implicit within this notion of American whiteness is a presumption of heterosexuality.[26] Nearly 50% of all visitors travel in couples, not alone and not with children, extended family, or friends. Honeymooners abound. I have detailed throughout the preceding chapters how the Edenic vision of Hawaiʻi was built up over the years and clusters around heterosexual assumptions of sensual enjoyment and "the natural" associated, for whites, with the icon of the hula girl and brought to life vividly in the mass-market lūʻau shows. The embeddedness of these assumptions and the linkage of nation, race, and sexuality with idyllic nature sutures these components together as "pleasure," naturalizing and reinforcing a conservative vision of social relations.

To test how fully these presumptions can saturate tourism, and how dependent they are on concepts of physical foundationalism for their power, I want to look beyond the human realm. "Animal tourism" provides an arena where different pleasures seem to be offered for sale, and it forms the basis for the next chapters.

Part II **STAGING**

THE NATURAL"

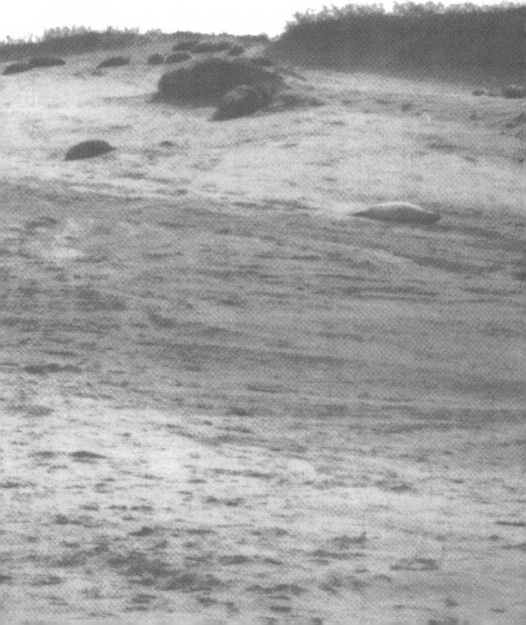

Looking at Animals

The Consumption of Radical Bodily Difference

n June 1997, debates over plans for a world-class aquarium in
Waikiki elicited a passionate letter to the editor. Pomaika'i Souza proposed an expansion of the current aquarium to include the old Natatorium, a large outdoor swimming pool built after World War I as a
peace memorial: "The pool itself could then [feature] sea lions that
dance hula, surfing penguins and everything else such a large 'stage'
could accommodate [as] the grand finale" to the aquarium visit, suggested Souza.[1]

Souza was probably joking about the sea lions doing the hula and
penguins surfing, but he was not that far off-base in his implicit linkage
of Hawaiian cultural tourism and animal tourism. It is no coincidence
that cultural tourism and nature tourism are both big industries, mas-
sively popular in their current incarnations, and share a commercial
history of increasing commodification during the last hundred years.
Both share a particular historical relation to imperialism and the
process of nation building. And both continue to constitute a contemporaneous sense of what their viewers are by showing them what they
are (supposedly) not. This is true whether that difference, always coded
as more "natural," is packaged as cultural difference (a lū'au) or as
species difference (sea lions bathing at the Natatorium).

A hundred years ago, the display of humans and of animals from "far-
off lands" symbolized the power of the displayer. For example, the 1901
Buffalo Pan-American Exposition featured not only a zoological garden
but also an Evolution of Man exhibit, both managed by the same man,
Frank Bostock. Jennie Wilson danced the hula at the exposition's
Hawaiian village, one of several exhibits devoted to the newly annexed
U.S.'s colonies, including Cuba, Puerto Rico, and the Philippines, all of

144

which were booty from the Spanish-American War. Not too far from her, Bostock's Wild Animal Show featured the "missing link" from animal to human in Darwin's evolutionary schema—a performing chimpanzee named Esau, dressed in a suit and top hat. As Robert Rydell has argued, such a presentation "reinforced the lessons of racial hierarchy that saturated the artistic dimensions of the fair and the living ethnological shows" and made implicit and explicit arguments about "progress."[2] In doing so, such exhibits also confirmed the emergent U.S. position as a colonial power and the dominant position of western and northern European–origin populations within the U.S. mainland. The non-European populations were arranged in village exhibits, often complete with associated exotic animals for decor, and were hired on the basis that they would authentically and accurately display the proper physical characteristics and cultural activities associated with their group.[3] These early expositions offered a form of cultural tourism (complete with the demonstration of culturally specific enactments) where the spectator could tour the globe in a matter of hours, just as zoos offered the chance magically to encounter animals from Africa, India, and East Asia, all in the course of an afternoon's stroll, the kinesthetic embodiment of an imperialist eye.

The history of natural history, which categorizes all that is thought to be without politics or subjectivity, underwrites the Evolution of Man exhibit as surely as it does the Wild Animal Show. It posits as "natural" that which is outside the designator's realm of the "cultural." This is the link that still unites cultural tourism and animal tourism despite a century of social change. Tourism, in the kind of industries I am discussing here, promises escape into another more natural realm for those who see themselves firmly positioned in modernity or, more recently, postmodernity. Always antidotal, it shows its audience what they are not and most often does so through the talismanic display of physical difference. In the history of Hawaiian tourism, I have discussed this as the naturalization/racialization of culture. There is a corollary to this experience in animal tourism. Industries like zoos, animal theme parks, aquariums, and ecotourism sites sell a related but distinctive experience of the natural, one we also encounter through visual perception of bodily difference, a difference as fully commodified and staged as the lūʻaus in Waikiki. The second half of this book examines this industry based on looking at animals. Unlike part 1's historical investigation of tourism in one site, Waikiki, part 2 offers a multisited comparison of many contemporary sites ranging from aquariums to animal theme parks, to zoos and ecotourism.

LOOKING AT ANIMALS

My first visit to an animal theme park was slightly embarrassing. There I was, during the open training session at the marine mammal amphitheater, when the trainer asked for a volunteer. I jumped up and waved my hand wildly. The trainer noticed, smiled, and said, "I think we'll let a child do it this time." A lucky little towhead clambered down the bleachers toward the side of the pool; I sat down, a bit chagrined at having shown so much desire for an activity that was, of course, a big treat for a child. But I was struck by how much I wanted to do this, to go to the side of the huge tank of water, and to stand there waiting for the 10,000-pound killer whale "Yaka" to swim up beside me, push herself straight up out of the water, stick out her tongue (!) and wait for me to lean over, at the trainer's command, to receive her "kiss" on my cheek— all to applause from the spectators, but that wasn't the key. I didn't have the urge to be a performer so much as a participant. So much so, in fact, that walking through the park later I stopped in one of those instant photo booths, where for three dollars you can make a postcard of yourself posed against various fake backgrounds, and had my picture taken with a killer whale. By carefully positioning my height on the stool and looking at just the right angle into the camera, following the instructions to the letter, I received a photo postcard suitable for mailing with a grinning me and a seemingly grinning orca bussing me on the cheek against a background of palm trees. I am slightly *larger* than the whale, mind you, and magically suspended in the water, but that did not matter. It was the realization, or simulation of the realization, of a dream come true

I had thought I knew what to expect at an attraction like Marine World Africa USA. I'd seen the pictures of happy spectators and leaping whales at places like Sea World in Florida or San Diego. A little awe, a little fun, and a lot of show biz is what I thought I was in for. We would pay our money for the opportunity to "consume radical bodily difference." And I still think this is so. But I wasn't prepared for becoming so involved in the process. The act of consumption is not quite the right phrase. It is too discrete, too final, too unitary. It does, however, usefully imply a physicality and merging. But my desire was not slaked by such consumption. Instead, I wanted more contact with the huge animals. Why was this such a thrill, and why was I so drawn to these huge bodies? Why are we so eager to look at animals and so willing to pay a lot of money to do so? Just what is it they are selling at places like Marine World that I was so eager to buy?

The industries based on looking at animals, what I am referring to as animal tourism, sell an experience of the natural through exposure to wild animals, whether or not the particular animals have ever lived in or even seen the mythical wilderness they are tied to in our imaginations. Many animals spend their entire lives in zoos, for instance, having never lived in "the wild." Indeed, many would probably perish if released, since they lack survival skills like hunting, for which they have no need in a zoo. Despite these contradictions, the animals both stand in for the rest of "the natural" (as that outside human cultivation, one of the word's earliest meanings) and are seen as natural themselves, subject to natural forces or laws.

Like racial others, animals are defined as other on the basis of biological difference.[4] Such recourse to biology masks the culturalization of this category. That specific and important physical differences exist is undeniable, but the historical attachment of particular values and meanings to those distinctions is very difficult to detect in everyday operations of concepts of animal and of the natural.[5]

The intensity of public discourses of the natural rises and falls at different historical junctures and exists in complex relation to notions of religion, science, and civil society, as Raymond Williams has demonstrated.[6] Often, nature and culture play a dialectical tune of critique and redemption, with one or the other in ascendance at particular historical junctures.[7] It is precisely in the realm of culture that animals are differentiated from ourselves. Concepts of group or individual subjectivity are a precursor to the idea of culture as something humans produce. Animals, as part of nature, are metonymic of the wild; they may possess social organization but are not seen as producing social organizations, cultures, or cultural products. Nor are those organizations seen as subject to historical change and development. Conscious critical agency is associated with humans, but the forces of nature, though they may yield changing results through natural selection, are perceived as lacking such critical agency even if seen as the repository of "rational" laws. In other words, even the history of natural history proceeds naturally. Humans alone are both subject to the laws of nature and able to subject the natural world to their will.

The last twenty years have seen an intensification of concern about this issue of humans' relations with and mastery over a natural world, with the rapid popularization of the concept of ecology and its designation as something that we must save. But the beginnings of this conservation paradigm are much earlier. Raymond Williams has argued that the opposite, and yet double, of conservation is exploitation.[8] With the intensification of our separation from the natural world, in the turn from an agrarian-based economy to an industrialized, urbanized one, we can trace a concomitant idealization of nature. Bits of it are cordoned off and set aside as public parks and nature preserves (private parks and preserves predate these). This is apparent especially from the nineteenth century on in Europe and the United States and can be seen in the commitment to city parks, to the emphasis on rejuvenating travel to unindustrialized parts of the country, and on the establishment of federal park systems. In these cases, nature was what was leftover, saved, or left empty. This double ideological move simultaneously commodifies nature while positing it as outside commodification. As Williams has noted, we "consume it as scenery, landscape, image, fresh air."[9]

The animal theme parks, ecotourism sites, zoos, and aquariums discussed in these chapters are contemporary extensions of this commodification. They meld commerce with the salvage paradigm of a vanishing wilderness. They are, in fact, huge industries based on the idea of nature as one of the last bastions of idealized authenticity in the postmodern era and on animals as exemplars of wildness. And within these industries, mammals are supreme. They are presented as our interlocutors, living on the border between the categories of humans and nature.

John Berger has commented on this relationship between an increasing marginalization of animals in terms of our daily lives and a simultaneous increase in their commodification.[10] While substantial changes mark the dominant relations between humans and animals over the course of the last several centuries, Berger argues that at least since the eighteenth century there has been a nostalgic regard for animals. With increasing commodification of human labor and its increasing separation from the use of animals, we can trace a concomitant rise in the commodification of interacting with animals.

Berger divides this latter commodification into two realms: as part of the family unit and as spectacle.[11] He notes, for example, that children in the nineteenth-century industrialized world were surrounded by images of animals in toys, decorations, and pictures. Animals were also brought into the family as pets, a trend which has reached gigantic proportions today. Pets and animal toys, especially stuffed animals, serve as totems of domesticated wildness, as an interface between human culture and animal nature.

Stuffed animals had their parallel in living animals put on display. The first stuffed animals became popular toys at roughly the same time that public zoos were being established in the early to mid nineteenth century and later.[12] "The zoo to which people go to meet animals, to observe them, to see them is, in fact, a monument to the impossibility of such encounters," notes Berger.[13] In addition, zoos like the London Zoo, established in 1828, or the Berlin Zoo, in 1844, brought prestige to national capitals by displaying exotic animals from faraway lands. They were, as Berger has noted, symbolic of imperial conquest of the lands themselves.

Zoos also demonstrated a civic function of public enlightenment, displaying natural history exhibits for all classes. Not unlike the popularity of stereoscope travel photographs or early film travelogues, zoos democratized access to the exotic. The "heritage" of nature was presumed to be the right of all. This blend of educational and imperial discourses continues today in distinctive applications.

Berger notes that part of our fascination with animals is a result of their similarity and difference from ourselves. This oscillation of similarity and difference operates on two related planes, the physical and the social. My contention in the next three chapters is that our visual observations of physical difference form the bedrock for concepts of social and psychological difference as they are developed in the structure of animal shows and in the educational and entertainment discourses that surround and extend these shows. Ultimately, whenever we talk of animals, we talk of ourselves, for the presentation of nature is simultaneously a buttressing or critique of certain conceptions of human cultural practice which the animals are compared with and contrasted to. The problematic of the natural is also that of the cultural, and these two poles are in constant dialectical motion. The category of mammal as that most similar physiologically to humans is the arena where the most intense preoccupation with the nature-culture divide is acted out.

Animals' identities as authentic representatives of the natural are ultimately presumed to reside in their bodies, in their physical difference from humans. Their division from us articulates the Cartesian and Christian mind-body or body-spirit split. Even when these conceptual boundaries are smudged, animals are seen as fundamentally more embodied than humans, that is, as more determined by their bodily aspects. In a Judeo-Christian philosophy that values mind/spirit over body, animals are placed lower on the hierarchy of valuable beings and therefore more subject to domination. Theatrical structures construct and present this idea of physical authenticity across a wide continuum of viewing situations which will be considered in these chapters.

With variations according to the genre of display, the animals are presented as aestheticized bodies. Often seen at rest, the stasis of such bodies heightens their objectness and allows for our leisurely contemplation of discrete bodily details. This is related to the allure of taxidermy, of the preparation of "trophies" which display "an animal frozen in a moment of supreme life . . . muscles tensed, noses aquiver," as Donna Haraway puts it.[14] These trophies elicit a fetishistic response, a substitute of desire for one object (the animal that lived) with pleasure in the fascination of another (its stuffed resurrection). But we also have a desire to see these bodies in motion. People's zoo behavior, feeding or taunting the animals, often aims at getting the animals to move, to *do* something.[15] Instead of the fetishistic pleasures of taxidermy, living animals offer a kinesthetic show of movement, of rippling muscles; they give off a smell, and invoke not just awe but the frisson of danger should they decide to come roaring our way. Animal movements and behaviors provide further evidence of a species' particular characteristics. Such behaviors are often perceived in a matrix of similarity and difference from human actions and interactions. We watch animal male-female interactions in these terms, for example.

But our perceptions of animal behavior are based on synecdochic evidence. The notion of natural behaviors is constructed in zoos through key omissions and rearticulations. Hunting is not permitted, breeding is tightly controlled, and most species only interact with others of their own kind. In addition, some behaviors, like obsessive pacing, reflect the dynamics of captivity and the physical limitations of some display modes. Selected, permitted actions, like grooming, are taken as evidence of the animals "being" themselves, that is, performing natural behaviors.

Newer zoo designs address this issue of presenting natural behavior by increasing realism in habitat design, therefore providing more of the conditions of possibility for natural, that is, wild, behaviors to be seen. There may be more room to run, for instance. But the key omissions of hunting, breeding, and species interaction remain, resulting in a false realism based on the material presence of the body but divorced from the full range of bodily practices. In contrast to the more static display mode of zoos, animal shows offer us the opportunity to see the bodies in spectacular motion and to see interactive behaviors, most often with people, but occasionally with other animals of the same or different species. While the key omissions remain, the discourse of the natural is complexly played out in terms of actions in these shows, as later discussions will detail.

The viewing structures of zoos, whether cage or habitat oriented, seem to depend on a rather straightforward sense of realism. In the simplest cages, bodies themselves are presented as "facts." The animals are there, and we stare at them. The representational mediation that structures zoo viewing becomes more and more apparent when the display context becomes complex, presenting a simulacrum of habitat of origin. Then the goal is not just to show bodies, but to show bodies in motion and in (selectively engineered) ecological context. But when animals appear in shows, as performers, a different level of more obvious mediation occurs. In these cases, as will be discussed in terms of performing sea mammals especially, the current style of display encodes action as extensions of natural behaviors. Whereas zoos present either a photographic, iconic sense of animals (displayed in cages) or a panoramic view of animals in a built environment, only performances display intense interaction between the animals and their environments, other animals and humans.

In contrast to the slow, muted pace of a PBS-type of animal documentary, which our experience of watching animals in environmental contexts resembles, these shows have an MTV sensibility. They string together fast bits of ever-changing actions, like rapid cuts of choreography in a music video. These motions and interactions are highly scripted and choreographed. The execution of specific actions on cue turns the animals into performers while denying them the subjectivity of human performers who both perceive and produce the fictive aspects of theatrical performance. The animals thus perform a fiction of themselves as wild, and they do so within the context of an obviously constructed theatrical vehicle for their display.

Spectacle at times disrupts the fictive aspect of the shows, presenting moments of sublime visual and kinesthetic pleasures for the audience. We can be overwhelmed by the scale of powerful jumps by the killer whales, for instance, while forgetting the frame of the show as a show during that moment. The spectacle of the bodies in motion stands in for wildness and uncontrollability, not subject to the constraints of culture, while simultaneously being wholly produced by it in the theatrical framework.

Animals, not being human and therefore outside the possible realm of culture, present an idealized authenticity, unchangeable because it is conceived of as a product (bodily essence) rather than a process (culture) subject to variation over time. As an ever-vanishing horizon of the authentic, animals perform their role of nature in ways that depend on their bodily display and its constant reworking as more or less similar to our own. With intense irony, these representatives of the wild exhibit through their performances their ultimate domination by and dependency on the humans who have captured or bred them. Their role is to help define the cultural through the display of what it is (supposedly) not. As Alexander Wilson has noted, while zoos and animal shows purport to be about animals, they are really "explicit, even intentional, models of relations between human cultures and the natural world."[16]

The following chapters consider various models of these relationships, analyzing a continuum of viewing experiences I call "in-situ," "out-of-situ," and "in-fake-situ." Ecotourism sites, zoos, and shows at animal theme parks will provide examples of each of these nodes on the continuum, each encoding specific notions of bodily authenticity, display, and human/animal interaction within an elastic discourse of the natural.

SEVEN

The Industries of Species Tourism

A huge and diverse industry supports our desire for looking at animals. Wildlife facilities attract more than 100 million visitors a year in the United States.[1] In 1997, a remarkable 40 percent of all adults in the United States visited a zoo, aquarium, or wild animal park.[2] There are other venues too: circuses, ecotourism, public television nature shows, even dog and cat shows.[3] Take, for example, the membership of the American Association of Zoological Parks and Aquariums, which issues accreditations to facilities meeting rigorous standards of animal care. It now has about 160 members. However, they represent merely one-tenth of all institutions, organizations, and businesses involved in the public display of animals in the United States. The U.S. Department of Agriculture issues exhibitors' permits to more than 1,700 animal collections.[4] These can range from large metropolitan aquariums, to shopping-mall petting zoos, to roadside tourist attractions like exhibits of snakes and alligators, or even bars and hotels or magic shows. The well-known Las Vegas magicians Siegfried and Roy use rare white tigers in their acts, for example, and a bar in Chicago was reputed to have two dolphins called "Scotch" and "Soda" on display.[5] Certainly the USDA numbers underrepresent the number of animal attractions in the United States.

Given the variety of venues involved, it is impossible to generate figures on the income of this industry for looking at animals. The full range of this activity on a global scale is gigantic. Consider just one segment of the industry, zoos, which are still the single most popular form of live entertainment in the world. According to the latest figures available, more than thirty-five million people visited the world's 900 zoos in 1978.[6] Undoubtedly, that figure has grown significantly in the last two

153

decades. In 1990, the San Diego Zoo alone, one of America's most popular, attracted more than 3,300,000 people. Its membership comprises 170,000 households, the largest of any such organization in the world. Even calculating at the low end of average ticket prices, the gross income for this one zoo must be at least $50 million a year.[7]

Looking at animals is not merely a contemporary fascination. The earliest records of menageries date back as far as 2,500 B.C.[8] Nor is it a socially segmented one: this is an activity that cuts across social lines of class, race, gender, age, religion, region, and nationality.[9] Why do so many people pay so much money to go to special places to engage in the activity of looking at animals? In this chapter and the ones that follow, I consider this social activity of looking at animal bodies across a range of contemporary venues. I give special attention to marine mammal bodies, which form the basis of one of the fastest growing segments of this industry and yet have received the least critical analysis.[10]

LOOKING AT ANIMALS: A PARTIAL HISTORY

The creation of opportunities for humans to look at animals has a long and wide-ranging history, of which I will only sketch a portion here. Menageries, zoos, circuses, dime museums, carnivals, and safaris are all precursors of the modern animal theme park and its cousin in conservation, ecotourism. The linkage of privilege, rarity, ownership, exotica, and looking is evident from the earliest records of zoo-style collections. Pictographic remains in archaeological digs in Siqqara, Egypt, show pet monkeys, hyenas, ibex, and gazelles dating as far back as circa 2,500 B.C. Exotic plants, birds, and mammals from Syria were kept by Thutmose III in Karnak during the fifteenth century B.C. Similar examples can be drawn from ancient Chinese, Greek, and Roman history. One of the largest of these early collections was assembled by Ptolemy I in Alexandria during his rule of Egypt. His successor, Ptolemy II, enlarged the zoo, sending collecting expeditions into Ethiopia and bringing the first chimpanzees into captivity. The scale of these endeavors is demonstrated in a feast celebrating Dionysus circa 285 B.C., which featured a parade of captive beasts. This giant procession included 96 elephants drawing chariots, 2,400 hounds, and lions, leopards, camels, cheetahs, huge snakes carried by groups of slaves, a giraffe, a rhinoceros, and 150 men carrying trees to which birds and other wild animals were chained.[11]

Two things are striking about this image. One is the similarity to today's big-draw animals at zoos—lions, elephants, camels, giraffes. The other is the chaining of the birds to trees, a crude sort of habitat display. The parading itself reverses one aspect of the visual economy of zoos, where animals remain relatively confined and the people move, but it provides a similar experience for the spectator of a changing sequence of exotic variety representing geographical range. Much like a modern-day arms parade, such a display signaled the wealth and power of the sponsor and his geographical reach.

To own "the other" and to subject it to a particular theatrical aesthetic enact a politics of vision based on differential hierarchies of power. This underlying structure still forms the basis of zoos and animal shows, but its negotiation, meaning, and particularities of enactment are always subject to change and contestation. For instance, the current paradigm for zoos is as animal conservation organizations involved in complex and globally expansive breeding and tracking programs for endangered species.[12] Related to this mission is public education about animals and animal habitat, which underwrites the necessity for public display. The San Diego Zoo puts it this way: "If even a fraction of [these projected] environmental catastrophes happens, wildlife in its natural setting is doomed. In all likelihood, endangered plants and animals will find sanctuary only in the protected confines of zoological parks and preserves. Thus, those institutions which began as the playthings of royalty have become sanctuaries for the world's wild animals. Zoos are responding to this moral imperative. . . . A successful conservation effort requires public support. That will come only with education. Conservation education can best take place as the public's interest is sparked. What better way to fan that flame than with the wholesome, family-oriented entertainment offered by zoos?"[13]

A remarkably packed paragraph, this statement from the glossy zoo souvenir book casts zoos as saviors, enacting a moral imperative to rescue doomed animals. A careful reading teases out the links between money and politics. Conservation requires "public support" (i.e., money and votes), which in turn requires "public education" (the information which will presumably persuade people to give their support), which in turn requires sparking the public's interest (so they will pay attention to this information) through "wholesome [i.e., natural, and what could be more natural than animals?] family-oriented entertainment." Entertainment becomes the means to a morally justified end—salvation—not merely a (potentially unwholesome, indulgent) pleasure in itself. Still, not everyone accepts this justification. The meaning of zoos is actively contested today. Vocal critics, often aligned with the animal liberation movement, charge that the emphasis should be on saving habitat, not on animal display, which they characterize as imprisonment, not entertainment.

The history of live animal display for human entertainment yields some very dark episodes, nearly unimaginable in their scale of mistreatment and in their production of sadistic pleasures. From roughly the third century B.C. to the sixth century A.D., "blood-sport" spectacles, featuring animals or animals and humans locked in combat, were popular in Europe. In a perverse early habitat re-creation, Nero flooded an arena so that gladiators in boats could spear seals while the crowd looked on. Writing in 1869, the historian W. E. H. Lecky described some of the massacres that took place during the Roman Empire: "In a single day, at the dedication of the coliseum by Titus, five thousand animals perished. Under Trajan, the games continued for one hundred and twenty-three successive days. Lions, tigers, elephants, rhinoceroses, hippopotami, giraffes, bulls, stags, even crocodiles and serpents were employed to give novelty to the spectacle."[14] In these spectacles, animals (like captive humans in other coliseum "games") were pitted against one another, fighting to the death, or they were tortured and killed by humans.

In such spectacles, the exoticism of the animal was important, as were its size, strength, and wildness. Nature was here subdued by men in an eroticized display of phallic power. Remnants of this coercion remain in attenuated form in lion and tiger shows in circuses and in bullfights. By extension, since most of these species came from outside Europe, the emperor simultaneously demonstrated his superiority over the regions whence they came. Since many of the gladiators were slaves, their bodiliness was matched against that of the animals, a category to which they were closely aligned. Animals and slaves were, in this context, both dispensable. It was the display of their physical capacity and prowess and its erotic, sadistic subtext that were valued.

One particularly gruesome "entertainment" took place in roughly 55 B.C. Pompey sponsored a game's finale in which "gladiators massacred twenty-one elephants that Pompey had acquired from Egypt only after swearing that the giant pachyderms would not be injured. The gladiators killed the elephants slowly, spearing them with javelins, the beasts flailing their great tusks, falling to their knees, trumpeting and wailing fiercely."[15] The elephants' resistance was a key part of the spectacle, simultaneously a signifier of their power and of the ultimately greater power of the gladiators who overcame them, and hence of the emperor who sponsored the spectacle. In these abhorrent performances, the animals played themselves. It was the authenticity of their natural behavior, fighting for their lives, that both signified their wildness and provided the foundation of the man-nature contest. Both the difference of their bodies from domestic animals and the display of the body's behaviors (enacting their fierce animalness) contributed to the spectacle.

Such blatant, state-sanctioned brutality toward animals died out with the Roman Empire, but royalty maintained animal collections during the Middle Ages, and, during the Renaissance, European travelers brought back both exotic animals and reports of zoos in other countries. Marco Polo visited a large zoo at the palace of Kublai Khan, which included monkeys, falcons, deer, camels, bears, and elephants, and Hernando Cortes reported on Montezuma's zoo in Mexico, which included pumas and jaguars in bronze cages, as well as giant turtles, armadillos, and huge aviaries full of quetzals, chachalacs, and condors. It was reported also that Montezuma also had human "freaks," like dwarfs and bearded women, placed in cages, where visitors could throw food at them.[16] This forerunner of the carnival sideshow indicates the disenfranchisement of the physically different and their banishment across the species line to the objectified status of the animals, indicated most dramatically by their being put in cages and "specimenized."

The sixteenth century gave rise to large private menageries, attesting to the power and wealth of their owners, as more and more animals were brought into Europe from expeditions to continents like Africa and Asia. Dresden, Prague, and Paris, among others, all built collections during this period. The emphasis on the exotic that seems to be a constant throughout the history of zoos, at least in Europe and North America, can be seen clearly at this time.[17] To this day, the big-draw animals (called "charismatic megafauna" by some in the zoo world) are the large mammals from Asia and Africa, the lions, tigers, elephants, and giraffes.[18] Indeed, it would be nearly inconceivable to think of a zoo without them.[19] The specific meanings of such importations may have changed throughout historical eras and as the zoos changed from private to public spheres, but the emphasis on conquest, and the attendant imperialism that it conveyed, remain.

Expeditions to bring animals out of Asia or sub-Saharan Africa were massive undertakings, costing a great deal in money and lives, of both men and animals. Large animals would be marched out of the jungle or savanna, hobbled. A crowd of water bearers and of domestic livestock, to be used for milk and meat on the journey, accompanied the pitiful parade. Untold animals died in this way.[20] These were trophy animals for the zoos, just as surely as a lion's skin and elephant tusks were trophies for Europeans on safari to Africa.[21] This lingering smell of colonialism mixes with the animal odors in safari parks in Africa and the United States today, even though the guns have been exchanged for cameras.

Little changed in the structure of zoos until the nineteenth and twentieth centuries. In the 1800s, European private collections began to be opened to the public, and publicly funded zoological gardens became very popular. The London Zoo, founded in 1826 by the Zoological Society of London, typifies this shift from private to public access. Although originally restricted to use by the upper-class members of the society, by 1846 anyone with the price of admission could enter. While some of the upper classes may have expressed annoyance that the new class of visitor exhibited "vulgar" behaviors like picnicking on the grass, others applauded their attendance, citing the zoo as an uplifting alternative to the public house.[22]

Before the establishment of public zoos, the wider public encountered exotic animals grouped together in traveling menageries or exhibited singly, like the llama from Peru put on display in Haymarket in 1805. Permanent commercial establishments also existed. Before the establishment of the London Zoo, for example, the major zoological attraction in that city was the Exeter Change Menagerie. Two rooms in a commercial district in central London were packed with animals in tiny cages stacked on top of one another. By hiking up the stairs to the second floor, visitors could see tigers, monkeys, sloths, a lion, leopard, panther, and a camel. Such attractions were not limited to the big cities. Traveling exhibits toured throughout the country, bringing panthers, ostriches, lions, and kangaroos to smaller towns like Norwich and Exeter, reaching patrons of all classes.[23]

Like the earlier private menageries of European royalty, these haphazard entertainments also encoded the power of imperialism in their displays of specific colonial booty, but the new movement toward zoos as public institutions made their civic purpose more explicit and more expansive. The Royal Zoological Society of Ireland, citing the recent success of opening its facilities to the working classes for a one-penny admission, boasted an attendance record of 100,000 in 1841, "confirming . . . the people in their improved habits" of respectability.[24] As Harriet Ritvo has suggested, such civic entertainments not only confirmed the status of Britain as an imperial power (the center to which animals from its colonies flowed), but also evidenced the triumph of humans (specifically Europeans) over nature.[25]

In the United States, the situation was similar. Small commercial traveling menageries moved from town to town, displaying individual specimens of various animals in rows of cages. But in the latter half of the nineteenth century, as part of changing social class formations, there was a growing emphasis on experiencing nature as an antidote to expanding, industrializing cities, and on public education, and several important zoos were established in major cities in the United States. For example, in 1859 civic leaders in Philadelphia, then the country's largest city and home to the first U.S. botanical garden as well as Peale's Museum of Natural History, created the Zoological Society of Philadelphia. Over the next fifteen years land was purchased, buildings erected, animals secured, and a professional staff was hired. The nation's capital followed suit, but not until 1891, when a zoological garden was opened as part of the Smithsonian Institution, with the express purpose of advancing "science and the instruction and recreation of the people."[26] In 1899, the Bronx Zoo was established, and by the early 1900s there were twenty-three professionally managed zoological gardens in U.S. cities.

The establishment of zoos was part of a larger movement to reform public spaces, to instil homogenous notions of citizenship, and to educate and "civilize" lower, often immigrant working classes. Also during this period we see the establishment of public libraries, parks, and museums. Theodore Roosevelt pushed for a conservation program in the United States, and most American cities responded to the "city beautiful" movement by bringing culture to the urban centers in the forms of grand civic buildings, ceremonial boulevards, and green areas. The natural was an integral part of this cultural movement, whether in the form of far-off nature preserves like Yosemite National Park in California or in urban zoos.

Nature, characterized, as Donna Haraway has noted, as a source of both health and purity, provided a model of social relations and citizenship when a white upper class feared "race suicide," embraced the eugenics movement, and struggled to Americanize massive waves of immigrants from southern Europe and elsewhere. Zoos and natural history museums were part of this effort to present an instructive nature. H. F. Osborne, president of the American Museum of Natural History in New York, encapsulated this goal when he wrote in 1922 that visitors could "become more reverent, more truthful, and more interested in the simple and natural laws of their being and better citizens of the future through each visit."[27]

The San Diego Zoo was established at just about this time. It began with a small collection of animals that had been housed in circus-like cages during the 1915–16 Panama-California International Exposition, held at Balboa Park, the site of today's zoo. Recalling the initial inspiration, founder physician Harry Wegeforth said: "On September 16,

1916, as I was returning to my office . . . I drove down Sixth Avenue and heard the roaring of the lions in the cages at the Exposition. . . . I turned to my brother, Paul, who was riding with me, and half jokingly, half wistfully, said, 'Wouldn't it be splendid if San Diego had a zoo! You know . . . I think I'll start one.'" Appealing to notions of civic pride, he raised money from San Diego's wealthy citizens, such as major supporter Ellen Browning Scripps, to establish a permanent exhibition.[28]

The birth of this zoo shows the confluence of several factors at the time. The international exoticism captured by the exposition, the sense that a well-developed city *should* have a zoo as part of its civic institutions to educate the public, and the active involvement of the upper-class industrial leaders in shaping such a civic culture for the lower classes, are all evident in Wegeforth's remarks. The enduring power of this philosophy is evidenced by the continuing emphasis placed on this story in the zoo's contemporary narrative about itself.

Not coincidentally, these same civic leaders and wealthy industrialists would have been prime targets of the emerging Hawaiian tourist industry, which was by that time advertising heavily on the West Coast. The international exoticism of the zoo at the San Diego Panama-California exposition was the same as that purveyed a few hundred miles to the north, at the 1915 San Francisco Panama-Pacific Exposition, where the appearance of Hawaiian musicians was credited with igniting a nationwide fad of Hawaiian music and dance. Both expositions depended on displays of "the exotic" to articulate a new sense of nationalism at the beginning of World War I.

A History of Exhibition Styles

Zoos necessarily articulate social constructs of the relation of knowledge to vision, since they operate at the intersection of theatrical and scientific frames. They use techniques of visual display to reveal information and to construct a specific relationship between viewer and viewed, humans and animals. These exhibition practices and the relations they construct shift over time. The animals at the 1915 San Diego exposition were displayed in what Jon Luoma describes as the first of four stages, a "bars-and-shackles menagerie" style, still evident in many zoos today. Barred cages were usually arranged along both sides of a pathway, so the visitors could stroll through this living taxonomy, arranged one species per cage.[29] This orderly arrangement reflected older notions of the natural sciences as a cataloging of differences and the presentation of evidentiary specimens. (Later exhibition techniques would emphasize the functioning of the body, not just its external construction, indicating a parallel development in the nascent sciences of anthropology and ethnology.) The relationship of animals to their species, to other species, and to their environment was not part of such cage displays. The pathway arrangement encouraged people to talk, look, and stroll and focused the attention of the viewers as much on their own social interactions as on the animals.[30]

This bars-and-shackles stage had seen development during the nineteenth century, with a shift in some zoos to an emphasis on "heightening the sense of theater by setting a mood believed compatible with an animal's origins, or its perceived origins. Curiously, all the mood-setting exhibits showed the creature not in relation to other fauna or flora, but to human cultures. At Cologne, for example, the elephant was housed in a building of distinctly Moorish design, complete with tiny, minaret towers."[31]

At the Budapest Zoo in 1992 I visited just such an elephant house, still in use. Its exterior resembles a Byzantine castle, with domed ceilings and an elephant head bas-relief decorating the center arch of the entryway. Inside, the first animal one sees is a lone elephant, framed by a scalloped prosceniumlike archway fronted with thick, widely spaced bars. Golden light streams down from above, spilling in from windows in the vaulted ceiling and accentuated by additional spotlights focused on the animal. Just in front of the bars stands a lone palm tree rising twenty feet into the air and topped with a scraggly tuft of leaves. Striking lighting, arched framing, the soaring architecture, and the sole palm tree in Budapest theatricalize this display of the captive animal. In the pen, nothing but a bale of straw. For the animal, nothing to see, to do, to smell, or to hear but the stream of visitors, who are never more than fifteen feet away. As in the barred cages that preceded these barred rooms, the animals can never get very far away from us.[32] This theatricalization, this Orientalization of the elephant, provides the visitor with a context with which to view the animal and to construct the meaning of that viewing. Unlike many of the habitat exhibits of today, which attempt to re-create the habitat from which the animal comes, this exhibit represents the cultural imaginary of mid-nineteenth-century Budapest, with the elephant serving as a symbolic marker of the human other with which it supposedly shared its home terrain.

The second stage of zoo exhibition practices, commencing in the early years of the twentieth century, focused on the clinical health needs of the animals and reflected a more scientific approach to zoo keeping. This emphasis extended through the mid-1950s (and continues to be a primary concern today). It wasn't until 1956, for example, that the first lowland gorilla was born in captivity, evidence of the increased attention to the animals' physical requirements.[33]

Stage three emphasized the barless "naturalist" approach, which had been pioneered by Carl Hagenbeck in Germany in the early years of this century. Hagenbeck wrote, "I wished to exhibit them not as captives, confined to narrow spaces, and looked at between bars, but as free to wander from place to place within as large limits as possible, and with no bars to obstruct the view and serve as a reminder of captivity. . . . A certain point must be fixed in the garden from which might be seen every kind of animal moving about in apparent freedom and in an environment which bore a close resemblance to its own nature haunts."[34]

To provide this illusion of freedom-in-captivity, Hagenbeck pioneered the construction of habitats utilizing invisible barriers—moats concealed by vegetation, or water barriers disguised as ponds and integrated into the landscape. As Nigel Rothfells has noted, Hagenbeck experimented to determine the vertical and horizontal jumping abilities of animals and then used those statistics to design barriers that would work effectively for each species on display.[35] Such a technique seemed to remove the barrier between animals and humans, finally banishing the thick iron bars that bisected vision.

The San Diego Zoo was one of the first in the United States to try the Hagenbeck model. Ellen Browning Scripps donated funds for the lion grotto exhibit, one of the zoo's first barless, moated enclosures. This exhibit is still home to the lions and was very progressive for its day, when such display techniques were just being tried in Europe and were nearly unknown in the United States. An old photograph of the exhibit shows Scripps, walking stick swinging out in front of her, striding by the enclosure dug into the side of a hill and inlaid with concrete walls.[36] The frame is exactly like a proscenium stage, with the top wall tilted down at a forty-five degree angle to meet the sloping earth. Narrower at the top than at the bottom, the rim outlines a space like a truncated parallelogram. Our vision is focused inward and upward toward the cavelike recess at the back of the terraced stone interior. Even in these recesses the lions remain available to our gaze. The narrowish ledges of the terraces encourage walking or patrolling, displaying the animal to us in side view, in motion, and recalling the Edward Muybridge photographic studies of bodily motion in animals and humans during the 1880s.

In these aspects of Hagenbeck's design we see more clearly not only the idealized fiction of peaceful coexistence of humans and animals but also Hagenbeck's long experience as an animal trainer. The same entrepreneur who staged animal shows for 6,000 spectators each night in his private pavilion at the 1893 World's Columbian Exposition in Chicago designed the lion grotto.[37] His Chicago pavilion featured camels on roller skates, bears walking a tightrope, and lions driving a chariot pulled by tigers, and the grotto, while seemingly light-years away in its conception of animal display, was equally theatrical. It provided an arena where natural behaviors were forcibly presented to view and literally framed, through the design of the structure, like an act on a stage. Theatrical and scientific visual discourses are united in this exhibit, as they are in ensuing zoo-display techniques up to the present.[38]

An unobstructed view, movement, the illusion of freedom and natural habitat, and a privileged point from which all is visible—these are the key components of Hagenbeck's concept and are the ideological underpinnings of such fake in-situ approaches to animal display. Moats, ravines, Plexiglas, and invisible netting today facilitate such visual sleight of hand and allow predators and potential prey to exist visually side by side in unnatural naturalism, precisely Hagenbeck's vision of zoos as a "paradise" where "animals would live beside each other in harmony and where the fight for survival would be eliminated."[39] Humans and animals seem to exist in harmony too. As Alexander Wilson notes, "Hagenbeck's sensitivity to sightlines and cross-viewing [of different species] were key contributions: the moats, groves of trees, artificial lakes, mountains . . . not only framed these vistas but also prevented zoo-goers from concentrating their gaze on other viewers."[40] In other words, we became part of their world. In describing Hagenbeck's achievement, naturalist writer Jon Luoma says: "Suddenly, they were no longer just animals on exhibit, but animals in some relationship to their own environmental framework. It was no longer just lions and gazelles, but a vision of Africa, of creatures of the savanna inextricably linked to the land and to one another . . . the framework for the zoo of the twentieth century, and perhaps beyond."[41]

The fourth stage in zookeeping extended this notion of environment to that of habitat, surroundings which would be behaviorally satisfying to the animals. "The architects should be the animals," argues one recent working group on zoo ethics. "The goal is to create an environment that maximizes the opportunities for the animal to express its natural behavior."[42] Animals need territory to mark and defend as their own and social groups in which to live. Such habitats would fulfill "the animals' powerful behavioral and social needs" and have become "part and parcel of ethical zookeeping."[43]

This vision of ecological "systematicity" parallels the desire to see a display of living culture, enacting its authentic self. The visual aesthetic of authenticity creates this illusion, while the missing ingredients, such as the key forbidden behaviors, like hunting, and the unseen moats, are rendered insignificant through their invisibility.[44] The illusion is that we are seeing not only authentic animals but authentic performances of species-specific behavior as well. In fact, what we do see in this display of wildness is a display of total dependence on humans for food, care, protection, and survival.

Along with this contextualization of the animal in a habitat is a parallel emphasis on seeming to place people in the same habitat, the inklings of which were already apparent in Hagenbeck's early exhibits. Since the 1980s, this style of design has been known professionally in the landscape trade as "landscape immersion." "If older exhibits aimed for naturalism, contemporary exhibition technology aims for realism," notes Alexander Wilson. It "conceals the barriers between people and the animals so well that we're never sure whether the animals can approach us or not."[45]

One aspect of this type of design is the replication of habitat specific to the animal's wild environment, that is, the appropriate plants which can be used for food, and it even involves designing the service buildings in the appropriate architectural style, like thatch or adobe. Interestingly, these habitat recreations are often faked organic realisms. For example, in its African region exhibit, the North Carolina Zoo uses hearty "look-alike" plants to impersonate tropical plants that could not survive in North Carolina's climate.[46] Keys to landscape immersion are zoo-geographical fidelity, proximity to the animals (but also no private areas for them), and the lack of visual distraction for visitors, notes Wilson.[47] The use of nonglare glass, covered buildings and service objects, and even piped-in sounds add to the immersion illusion.

The Gorilla Tropics exhibit at the San Diego Zoo is an excellent example of this style of display. This two-and-one-half acre "simulation of an African Rain Forest," comes complete with thousands of botanical specimens representing foliage appropriate to African locales, like Rwanda and Gabon. Birds and small primates coexist in the exhibit, which is anchored by a 8,000 square foot enclosure, where a troop of western lowland gorillas lives. Taking part of their food from the exhibit growth, they thus exhibit more natural behaviors. But even this introduction of food gathering is staged, for the actions depend on where the foliage is planted relative to the viewing spots.

Visitors walk along landscaped tropical garden paths as if strolling in the rain forest, until they come upon the specific areas staging the gorillas. The one closest to the gorillas is a semi-enclosed area fronted by

Plexiglas, with stations for viewing on a series of steps lined up in a row. "Actual environmental sounds of the African rain forest" come from hidden speakers, to "enrich the visitor's experience, as well as to add to the animal's comfort and security." Other viewing areas "are revealed as you wind your way around the sunny mesa that makes up a large portion of Gorilla Tropics," some of which are near several cascading waterfalls. The "exhibit attempts to capture the look and feel of the African rain forest . . . and encourages animals to climb, play, build nests, or otherwise express their natural abilities."[48]

The exhibit is open to the sky, with fake rocks rising to wall the gorillas into their part of the rain forest. The rolling terrain seems to blend seamlessly with the rest of the Southern California landscape, extending our sense of immersion. Once on the paths, we are enclosed by foliage, and the exhibit seems boundless, as if we were transported to the greater African landscape, but one where the foliage is labeled by name and with the name of the benefactor whose cash contribution made it possible. These exhibition styles reflect a conception of human and nature relationship shaped by the popular ecology movement and by the growth of ecology as a science during the last thirty years. Humans are seemingly conceptually placed in (and as part of) nature, which operates as a complex system, an ecology.

However, what seems on the surface to level the hierarchy between humans and animals, placing both within a larger system, and to provide the animals with a more natural environment, has a more sinister aspect as well. As the realism quotient in display practices increases, so does the sense of voyeurism. The implication is that more realistic habitats yield more natural, that is, realistic, behaviors. We seem to be seeing the "real" natural, which is more fully exposed to our view.

Certainly the spectrum of observable and allowable behaviors has been increased, as the inclusion of some foraging on the planted foliage indicates. But the idea that increased realism automatically yields an increase in animal welfare also covers up the fact that an increase in performative behaviors provides the viewing audience with a more entertaining experience. The gorillas do more, they exhibit their bodies in action; their strength, agility, size, and mass all become more visible. They are, in a sense, unwittingly performing themselves, or demonstrating their species. The mediating effects of the visual structures frame their behavior as a performance, theatricalizing actions for us, and turning them into observable signifiers of species-specific behavior, of "gorillaness."

The direct act of looking and the force required to contain the animal for our view, which was underlined by the old bars and cages mode of display, are less obvious to us here. As we become more hidden, so do the power relationships that subtend the visual structure, for, while in both habitat and bars-and-shackles designs the animals may occasionally "return the look," we still hold the keys to the locks. The commodification of bodily difference, of the natural, and of authenticity that zoos both provide and are based on is ultimately only reinforced by the rise in realism.

THE STRUCTURE OF SPECIES TOURISM: BODIES AND VENUES

Two powerful categories of differentiation structure the animal tourism industry. One concerns the situations in which viewing takes place, and the other concerns the bodies on display. Each of these categories can be thought of as a continuum. I want to discuss three categories of venue, which I am terming "in-situ," "in-fake-situ," and "out-of-situ." These form nodes on a continuum from real or natural to fake or artificial. But these terms are not mutually exclusive or rigid. Elements of more than one may coexist at any site. The second continuum concerns animals' bodies. Here I am proposing a gradated range of similarities to and differences from human bodies. Various animals present greater or lesser possibilities for anthropomorphization and spectator identification. However, both striking similarity to and striking difference from human bodily structures can exert a fascination for spectators. And in some marine mammal shows it is precisely this combination of similarity and radical difference that gives the shows their charge and their structure of meaning.

A Theory of Gradation

Mammals are usually the biggest crowd pleasers at zoos and oceanariums. Their biological similarity to us is important. Like us, they have intercourse, give birth to babies, nurse them, have warm blood, and have skin/hair/fur analogous to ours. Most of them, like lions, tigers, bears, elephants, hippos, and giraffes, also have facial structures that look like ours, with recognizable noses, eyes on the front of rounded skulls, ears, and mouths with at least a suggestion of lips. Most of them make sounds, even if we may never have actually heard them (have you ever heard a giraffe call?). Thus, there is at least the conceptual possibility of animal "language." This humanoid face quality facilitates our identification with these animals, with what we imagine their senses to be, and with what we imagine to be their sense of perception of our shared environment. (If it is hot out, we imagine a polar bear must be really hot, because we would be sweltering in a fur coat in that heat, for example.) I don't mean to suggest that this sort of identification, at least for adults, proceeds in such a literal or conscious way as we look at these animals. But their biological structure is *comprehensible* to us in a way that other animals' are not.

Take eyestalks, for example. Now *there* is a real impediment to identification. And the hard-shelled bodies of crustaceans in general, like the thorax—abdomen divisions of insects—or the cold-bloodedness and scales of reptiles, are similarly incomprehensible from the perspective of our sensory imagination. At the phenomenological level, some animals just live in a different world than we do. Usually, these animals, like lobsters or sea slugs, do not gather a great public.

But sometimes the radical difference can become a draw in itself, especially where it can be successfully transmuted in display from "ugly" to aesthetically pleasing. The spring 1992 display of jellyfish at the Monterey Bay Aquarium is a good example. These fish aren't really fish at all, but coelenterates of remarkable variety and shape. Nearly transparent, these "jellies" (as they are called in the trade) float diaphanously through the water like geometric ghosts. Drifting tentacles three feet long wiggle to the pulsing movement of the moon jelly, with its half-dome top. Others are like delicate disks, fringed with tiny tendrils or decorated with long, streaming tails.

These improbable beings are displayed in special $500,000 tanks, and New Age music provides the atmosphere for contemplative, transcendent viewing. Sensuous, sustained, and continuous movement animates the white edges of these nearly translucent animals as they drift by or move through the water with propulsive openings and closings of their bodies. Glistening against the black background of their tanks, they look like diamonds at the jeweler's, white against a soft black velvety background and lit with the intensity of a spotlight on stage. Behind them the blackness recedes like outer space, recalling the mysteries of unknown worlds and banishing our preconceptions of these gelatinous things as prickly stings merely to be avoided while swimming. These jellies are so abstractly beautiful in shape and movement they are nearly aestheticized right out of the category of animal. They become surrealistic white shapes, odd mixtures of volume and line continually changing against an ebony background, ebbing and flowing without sharp punctuation, just like the music that "accompanies" them. Of course, the fact that these are jellyfish makes this gossamer art display all the more remarkable. That lowly jellyfish can be so aesthetically pleasing is part of our pleasure. After all, who would have imagined?

In this case, their bodily dissimilarity to ours, with no face, no bones, no blood, no skin, becomes an occasion not for disgust or distaste but rather for marveling. But while we enjoy the jellies as beautiful objects (living objects), we do not identify with them as sentient beings. This transmutation of nonidentification into aestheticization seems to be working very well in developing a public for these creatures. Aquarium spokesman Hank Armstrong reports, "Attendance is way up. The jellies are motivating people. No one was predicting anything like this. But if you enjoyed our sharks [exhibit], you will turn to mush for the jellies." The jellies exhibit has shattered attendance records.[49]

Marine mammals interestingly fall in between categories, and this is, I believe, one of the reasons for their popularity. Marine mammals are both radically different from us and reassuringly similar. Living in a foreign medium, water, they are separated from us in a fundamental, though temporarily bridgeable, way. We can swim, snorkel, or scuba dive; they can surface and even survive out of the water for limited periods. But they are also very similar to us, being mammals, raising their young, having flippers that can clap like arms (sea lions) or little "hands" with claws (sea otters), and, with whales and dolphins at least, "dialects" and speech systems. There is a tension between the mammalness of whales and dolphins, and their "fishness." Living in the water, having fins if not scales, flippers and not arms, blowholes and not noses, they can remind us of fishes even though technically they are mammals. At the same time, their "faces," especially the jaw structure of whales and dolphins which can be reminiscent of perpetual grins, make them anthropomorphic candidates, as does their communicative and interactive ability.

Living Cultures: In-Situ, In-Fake-Situ, Out-of-Situ

Aquariums, oceanariums, theme parks, and ecotourism sites all offer the opportunity to see sea creatures on display. What are the relationships among these types of sites, and between them and museums, cultural performances, and other forms of entertainment?

Central to each of these modes of presentation, whether in an art museum or at Sea World, is the idea of collection and presentation or demonstration. Knowledge or entertainment is usually the stated goal. For marine mammal shows and tourist shows, the combination of education and entertainment, sometimes dubbed "edutainment," characterizes the display. Museums and aquariums may put more emphasis on the "edu" part of edutainment, but they too are pleasure-producing places, although information is perhaps rated as important as display in these venues. Pleasure may be broadly defined in this context as visual pleasure, intellectual stimulation, and possibly the pleasures of participating in activities associated with certain social classes (art museums or whale watches, for instance). These pleasures are different from those in other types of entertainment, such as going to an amusement park, where the rides provide kinesthetic pleasure, or going to a sports event, which shares many of the dimensions noted above, but with the addition of competition as the structuring relationship.

In each of these cases, animal tourism, people tourism, and museums, we go to see things we don't see everyday. They promise a distinctive, out-of-the-ordinary experience. Dogs and cats are not featured in zoos, for instance (although performing dogs may be part of a circus act). Similarly, ecotourism provides the opportunity to come close to animals we usually cannot see or see only at a great distance or through representations. Watching cockroaches in the kitchen or rabbits in the backyard doesn't count as ecotourism. Likewise, museums usually feature art and artifacts produced either by artists deemed exceptional or professional (as in the Museum of Modern Art) or by groups other than ourselves (Museum of Natural History, and anthropological museums in general).[50] In either case, uniqueness is offered. In each venue, specimen selection, arrangement, commentary, and physical display are of the utmost importance. Zoos, like art museums and performing animal shows, have curators who perform these tasks. In museums, most of the things on display are inanimate objects, although a live performance may complement some particular exhibit. By contrast, in all the other categories of display noted above, living creatures or humans are what are being displayed. Associated artifacts are secondary.

In all of these exhibition venues, the collection of good specimens is important. Performing whales that can't jump high, or small specimens of gigantic snakes, or ecotourist sites with sickly inhabitants are undesirable. Similarly, the museum curator seeks a good example of a Shoshone basket, while the tourist-show producer seeks good dancers or, for the nightclub shows, attractive ones. Quality and value are produced in accordance with specific standards for each field of display.

In each display genre, these elements of selection, presentation, and valuation reveal the formulation of a specific underlying problematic of the cultural (as is the case with art or anthropological museums or tourist performance) or of the natural (as in zoos, animal theme parks, ecotourism sites). Ultimately, these two poles are part of the same dialectic, and the similarities and differences in presentation represent the defining framework of these problematics as well as the oscillations, redundancies, surpluses, and "noise" that erupt in the continual production of these systems.

Subjectivity and Realism

Museums and zoos have changed their visual formats. With turn-of-the-century dime museums, for example, objects were presented in curio cabinets, as objects. It was their physical presence which made the museum a museum. The objectness completely overshadowed the context in which the object had existed before it was collected. Later, dioramas provided a visual context for objects. The objects were "real," while the context was represented. Now in aquariums, for instance, and in many zoos, context is both presented and represented.[51]

Many habitats at zoos now function as theatrical peep shows. The Gorilla Tropics exhibit at the San Diego Zoo, discussed earlier, is a good example. Re-created habitat surrounds the animal on three sides, with a fourth wall constructed of glass or acrylic for the viewing public. In these habitat displays, real organic material is employed (real grass, real water, sometimes real trees), along with manmade items like plaster trees, rocky landscapes, and caves. An animal's habitat is realistically represented or in some cases re-created, as in the two-story high Plexiglas-enclosed kelp forest at the Monterey Bay Aquarium. Wild animal parks remove the fourth wall and proscenium-scape approach. Or rather they reposition it, so that as we ride by on the monorail we are above the animals looking down, or sometimes merely separated by uncrossable moats and seemingly within their habitat.

The ultimate in contextual realism is approached through ecotourism, where all the props for the context are real, and it is the public viewing and its visual and ideological framing that turn the animals into a display. On this continuum of realism, the marks of construction, both material and conceptual, are increasingly invisible, literally removed from sight. The animals become increasingly "subjects" along this continuum, situated in relation to others of their own kind and of other species and able to act upon and respond to their environment.[52] In popular and even some scientific discourse, certain species are granted status not only as actants but also as subjects possessing a psychological interiority. Both popular anthropomorphism and scientific intelligence or communication experiments with mammals reinforce this gray area of animal subjectivity. However, their objectification never fully ceases, because our species tourism places a fundamental emphasis on their bodily difference and subjects it for pleasure to our gaze. The entire structure of animal display is predicated on the value of this gazing and the hierarchy of control that it reveals.

An example in human presentation is provided by the Polynesian Cultural Center (PCC) in Hawai'i. It offers representative bits of architecture and traditional activities, like woodcarving and cooking, enacted by contemporary representative of seven Polynesian countries, like Samoa and Fiji. However, here the presentation and representation overlap, because those hired to "be" in each village re-creation must in fact be what they represent, that is, a Samoan or a Fiji Islander. They must be authentic on the bodily level and also on the cultural level because they must be knowledgeable about the traditional songs and dances of their communities.[53] The historical nature of the re-creation is not emphasized, and what are often residual modes of cultural practice in increasingly urbanizing island communities are here presented as embodying popular living cultural practices. The PCC in Hawai'i is parallel to the Wild Animal Park in San Diego, where animals are placed in re-created habitats yet carefully separated one from the other. We ride through the park on a monorail, traversing continents in minutes, and at the PCC we make a similar journey by boat, gliding by one island representation after another. The inhabitants of both parks are in fake in-situ.

The continuum for animal viewing from in-situ to out-of-situ is based on increasing human intervention in the exhibited behavior as well as varying degrees of realism. The animals in-situ are presumably being themselves, as they would were no humans present. This as-if-ness is constitutive of ecotourism and is constantly negotiated both in the discourse of ecotourism and in the physical proximity between animals and humans. The animals totally out-of-situ, in a tiger show, for instance, are performing behaviors they would presumably never perform in the wild. The complex discourse of naturalism, that is, performed behaviors as extensions of natural behaviors, will be discussed in detail later, but it is clear that the choreographed movements through space, and their temporal and spatial coordination with that of other animals or humans in the act would never be seen in the wild. For instance, we would never see six tigers sitting up on their hind legs in perfect unison.

The in-fake-situ category, like the Gorilla Tropics exhibit, is particularly interesting. Presumably the animals are performing behaviors similar to those they perform in the wild, for example, caring for their young, establishing social hierarchies, and grooming. However, these behaviors are separated from the full complex of behaviors in which they would otherwise engage, such as breeding, fighting, and hunting for food. We come to see an attenuated performance of natural behaviors which stand in for the whole.

Structures of Vision: What We See and How We See It

I have already mentioned some of the ways in which our vision is structured in these various situations. Ecotourism takes us as close as possible into the environment inhabited by the animals. Performances totally out-of-situ, like the circus or Sea World, place us as theatrical spectators at events where the performance and viewing spaces are rigidly separated. Spaces like the Monterey Aquarium and the San Diego Wild Animal Park attempt to provide us with views "as if" we were part of the animals' environment. We may ride a monorail through the reserve, or we may view the full height of a kelp forest as if we were diving in it, with viewing stations showing us underwater views two-stories high.

The act of viewing is slightly different in each of these places. Visiting a nature preserve, we move through the space, creating a constantly moving panorama, like a diorama come to life. At the circus, our viewpoint is stationary, and the animals move in a circumscribed space, usually presenting all sides of their bodies to our vision. This is also the case in animal performances at theme parks like Sea World and at zoos. At the aquarium, we see the animals moving in their environment, and we can simultaneously position and reposition ourselves at varying angles and heights to view the animals from above, below, or head on. We actively participate in constructing the view we will have, within the limits of possibility determined by the structure of the display tanks. Here the duration of our looking is self-determined.

If something happens, that is, if there is movement rather than stasis, we are likely to look longer. Zoos have experimented with ways of getting the animals to do something, to perform a behavior, to move, so that people will be more interested. The irony is that many activities, like hunting and mating, which provide spectacles of movement and titillating drama in animal documentaries, are forbidden in the zoo. Sometimes zoos' experiments to manufacture an activity backfire. For example, Minnesota Zoo employee Jim Pichner commented on the use of devices to get animals to display behavior: "We've tried a few things here. We had a hydraulic feeding system for otters that was supposed to release a fish so that people could see the predator-prey relationship when the otters slid into the pool and caught the fish. But in practice, we didn't get squat out of it. The otters learned after a few times that the sound of a motor or a click or two at the back of the exhibit meant that a fish was about to be released. They'd swim over to the device and—wham—they'd have that fish the minute it was out."[54]

In a sense, these viewings encapsulate miniperformances, where the animals do something (or don't) and we watch. Each act of viewing has a beginning, middle, and end, at which point our attention shifts to another animal or exhibit. Animal shows, which are increasingly popular not only at animal theme parks but also at zoos, take this urge to see the animals do something even further. Temporarily trading the in-fake-situ display habitat for the out-of-situ stage, zoo shows choreograph behaviors in a way the experimental fish machine in Minnesota failed to do. Such shows reveal the strong parallels between this notion of a staged enactment of species specificity (hawks soaring, seals swimming like torpedos) and the staging of cultural (ethno)specificity, as discussed in part I.

Condensation

Another aspect shared by both people tourist shows and animal viewing structures is the emphasis on condensation and selection. We don't see all animals, even from a particular geographical region. Similarly, we don't see all extant dances from a particular region. Decisions have been made about what is worth looking at, what is distinctive, even essential, and worthy of our time and effort as well as representative of the culture or species we have come to see.

The criteria vary historically and from circumstance to circumstance, but in each case there is some consideration of what makes a good show or exhibit. Drama, variety, surprise, humor—these are some of the qualities of experience that the designers of people or animal presentations may strive for. The choreography of the show, its costuming, the musical score, the verbal narration all shape our experience of the culture on view. In a museum or aquarium, for example, the correlative decisions become architectural. How is the spectator moved through the space? What sequences of viewing are facilitated or made more difficult by the spatial formation? How are the exhibits lit, where are the viewpoints for looking constructed? What relations among spectators and between spectators and animals do such pathways and viewpoints prescribe? In animal theme parks, both the theatrical structures and the spatial structures are operative. The viewing of the performance is spatially and temporally situated as part of a larger range of park activities.

Compression occurs in both the temporal and spatial dimensions. In the Kodak Hula Show, for instance, we see renditions of both ancient (*kahiko*) and modern ('*auana*) style of hulas, and at Germaine's Luau we see dance forms from Tahiti as well as forms developed in Hawai'i. At the PCC we walk from Samoa to New Zealand. In a zoo, we can metaphorically cover the earth in our afternoon's visit, skipping from the Sumatran tiger exhibit to the penguin habitat in merely minutes. Like a fantastical armchair traveler, we skim the globe while walking a quarter of a mile, peering in at reproductions of African savannas and Amazon jungle. For example, the Minnesota Zoological Park has a one-and-a-half acre building that "claims to offer a sample three-thousand-mile walk through . . . the humid forests of Southeast Asia." Five stories high, it gives us a journey through vertical as well as overland space. We can descend from the top of the forest, where free-flying birds accompany us, down past cliffs and waterfalls to sea level, where dolphins swim in a pond.[55] These presentations of animals in-fake-situ allow us to reap some of the rewards of tourism without the cost and inconvenience of travel. It is, in effect, the experience of travel that is being simulated as much as it is the recreation of natural habitats. Class privilege is leveled in this democratizing access to the exotic.

Bodies, Actions, "Identity"

The discursive limits of each of these formats—in-situ, in-fake-situ, and out-of-situ performances, like the circus—are based on the species boundary of animal/human. In each case we are predisposed to view animal movement and animal behavior, as expressive of (a) animality and (b) particular species identification. Tigers act like tigers and, conversely, actions by tigers are tigerly. The evidence of the body determines the species division, and the actions we see are perceived of as species-identified behavior—unless, of course, the actions are perceived as reproducing human behavior.

The more explicitly anthropomorphized behaviors, like seals clapping or a chimp waving and "smiling," similarly take their meaning from the humanness of the actions and the nonhumanness of the performers. In each case, the bodily difference of the animal is the foundation through which the action gains its meaning. Whatever an animal does ultimately reaffirms our concept of it *as* an animal, given the resilience of the human-nonhuman divide. Animals may be "cute" when they exhibit behaviors coded as human, but they never stop being perceived as animals. In fact, it is precisely the gap between humans and animals that is revealed through these mimicry constructs.

What do "extensions of natural behaviors" imply in this context? By definition, we might expect an extension of natural behavior to mean an amplification of naturalism. In practice we have seen that these extensions merely choreograph behaviors which it is possible for the animal to do. For example, to see the tigers at Marine World USA play leapfrog is not to see them being more tigerly; it is to see the abstraction of tigerliness (capacity to jump) into a framework that takes its intelligibility from human actions. Humans play leapfrog. (Presumably even frogs don't leapfrog, as the term refers more to the position of the body, hands in front, legs bent and spread in the air, that recalls a frog jumping.) Similarly, coordinated acrobatic behaviors, such as ten tigers sitting up balanced on their haunches at once, are intelligible and applaudable through the human matrix of precision behaviors, like acrobatics, and the "ta-da" picture moments of held poses at climactic moments in a traditional ballet. Animals always reveal their difference from ourselves even when they are performing their similarities. No matter how elastic the animal/human, nature/culture distinction, it is continually reasserted, as the following case studies of "in/out of/and fake" situ reveal.

EIGHT

In/Out-of/In-Fake-Situ

Three Case Studies

In 1992, I moved to the West Coast for a year. Searching for a little relaxation, I started visiting local tourist sites. First, just down the road from Santa Cruz, it was Año Nuevo State Park, home of breeding elephant seals. Then it was a weekend trip up north to Vallejo to Marine World Africa USA. Other excursions took me south to the Monterey Bay Aquarium, and then eventually further south, to Sea World in San Diego. Living on the coast, I suddenly felt surrounded by marine attractions, never a big part of my life during the preceding decade in North Carolina. Just like that fateful first visit to Hawai'i, when a vacation inaugurated an intense engagement with issues surrounding cultural tourism, I found myself thinking more and more about animals. I couldn't get them out of my mind. One day I was talking about the elephant seals with a colleague, who casually remarked, "You know, animals occupy a whole floor of my mind." Somehow that one sentence validated my growing need to think carefully about these fishy bodies and the huge industries they support. I realized I had crossed the species barrier in my study of tourism.

This chapter investigates three of these sites, Año Nuevo, the Monterey Bay Aquarium, and Marine World Africa, in extended case studies. Ranging along a continuum of degrees of "realism," each of these tourist sites embraces particular conceptions of animal subjectivity, notions of authenticity, and models of human-animal relationships. Each represents a different relationship to the concept of "situ."

The higher the perceived realism quotient for each site, the more difficult it is to detect the staging of the natural. Ecotourism sites, like Año Nuevo, represent the maximum end of the realism continuum, where the intervention of humans and the culturalization of nature are most masked. Performing animal shows, like those at Marine World Africa, where the ecological context for the animals is only referred to but not represented, operate on the lower end of the realism continuum. At that end, the intervention of humans in presenting the natural is most apparent. But even at this low end of the range, complex visual and verbal rhetorical structures work to activate the concept of the natural, here encoded as authentic (wild) animals performing extensions of natural behaviors. In between on the realism continuum are sites like the Monterey Bay Aquarium. These feature elaborate constructions of representations of the real, rather like docudramas. Ultimately, in each case the repository of the natural lies in the bodily evidence of the animals on display.

IN-FAKE-SITU: THE MONTEREY BAY AQUARIUM

The entire Monterey Bay Aquarium presents itself as a transitional space, with the goal being to bring the outside in, or us into the outside, and to exchange our above-water position for the below-water world. Built in 1984 on the edge of the sea in Cannery Row, the architecture retains the blocky flavor of the old canneries but punctuates its space with huge expanses of glass, balconies, and walkways out over or overlooking the ocean bay. Telescopes on these breezeways allow a closer look at sea lions and birds perched on nearby rocks, technologically extending our eyes and bodies out over the water and seemingly extending the aquarium even further out into the bay.

Monterey Bay was made famous by John Steinbeck's novel *Cannery Row*, which portrayed the area as a tough, male site of scrabble and struggle. In its current incarnation, it is still selling fish, just as in its heyday as a canning operation, only now the fish are for looking, not for eating. Monterey now flourishes as a wealthy recreational site amid farmland tilled by migrant workers, and the lower-class maleness nostalgically associated with the site is transposed into institutional power, a cannery-style museum of the sea that retains in its architectural design the traces of its marketable past. Given the aquarium's goal of getting us to know the world below the water, the ideal would have been to sink a glass building under the bay, bringing us into that watery world but, that being impossible, the designers have settled for re-creating the bay on the edge of it, using the same salt water that flows freely by the doorstep.[1]

This is ecotourism for people without scuba equipment, a keep-your-feet dry sea adventure that features a thirty-foot-high kelp forest exhibit of tons of water, plants, and fish. The "nature immersion" zoo exhibit format described by Alexander Wilson seems a particularly apt description here, with the added twist that this aquarium of and on the bay replicates the site it sits on. It thus gains a double layer of authenticity, one from the discourse of science as real knowledge of the real, the other from its docudrama format of using itself (kelp from the bay outside the glass) to represent itself (the "same" kelp forest and fish inside the glass). Here nature is posited as both system and material. Using real material to re-create the system on the same site where it exists naturally helps hide the culturalization of nature through doubling and proximity.

Producing this "real simulacrum" requires complex ideological work, as the two poles of the nature/culture division are brought together under the oscillating sign of the real/not real. Such a feat also requires significant physical and economic resources. For example, the influx of real sea water into the exhibits requires a massive infrastructure of pumps, filters, and wave machines. More than two-thousand gallons per minute are pumped in day and night. When the aquarium is open, "sand filters improve on nature's work, turning the bay's cloudy water clear. Then, for a few hours each night, when the visitors are gone, unfiltered water is pumped in, feeding those creatures that filter food from it."[2] In this revealing statement resides the irony of such hyperreal recreations. The natural water that feeds the animals is denaturalized to present nature more clearly (literally). However, in the process life-sustaining resources are removed, making the wild organisms domestic, totally dependent on the human apparatus for their continued survival. This management of and improvement upon nature is typical of the in-fake-situ approach.

Building a building to contain a portion of the ocean isn't easy. A new wing, opened in 1996, contains even more water than in all the previous exhibits combined. The project required several years of construction and cost more than $60 million. The centerpiece of this addition is a one-million-gallon exhibit showcasing the plants and animals that live in the outer bay, where the open ocean begins. Most striking among these is the *Mola mola*, a giant ocean sunfish that can grow to a diameter of ten (!) feet and weigh a ton and a half. This vision extends the reproduction of nature from the confines of the bay to the border of the ocean. If the bay is a place where humans and nature interact, the ocean is more distinctly conceived of as purely the natural realm. By extending the conceptual reach of the aquarium, the design also extends the border of the cultural further into the natural.

The massive scale of this undertaking underlines its ideological importance. To give visitors the sense that they are really looking at the ocean, the fish are kept in a seamless tank, fronted by an acrylic wall forty-five-feet long and fifteen-feet high. "You'll see no surfaces at all. You'll just be looking out into the blue," remarks aquarium director Julie Packard.[3] This architecture makes it possible for the viewer's peripheral vision to be completely filled by the "ocean" and its inhabitants. Pressing our noses to the glass, it is almost possible to imagine we are out there under the sea. Hushed audiences wait in the dark for the arrival of the behemoth, erupting into oohs and aahs when it swims into view.

In addition, the new wing houses the world's first live deep-sea exhibit. Deep-sea creatures have rarely survived in captivity before, but this exhibit houses dozens of creatures "never before seen live in an aquarium." The emphasis on bringing the sea inside and on the creation of one-of-a-kind displays reminds us that both authenticity and uniqueness are hallmarks of tourist destinations, and bringing them together is necessary for commercial success.

The centerpiece of the Monterey Bay Aquarium is just such a unique exhibit. Rising two stories and cutting through both floors of the building is the world's only kelp-forest exhibit. Like trees underwater, thirty-foot-high kelp plants stretch upward toward the mixture of artificial and ambient sunlight at the top. Rooted on rocks at their base, the long stalks of broad flat leaves are buoyed by tiny air sacs, like balloons that keep them floating, waving rhythmically in the fake tide that is essential for their processing of nutrients. At the top, the yellowish-green plants open out into a canopy three feet thick.

We stand in semidarkness, looking into the huge lit box. Black metal strips divide the sixty-six-foot-long expanse of glass into tall rectangular panels fifteen feet high and eight feet long. The framing effect gives the feel of looking through a big bay window into the sea. Our world becomes muted as the lighted space before us pulls our gaze deep into the blue-green water. In this vertical, cutaway ecosystem, each area has its inhabitants. Crabs and crevice kelp fishes hide in the bottom in red algae, and brick red starfish cling to the rocks. Sea cucumbers scavenge on the sea bed, and turban snails slide up and down the fronds. In the upper reaches, schools of fish swim by, again and again, each one sticking with it own kind. Sheepheads, perch, and golden senoritas cruise the tank in endless motion. Rockfish, their fins motionless, drift by in a school with the eerie stillness of a submarine. Tiny anchovies, glinting gray, circle in a school in the upper-right portion of the tank. Below them, a school of slightly larger sardines makes a bigger circle. The "sunlight" comes filtered through the water and spangles the white-gray scales. The motion is endless, the schools ever circling in this mini-ocean. Their limited pathway keeps them within our vision.

Between these fish highways swim more solitary fish. There is continual movement here across every plane—close to us, in the far distance, and in the middle distance, fish are swimming. The endless, unpunctuated motion is mesmerizing. Against this horizontal movement is the vertical line of the innumerable kelp plants stretching toward the water top and swaying with the never-ending fake tide motion. Our attention constantly shifts back and forth from the large-scale sense of movement to our own sudden "discoveries" as particular inhabitants catch our eye, drifting into range or rewarding our intense scanning of the nooks and crevices.

Having seen the kelp forest from its bed, with the sardine school at eye level and the kelp stretching far over head, one can then walk up to the second floor and look down from above or stop by a window shaped like a huge porthole and have a look at the upper portion of the forest. Like a television set that is always on, the window frames a continual flow of constantly changing visuals, all of which are basically the same. Except for the twice-daily feeding times, when a scuba diver enters the tank to feed the fish, the motion rarely shifts from its hypnotic moderate speed. There is a guide nearby to answer questions (such as, "Do fish sleep?"), but the labeling is minimal. Seeing is all. As if watching a movie without a narrative, we continually shift from one scene to another, our eye drawn by motion, color, and shape into an almost abstract pleasure at this vision of the sea.

The emphasis on the visual throughout the aquarium is very important. It implies that knowledge can be obtained through vision alone. It places a premium on perceptible bodily difference and implies that in itself such difference is meaningful. We learn little about how these bodies work, how they function in their particular habitats. The visual emphasis also links the entertainment value and spectatorial habits of film-and-television watching to the museum/aquarium experience. This linkage brings together popular-culture visual pleasures with the more elite, class-identified pleasures of museum going and educational pursuits. It also increases access by implying an equality among viewers. Age, class, and literacy distinctions are not brought to the fore, although they may shape the demographics of the visitor population. The implications are that nature exists as a knowable physical realm that is not the cultural (i.e., does not require or display knowledge specific to distinctive cultural groups), and that it is visible, accessible, fun, and of importance to all.

The spectacle of scale that characterizes the kelp forest is transposed into a more delicate and even more highly aestheticized mini-exhibit nearby. I've christened it the "sardine can," after the cannery days, and it consists of an acrylic cylinder five feet across and roughly four feet high, resting on a base. Inside are a couple of hundred sardines (at least), a far cry from the record catch of 235,000 tons in 1945, but still a good number of fish.[4] The sardines fill the tank with a stream of silver, forever swimming counterclockwise around their confining quarters. All of the fish move at the same speed in the same direction, never stopping. It's quite remarkable really, like a mobile, or a moving painting, something one would put in a showy modernist house. Peering in we can see the other viewers opposite us, their faces bulging large through the curving glass. Individual fish bodies are abstracted through motion into an almost solid sheath of glinting silver. The lowly sardine, re-canned, has become an aesthetic object, lit like a jewel.

Viewing

As I mentioned earlier, the visual parallels with museums, movie houses, and theaters are quite apparent in the aquarium. The small exhibits especially are reminiscent of museum display, where important objects are laid out in acrylic containers (look but don't touch), lit for maximum drama, or at least unobscured vision, and labeled. Flowering sea anemones, animals that look like plants, are displayed in this way. And tiny sea slugs, only an inch or two long but boasting brilliant coloring, are similarly glamorized. Some animals are thus displayed as unique objects, while others, like those in the kelp forest, are presented as constituent parts of a larger whole.

The latter provide the pleasures of large-scale spectacle, whereas the former provide the intimacy of investigation. Each invites a different and opposite sense of the nature/culture problematic. The intimate exhibits position us as separate from, but powerful over, the objectified physical oddities on the other side of the glass. In contrast, the huge exhibits dwarf us in scale and position us as separate from this natural world. Were we really to enter it, rather than pretend to enter its simulacrum, it would literally overwhelm us and we could not survive. One of the pleasures of the aquarium is this attenuation of danger and its linkage to desire through a transposition of a physical encounter into a visual one.[5] The physical presence of the living animals rather than inanimate representations is essential to this dynamic.

The visual format of the kelp forest is somewhere between a movie and a live theatrical show. The huge size recalls a wide film screen. The seven-inch-thick acrylic layer between us and the animals, and the tons of water that would inundate us were it not there, give a sense of separation that is more like movie viewing than live theater. The "actors" in this case may be live, but they proceed behind the seven-inch-thick acrylic panels without responding to our presence, or so it seems. Like movie audiences, we have no effect on the unfolding of the movie on the screen or the actions taking place before our eyes. The exception to this is the touch tank, where a streamlined bat ray may elude our touch if it wishes.

Viewing practice is continually negotiated in relation to the framing provided by the architectural design of the exhibits. Rectangular viewing tanks, like picture frames, or round windows, like portholes, focus our attention into the smaller tanks. In the huge exhibits, of course, the big walls of glass reject the framing idea and instead emphasize limitless expanse, filling our eyes full of the ocean, putting us, as nearly as possible without a wetsuit, in that environment. But, whether in the large or the small exhibits, it is clear who is viewing and what is being viewed. The exhibits are lit, but we are in darkened rooms. Like peeping toms staring in through a lighted window, we observe unobserved.

As viewers, we are very active. I've mentioned the oscillation between mesmerized contemplation of movement, shape, and color, which is so striking in viewing the kelp tank, and our focusing in on specific animals. Our gaze shifts from long shot to close-up continually, and from deep focus, to middle ground, to near space. We put together a series of views, of visual investigations into the continual stream that moves in front of us. This emphasis on active viewing is due in part to the lack of narrative. We are guided visually by the architecture, lighting, and interior design of each display, but how and where we look within those frameworks is quite open. This means that each viewer's experience will be considerably different from another's. It also encourages a collage style of viewing, similar to MTV editing, a type of visual pleasure based on juxtaposition and image rather than character, story, or linear development. In addition, this spectatorial freedom opens the possibility of collaborative viewing. Nudges and "Oh, look!" exclamations in the dim lights provide evidence of this type of social exchange.

The importance placed on the framing of our viewing is underlined by the emphasis on taking pictures. The back of the aquarium visitors' guide brochure lists a series of "Kodak picture taking spots" throughout the aquarium. These are marked on the map too. The brochure even provides "suggestions for great photos." At the Touch Pool, for instance, we are advised to try "a close-up with subject, tide-pool animal and aquarium guide in frame," and are reminded to "shoot with the windows behind . . . to reduce glare." At the Great Tide Pool it seems that "several angles are possible." We should "try at least one with Monterey Bay in the background." And from the outdoor decks, there is an "excellent view . . . from the top of the pump house." Remember, "Get the ocean in your photos from the decks." Each of these instructions tells us how to enact and picture the transitional space of the aquarium. We should document our interaction with the animals in the tide pool, the bridging of the worlds of air and water, and we should also stage for our lens the aquarium as bridge or borderland, uniting the ocean and the land, the bay and the exhibits.

As with the emphasis on photography in other forms of tourism, the documenting of the difference of the "foreign" inhabitants, as well as our contact with them in their homeland (or a representation of it), is an integral part of species tourism. Free use of cameras, shops selling film, slides and postcards, and the provision of photo spots to stage the memory along with guidelines for producing good photos, all underline the importance of visual consumption, visual framing, and visual documentation of bodily difference to the tourist enterprise.

The aquarium involves several of the characteristics of animal viewing that I discussed in the preceding chapter. Geographic habitats are condensed, although less so than in many exhibits, since this aquarium concentrates on life found in the Monterey Bay region. But still we travel from the tidal channel to mudflats to marsh, dunes, and ocean. And interesting or visually striking animals tend to be featured. Only selected species are displayed in exhibits that purport to be realistic and comprehensive. Predators and prey must be kept apart for the most part, although in some cases coexistence is possible because each is so well fed. (The sharks, for instance, don't bother with the mackerel.) Even that is an odd type of faux realism—predators coexisting without predation! And in the kelp forest, several species are shown together that wouldn't normally inhabit the same territory, but would come and go as the temperatures change with the seasons. There is no "weather" in this kelp forest, though.

Still, the ecosystem approach of the exhibit, which seems to show us a whole community of plant and animal organisms in dynamic relationship, would lead us to believe that what we are seeing is real, a full slice of the ocean life just brought in a few feet from the sea and resurrected behind the glass. A sort of in-situ transplant, made all the more believable in this case because of the aquarium's particular emphasis on the Monterey Bay that we see right in front of our eyes every time we lift them from the exhibit to look out the window.

We also assume that the behavior we see is realistic. Fish do not make great trained performers! But, in fact, the tight circling of the fish schools which contributes to their visual abstraction is very different from their mile-covering behavior in the ocean. In the aquarium, it is not training that extends natural behaviors, as it does with marine mammal shows. It is, rather, the missing interactions and the rechoreographed behaviors caused by the confinement that rework the meaning of "natural" in this fishy world. Although it appears that the kelp forest is an organically developed community, it is in fact constructed of re-assembled inhabitants mimicking natural or wild behavior.

Fish are far away from our bodies on the similarity continuum and do not exhibit behavior that can be framed in terms of personality. They are not great candidates for anthropomorphism.[6] Nevertheless, there is one area where the power of anthropomorphic framing asserts itself against all odds, and that is in the ways that reproduction is presented. Although there is not a lot of discussion or many wall labels at the aquarium, the souvenir booklet goes into some detail about the reproductive behavior of kelp-forest inhabitants. The intense cultural overlay on what is presented as perhaps the most natural of all natural behaviors indicates our heavy ideological investment in sexual difference. Many sea creatures aren't obviously sexually dimorphic, and visible differences cannot assist the casual viewer in determining the biological sex of the animals. And in some invertebrates, like the moon jellies, or sea anemones, the question for all but specialists seems moot.

In many cases, intercourse doesn't take place, rather the male swims over the eggs and sprays them with sperm to fertilize them. Interestingly, some fish exhibit a most progressive approach to biology. Consider the enviable gender fluidity of the rockfish, for example. When there are no males present, one of the females will change shape, size, color and gender to become one. The piscene transsexuals would surely have gathered more of the public's attention if they were mammals and not fishes.

Feminist scholars have pointed out the gendered structure of some scientific research and reportage. Valiant sperm are always battling their way to penetrate desirable eggs in these patriarchal narratives. While we might expect to find this anthropomorphic conceptualization at the cellular level with regards to human reproduction, it is interesting to see it applied to invertebrates and even microscopic animals. It seems that the biological process of species reproduction is very difficult to frame in any way that does not resemble the traditional heterosexual human narrative. The language of such science frames our conception of the behavior we do see and of that we imagine as we ponder these seagoing bodies. Here are a few examples of descriptions taken from the aquarium's book on the kelp forest:

> Summer and winter, night and day, there's almost always some reproductive activity underway in the kelp forest. With sexual encounters or sexual arrangements, the plants and animals lay the groundwork for future generations. Some creatures keep it simple: they reproduce by dividing in half. The beautiful diatoms of the kelp forest plankton use this asexual method. . . .
>
> . . . Sex complicates life for many plants and animals; it adds the problem of finding a mate to the rest of life's challenges. To its credit, sex offers a reshuffling of genes. . . .
>
> . . . Snails, clams, and vertebrates, like mammals and fishes, rely exclusively on sexual reproduction despite the problems of getting together with the opposite sex. Many organisms take the best of both worlds, fragmenting or cloning some of the time, while maintaining sex as an option when the time is right.
>
> . . . Some kelp forest creatures are hermaphrodites, with both male and female sexual organs. A few hermaphrodites can fertilize their own eggs. Others, like the showy sea slugs—the nudibranchs—can maximize each sexual encounter. Any two nudibranchs can mate, and when they do, twice as many eggs are fertilized at one time.[7]

One of the pictures accompanying this section of the book shows a pair of white-speckled burgundy-brown sea slugs joined head to tail and mating in what looks like a whirling dervish dance. The application of this sexual discourse about finding mates, waiting till the time is right, and having profligate sex with anybody is quite remarkable for the way in which it attaches so much meaning to whether the animal produces sperm or eggs. For surely the sex act often bears little relation to the cycle of arousal that humans associate with sex. And for many animals, like the star fish, the sex act involves no physical contact at all. They merely release their eggs and sperm directly into the water.

An enormous discursive and imaginary effort is required to translate information about species reproduction into such highly sexed tales of mating. That such a discourse can successfully be attached to something as morphologically different from ourselves as a sea slug is a testament to the power that the concept of sexual dimorphism (and by extension the gender characteristics that are socially attached to such marked bodies) still exerts on scientific and popular attempts to conceptualize all forms of life. As Donna Haraway has noted, "Animal societies have been extensively employed in rationalization and naturalization of the oppressive orders of domination in the human body politic . . . and in the reduction of the body politic to sexual physiology."[8]

The culturalization of nature proceeds here in casting biological reproduction as "sexual encounters" and in continually reasserting the categories of male and female even when such divisions are basically meaningless. Such explanations of reproduction attempt to make bodies which are radically different from our own comprehensible by inscribing a sexual difference even when none is visible. This construction of the natural as sexual obversely functions as evidence of what is natural in the cultural. Ideologically, such discourses of nature naturalize the attachment of sex as a gendered activity to sex as a biological category.

The Monterey Bay Aquarium as an "in-fake-situ" site provides us with a simulacrum of the very site it sits on. It sells the opportunity to look at fish while keeping our feet dry and relies foremost on reciprocal notions of the visibility of nature and the naturalness of vision to structure its product. Its claims to being/presenting authenticity, and hence true knowledge, lay in the physical evidence of the fish on display and the invisibility of the design elements that structure their relationships to one another and to the habitats provided for them. What is invisible is most important in this museum of the visible. If the operations of these invisible structures and their implied constructs of the problematic of the natural are sometimes hard to see owing to the discourse of realism that pervades these displays, they are less visible still in the next category on the realism continuum, ecotourism.

IN-SITU: ECOTOURISM AT AÑO NUEVO

If such in-fake-situ environments as the Monterey Bay Aquarium promise a high degree of naturalism, there is still nothing so natural as nature. Ecotourism promises the ultimate immersion and the greatest guarantee of authenticity and realism. Such tourism involves going somewhere to see something natural with the intent of disturbing the destination as little as possible. It is a growing part of the tourist industry, and I had my first formal encounter with this phenomenon as I made plans to see the northern elephant seals during their breeding season at Año Nuevo State Park south of San Francisco. At Año Nuevo, I would be seeing elephant seals in their natural coastal environment, doing what they naturally do, in this case, breeding. But before I could enter into this primordial space, I had to buy a ticket.

I called the toll-free phone number for tickets and found that they were cheap, only $2, in keeping with the state park mandate of accessibility for the whole population. What was most impressive was the amount of lead time needed to get a reservation. The breeding season runs from December through March, and tickets must be purchased a minimum of ten days in advance for one of the guided nature walks, which are the only way to see the seals. Weekend walks sell out quickly, and most were booked for the rest of the season when I called in mid-January. So I signed on for a midweek tour, little suspecting that my fellow walkers would be mostly under ten years of age—a Cub Scout group out earning their badges.

The seriousness of this entire endeavor was underlined when my tickets arrived in the mail with an information sheet warning in bold print that "the walks leave on time and you forfeit your reservation if you are late." Like a show with no intermission, latecomers would not be seated. And, it seems, a certain amount of commitment is required, for this is not a passive watching experience. "The walk is 3 miles round trip and takes approximately 2.5 hours to complete. A portion of the walk is located on sand. Be prepared for possible wind, rain, and sun and wear layered clothing and appropriate shoes. Rain gear is advised. . . . The walks proceed as scheduled, rain or shine. There are no refunds for cancellations," warned the information sheet.

The physical set-up of the preserve constructs the experience of viewing the seals as a journey from our world to the world of the elephant seal, literally from culture to nature, the border between the two consisting of a one-mile walk out across scrub lands to the sand dunes area where the seals congregate. At the staging area where the dunes begin, we were met by a second ranger, having been first put into our group by another ranger at the entrance to the park. Now the walking became more difficult, and the highway and even the visitors center receded from view. As we walked, the ranger talked about the natural habitat surrounding us, pointing out plants and telling us how to behave around the seals, that is, how best to be an audience in this situation. He was both our tourist guide in the foreign territory and the protector of the seals we came to see. It seems there is danger on both sides though—we were told to stay twenty feet away from the seals at all times (a state law), not only for their protection but for our own. Riled elephant seals can cover that distance in three seconds and have been known to charge intruders when they perceive danger to their pups.

I knew there would be a great many seals, and I knew we were getting closer, but still I wasn't fully prepared when we crested the top of a sand dune and saw the first pup dozing in the sand ten feet away. Somehow the word "pup" doesn't give the right impression. Newborn baby elephant seals weigh sixty pounds, and pups grow to three-hundred pounds after nursing for a month, at which point they are called "weaners." The term is apt because not only have they been weaned, but they also look like wieners, like fat sausages, tapered at each end, sleeping. "Super weaners" can get even bigger. Stealing fat-rich milk from more than one female, some males can reach 500 pounds in just two months.

There was the pup, just lying there, being an elephant seal in its habitat, which was exactly what I came to see. Over the crest of the next dune, the landscape opened out to a wide sandy area, dotted with groups of elephant seals and scattered individuals. Everywhere I turned there were elephant seals, lying around motionless, like a living museum display. The count that day had been 490 females, 355 males, 350 pups, and 1,002 weaners. In these groups were some truly huge animals, the males, especially the so-called alpha bulls, whose size gave them top ranking in the community of seals. Such animals can reach fifteen feet in length and weigh three tons.[9] Giant masses of gray-brown flesh, these males occasionally woke, snorted, and rearranged their bulk, their big fleshy snouts wobbling at one end of their ill-defined bodies.

In this type of ecotourism, the animals are basically being spied on. We look at them, but they do not look at us, ignorant of or ignoring our presence (or so it seems). Basically, the visual structure is a theatrical one, with the animals performing themselves and the humans providing the paying audience. Each groups stays in its assigned spot for the duration of the viewing, which has a defined beginning (long entrance prologue), middle (being in the middle of the animals' space), and end (the long walk out of the reserve, passing the next group coming in for the next "showing").

But even though all the participants in this visual equation are live, and there is no screen or glass panel separating them from us, we also have the voyeuristic sense of watching a movie. The animals do not interact with us and they rarely move, so the nearly static scene unfolds on the landscape like an early Warhol film, like *Sleep,* that will run its course with or without us. But this is a movie that might change into a riot at any moment. There is always the possibility (and danger) that this stasis will break and suddenly we will be confronted not with 1,000 sleeping sausages, but with three tons of raging flesh in motion, charging toward us. This ever-present but latent potential for interaction, for movement, for a return of the gaze, is one of the ingredients in this experience of realism and is one of the defining characteristics of live theater of any kind. Ultimately, the tension between stasis and latent mobility, between the bodies as part of the inanimate landscape and as active agents in it, results in a surreal sense of the natural rather than a realistic one.

Part of this surrealism stems from the fiction of our nonintrusive intrusion. By definition, ecotourism precludes interaction, substituting for it the incompatible value of seeing the animals as if they were undisturbed. However, visitor figures reveal the fiction of this supposed human invisibility. At peak times during the breeding season up to 500 people a day pass through this reserve, making the ratio of animals to humans roughly four to one.

For instance, ours wasn't the only group out there gawking that afternoon. Right beside us was a Japanese film crew making a documentary on the elephant seals. They'd paid the state of California for forty days of shooting time, our ranger told us. In fact, they took pictures not only of the seals but also of us looking at (and taking pictures of) the seals. I took pictures of them taking pictures of us taking pictures of the seals, just for documentary purposes. A basic question becomes, Why were we all there and why were we taking pictures? What was the experience we had paid for and were documenting for future reference?

A key ingredient in this experience is the closeness to the animals, to wild animals, who are supposedly unaffected by our presence. The behavior we see is presented as authentic, since such wild nature is by definition natural, that is, not shaped by humans. These are not trained behaviors, or caged behaviors, or even behaviors in re-created habitats in which the animals are obliged to be. Unlike zoos, where the "wild" animals stand synecdochically for nature, here the equation is authentic bodies in authentic setting yields authentic behavior equals real nature.

This ecotrip has something of the magical journey about it, because this is precisely their world we are entering, not their world that we are re-creating for them to be in, or our world that they are transported into. This is a journey which takes us to see something both rare in occurrence and spectacular in scale. After all, this is not just one, happenstance run-in with a lone deer or elk in some less-populated area but rather an encounter in a habitat periodically and annually claimed by the thousands of seals that return here as part of their yearly migration pattern. So the number of animals has its importance not just in determining the scale of the spectacle but also in creating and defining the land as seal land, into which we enter in tightly controlled access. Like a cordon sanitaire, literal pathways into this foreign and exotic "culture" are created daily by the rangers moving guideposts among the animal groupings. Vision can cross this line, but not bodies.

Crossing from our world into theirs provides a fantasy of returning to our origins, of becoming part of the natural world ourselves, at least for the duration of the visit. The natural is privileged as a "truer" real, one to which we have lost access in daily life yet can regain in these special pilgrimages to sacred sites. The ritualized procedures for access and behavior at the site all emphasize this pilgrimage aspect. Religiousness comes through also in the hushed voices and sense of awe evoked by the scale of the spectacle. Nature here means not only the natural world but the transcendent forces which supposedly animate it and control fundamental processes like reproduction, growth, death, and prescribed sex roles, all of which feature prominently in the Año Nuevo educational rhetoric. The unstated belief is that these forces are acted out unimpeded in the preserve, thus creating it as a utopian site of purity, one which must be maintained because it represents something of inherent value.

Central to this construct is the assumed need to control human access while providing immersion in the space. The boundaries between the natural and the cultural must be rigidly maintained in order for ecotourism to work, yet simultaneously this boundary must be permeable; we must be able to cross it without disturbing it. The Monterey Bay Aquarium gives a simulacrum of this type of immersion by building its kelp-forest tank two stories tall, so that it's as if we were in the water with the fish, which are at our eye level, and above and below as well. At Marine World Africa, the animals are trained to come into our environment. Hawks soar over our heads, killer whales rise from the water to kiss us, and llamas stroll about by the concession stand to be petted and introduced by name by their trainers. But at Año Nuevo there is no "as if," and there is no training. What we are consuming is the minimal constructedness of the experience (which is not to say the meaning of the experience isn't heavily determined by various discourses). The structuring absence is not, as in Monterey, the unmarked choreography of animal life and the visual structures of the design but, rather, the fiction of our own bodily presence as absence, our unobtrusive intrusion.

This is related to other kinds of tourism, of course, that is, to the trips where we go to look at people and their products rather than at animals. In these cases, too, there is an ethos of not disturbing the culture that we went there to see (a Hilton or two is OK, but don't build it so it looks just like home!). There too we have the fantasy of seeing, even participating (buying a souvenir in the local market, for example), without fundamentally changing that which we came to see.

Ultimately, it is the animals that hold the final card. If they are too annoyed with the tourism, they can (a) charge the visitors (physically, not monetarily) and cause mayhem or (b) leave this site and seek out another. At least in the short run, their agency gives them the upper hand in setting some of the limits of contract between seer and seen. But in the longer run their existence depends on our interest in preserving such habitats. Their continued use of this land depends on our tourism just as surely as the economies of some small nations depend heavily on tourist dollars. The natural, defined as that which is outside human intervention, or, as Raymond Williams, said "that which is left over," is fundamentally dependent upon humans for its continued existence.

It is not inconsequential that the tourism that helps support the preserve is heightened during the breeding season. Watching animals breed, at least those that do so by means of some type of intercourse, provides one of the few socially sanctioned (under the rubric of education) occasions for viewing procreative acts. Like the privileged views of human and interspecies violence sanctioned by the state during the Roman Empire, the preserve similarly sanctions group viewing of that which is usually outside of social acceptability. Were these humans, of course, the site would be closed down immediately. But sex among animals is nature at its most natural.

The intercourse of these large blubbery mammals, with the huge, awkward male lumbering onto the female, isn't very sexy, but it is sex. There is a mystery to the sexual organs of these animals. These large sausage-shaped masses seem nearly undifferentiated, and with the eyes closed, as they mostly are, since the majority at any time is sleeping, facial expression is nil. Huge, dangling proboscises of drooping flesh characterize the male faces. Necks are nonexistent, flippers nearly useless on land, as these animals lurch forward like huge, ungainly inchworms.

Despite our inability to locate primary and secondary sexual characteristics (relative male and female size is the best clue for the casual viewer), the sex act itself, consisting of penetration of the female by the male from behind, is a familiar category of activity. Penetration, invisible though it may be, and with a male organ we cannot see or even perhaps visualize, still provides a category of anthropomorphic possibility for us to frame the activity within. This unknowable similarity is perhaps one of the attractions of the site. They do it and we do it, in ways that are at the least analogous, and that reinstate a sex differentiation as formative of elephant seal "culture." No matter how different they may be, the sexual differentiation gives us something to hold on to in calculating similarity to and difference from ourselves. It reconfirms our voyeuristic role, too, putting the element of sex into the pleasure of viewing bodily difference.[10]

On our group outing we did glimpse mating on the seaside area below us. As the ranger explained it to the Cub Scout who asked what was going on, the male bites the female on the neck to hold her down while they mate. "Can't she leave?" asked the boy. "He's too heavy for her to get away." As the talk develops, the ranger explains that the females are stuck in whatever "harem" they join. The ruling male protects them from "molestation" by other bulls. "Sort of like keeping one abusive husband rather than many abusive suitors," remarked one of the adults in our group. The females, it seems, won't leave their pups in the group and strike out alone. The subtext of wife abuse structures the exchange.

Sexual habits, I suspect, would have been discussed more frankly had our group not been dominated by young children. The sociobiology subtext is developed extensively in the writings on these animals, particularly those of leading authority Burney Le Boeuf, a University of California at Santa Cruz researcher, who has studied the seals for the last twenty-five years. His writings characterize the bulls as sexual dominators, while a more feminist response appearing in a companion book by Sheri Howe characterizes the sexual activity as rape.[11] The intensity of these debates and the inquisitiveness of the tourists reveal the truth value and utopianism still attached to the natural, and its presumed basis for the cultural.

Our stake in scrutinizing animal reproduction, called sex, is not so much to find out how they do it, but why we do it. It reveals also the bodily foundationalism underlying the category of both the natural and the cultural. By positing the natural and the cultural as distinctive spheres, sometimes opposite yet with the natural as originary, and taking sexual dimorphism as a founding principle, the naturalization of the cultural proceeds. The category of the natural functions as a rudder, bringing us back to biology as if it were a neutral, natural, originary category.

If the emphasis in the ecotourism model is equally on the animals, the site, and the placement of people in the site, something quite different happens in the staging of the natural at out-of-situ sites like Marine World Africa USA. Here the focus is very much on trainer-public-animal interaction as opposed to the denial of human presence at Año Nuevo. Activity rather than stasis characterizes the animal presentations, and little effort at all is expended in creating the illusion of habitat realism. This site represents the low end of the realism scale. The removal of real or not-so-real context means that our perception is focused even more firmly on the animal bodies and actions.

OUT-OF-SITU: MARINE WORLD AFRICA USA

Marine World Africa USA, as the polyglot name implies, combines aspects of a number of genres of public activity. Part zoo, part theme park, part circus, even part carnival, it blends these formats quite effortlessly throughout its 160 acre grounds in Vallejo, California. Created through a merger of Marine World (which opened in 1968 in Redwood City, California), and Africa USA, an exotic-animal training facility in southern California, it is now a nonprofit foundation for research and education, "devoted to furthering people's understanding, appreciation, and concern for the world's wildlife."[12] It is the first nonprofit foundation of its kind, sponsors research projects at the park and abroad, and does extensive educational outreach in the northern California area, as well as providing animals for media events.[13] (Some of the elephants, for instance, were featured in Eddie Murphy's movie *Coming to America*.) The physical layout of the park is like that of a theme park, with many separate areas, theaters, activities, and showcases. There is almost no effort to provide realistic surroundings for the animals. We see them in shows or strolling around the landscaped grounds, but extensive energy and money have not been spent on habitat re-creation. As one of the animal trainers noted, "Realism is for people; [it isn't necessary for] the animals."[14]

As the visitor's guide states, the goal of the park is to "provide education through entertainment," to bring out "a serious message of conservation," and to "enable people to come as close as possible to exotic wildlife," so that visitors will "leave with a better appreciation of the other species that inhabit our earth and an understanding of what you can do to save them."[15] The idea is that, if we get to know and like these animals, we will care enough about them to work to preserve them and their environments. In fact, this "knowing" is framed less in terms of educational facts about the animals, despite the heavy emphasis on a discourse of education, and more in terms of personality and individualism. Neither of these latter aspects features prominently in the construction of experiences at Año Nuevo or the Monterey Bay Aquarium.

What are these animals, and how are they showcased or portrayed so that we can get to know them? The overriding impression one gets from spending time at the park and from reading the program booklet (which features brief bits of information about the separate shows, individual animals, individual trainers, and more scientific information about life span, eating habits, and training procedures) is that most of these animals are beautiful, charming, intelligent, inquisitive, often playful, and dying to meet us. They come across as just the sort of "people" we would like to have as friends: trustworthy, fun, clever, responsive, and good looking.

The most popular exhibits and shows feature lions and tigers, elephants, dolphins and whales, sea lions and harbor seals, chimpanzees and orangutans, and birds. There are also butterflies, reptiles, fish, rhinoceroses, and flamingos, but these are not the big draws. Those in the first list are featured daily in a number of "shows" in specific "theaters." An exception is the elephants, which have their own "encounter" area, where they perform a variety of behaviors, including a logging demonstration and "traditional performance" (i.e., circus-type activities), give rides to adults (myself included) and children, and engage kids in a tug-of-war competition.

In addition to the animal shows, there are people shows, or rather, people-only shows, because there are human performers in all of the animals shows, too. The people shows consist of performances by the Marine World International Ski Team, who mogul and slalom their way across the parkside lake, competing with each other in "gravity-defying jumps, acrobatic flips, graceful and daring doubles routines" (as the park booklet states), and the "Incredible Acrobats of China," from Shanghai (subject of the only full-page photo in the entire booklet), who "perform incredible feats of balance, precision and strength, continuing traditions that date back over 2,000 years." Since my visit was during the off-season, neither of these people shows was on the schedule, but it is interesting to note two things. The emphasis on marine mammals in the park is carried over into the waterski team demonstration. And the emphasis on the exotic, the ancient or timeless, and on feats of physical skill, strength, coordination, cooperation, and precision, which is conveyed by the blurb for the Chinese acrobats, could easily describe any of the big animal performances as well. For instance, the killer whales also perform gravity-defying jumps, acrobatic flips, and graceful and daring doubles routines at high speeds, and the sea lions also excel in feats of balance, precision, and strength. Both animals and humans can learn and perfect similar spectacular feats (presenting a sort of artistic product or cultural artifact), owing to their "natural" physical abilities and intelligence.

Constructing the Animal-Human Relationship

The animal-human relationship is emphasized throughout the park and its literature. There are two axes to this relationship. The first is that of the trainers and their animals. The second and parallel one is of the visitors and the animals. In both cases, the subjectivity of the animals is emphasized and framed in terms similar to and usually equal to that of humans. "Trust, respect, and affection" are the key to training animals, we are told in the visitor's guide, in what sounds like a marriage counselor's holy trinity. And the romantic and familial subtext is not far off. Trainers often hand-raise the performing animals, many of whom are not wild at all, but born and bred in Vallejo, California. The park features a nursery where we can see bottle-feeding in progress. And the trainers all develop one-to-one bonds with their performers, often living with them for years at a time, as surrogate parent and friend.

When their animals are not performing, many of the trainers walk around the park with their charges, answering questions from visitors and allowing the visitors to interact with the animals, and sometimes even to touch them. The trainers all work with specific animals which they train, display, and physically care for. Throughout the program book are photos that demonstrate these friend/family relationships. The blurb on the chimpanzee, for instance, includes a family photo that could stand on any coffee table. Smiling mom and dad sit in a field of wild flowers, arms around their hirsute children. Only in this case the children are all chimpanzees, and "their two trainers have become part of the family and are recognized as its dominant members."

And in the tiger habitat area, called Tiger Island, two male trainers "swim, wrestle, and relax" with their adult Bengal tigers, which resemble huge, rambunctious house cats. The bonds between trainer and tiger are so strong that "when a female tiger on Tiger Island gives birth, the trainers are right there, assisting with the birth and helping her nurse her cubs." This is a permeable boundary zone between animal and human life that temporarily blurs the species barrier. The trainers inhabit this zone, and so can we, in fantasy, as their surrogates. This is very different from the aquarium site, which offered the "as if" experience (as if we were underwater in the kelp forest), or the Año Nuevo example, where we move into the natural world but mustn't interact with the inhabitants or risk destroying the naturalism we came to see.

In the middle of the booklet is a section called "familiar faces," which features photos and biographical sketches of three of the most important trainers. Like any other theater playbill, these sketches are complete with head shots, a listing of experience and how they got started. Mark Jardarian, for instance, "answered an advertisement for a parking lot attendant at Marine World" eighteen years before and rose through the ranks to become manager of the Wildlife Theater. Ron Whitfield, lion-and-tiger trainer and owner and perhaps the most notable human star, is featured in a portrait shot with his favorite lion, Zamba, which has been with him for twenty years. Ron and Zamba lie together in a field of gold-tipped hay, both their manes of hair burnished by the sun, both looking out at the camera, heads tilted to one side. They are a couple, out for a day in the country, completely at ease with each other, lounging with elegance in a beautiful natural setting. Debbie Marrin-Cooney, trainer of killer whales and dolphins, is pictured in the water nose-to-nose (so to speak) with one of her dolphins, sun dappling hair and water and glinting on her teeth and his as the dolphin "grins" and she tickles his chin.

The emphasis on animal subjectivity plays itself out through a highlighting of animal intelligence and of individualization. In every big show, not only are the trainers named as stars, but so are the animals. Every animal. And an emphasis is placed on the individual animal's likes, dislikes, and particular "personality." At the elephant-ride concession, for example, everyone placed atop a pachyderm is told the name of her or his particular elephant, each of which is featured with a "profile" and individual picture in the guidebook. For example, Ginny, the oldest elephant at Marine World at fifty-two years, is an 8,500 pound Asian female elephant (most names are gender coded to the sex of the animal) and likes to peel her oranges and shell her peanuts before eating them because she is so "fastidious."

Featured in the program booklet, and given a lot of time on the official souvenir video, is "Tasha, the snow leopard," and her trainer, Karen Povey. Tasha serves as a heightened locus for the human-animal bond, because she is blind. "Karen is a 'seeing-eye human' for Tasha and says she gets great satisfaction from providing an excellent quality of life for the cat." The level of dependence of these animals, some of which, like Tasha, work for years with only one trainer, is highlighted in this case. But lest we feel sorry for the snow lion, the booklet assures us that "Tasha, however, does not realize she is different." This disabled snow leopard is able to lead a full and satisfying life thanks to Marine World Africa.[16]

The amount of physical contact between the trainers and their animals is enormous, and the intimacy of it is symbolized by the shots in the program booklet (roughly 90 percent) that feature embraces, kisses, or at least touching between animal and trainer, or animal and human audience member. It is encapsulated in the walkarounds, where visitors are invited to get close to the animals led by their trainers, and it appears throughout the shows, where, through the vicarious identification with the trainers, the visitors can be within touching distance of the animals. In the case of the whales, this contact space extends through the first six rows of the amphitheater, the "wet zone," where viewers will be sprayed with water as the huge animals purposefully belly flop for spectacular splash effects.

This emphasis on cross-species bonding invokes many fantasies and works on a number of ideological levels at once. These bonds create an Edenic vision, as does the whole park, of "Man" in harmony with "Nature." And it goes beyond the goal of harmony to a suspension of the boundaries that separate species one from another and to a merging of individual animals and individual men and women into pairings of long-lasting, mutually loving, and respecting relationships. An idealized, nonconflictual relationship is shown, one which few human pairings can approach. The natural realm here acts as a blueprint for the social.

The natural may open out also to a nostalgic prototype of Eden, reminiscent of that promised in Hawaiian tourist advertisements, evoking a rural, agrarian past when life was supposedly lived with and on the land, not in contradistinction to it. The green rolling hills of the theme-park setting activate this sense. The park is set off from the city of Vallejo yet abuts suburban housing, which peeps in over the hills. Simple, enduring, meaningful social relationships are associated with the park setting in contrast to the built environment of cities or the anonymous tract housing of suburban sprawl. Purity, harmony, simplicity, trust, and morality are the underlying themes for social harmony built on a familial model and encapsulated in the animal-human dyad.

The animals, it appears, "love" just as we do, developing their primary bonds not with one another but with their trainers, on whom they are dependent for food, exercise, freedom or confinement, and physical care. The dominance in this bonding is submerged and also counterbalanced by the wildness of the animal, or ability to reject the intimacy, even to react by inflicting physical injury should it so choose, given the physical supremacy of each of the main animals, such as lions, tigers, elephants, whales, dolphins, and orangutans. The animal appears to choose to be with the trainer in so loving and trusting a way. Force, domination, restraint, and confinement, all necessary to the production of a site like Marine World Africa USA, are invisible. Resistance is hidden by training. The implication is that all animals and all humans could reflect this intimacy and trust if only they could get to know each other as well.[17]

Along with this sense of pleasurable innocence, of Eden before the Fall, there is a submerged sexual subtext. Expressions of human-animal bonding are represented through interspecies kissing, embracing, and lolling about together. The trainers and animals act out human-to-human behaviors, framed by human body language (the whale kiss, the orangutan embrace, tickling the dolphin under the chin) that indicates affection, and if done by humans, would often express sexuality as well, especially mouth-to-mouth kissing.

This submerged subtext of species miscegenation banishes bodily differences though analogous actions and postures for the humans and animals. And it temporarily moves the flexible boundary of the nature/culture divide to place humans and animals on the same side of the line. Interestingly, although wild animals like lions and elephants usually stand in for the natural in zoo-style settings, in this case the animals, shown in stadiums or walking along the paths with their keepers, seem to be so closely paired with their humans (and by extension with us), that they become decontextualized from the natural. Not free, not fully domesticated, they exist with us in a borderland of postsuburban rural bliss. The older cultural form of rural life becomes nostalgically reconfigured into uncorrupted pastoralism. In the visitors' guide, photographs illustrate and document this transcendentalism. For example, one pictures a Michelangelo-like touch between the furry fingers of a chimpanzee and a white male hand (god?), and another features a lip-to-lip kiss of orangutan and male trainer, locked in an embrace, back-lit by golden sunlight that gives them both angelic halos.

Alexander Wilson has commented on the possibilities anthropomorphism present for eroding human/animal speciesism. Anthropomorphism, "as a cultural strategy for addressing relations between humans and the natural world," can, he notes, allow "animals to be addressed as *social* beings, and nature as a *social* realm. This suggests a breach in the species-barrier between human and animal. [Many] conservation and preservation documentaries insist on that barrier and reject the possibility of interspecies intimacy. Anthropomorphism is . . . an historical and strategic intervention, a step on the way to understanding that the wall between humans and the natural world is not absolute. It is permeable, movable, shifting, able occasionally to be leaped over—as it always has been by hags and shamans."[18] Wilson is right as far as he goes, but this shifting of boundaries is not innocent.

Each shift relates to specific conceptions of the natural and the cultural and the dialectical relationship between them. And each shift invokes a different sense of the possible, the moral, the desirable, and the true. In the case of Marine World Africa USA this shift activates a whole complex of social values based on concepts of family values and transcendental pastoralism. This ideology is encoded through the medium of animals, the display of their bodies, and the imaginary of intimacy and desire that subtends the shows. Whereas nostalgia for an exotic primitive frames the selling of Hawai'i, Marine World's nostalgia is in some ways based on less difference, not more. Intense ideological work throughout the park makes the animals more like us despite their obvious dramatic physical differences. In Hawaiian tourism, the reverse is true. Bodily difference must be emphasized, and cultural difference must be distinctively portrayed not downplayed.

Souvenirs

The staging of nature that motivates the many shows at Marine World has a miniversion in the park's many opportunities to create a piece of memorabilia of your trip. One booth offers the opportunity to picture yourself perched atop a fifteen-foot-long leaping whale (made out of plaster) against a background of a huge wave. If this photo souvenir isn't enough, you can have it embossed on something useful, like a coffee mug or a tee-shirt. Or you could have yourself pictured kissing the killer whale, or next to an elephant, through the magic of photocopying.

These souvenir creations offer the chance to act out, or to "fake" a realization of, the fantasy of coming close to the animals. That is the guiding principle of Marine World's whole format, from the "have lunch with the animals," when the trainers stroll by the snack bar with their petable animals, to the elephant rides, to the flyover by the birds in the show, to the "wet zone" and kisses during the killer whale show. I was surprised that they didn't have photographers ready to take your portrait with your family atop the elephant during the elephant rides.

Unlike the opportunity to dress up in hula clothes for a souvenir photograph offered at the Kodak Hula Show or at the Polynesian Cultural Center, no such chance is presented to "become" temporarily, at the bodily level, that which you came to see. At Marine World, the closest approximation would be having one's picture taken with a (fake) animal, just as tourists clamored for the chance to pose next to the dancers from the Kodak Hula Show, to document their contact with these representatives of another culture. And the "kissing the killer" photo is another way of documenting that contact even if, in this case, I outsized the whale in the photograph. I suppose it would have been too tacky to have a booth where people could dress up like the animals and have their picture taken in midleap or midroar. Children might be able to get away with that without appearing to make fun of the animals, which would be unforgivable given the conservation orientation of Marine

World.[19] Also, our goal here is not to become temporarily nativized (or "animalized"), which is one of the pleasure subtexts of a romantic vacation in Honolulu. Rather, it is to establish physical and emotional contact with the animals. The animal-human boundary must be maintained at the physical level in order for the prescribed cross-species social and psychological intimacy to be meaningful. These souvenirs offer the opportunity simultaneously to stage and document this desire for boundary permeability and its imaginary fulfillment.

Extending the Natural: Trained Behaviors as Extensions of Natural Abilities

The success of a park such as Marine World rests on a tension between this humanizing and the maintenance of the authenticity of the natural, which must be carefully managed. The discourse on training provides an example of this management. "All training, whether of land animals or marine mammals, begins with understanding the animal's natural instincts, behavior, and intelligence," notes the guidebook. "Working with animals requires an unfailing respect for the animal and its physical abilities and instincts," and it "requires hours of dedication and patience. . . . Our trainers must give endless praise and reassurance in the form of pats on the head, belly rubs, tongue tickles (for whales and elephants), and ear scratches. It's all in a day's work for these dedicated professionals."

The animals, then, are really like completely reasonable human beings, having moods, expressing feelings, and being capable of being understood if only we work hard enough at breaking a code based on individual personality, instincts, and behavioral traits. Here it seems that it is really only the instincts that separate them from humans, although granted some species may be more intelligent (i.e., more like us) than others. What these instincts might be is never specified, but it seems an essential part of the equation which reads: natural instincts and behaviors—plus shaping by human contact and training based on understanding of instincts and behaviors—equals successful performances. This discourse presents humanized animals that remain different from us but comprehensible.

Training, a culturalization of the natural, is presented as a beneficial improvement on nature. The program stresses that "the benefits of training go far beyond entertaining and educating guests. Trained animals enjoy a greater range of physical and mental activities than their untrained counterparts." For instance, in the case of elephants, "Training also incorporates the animal's natural desire to form strong relationships and belong to a structured group, and taps into their need for intellectual challenges and ability to learn accepted ways of behavior." The proof, it seems, is in the pudding. Elephants at Marine World can live almost twice as long as nonworking (i.e., zoo or wild?) elephants.

In the section on training in the program booklet, a distinction is drawn between trained animals and "tame" ones. Wild animals are never completely tamed, it seems, because they "will always have . . . natural instincts." But these natural instincts do not make for unpredictable, savage behavior. Rather, there "is a reason, a motivation, for every behavioral trait an animal displays, whether it is affection, fear or aggression. . . . The ability to 'read' or understand the animal's thoughts or moods is only accomplished with a great deal of patience, love, and dedication. All training, whether of land animals or marine mammals, begins with understanding the animal's natural instincts, behavior, and intelligence."

A discourse of the natural is maintained through this distinction between trained and tamed animals. But the tripartite linking of "instincts, behavior, and intelligence" implies a homology among the three and softens that distinction. Instincts (nature as hardwired) almost become a kind of intelligence, the key to which the trainers must find. Thus aspects of human subjectivity such as emotional attachment, critical intelligence, and the act of choice that such implies, as opposed to behavioristic determinism, combine to present animals as radically different in body but similar in a supposed psychological interiority. Each species is framed differently in terms of more or less similarity to humans, as the format of the different shows indicates.

I will consider four different shows at Marine World Africa USA. The bird show is the most heavily narrativized, the lion and tiger show the least, and the "Magic of Animals" and whale and dolphin shows somewhere in between. How is the dialectic between natural and trained (or unnatural? or man-made?) played out in these main shows? And how is that tension related to the bodies of the animals and how they are displayed?

For the Birds

The bird show takes place in an amphitheater that holds approximately three hundred on bleachers. At the entrance up top is a sign for the Bates Motel, and on the stage is a worn wood, ramshackle building that is overcast with the spooky aura of Hitchcock's *Psycho,* with its evocations of stuffed birds and maniacal humans. The show itself, however, is not at all macabre. There are two human female characters in this show and several birds. The plot is thin and centers on a search for "Max," the missing turnbill, who does whatever he wants, it seems. Ins and outs, appearances and disappearances, give this piece a slightly comic, farcical touch, but these are not professional actors, rather actor-trainers, so the drama is not exactly first-rate. The birds, however, are wonderful, entering on cue from inside the motel set, or flying in from a nearby field when called. Bits of information about the birds' dining habits and abilities are recounted or displayed. At one point, for example, a scarlet macaw puts together a three-piece jigsaw puzzle while the theme music from the game show *Jeopardy* plays, further anthropomorphizing the animal into a feathered contestant. The *Psycho* and *Jeopardy* citations provide additional human framing for the birds, which are less like us physically than mammals and therefore somewhat harder to personalize.

The audience is physically involved in two ways. At one point, one of the actor/trainers asks for a volunteer, who holds out a dollar bill in her hand, and a bird flies out to her, picks it out of her hand without landing, and swoops back onto the stage, a feathered pickpocket.[20] This closeness of contact is later extended to the whole audience. At the end of the show, a hawk soars in close over our heads from a birdhouse on the neighboring hillside, circles the amphitheater and lands on the trainer's arm on stage. The trainers urge us to "look to ourselves" for a solution to the disappearing rain forests, and a strikingly colored parrot swoops over the audience to end the show. "A beautiful bird in flight is not easily forgotten," runs one of the closing lines. And it is true. I gasped when that bird soared right over me.

The thing about birds is that they can fly. This is one of their defining characteristics, one of their main differences from us, and the source of a great deal of human fantasy, as well as an inspiration for aviation. This is a fundamental bodily difference between them and ourselves, and in this show it is the culminating moment of the performance, the punctuation mark to a plea to save endangered species and their habitats. What is even more remarkable is that these birds, the flight of which represents freedom, escape, and existence in another stratum of the world from our own, "choose" to fly on cue, to soar out and not to leave, to return to their keepers. The contrast between freedom and docility, instinct and training, is contained in and enacted through these dramatic flyovers that are the highlight of the bird shows.

But why does the presentation of the birds require a narrative excuse, whereas the shows for other animals, like the tigers, do not?[21] Does it have to do with their size, our perception of their intelligence, the type of press they receive, perceptions of aloofness, of nonaffection (compared with domestic catlike tigers, for instance) or is it that they are physically more different from ourselves? Their wings are somewhat analogous to arms perhaps, but the eyes are often small and beady (associated with rodent eyes?), and for all the softness of their feathers and the attraction that brilliant colors bring, they cannot be easily nuzzled or petted. The beaks are problematic too—no lips—even if they can mimic human vocalizations better than other animals, and even if they have an elaborate repertoire of songs and calls with which to communicate with one another. In the popular imagination, birds do not make as intimate pets as mammals. They are heavily narrativized, made in some sense into characters in the play, in order to personalize them more fully, making the mission of Marine World, the one-to-one contact of visitors and animals, more possible.

Lions and Tigers

At the other end of the spectrum of narrativity is the lion and tiger show, held in the Jungle Theater, a three-quarter thrust stage with amphiteater-style seating around a central performance area enclosed in wire mesh. It's about forty feet wide and decorated with a backdrop mural of grazing zebras in an African savanna. The rim of the stage area is punctuated with crests painted on the concrete, featuring chimpanzees. In the back, barely visible, is a cage area with iron bars. This is noticeable only as the animals enter and exit. The wire mesh which surrounds the playing areas is strong enough to make us feel safe in the audience (in the first row I was only ten feet away from the animals), but not so massive as to be intrusive. We are aware of the separation between the animals and ourselves, but importantly they do not seem caged.

The show begins with lion owner and trainer Ron Whitfield entering the arena. He is handsome, fit, energetic, and dressed in khaki pants, a polo shirt, and sneakers. He hardly fits the slick-haired lion-tamer stereotype. He looks more as if he stepped out of a Ralph Lauren advertisement. Throughout the show he will speak, move the big cats, adjust the various apparatuses, pushing stands together or apart for different parts of the show. Sitting close, I can see how hard he is working. He makes it look easy, and the show flows well, almost covering the potential danger that exists in being the lone human in a closed space with twelve tigers and a lion. There is no whip, no chair, no gun, just a short stick that he uses as a prod, a guide, to direct the animals' movement.

The force of domination is nearly invisible here, with almost all of its trappings removed. So is the power of reward. Ron tosses the cats tidbits of steak after each action, but this motion is so swift and neat it is unnoticeable. The meat comes from a discrete pouch on his belt and is quickly restocked by his assistant whenever needed. We hardly notice the ingestion of the reward either, because our attention is always drawn to another animal just starting a new trick. Of course the bars do remain, reminder of latent danger to ourselves, and occasionally a cat will passively resist a command. But these moments are usually passed off with humor, not increased assertiveness on Ron's part.

Whereas in the circus the danger element would be foregrounded, here it is very understated. In keeping with the Marine World Africa philosophy, these animals are presented as partners in the show, each with its own name and distinctive personality. Ron explains that what we will see are "extensions" of "natural behaviors," not "tricks," a term he says implies slight of hand, hence deceit. What we will be seeing is, by implication, truthful, not deceitful or unethical.

In every case, in fact, throughout the park, the performances are based on extensions of natural behaviors. What does this phrase really mean? It is key to the park's philosophy, to the underlying ideology of the presentation of animals to humans, and frames our perceptions of what we see in each of the shows. "Natural behaviors" can mean either behaviors that occur naturally (i.e., without training) or behaviors that occur "in nature." There is a slightly different implication in each reading of the phrase. Behaviors that occur in nature would include courting and breeding behaviors, food gathering, fighting, and social interactions. Some of these behaviors are perhaps desirable in the park (breeding, for example, when controlled), and others, like fighting, would be undesirable, considering the vast expenditures invested in these animals. Given that the animals are not in "the wild" and furthermore that most of them have never been, having been born and hand raised at the park, natural behavior can also refer to those actions that are instinctual, or hardwired into the central nervous system of the animal. These behaviors could include ways of using the body, for example, jumping, standing, lying down, and reactions to other species which may be enemies.

By reassuring the audience that what they are seeing are all extensions of natural behaviors, the trainers imply that what we are seeing is still natural, perhaps even better than natural, as in heightened abilities. We can train them to do things they are capable of naturally, but in ways that are more spectacular or more controlled, or more designed, or on cue. In this case, humans improve on nature, molding it, shaping it into a regulated, improved, and enhanced version of itself.[22]

There is in this tiger show something of the Fordist body, a body whose movement is regulated, standardized, performed in coordination with others, under direction from a management source to produce a product which can be sold, in this case "tiger performance." For example, at one point in the show, three tigers lie down and roll over in perfect unison, just like a small corps de ballet. At another point, two tigers alternate jumping over each other repeatedly in a remarkably fluid leap frog. But these are happy workers, well fed, and stimulated by the work they do, or so the story goes. The pleasurable connotations of "stimulation" code the animals' work as fun. In this regularization, in this discipline, lies the transformation between animals and humanness, and it is coded in the language of desire. The animals *want* to do these actions, we are told. Again the attributed subjectivity and the implied choice for each individual animal mask the human-animal power differential that structures the show, and their very existence in the park. Such a masking presents labor as fun and entertaining, for them and for us, and rides on a notion of self-fulfillment and unalienated labor that coincides with the transcendental pastoralism of the park.

Once all of the dozen tigers have entered and are on their pedestals, the first "behavior" consists of a salute to the audience. The tigers, arranged in a semicircle around the stage, all sit up on their haunches to welcome us. One lion is also in the show, but he remains up high in the back part of the stage until the very end and is kept separate from the tigers. The opening section of the show introduces Ron by a voiceover from the production booth in the back, coordinated by Mike. Throughout the show, the male announcer will alternate with the male trainer in telling us about the cats and the behaviors they perform. Music will come in at appropriate moments to heighten the mood, and two unnamed but muscular male assistants will roam the outside of the ring area, pushing the cats from behind to keep them in proper form. A little educational patter is slipped in. We are told that all tigers are endangered and that some are more compatible in groups than others, since tigers in the wild usually live solitarily. Given their solitary lives, it is difficult to see how group performance is an extension of natural behaviors.

The cats are introduced by name, and one, "Lucy," dominates the show. She has the closest relationship to Ron, who incorporates her general recalcitrance into the show as a form of humor. "Sit up and look like a tiger," meaning proud, alert, powerful, he jokes to the supine Lucy, always sleeping on the job. The cats, like humans, all have distinctive faces, which makes it easy for him to tell them apart. They also have distinctive stripe patterns, "like our fingerprints." Named, identified by face and "fingerprints," and exhibiting distinctive personalities, these cats are personalized.

The behaviors consist of jumping, rolling, and sitting in various combinations. Again the exclusion of some behaviors (fighting, sleeping, urinating) is paired with the heightening and condensation of others, just as was the case at the Monterey Bay Aquarium, owing to the physical design and fish curating. Our desires at the zoo to see the animals "do something," to display their bodies in movement, and to interact with one another and us, are satisfied by the show format. The animals do a lot, a lot more in fact that animals naturally do in the wild, given that most time is spent resting, and that vigorous activity like running, leaping, or hunting occurs only in spurts. Like a greatest hits album, the show presents only those behaviors deemed worth looking at. The tiger bodies are the ultimate visual evidence of wild nature. Its portrayal in the tiger show culturalizes that physical difference through aestheticization, amplification, and choreographed display. This display intensifies as the show progresses.

The "most spectacular" behavior, Ron says, is the leap through a burning ring of fire. He warns us in advance that this will be a "good photo opportunity" so that we can get our cameras ready. This is definitely a circus trick, so indicative of "circus" in fact that it is often depicted in circus posters.[23] But there is none of the whip snapping and drum rolling usually associated with our images of circus tricks. Ron is careful to assure us that the fire doesn't bother them at all. This way we can have our circus and our ecotourism, too. Tigers gladly perform tricks that aren't tricks for the reward of mental stimulation (and presumably for the sense of pride in a job well done), with a little meat inconspicuously thrown in on the side. They are not bothered by jumping through a ring of fire, which presumably is an extension of natural behavior. Is it natural to be unafraid of fire?

In the next behavior—jumping through a suspended, paper-covered hoop to triumphal strains of brass music—Ron demonstrates that tigers can overcome their natural perceptions, although he doesn't put it in those words. Tigers, he tells us, think that when something looks solid, it is solid. Therefore, to get them to jump through a paper covered hoop is not easy. They have to train the tigers to jump through ever smaller openings in the hoop until they are willing to burst through the paper ring. Here natural perception is overcome so that we can enjoy the unnatural spectacle of a tiger leaping through a paper ring while demonstrating their natural agility. The show patter links this ability to unlearn tiger perception to intelligence when Ron jokes that one tiger, Kenny, "never figured out paper." So it appears that it's good to do tigerly things except when those tigerly "instincts" conflict with the choreography of a good show. This moment is symptomatic of the tremendous flexibility of an ideology of the natural which can constantly be reformed to accommodate conflicting data.

Toward the end of the show the patterned choreography of the bodies is more evident. One tiger, in an upright sitting position, hops across the stage on its hind legs. Although Ron notes that the big cats sit on their hind legs when fighting, he fails to note that this is a momentary behavior and one that occurs not in perfect balance but in contact with an opponent. Here, the repeated action requires perfect verticality and serves no purpose other than our entertainment. What is it we applaud with a trick like this? Is it the skill of the trainer, the skill of the tiger, or the anthropomorphism of the act which transforms the horizontal natural body posture of the feline into the vertical posture of humans?

At the end of the show, the lion, introduced as the 500-pound "Chad," which has remained stationary throughout, performs a similar act. He is, we are informed, the only lion in the world trained to perform this behavior. (We might ask why even one lion is trained to do so.) Here the issue of mastery emerges more clearly. This lion, king of the jungle, more massive even than the tigers, is momentarily turned into a pet, a house cat begging for food on his hind legs.[24] Domesticated, this "other" obeys and, we are led to believe, enjoys doing so. "I never saw a cat do anything he didn't want to do," says Ron. The lion, idealized synecdoche of the natural world, is metaphorically miniaturized in this action. In this powerful rhetorical doubling lies the special pleasure of this moment. Pets represent a domestication of wild animals, which in turn stand for the whole of nature. Telescoping nature into the figure of a begging house cat moves the nature-culture boundary still further, so that the culturalization of the natural is completed in this act of imaginary bodily transposition.

The "Magic" of Animals Show

Of all the shows at Marine World, "The Magic of Animals" show comes closest to presenting animals as humans. It takes the place of the Chinese acrobats performance in the winter season and is played in the largest outdoor auditorium of them all, seating about 2,000. The day I attended, with cold and blustery weather, in the middle of winter, there were only about twenty people in the audience, including some of the staff from the other shows.

In this show, Marine World becomes most transparent about using animals as vehicles for entertainment rather than justifying entertainment as the frame through which to educate. This was the only show in the park where the verbal emphasis was not on the abilities of the animals but on a theatrical theme in which the animals were players but not the stars. Even so, facts about each animal are woven into the patter to retain the educational cover.

The concept behind this show is to perform magic tricks with animals. Once the structuring gimmick is decided on, a show is woven out of the raw materials available, depending on which animals are not already in other shows and the specific behaviors those available can perform. These animals and specific actions are then woven into a loose story line. Finally, the verbal script is written and a complex musical score is assembled to accompany the actions. This show had thirty different bits of music accentuating the tricks and providing emotional cues and atmospheric shading. The sound cues are taken from the verbal script, not from behaviors, since animal actors can be less predictable than humans. Like any other theatrical show, the production also requires a director, sound designer, scenic designer, costumer, star, and supporting players.

The backdrop for the magic show consisted of a painted Mayan temple, giving the tricks a vaguely jungle-like setting. The star is a young male actor, dressed as if he stepped out of *Raiders of the Lost Ark* in dapper hat and bush vest. First, he produces a dove out of his hat in a typical magician's trick. Then he moves on to bigger things. Trainers, dressed in khaki, roll in an empty cage and cover it with a cloth. Whoosh—the cloth is pulled away to reveal a puma in the cage (facts about the endangered status of pumas follow). Next, he makes one of the female trainers disappear and later suspends her magically in midair, passing a hoop around her body so that we can see the absence of hidden strings. The typical male-female relationship of magic acts is repeated here, with the female body being subjected to superhuman control by the magician. This relationship also, not surprisingly, aligns the female with the animals, which were also acted upon by the magician's "will."

Since most of the actors in this show are animals, not humans, sometimes things go wrong. For instance, at one point the orangutan (Jolyn) is supposed to pop out of a suitcase. During one rainstorm, Jolyn got scared and couldn't or wouldn't do the trick. In these cases, they have to try to turn it into something positive; no coercion can be displayed. "Here at Marine World, we never make the animals do anything . . . ," they might joke, with revealing irony, to cover a gaff while retaining audience goodwill. In these cases, the animal is never forced to perform the trick, but neither is it rewarded. Similarly, when timing doesn't go as

planned, the actors have to fill in time between stunts by verbal vamp-
ing, such as in vaudeville, but in this case the patter consists of educational facts about the animals.

In the other shows, like the lion and tiger show, the trainer directs the
animals, and there is less uncertainty. But here the lead character is an
actor (one of the few professional actors on staff), and the animal trainers or handlers are kept in the background, getting the animal to enter
and exit and stay in position as needed for the illusions. There is pro-
portionately a looser chain of command, and more uncertainty results,
revealing the usually masked control of the humans over the animals
through these "mistakes." These resistances were not so much aggressive contestations, but passive refusals or ignoring of commands. The
animals might pay attention to something else besides the directive cue
or want to loll about or play with the trainer. Natural actions or responses replace trained extensions of natural actions in these revealing
moments of wandering attention, thereby marking through contrast
the intense structuring and training that goes into presenting the natural in the other shows.

Toward the end of the show, the orangutan appears, in a humorous
segment, in the only instance in the park where I saw an animal dressed
up like a human. Jolyn appears wearing black running shorts, blows her
nose using a hanky, gives the magician a kiss, and grins, revealing a
toothy smile. Cast as a humanoid, the orangutan plays the crowd
against the magician as she foils a simple trick where an orange is supposed to disappear. Using this staged usurpation as his cue, the magician gets in a plug for conservation. "We have fun up here," he says, "but
it's not fun that orangutans are disappearing in the wild." The show then
closes with an animal "fax," as a tiger cub is magically transferred from
a cage on stage right to one on stage left. At the end of the show, audience
members are invited to come up and talk with the trainers, meet the
tiger, and ask questions.

It is significant that the only animal to be dressed up was the orangutan, the most human looking of all animals in the park. None of the
other animals was costumed, although several engaged in behaviors
that mimicked human actions, like waving. What is permissible with a
primate would not be permissible with marine mammals or with the big
cats, perhaps because it would invoke a circus atmosphere and seem to
take away the dignity that the shows try to give them. The orangutan,
inheriting the chimp's reputation for human behaviors, can be gotten
away with. We are not making Jolyn into a human so much as we are
laughing at the recognition of the fact that she is almost (but not quite)

human. The orangutan is thus conceptually positioned just on the other side of the animal-human divide. With a little costuming and choreography she can almost step over it.

On the realism continuum of in-situ to out-of-situ, this show presents animals on the far edge of the out-of-situ range. Not only is no habitat context provided, but the heavy narrativization and characterization used to present the animals and their behaviors reposition them firmly in our world, cloaking the natural world associated with the symbolic presence of the tiger cub body, for example, in the high-tech framework of an animal fax. That this is a tongue-in-cheek magic show facilitates this importation of the natural into the cultural. Orangutans use handkerchiefs, wear clothes, laugh, and go on trips.

The magical fantasy of anthropomorphism is an extended instance of domination through incorporation, here presented as humor. Like the concept of racial assimilation, which is dependent on the idea of different social groupings called races, anthropomorphism makes the partial or temporary erasure of social difference its focus while retaining physical differences (between the category "animal" and the category "human") as the ground of meaning. The humor is manufactured in the gap between the difference and similarity between human and animal. Anthropomorphized animals are both like and unlike us, and obversely we are both like and unlike them. Sometimes humans are considered a part of the natural world; sometimes they are defined against it. The humor of the Magic of Animals show reveals and is dependent on the motion of the ever-shifting boundary between the natural and cultural.

Orangutans hold quite a different place in the public imaginary than whales do though, and the relationship between animals and humans is played out differently in the emphasis on spectacle rather than narrative that characterizes the marine mammal shows at the park. Even here, though, anthropomorphism is not absent.

Killer Whale and Dolphin Show

The killer whale, referred to earlier in the section on kissing, is the premier symbol of Marine World Africa. Its picture is the most dramatically featured on all material about the park. Its leaping black-and-white torpedo body appears on the cover of the program booklet, in a two-page spread on the publicity pamphlet used to advertise the park, and on the cover of the souvenir video. What do this particular animal and its representations convey, and how do those relate to what we see in the show?

One of the most stunning aspects of whales is their size and power. The two female killer whales in the show weigh in at ten thousand pounds and is twenty-three feet long, for the twenty-three-year-old Yaka, from the North Pacific, and six thousand pounds and seventeen feet long for the younger, more diminutive twelve-year-old Vigga, from the North Atlantic. They are marked dramatically in black and white, like early Rauchenberg paintings. The black is absolutely black, covering their backs from the tip of the snout to the tail. The bellies are glistening white, again starting at the snout tip, thinning in the middle, and swirling outward on the ends of the bodies. There is something important about this coloring. It gives their bodies a definition that all-gray whales lack.

The top jaw is black, the bottom snowy white, the long line of the two meeting colors gives a sense of a mouth, of lips. And behind their small, dark eyes, on a background of black, are large oval circles of white, looking like eyes, or maybe like eyebrows, but somehow giving definition to the face of the animal, a face that must be imagined, because the rocket shape of the marvelously streamlined and blubber smooth bodies does not differentiate between head, neck, and belly. But the short, wide black flippers intersect the white underbelly just about where arms might be and give an impression of a torso. Looking improbably like large five-ton penguins, these animals soar out of the water and through the air. They are striking in their markings, "cute" in their short-armed flippers and long grin. They look almost like a Disney version of whales, just as Mickey Mouse is a Disney version of a rodent. Photogenic, with markings and "arms" that provide requisite fodder for anthropomorphism, Yaka and Vigga combine awesome size, strength, and power with aesthetic beauty, personality, and cuteness. They are the emblem of Marine World.

The show opens with a painted backdrop of the Pacific Northwest, mountains and fir trees, backing the large performance tank. It is surrounded by a large outdoor amphitheater, which seats several hundred. A young man in his twenties plays the master of ceremonies. He is dressed like a fur trapper in buckskin and boots. The Indians of the Northwest, he tells us, once worshiped the whales and thought them gods. A few tidbits of information are thrown in about their eating habits and habitat, then the two whales surge into the tank, the music swells to Olympian proportions, and they introduce themselves with huge leaps out of the water. Then two women are introduced as the trainers; they give the cues to the animals throughout the show, as the MC provides narration.

The animals zoom around the tank at forty miles an hour and then slow to an adagio tempo, showing us their flukes. (This is part of the trained medical behaviors, behaviors that allow the animal to undergo medical tests like examinations and the withdrawing of blood without undo stress. These very valuable animals receive better medical care than most humans in the world.) After the MC tells us about the medical behaviors, it is time to boost the tempo again, this time with appropriately triumphal music. The two orcas breach, that is, soar out of the water and purposely crash back onto its surface, creating a huge splash. The sound and flying water emphasize their magnitude. In comparison, human belly flops are a pinprick of sound and a few drops of water. The power that translates from these breachings carries a frisson of danger, too. Humans cannot compare in terms of size, strength, mass, or power. It is thrilling to see such a demonstration up close.

But the orcas are only huge in comparison with people. Compared with most whales (technically, the orcas are the largest member of the dolphin family), orcas are downright diminutive.[25] Whales, in common mythology, are supposed to be big—think of the biblical story of Jonah and the whale, or *Moby-Dick*. The orcas are big enough to be big, but small enough to be approachable and believably "friendly," with a body size that is not so out of scale to our own as to be too terrifying. This is a controllable sublime, in which size, activities, facial markings, and body shape all combine to make the orcas the perfect whale performer for these shows.[26] We can desire to be close to them while simultaneously being impressed with their capacity for physical dominance of ourselves.

Another part of the aesthetic of this show is the demonstration of control and smooth, sustained movement that could be described as graceful. No sudden changes of speed, energy usage, or direction detract from the elegance of the next segment, called the "ballet of the killer whale." Yaka and Vigga roll on their backs and swim around the tank upside down, their milky white bellies exposed to the audience. There is in this emphasis on grace a sense of channeling and containing all the power (and potential wildness) that were demonstrated moments earlier by the breaching. There is reassurance and safety here in the knowledge that such huge, powerful animals can be so trained/tamed as to restrain themselves on command to produce the movement coded as "beautiful" by the ballet reference.

Animals as Professional Performers

"Have you stopped to think they are watching *you?*" asks the MC. This is an interesting moment in the show. This is a casual, funny aside, surely, yet underneath it lies a host of issues. *Are* they watching us? And if they are, what does that reversal imply? Can whales "return the gaze"?

To do so, they would have to possess a subjectivity capable of understanding themselves as both watcher and watched. This might be going too far, but the question of the animals' subjectivity, which is heightened in so many ways throughout the park and in a great deal of the popularization of the research on marine mammal intelligence, is interestingly brought to the fore. Do we grant them a subjectivity but not a consciousness, or a self-consciousness? If so, what is the tension between the anthropomorphism of body and body language, as well as vocal language in some cases, and the lack of self-consciousness or self-awareness that is implied in the show situation? The animals, it seems, perform for their trainers, and, to be crass about it, they perform for that smelt that they will receive as a reward for good behavioral production.

For all the framing in terms of their enjoying the activities, needing the mental stimulation which the training provides, and getting tactile rewards from their trainers, the animals are never performing for the reward of audience applause. They would only be performing directly for the audience if we arrived with our pockets full of fish. The applause then is for whom? To express delight, approval, awe at what we see? As a reward for the trainers and production designers? Are we applauding the animal for being itself (i.e., the mass of the body that makes a big splash), the choreography of the show, the innate abilities of the animal ("intelligence"), or the skill of the trainers in shaping the behavior?

What would it be like if the trainers were invisible during the show? Maybe they could give all the cues through underwater windows or underwater signals. Imagine a show that, like a ballet, consisted only of dancing dolphins or whirling whales moving to music against a painted backdrop. Pyrotechnical skill could be highlighted in solos, and unison work featured in the group movements of the corps de ballet. Entrances, exits, tempo changes, could all happen on cue, seemingly without the direction of humans. This is the next logical step in showcasing these animals as intelligent individuals. Then, they could take their reward in applause, bowing to the audience. We would never need to know that a feast of fishes awaited beyond the gated exit. But it appears that the duration of behavioral sequences must remain relatively short in between gustatory reinforcements. This places the animals, trainers, and audience in a triangulated position. The animals desire rewards from the trainers (smelt or praise), the trainers seem to desire rewards from the audience (appreciation for the animals and for their own skill) and from the management that pays their salary, and the audience desires spectacle from the animals.

These shows are different from traditional Euro-American dance or theater performances because the expressivity and creativity of the animal as performer are not among the ingredients. (In those types of performances we may recognize the importance of the designer, writer, or director, but the contribution of the performer is not merely to reproduce their directions faithfully but also to do that while bringing him-or herself to the role, that is, making his or her rendition distinctive. Each actor would strive to do "his own" Hamlet, not Olivier's, for example.) And these shows also differ from sports because, although trained skills are important (as are coordination and the ability to execute the plays called by a coach), individual responsiveness to changing circumstances, key to making a spectacular pass in basketball, or driving toward the basket around a shifting field of defenders, is not operative in these shows. The improvisatory use of learned skills within predetermined structural parameters is not granted to the animals.[27] What would it mean if they were? It would grant the animals an agency in the process which is now limited to choosing or not choosing to fulfill a particular prescribed bodily motion.[28]

However, these divisions are not absolute. There is an emphasis on the species capability (to breach, to swim speedily) paired with an individuation of the performers which stops short of granting creativity to them. Trainers will develop behaviors for specific animals depending on abilities they show and they will incorporate individual personalities (even recalcitrance) into the action and narration of the show, as with the tiger Lucy, but they will not frame the animals' public performance in terms of creativity or problem solving.[29] The performance of specific movements of the body through prescribed paths in space and at specific times and speeds is what is rewarded, whether that be whale soaring in the air on cue or tigers leaping through a hoop of fire. We applaud what they can do, that they do it (choice, training), and that they do it on cue.[30]

These distinctions reveal the particular mediation of performance that occurs when the performers are animals. With humans, performance in the theatrical sense places a set of quotation marks around a set of actions, heightening their symbolic content, and supplying the sense of "as if" that unites the audience and performers for the duration of the event. The actress speaks as if she were the character Ophelia, for example. For the audience, cognitive awareness of the boundedness of the performance situation, of its production as a representation, of the behavioral contracts between audience and performer, and of the emphasis placed on symbolic rather than instrumental words and behaviors all characterize human dramatic performances. In tourist performances like those in Waikiki, however, the as-if-ness, the fictionality, is replaced by a presumption of nonfiction, of documentary. The expressivity of the dancers is presumed to be real, not acting, since by definition they are performing themselves.

At animal performances like Yaka and Vigga's at Marine World, a splitting of documentary and fiction occurs. The human performers, like the show's MC, are perceived through a theatrical frame that recognizes them as actors portraying a role. The stars of the show, the animals, are not. While their actions may still generate the double meanings of what is done and what is implied, like the fake shooting of a protagonist in a play, they do not themselves produce this distance between the act and its meanings. In other words, the orca that busses me on the cheek is not pretending we are in love; rather, it is matching its nose to a target. Behaviors which are instrumental (i.e., they yield fishy rewards) are perceived as symbolic, referential, aesthetic, or emotionally expressive, depending on the framework of the show. In tension with this is the bodily presence of the animal and its physical size, mass, and capabilities—its facticity. The demonstration of these aspects of the animal tend toward the production of spectacle, with its emphasis on the visual and iconicity, but they function on the symbolic level, too, as evidence of realness, and of species specificity.

The alternation of these aspects of performance is highlighted in the next segment of the whale show. The kiss comes next, like the one I described in the opening during the training session, only this time accompanied by a big smooching sound on the microphone. Humor is yoked to anthropomorphism again. Then we shift gears from the intimate to the spectacular with a demonstration of strength and power in the dramatic "speed run." In this segment, the two whales race around the perimeter of the seventy-foot tank in opposite directions. But this time, they make a mistake, going the wrong way, so they are recalled. No improper behavior can be tolerated, even in public. This reminds us they are animals. It was their mistake, presumably, not the trainer's, that got them confused. They try it again, this time passing the center of the circumference in perfect unison, and kicking up big waves in their wake like huge speedboats. The speed and the displacement of water once again serve as impressive demonstrations of physical mass and strength.

We are close to the end now, and the alternation between personalizing behaviors and those that demonstrate species specificity continues. The MC demonstrates the hand cues they use to get the whales to vocalize, but this time the whales won't stop talking. The trainer and MC exchange helpless looks, until finally the whales pipe down. When he asks them to speak next time, they emit loud farting sounds and shake their heads "yes" in approval. This segment produces humor by giving the whales the appearance of agency, like smart-alecky kids who thumb their noses at the teacher, ignoring commands and dipping into scatological body humor. But this is a staged resistance, therefore humorous. No real resistance can be tolerated, both for safety reasons and for ideological ones.

The show closes with another round of spectacular behavior as smart-alecky kids become once more denizens of the deep. We are cued to get our cameras ready, because aerials are coming up, and they "make the best pictures." The whales jump into the air in unison, one sailing over the other, and then they execute a series of jumps rising fifteen feet out of the water, touching their noses to a suspended target with the kinesthetic eloquence of Michael Jordan making a basket. The big bodies are fully revealed for our cameras; what is normally hidden under water is suspended vertically in full view. Then they land in big, breaching splashes as the water explodes into the air. The spray rains onto the audience, their bodies directly affecting ours. The music cues our applause, and the MC closes by telling us, "We hope you leave with a better understanding of the animals and why they were even worshiped by the Northwest Indians."

Massive, powerful, athletic, spectacular, funny, friendly, kissable, and sublime, these orcas have earned their keep this day. But, as impressed as I was, I hadn't seen anything that would compare with the presentation of Shamu at Sea World.

NINE

Performing Nature
Shamu at Sea World

What Mickey Mouse is to Disneyland, Shamu is to Sea World.[1] Marketing symbol, ambassador, embodiment of dreams come true for children (and adults), Shamu, the most celebrated orca whale of all time, is the synecdoche of Sea World. The orcas at Marine World Africa, Yaka and Vigga, shrink in comparison with the megastar personality of this mighty marine mammal and the industry of marine theme park which has sprung up around it.

The ideological work of Sea World is based on the trope of family as the conceptual frame around which to construct a problematic of the natural. We saw a similar construction operating at Marine World Africa, but it is much more intensely played out here and is articulated through the choreography of the show (exactly what actions are performed and how they are presented), the specific bodily relationships between the trainers and the animals, the relationship posited between the audience and the animal and human performers, and the verbal narration that goes along with the presentation. In addition, special technological effects reinforce certain aspects of these actions and our perceptions of them.

By uniting the idea of family with nature, both sides of the equation are reconfigured. Families as specific social organizations are naturalized as paradigmatic of all relations, whether on a global scale or between humans and animals. Obversely, nature becomes part of the human family, completely culturalized and incorporated. Complex tensions pull at the edges of these formulations and are revealed in the structure of the shows at Sea World. But even with these competing tensions, the shows ultimately promote a utopian view of Americanism tied to corporatism and world leadership.

The Shamu show notion of family binds all animals and all humans together in a vision of harmony. The diversity of shows and exhibits at Sea World, which includes penguins, walruses, seals, porpoises, dolphins, and reef-dwelling animals, emphasizes this idea of a family of diverse species coexisting in the ocean world. This represents a sort of horizontal unity. A vertical unity between animals and humans is complementary and leaves us on top, just as parents are in positions of control within a family. The specific values associated with the family paradigm and promoted during the show include trust, affection, mutual respect, and a high degree of individuation. What are not allowed are a visible show of force, aggression, competition, or violence of any kind. However, the lines of command remain clear even though unarticulated or covered over by assertions of mutuality and equality.

In the invisible assertion of this control and in the aesthetic design of the shows, the shifting boundary of the natural and the cultural is continually redrawn to accommodate the conflicts inherent in such a familial paradigm. The mode of display aestheticizes the animals in two senses, producing the natural both as a cultural artifact and as the complementary concept to the cultural. In the first sense, the careful design of movement in terms of symmetry, grace, and geometrical patterns aestheticizes the whales as "art," the most historically recent sense of the term "culture," as Raymond Williams noted. But at the same time, the earliest sense of culture as "to cultivate" is also invoked.

At Sea World that which is cultivated is nature itself, designed through the choreography of the whales into pleasing shapes and forms just as plants are designed into formal gardens. One key difference is that plants exceeding the bounds of cultivation do not pose a deadly risk to the gardener. With the whales, the other sense of nature as a set of forces that organize life and must be either obeyed or contained (depending on the particular philosophical juncture) is ever-present. Wayward whales on a rampage are uncontainable; such forces of nature unleashed against humans would be terrorizing.

Unlike the early Roman spectacles of human-animal combat, which depended upon an antagonistic construction of the human and natural worlds, such aggression (or the spectacle of its containment that structures the traditional lion-tamer act, for instance) is deemed neither morally supportable nor economically viable. Instead, this constant threat is submerged, providing the shadow base from which the utopian unity is constructed and, indeed, is the basis which makes such unity utopian in design. The utopian aspects of the family vision depend on a simultaneous assertion and denial of the distinction between the natural world and the cultural world, between animals (standing for that which is "wild," "natural," and "free") and humans. If this division is not asserted, it cannot then be overcome in the discourse of transcendent familialism. In the transcendent moments of the shows (like the whale ballet, audience interactions, and the most spectacular acrobatic moves), these wild animals are fully incorporated into the family of humans. The culturalization of nature is complete. The product is a controllable sublime, and it is best marketed through the figure of a giant, smiling, dangerous but cuddly killer whale—Shamu. The huge scale of the park represents both the enormous capital investment in this animal and in her display, as well as the profitability of such ideological work.

SEA WORLD SAN DIEGO

In 1964, four graduates of UCLA opened Sea World on twenty-two acres of land in San Diego. Today, more than thirty years later, the "marine zoological park" sits on one-hundred-fifty acres on San Diego's Mission Bay. Purchased in 1976 by Harcourt Brace Jovanovich, Inc., ownership of all four Sea Worlds transferred to the Anheuser-Busch Companies, Inc. in 1989 for a price of $1.1 billion.[2]

Nature is big business, as the above fact makes clear. And within the nature industry, marine mammals are rapidly becoming the rising (and bankable) stars of this growing entertainment field. The "seaquarium" industry generates revenues of at least $600 million a year.[3] While the Busch entertainment conglomerate does not release annual theme-park attendance figures, their publicity materials state that more than 160 million people have visited Sea Worlds in the last thirty years.[4] Susan Davis has estimated that the four Sea Worlds together attract at least 11.35 million paying customers a year, mostly from North America. The vision of the park reaches much farther than that, too, through television specials and educational shows. Davis reports that an additional sixteen million viewers are exposed to Sea World through direct satellite broadcasts to schools throughout the United States.[5]

"Sea World: It's not another Park, it's another World," declares the sign at the Sea World entrance. And this world is extensive. Five aquariums show sea and freshwater fish and marine invertebrates, and more than twenty "major educational exhibits" are featured, including the world's largest display of sharks. We can also "touch and feed bottlenose dolphins" in the dolphin pool, and see 400 penguins in the "Penguin Encounter."

There are many additional services and products: nautical gift shops, places to have a picture taken with Shamu (represented either by a fifteen-foot statue or by a person dressed in a Shamu suit), food concessions and restaurants, a space needle ride, souvenir shops, a play area called Cap'n Kids World, and the Busch pavilion, where visitors can sample a wide variety of Busch products. Products, services, exhibits, shows, and souvenirs are so heavily cross-referenced that, as Davis notes, they provide an "intricate maze" that collapses publicity and entertainment.[6]

All of this is set in a beautiful park, carefully groomed, squeaky clean, wholesome, and full of carefully tended plants and animals. "Family entertainment at its best" is what the brochure for the theme parks promises. The same threats of violence that are banished from the human-animal interactions in the shows are also absent here. A rural, small-town sense of safety, scale, and simplicity governs the physical design. Sidewalks wind gracefully from exhibit to exhibit; trash is immediately whisked away. The city of San Diego, set off from the park by a very long access drive, is not even visible from the complex. Urban components like crime, dirt, pollution, noise, and different groups of people with competing needs are not found here. A day at Sea World is a vacation from these tensions and differences.

Parkgoers represent a relatively homogeneous population in terms of racial and class background, although there is some variation. Sea World keeps close track of these demographics through extensive market research. As Susan Davis reports, at Sea World San Diego, 51 percent of customers claimed an annual income of at least $40,000 a year, with 33 percent reporting more than $50,000 a year. Nearly 90 percent described themselves as "Anglo," and the rest as "non-Anglo," the only two choices given in surveys. Given the much more diverse balance of populations in southern California, Davis argues that Sea World consumers (unlike those of Disneyland, for example) are self-selecting from the white middle to upper-middle classes.[7] As important as this homogeneity is perhaps the shared sense of a community goal among all of the visitors—to play, to have fun, to escape from daily routine, and to see nature. A nostalgia for a simpler, safer, small-town past is transmuted into a nostalgia for an Edenic community of animals and people that coexist in harmony.

The theme of education structures all of this promised fun, and takes away the obvious, that performing animals are captured and exhibited for profit. The counterdiscourse to this commodification of the natural for profit is the presentation of nature for education, conservation, and research, that is, nature as nonprofit enterprise. Like Marine World Africa, Sea World, too, is a hybrid, combining nonprofit research behind the scenes with for-profit "edutainment" up front.

Sea World sponsors research through the Hubbs–Sea World Research Institute, founded in 1963. Assistance is provided by Sea World and the Anheuser-Busch companies through cash contributions and through making "Sea World's unparalleled collection of marine animals available for study by qualified researchers."[8] Marine-life education classes reach 200,000 San Diego schoolchildren a year, and Sea World is an accredited member of the American Association of Zoological Parks and Aquariums (AAZPA). "As such," their publicity asserts, "Sea World meets rigorous standards of ethics, professional training and animal care and actively supports the AAZPA's wildlife conservation programs." "Your visit today makes possible our education, research, beached animal rescue and conservation programs," notes the park-guide brochure handed to every visitor. "Research" and "conservation" legitimate the commodity and entertainment aspects for the predominantly middle-to-upper-middle class audience, 40 percent of which hold college degrees.[9] But there can be no doubt that the for-profit aspects of the park outweigh its not-for-profit side.

The hierarchy among these categories is easily read through the material resources devoted to each in the outlay of the park. Most of the site's physical area is devoted to show stadiums, exhibition tanks, and guest services in the form of restaurants and shops, not research facilities. But the guarantee of education, research, and conservation underlying all the fun allows guilt-free pleasure and a justification for the steep entrance prices, which run 20 percent higher than those of Marine World Africa USA. Adults enter for $23.95, children (ages three through eleven) for $17.95, and toddlers get in for free.[10] This brings the price for a day's entertainment for a typical family of four to $83.80, plus the cost of lunch, snacks, and the requisite souvenirs. All attractions and exhibits in the park, with the exception of the two rides, are free once the entrance fee is paid. Even so, taking the hypothetical family of four to Sea World for the day is easily a $100 proposition.

The corporate structure of the Sea World empire is further emphasized by the presence of various major corporations that "sponsor" particular shows or exhibitions. For example, the Penguin Encounter is "presented by ARCO." Public relations information notes that "Sea World's relationship with these firms involves participation in national and regional consumer promotions, joint construction, display of educational graphics and mutual institutional advertising programs. Sponsors are ARCO, Southwest Airlines, Adohr Farms, Pepsi, Kodak, am/ pm mini market and HomeFed Bank." The newly opened Busch products pavilion, called the Clydesdale Hamlet and Hospitality Center, is a quintessential example of this linkage of corporate/commodity/"edutainment." The licensing of Shamu representations, such as stuffed animals and tee shirts, the commodification of the personification of the natural, is also tightly controlled.

In these mutually beneficial institutional advertising programs, the affiliates garner goodwill for their support of conservation programs, but even more importantly they get to be associated with the very positive and powerful image of Shamu.

SHAMU

"I Love Shamu" reads the bumper sticker I bought as a souvenir. Note that it doesn't say: "I Love Sea World." Shamu, like a movie star or any well-known public figure, is a character, a personality, a locus onto which we can project our fantasies. She is the only animal at the park to be so personified, blazoned on tee shirts and mugs, reproduced in cuddly form in Shamu stuffed whales (available in graded sizes, and costs, from three inches to four-feet long). Although other animals at Sea World have names, only Shamu has been accorded emblematic status. Her picture dominates every piece of literature coming out of Sea World, the sleek black-and-white torpedo form lending itself well to abstraction and to graphic reproducibility on everything from brochures to shopping bags to corporate stationery.

The visual impact of the body cannot be underestimated, and it has contributed immeasurably both to the commodification of Shamu and to the development of a public for the whales. By comparison, Nancy Hotchiss, education director of the AAZPA, notes that nobody cares about freshwater dolphins. These dolphins are often less sleek of shape, paler in color, and more sluggish than saltwater dolphins, the category of cetaceans to which Shamu belongs.[11] They do not offer the same imaginary of graceful, powerful, playful friends nor the abstractable graphic visual possibilities.

Of course, like Lassie, which was played by a series of collies, Shamu isn't really just one whale. There is a "Shamu" at each of the four Sea Worlds.[12] Her presence is not only necessary; it is constitutive of Sea World sites. Physical form, personality, and physical presence are all condensed and compacted into the idea of "Shamu." The whale's physical body and its actions come to represent the complex of feelings, ideas, and fantasy that represent the ideological subtext of the park.

Constructing "Shamu"

Star personas are built over a period of time and through numerous representations.[13] Shamu has emerged as a megastar over the past quarter-century and through several modes of representation. These include the live shows; the entire rhetorical, ideological, and material structure of the Sea World parks, which support and depend upon the Shamu signifier; and the numerous representations of Shamu in newspaper articles, publicity reports, and souvenir memorabilia. In this section, I want to concentrate specifically on the construction of the centerpiece of Sea World San Diego, the Shamu show in Shamu Stadium.[14]

A publicity release notes: "'Baby Shamu Celebration' is Sea World's signature show. Every day, thousands of visitors to Shamu Stadium walk away with a deeper appreciation of the beauty, mystery and power of killer whales. Baby Shamu, Shamu, Namu and Nakina have mastered a repertoire of hundreds of show maneuvers including crowd-pleasing (and often drenching) breaches, spinning leaps and graceful arching bows—interestingly, all extensions of natural behavior."[15] This one paragraph provides several clues to how we are to relate to Shamu. What we will see is natural, fun, aesthetically pleasing, interesting, and masterful. It is also a celebration of babies, and thus of family.

As the signature show, this performance is clearly the most important event of our day at Sea World. To miss it would be unthinkable. The importance is underlined by the size of the stadium, the largest of the three marine mammal show areas (the others are for the whale and dolphin show, and the sea lion and otter show, in order of decreasing stadium size). This outdoor stadium, built in 1987 at a cost of $15 million, is the largest marine mammal complex ever constructed.[16] It holds five million gallons of blue water, and seats 6,500 people per show. There are several shows a day during the peak season.

The pools are stunning. Acres of azure water spread out in a huge horseshoe shape, with the viewing stands rising in a semicircle around the front curve of the pool. Only a chest-high clear acrylic wall separates this raised lake of water from us, and we can see right through the sides, the water brimming full to the top. The lip of the wall curves in slightly at the top, giving the sense that the liquid is barely contained, a slice of the sea somehow magically misplaced on land.[17] And this is travel-poster water—sparkling clean, clear, aquamarine, and tipped with white from splashing waves as the orcas jump and breach.

The frontstage and backstage parts of this performance area are both visible and are linked by a flat cement area at water level.[18] The four to five trainers who work each show use this as a home base. Behind them rises a forty-foot screen, a Sony Jumbotron. Today it acts only as a blue backdrop, separating the performance pool from the holding pools behind. But it will be actively used in new shows. Cement pathways and catwalks connect the central stage area to the sides of the pools, where audience participation segments are staged. And right in the middle of the semicircle, the pool opens out in a square, like a tongue sticking out, jutting into the stadium. This is where the orcas will take their bows, sliding right into the seating area.

From the whales' point of view, the stadium stands are always visible, blocking the horizon and the world outside Sea World. We look "in" at the whales during the show, visually placing them and ourselves within the "world" of Sea World, our backs to the ocean and to San Diego. Like other theme parks, Sea World operates by creating a world within the larger world, a world that is nearly completely self-referential, a world literally looking in on itself and masking the boundaries which separate it from outside.[19] Physically set off from San Diego by acres of parking, a long winding access route, and an undeveloped belt of greenery, Sea World is similarly psychologically set apart. As audience, we join the whales in a shared nautical world for the duration of the show. This overarching theme of a nautical world is reinforced throughout the park in every show, exhibit, and even in most of the restaurants and the vast majority of souvenirs. We are joined with Shamu in a world apart from our modern urban one, but, simultaneously, Shamu moves into our world. She crosses the watery divide literally at special moments in the choreography of the show and metaphorically by surrounding us with her images and simulacra, which abound in the park.

The Show: "Baby Shamu Celebration"

The crowd has been filling the stands for the last half-hour. The music from the preshow tape fades down with the words "to touch eternity," cuing us to the utopian dimensions that will be brought out throughout the show. Soaring electronic notes fill the stadium, and two huge black-and-white orcas enter the performance pool, zooming around its circumference. A male voice announces: "Perhaps the most awe inspiring, mighty, and majestic of all animals, the killer whale. . . . " On cue the two animals arc into the air, revealing the massive dimensions of their bodies, up to twenty-five feet long. Four trainers (male and female), clad in glistening red-and-black wet suits, run onto the cement platform and wave to us as the orcas exit through metal underwater gates.

Immediately two more orcas enter. Their breaching leaps into the air elicit loud "oohs" and "aahhs" from the crowd of several thousand. The triumphal sounds of brass underscore the whales' introduction as "masters of their world: Shamu and Namu!" This is so much better than at Marine World Africa USA. The scale of spectacle is easily three times as large; there are more whales, more trainers, and much more room to move in. The whales can gather speed, dive deeper and leap higher, and interact more directly with the trainers. Where spectacle is concerned, more is better, and there is much more size, power, and activity here.

At the end of this opening segment, the music softens, and the trainers introduce themselves, the facility, and the whales, including Baby Shamu, for whom the show, "Baby Shamu Celebration," is named. "This is the world's largest and most advanced breeding facility for whales. Baby Shamu is a milestone in marine science, the sixth calf born at a Sea World." Now eight-and-a-half feet long and weighing 800 pounds, the baby will be present throughout the show, at times actively mimicking the behavior of the older whales, at times flubbing a routine. (Too much discipline at such a young age might reek of child labor, and Baby Shamu participates in the shows as if playing freely, doing whatever she wants.)

At less than a year old, she has had minimal training so far, but her presence in this show is key. She not only points up the gigantic size of the adult whales (which can reach weights of five tons and above) through her (comparatively) diminutive counterpoint, but provides the "evidence" of family that the rhetorical structure of the show is built around.

The refrain of the Shamu song spells it out: "We all share the sky, we all breathe the air. Water means life, and we're part of the sea. Just like a family." The "family of man" is here expanded to include sea animals, especially those that are mammals like us. Although the song says "we're part of the sea," the reality at Sea World is that the sea is represented by the giant holding tanks. This simulacrum is literally imported into our world while the real sea rests just outside the park, unnoticed. Still, in a secular, ecological cosmology, we are linked to these marine mammals that bear, nurse, and raise young as we do, and breathe the same air as we do, their warm-blooded bodies covered with a smooth sensitive skin just like ours. The "babiness" of Baby Shamu evokes these physical similarities as well as the social similarity ("familyness," kinship system) between us and them.

Press releases attest to the popularity of Baby Shamu: "A few times every week, letters arrive at Sea World without an address . . . just the words 'Baby Shamu' scrawled carefully in crayon across the front of an envelope. There is little question the young whale has captured the hearts of children and adults nearly everywhere. Her daily appearances at Shamu Stadium are marked with eager and enthusiastic cheers. Baby Shamu's progress has been watched with affection since a summer afternoon in 1991 when 1,500 people witnessed her birth at Sea World." In this publicity statement, we are positioned as doting parents and our own kids become transspecies pen pals.

During the next part of the show, someone from the audience, as our surrogate, meets one of the whales. Today it is an adult, but children often participate in this segment as well. Mike, from Ventura, California, is led out to a small platform at the side of the pool. One of the trainers tells him what actions to perform to instruct the whale. Today Nikina is performing this segment, and, as Mike marches in place, she mimics his walk with a series of tail flaps. Next, Mike meets Nikina "up close." Blindly following instructions, he throws both hands up and jumps back surprised when, responding to his command, she squirts a stream of water toward him. Laughter ripples through the audience, the hapless human having brought the joke upon himself. Mike here is the straight man. Finally, Mike rewards Nikina by giving her sensitive skin a rubdown. As he leaves, she ducks her head underwater and waves her upright tail "good-bye."

Audience-participation segments like this are included in every whale show and in the dolphin show as well. They are one of the differences in how ecotourism, zoos, and Sea World construct our relationships with the animals. Sea World is the only place where such literal contact can take place, where, as Susan Davis notes, the animals seem to return our gaze directly, to reach out to us.[20] Audience-participation segments function to establish an individual link between each audience member and the individual whales through the identificatory mechanism of the participant. The trainers also function as avenues of identification, especially during the segments of the show when they are in the water with the animals. But their specialty training, their professionalism, sets them apart from us in a way that the audience volunteer is not. At Sea World, unlike Marine World Africa, they have done away with the whale kiss that I detailed in the preceding chapter. It is now regarded as too anthropomorphic and as obscuring the danger and power of the whales. This change in choreography represents a shift in the ideological framing of the animal-human relationship that I will discuss in the context of a history of the shows. Anthropomorphism persists in other behaviors, though, and subtends at least some aspects of the family trope.

Next comes the most spectacular and most moving part of the show, what the producers call the "whale ballet." It represents the fantasy of cross-species melding, of the vanishing of the natural/cultural divide. An elite artistic form, ballet, is used as a frame for our perceptions in the segment and facilitates the absorption of the human into the whale's aqueous world. The whale is aestheticized while the human is transformed into a marine mammal partner, equally at home in the water as the whale. The natural is culturalized while the cultural is naturalized, and this transformative process is framed as art.

The "Whale Ballet"

The opening lines of this segment's narration emphasize the close relationship between the trainers and the whales: "We create an environment for killer whales comfortable enough for them to breed." Breeding is a measure of success in re-creating enough of the natural habitat for them to participate successfully in this most "natural" of natural (family linked) behaviors. "We care for them twenty-four hours a day. We have a special relationship with them. . . . *We enter their world* . . ." With that, one of the trainers slips into the water with the whales for the first time. Throughout this segment, trainers and whales will work together in human-whale duets.

Like a ship's bowsprit, the trainer arches out in front of the orca, his feet balanced on the nose of the animal, arms extended to the side and behind him, like a nautical Nike. In this position, the whale pushes him all around the tank of water at a rapid speed, white foam flying from the trainer's chest. At the end of the circuit, the trainer whistles, and the whale drops him off at the cement platform, giving him just the right boost to hop out of the water and land seamlessly on his feet.

A second orca enters, and another trainer joins him. He stands on the whale's back, riding him like a surfboard, and then does a series of jumps off his back as the whale keeps moving apace beside him. The whale swims to the side for a big reward of fish, then they start again. This time the trainer pushes on the whale's face, wrapping his legs around the huge neck and balancing each foot on a flipper. Together they rocket up out of the water, the trainer clinging like a gnat on to the giant body. They change to a barrel roll, the trainer walking rapidly in place as the swimming orca rotates under him like a living log in a lumberjack contest. Then the orca rolls to his side, one flipper in the air, and swims slowly around the pool in a display of control and precision of position like a ballet adagio. The trainer rides like a statue atop. A great many fish are consumed as a reward before the acrobatic highlight of the show begins.

In this ballet so far, we have already seen adagio partnering, movement in unison, supported display (like a ballerina who holds an impossible arabesque while pivoted by her partner), and lifts. Importantly, this centerpiece of the show is the only extended period when the trainers and whales are in the water together. The whole structure of the choreography and the theatrical aspects of its staging in terms of timing, visual focus, and sound score underline the concept of loving, equal partners that frames the traditional ballet duet. Just as a ballerina subtly cues her partner when she is ready to balance, the trainers give the cues to the whales through a series of nearly invisible presses, taps, and foot signals which are integrated into the continuous flow of the movement. There is no voiceover during the whale ballet, no verbal interference to distract from the visual display of man (or woman) and animal dancing together. The emphasis on sound rather than words helps construct the abstract qualities of this segment, heightening the artistic discourse. The literalness of movement mimicry is gone, replaced by expressive partnering. The synthesized music is melodious, sustained, full of soaring violin sounds, emotive.

Throughout the show, the musical score is very important, but nowhere more so than during the ballet. I was fortunate to be able to go behind the scenes up into the technical booth during the performance of one of the shows. This is where the sound (and for night shows, lighting) cues are run. The tiny wooden room faces out onto the stadium so that the sound technician can take his cues from the actions in the pool as well as from the trainer's spoken text. Stacked in the production booth are twenty or so music cassettes, labeled "slide out," "overture," "black and white ballet," and "husbandry." The sound engineer works furiously throughout the show, exchanging cassettes, fading in new sounds so that they hit full volume at the height of a jump, and so forth. He operates a twenty-four-track sound board, which means that separate tracks can be punched up to accent specific actions.

During the whale ballet segment, there are twenty-four behaviors that are possible, such as "anthropomorphic," "athletic," "slow activity," and "relational," and each has its own special sound. The tape for the ballet has eight different tracks, and each can be activated separately or in combination with any other. The calliope sound can be used for "fun" endeavors, for example. Within a specified range of ballet behaviors, the trainer decides exactly which actions to do that day and in what order, and the sound technician follows. This sense of improvisatory flow comes through during this segment of the show as the whale and trainer come together and separate and unite again in a series of actions of varying length and energy.

The necessity for structured improvisation is not just to keep the trainers interested. If the whales become accustomed to set routines, which
are then interrupted for any reason, they become belligerent. Also, the
chaining of behaviors seems to have a limit of about four or five different
actions. These require intermittent reinforcement, with a big reward at
the end. The whales will not perform more extensive phrases of movement without reinforcement. These technical and psychological requirements thus have a direct effect on the aesthetic structure of the show.

To the uninitiated viewer, the physical cues given during the whale
ballet section are nearly invisible. They meld seamlessly with the relational flow of action and interaction between the whale and trainer. For
instance, the trainer may seem to be hugging the whale in an affection-
ate or playful embrace, but that hug is really a press on the whale's ros-
trum, which is the cue for "dive down." Similarly, a slap on the water,
which may be read as a playful splash at the whale, is a signal for the
whale to return to the central staging area. Other cues are invisible.
When riding on a whale, the trainer may either fall off or jump off with
a hard press against the whale. The former action cues the whale to continue on to a separate spot, while the latter means "stay with me," so that
the whale swims alongside the trainer at his or her pace. Similarly, finger
taps, which look like the trainer is tickling the whale, signal the animal
to roll over, as do walking feet, when the trainer is standing on the whale
preparing for the barrel-roll maneuver.

Instrumental Movement Transposed into Expressive Behavior

The invisibility of these cues enhances the playful relational discourse
that the ballet segment (and its very name) presents. This is quite different from the more mechanical demonstration of broad cues that is
highlighted in the "meet the audience" part of the show. There the emphasis is on the directive, instrumental aspects of communication. Here
it is on the interspecies relationship. In this way the whale ballet sits at
the heart of the show, representing an idealized relational state between
human and animal, a relationship of equals where the lines of power
and their communication are washed over in the continuous aqueous
flow of partnering. We never see a command given; rather the coordinated behaviors seem to be the result of intuitive understanding. Note
also that the whale rarely jumps alone during this segment, emphasizing equality through shared location in the water—animal and trainer
swimming together, diving together, or the whale supporting the human as they breach the water together.

The ending of the ballet is one of the most memorable movements of the whole show. With an invisible cue, the trainer signals the whale to dive, and holds on, diving with her. Without warning, Shamu bursts out of the water in the center of the pool and rockets toward the sky. Sitting perched atop her nose is a trainer. The whale shoots straight up, thrusting its body nearly thirty feet in the air, the whole mass nearly exposed before the peak of the jump is reached. The trainer jumps off and the whale lands with a huge splash. We are stunned at the acrobatic quality of this feat, its grand scale of body-mass displacement, its suddenness, and the remarkable coordination between animal and trainer that it represents, for the maneuver requires that the animal go straight up, not at a slant or the human would fall off before the peak of the jump. It is the suspended moment at the top of the jump that emphasizes its height, thrust, and momentum as the whale hovers weightlessly for a split second before gravity accelerates the crashing return to the water.

"Get your cameras ready!" shouts the trainer through his portable microphone. And we do, for this moment is the highlight of the show, its punctum, the condensation of power, beauty, control, interspecies communication, and acrobatic aestheticization that the whole show is built upon. This time we are ready when the "spyhop" is repeated.[21] Positioned right in the center of the pool, Shamu explodes twenty feet into the air once again, and this time it is even more spectacular, because the trainer, who had to dive thirty-six feet to the bottom of the pool with Shamu to prepare for the leap, is now *standing upright,* balanced firmly but delicately on the tip of Shamu's nose, the only point of contact being the soles of his feet. Arms outstretched above him, the trainer doesn't just fall off this time, rather he dives off in a graceful arc, pushing off from the nose at the height of the jump, extending it, using it as a springboard for another movement in the ballet. Together, the trainer and Shamu enter the water to thunderous applause.

The first time this action is performed, the element of surprise is fully utilized. The invisibility both of the cue and of the preparation creates a sort of visual silence which heightens the explosion of the action. When it is repeated, the voiceover directs us to the pyrotechnical aspects of the feat. Our attention is drawn to the unison dive thirty feet below the water, before unnoticed, now marked as preparation, and our cameras are positioned to catch the leap at its height. This way we can enjoy the drama and aestheticism of the suspended leap the first time through, and its technical achievement during the repetition. Like a musical encore at a concert, the repeat reactivates the emotional charge that attended the first viewing, but (like an instant video replay) also tech-

32. Elephant House, Budapest Zoo. This is an early example of a "bars and shackles" exhibition style enhanced by orientalized decor. Photo: J. Desmond.

33. Lion House, Lincoln Park Zoo, Chicago, 1994. This display aims for a "naturalistic," not "realistic," effect, exhibiting the tiger against a dioramic background, as in a natural history museum. Bars in the 1912 building have been replaced with less obvious mesh. Photo: J. Desmond.

34. People as seen from the lion's point of view at the Lincoln Park Zoo. Photo: J. Desmond.

35. Viewing "nature" can serve as a means of naturalizing the heterosexual family. Note the copresence of live and stuffed tigers. Lincoln Park Zoo. Photo: J. Desmond.

36. The Lion Grotto, San Diego Zoo. Built in the early 1920s with funds from Ellen Browning Scripps (foreground), this exhibit utilized Carl Hagenbeck's ideas for a moated enclosure rather than barred cages. Copyright 1998 by the Zoological Society of San Diego; used by permission.

37. Great Ape House, Lincoln Park Zoo. In this example of the "scientific" or behaviorist approach, rings and ropes facilitate climbing, but no attempt is made to convince animals or humans that these are trees and vines. Lighted enclosures and darkened viewing stands emphasize the theatrical structure. Photo: J. Desmond.

38. Behind the scenes: an unidentified worker builds a fake tree at the Lincoln Park Zoo. Photo: J. Desmond.

39. Behind the scenes: a snow leopard looks in at her keepers at the Lincoln Park Zoo. Photo: J. Desmond.

40. Gorilla Tropics, San Diego Zoo. Gorillas, at lower left, are immersed in their habitat in this excellent example of the "in-fake-situ" approach. Edible plants, recorded environmental sounds, and a rushing waterfall are all designed to simulate an African rain forest and to encourage "natural behaviors." Copyright 1998 by the Zoological Society of San Diego; used by permission.

41. The Kelp Forest exhibit, Monterey Bay Aquarium. A wet-suited diver feeds the fish. Copyright 1993 by the Monterey Bay Aquarium; used by permission.

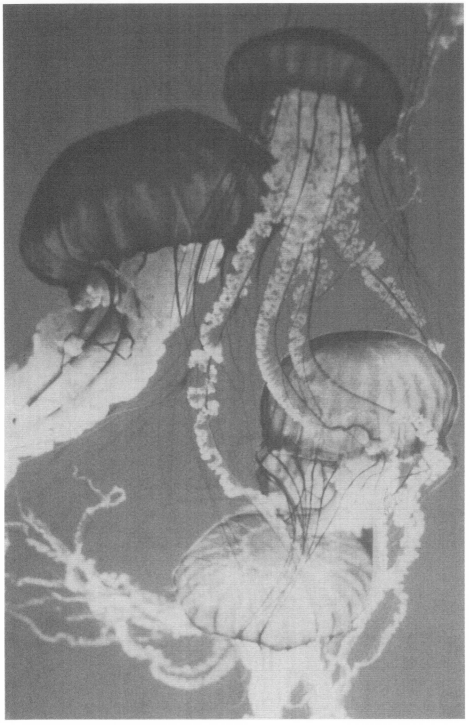

42. "Jellies" on display, Monterey Bay Aquarium. Copyright 1996 by the
Monterey Bay Aquarium; used by permission.

43. Año Nuevo State Park, near Santa Cruz. A park ranger leads visitors to elephant seal breeding grounds. Photo: J. Desmond.

44. Elephant seal bulls, females, and "pups," including "super wieners," rest in groups by the sea as tourists approach at Año Nuevo State Park. Photo: J. Desmond.

45. "Kissing the killer whale" is a fantasy come true through this $3.00 photo-booth creation from Marine World Africa USA, Vallejo, California.

46. A heavily narrated bird show at Marine World Africa invokes Hitchcock's movie, *Psycho*, with a reproduction of the Bates Motel. Photo: J. Desmond.

47. The tiger show at Marine World Africa. Photo: J. Desmond.

48. Animal bodies as tourist souvenirs at the Marine World Africa gift shop. Photo: J. Desmond.

49. A photo spot stages the family in Shamu's embrace at Sea World, San Diego. Photo: J. Desmond.

50. Shamu performs the "spy hop" maneuver with her trainer balanced on her nose at Sea World, Orlando. Photo: Erin Morgan.

51. A perfect interspecies duet: Shamu launches her trainer/partner into the air at Sea World, Orlando. Photo: Erin Morgan.

nologizes it. We are distanced from the act in two senses. First, by the attention to the technology of the action ("How'd they do that!!??") and, second, through the camera eye. In taking the picture we produce a static representation of the consummation of the event, the peak of the jump as the visual, aesthetic, and dramatic apex of the ballet, the punctum of the whole show. We also memorialize our experience for later consumption as a souvenir. We are already remembering the event (as the second leap is a reenactment of the first) as we reproduce it.

The spyhop is the punctum of the show, the moment most prominently featured in the publicity brochure. Our applause indicates a combination of awe at the physical force, mass, and power so dramatically displayed and approval for the human control that has harnessed it into an aesthetic display. Most of all, it acknowledges the visualization of the meeting of the cultural and natural spheres (their division based on essential bodily difference) and the interactive bridging of that divide. Animal and human are one in this moment. Underneath it all, we celebrate diversity, mutual love, understanding, and trust through the union of opposites, here elevated to the status of art. In this liberal, Enlightenment universalism lies the paradox of power and domination invisibly applied to achieve the fiction of a world living together in familial harmony modeled on a Christian notion of Edenic paradise.

The educational segment of the show comes next. It highlights notions of respect for the animals' intelligence and of an exchange between equals. Although it would appear that the people are educating the whales, in fact, the voiceover patter from one of the trainers tells us that it is the humans who have the most to learn. Speaking of Baby Shamu, he notes, "Our knowledge grows with them." This educational segment focuses on new research on the whale's ability to interpret audio systems of communication. The Sea World Research Institute is developing synthesized tones that the orcas can use as signals for specific behaviors. While the trainers stand silent and still, sliding sounds, like a loud pennywhistle, slice through the air. Two orcas swim to the center of the pool and jump on cue. More sounds, and the whales "vocalize" loudly, in "aarh, aarh" sounds. This is mildly interesting, but the tones for the cues are boring after the music of the first half, and the pacing of this section is slow.

Taking away the interaction of the trainers with the whales also lowers the emotional impact. It makes clear how much the power of this show depends upon and features the one-on-one interaction of each whale with each trainer. This is especially true during the whale ballet duets, but also during the other parts of the show. The whales and trainers must commune before each behavior or chain of behaviors. The whales are "stationing," or treading water (in a sense), in front of the trainer, and establishing eye contact while the physical signal is given. In this the trainer resembles a referee on the football field making a call or an airline attendant giving safety instructions. The gestures must be sharp, clean, and emphatic. There is no extraneous movement of any other part of the body to detract from the clarity of the message. This is purposeful, unambiguous communication in the sense of sending and receiving commands for action. This is exactly what is going on during all of the show, but only during the stationing is it so nakedly displayed.

The whales, having watched the message closely, with their heads sticking vertically out of the water, then take off to perform the denoted maneuver when the "go" cue is given. And after each chain of behaviors, they return to the cement platform to their trainer for a reward in the form of rubs, pats, hugs, or fish. In complex chains of behaviors, a whistle toot serves as a "bridge," or intermediate reinforcement, to let the whale know that it has performed correctly and should continue the chain of behaviors. The series of behaviors always begins with whale-trainer communication and ends with whale-trainer communication and reward. No reward is given for incorrect performances, nor is any "punishment" forthcoming. But mistakes are always redone, even during performance, so that the whale knows that mistakes are not tolerated. This is one aspect of the show where the human domination of the whales may peek through.

With four whales and five trainers working at once, this means that the audience attention is constantly drawn from one animal to another as each performs behaviors in turn. While one is being rewarded, the next is receiving instructions and taking off. And sometimes the whales perform together in twos or threes. This gives the show a much more rapid pacing than was possible at Marine World, which had only two whales and two trainers and one announcer. In the fast-paced sections of the show, we see highlight after highlight, and the preparations and denouements go unnoticed. The result is a series of fast, visual edits, each filled with motion within the "frame." This MTV pacing complements the longer, cinematic pans of the adagio sections, where our eyes follow the animal in uninterrupted flow. Decontextualized, without a framing narrative or more loosely conceived stage setting, as was the case at Marine World, the visual emphasis is always on the orca bodies, their abilities, our relationship to them, and the intimate bonds between the trainers and the whales.

At Sea World we applaud the bond between trainer and orca as much as we applaud the acrobatic feats they perform. This is especially true in the human-whale duets, but it is also operative during the rest of the show, underlined by the intensity of looking, hand signals, and physical reward giving that weave each action in the show together. There is something remarkable about the stationing behavior, the huge whale looking expectantly, alertly, directly at one trainer, almost literally nose-to-nose, and made smaller for the moment not only by the subordinated position of being below the trainer but also by the truncated view we have of the animal, only the pointed tip of the head thrust out of the water. This is the same view we have when the animal returns for a reward, during which the physical contact is even closer, with the trainer shoveling in a pile of fish to the open, sharp-toothed jaws, or wrapping his or her arms around the cone-shaped snout. It is in part the lack of these intense interactive communicative behaviors that makes the "educational" segment on communication research so dull. We aren't really there to see the whales respond to cues so much as to see them respond to the trainers.

John Spafford, show supervisor, finds the educational segment of the show too slow, noting that they always lose some of the audience's attention during it. However, it seems that a segment highlighting research is absolutely necessary to the framing of the entire Sea World venture as education. The disjuncture between what the audience is buying as pleasures (spectacle and familial transcendent fantasies) and the rhetorical packaging of those pleasures (as education) is revealed in the audience reactions to this part of the show.

The music cranks up again for the ending portion of the show. The synthesized sounds are bright and bouncy. "It's playtime!" announces one of the trainers. "We're going to get you guys wet!" Requisite education accomplished, it's time for fun again. One of the orcas swims slowly around the edge of the tank wall by the stands. He is turned sideways and makes huge splashes with his tail, purposely pushing the water over the rim and into the stands. Screams of delight move in a wave around the stadium as those seated in the "wet zone" get what they came for. Children and adults shriek and run to save cameras and clothing. Sitting on the far side of the stadium, we know it is coming but can't do anything to escape. The anticipation actually increases the delight. For a moment during that shower we share the orca's world, directly and physically affected by its movements. Like the trainers, but sans wetsuits, we "play" in the water, too, our behavior altered by the whale's.

Shamu dives and does a big tail splash, then zooms up into a huge jump. Four whales are in the pool now, each responding to a different trainer's command. On the far side of the pool, one orca drenches the bleachers with big tail swaggers, while on the opposite side another breaches and lands in a giant splash. The movement and the wild water spraying everywhere mark the power and strength of the animals. All four, including Baby Shamu, return for rewards, then on to the finale. They have saved the biggest booms for last, like a Fourth of July fireworks explosion. Now, the three adult whales swim in unison for the first time during the show. Side by side, like a chorus line, they jump, and then, in unison, they jet into the air and execute perfect back flips, rotating one-and-a-half times in the air like giant pinwheels whipping around. It is stunning to see that much strength and speed harnessed into unison precision and also to see the full bodies spinning in the air, suspended tonnage in motion with the perfect control of gymnasts. Once again we applaud not only the feat itself but also the invisible control and domination that is able to cultivate such "wildness."

Many hugs and tongue pats reward the animals for their efforts, and then two of them swim toward us once again, this time continuing right out onto the platform jutting into the stands. They slide out and arch their heads and tails upward, like a giant smile in black and white, taking a "bow." They have been on the border before, but this time they cross directly into our world, a place where their physical survival is ultimately impossible. The move represents a denaturalization of the natural. The music slows down, becomes mellower, dreamy. "Here she is—Shamu," says the trainer. She picks up a small child who is waiting and places him on the broad back of the whale. "New life is the most precious thing that there is," she reminds us, at once invoking a linkage of Baby Shamu and this child, all children, and the ecological cosmology that opened the program with the Baby Shamu soft-rock song which plays again now.

The audience claps its approval, the child is removed, and the whales can finally relax their bowing pose and slip backward into the water. "We build the future," sings the voice on the Shamu song as the crowd slowly gathers its things to exit. The trainers stand by the edge of the pool, ready to answer questions as we file out. Their suits are still wet from the show, and for the moment, like honorary marine mammals, they mediate between our dry world and Shamu's watery one.

Borders and Border Crossings

These ending moments encapsulate two of the predominant themes of the show: the mobility of or crossing of the species (hence, nature/culture) border, and the emphasis on family as the paradigm for all relationships. The final image of the child safely astride a gigantic bowing Shamu on dry land symbolizes both of these themes at once.

Throughout the show people, animals, and our lines of vision cross the divide between water and land, human and animal realms, and performance space and audience. This crossing is fundamental to the utopian appeal of the show. The architecture of the Shamu stadium, with its tall, clear, acrylic wall surrounding the edge of the pool (like a thrust stage), allows us to see the animals as they glide not only on the surface of the water but also for a portion of the way under the water as well, a position we could never take viewing these animals in the wild. We also have privileged views during the spectacular leaping segments, where an unimpeded view of the complete whale body is afforded at the moment of suspension in the air. Rarely do leaps in the wild exhibit such verticality. The completely visible whale body is also reproduced in the stuffed Shamu souvenirs, which allow us to hold the whale in our arms or gaze at the whole body as it might be seen out of the water. Both such simulacra and the show's leaping choreography extract the whale body from its natural watery environment.

There are other moments, too, during the show that emphasize these border crossings. Signals and perceptions can cross the border, as they do in the audience-participation segments. People can cross the border by slipping into the sea, as the trainers do during the whale ballet. And whales can move into our environment, as they do metaphorically during the "get the audience wet" segment, which confuses the boundary between the land and sea, wet and dry, and as they do literally in the slide-out maneuver at the end of the show. In all these ways both the trainers (as our surrogates) and the whales become hybrids, mediating between the two worlds of water and land. In these border crossings the amphitheater is constructed as a frontier of exchange.

But ultimately this is not a true exchange, although it is presented as such. The whales are literally imported into our world, placed in a huge (beautiful) container, completely out-of-situ. The conditions of possibility for the show are that wild whales are captured, transported thousands of miles, confined, trained, and forced to work for a living. They make money for the Busch corporation. To mask this reality, they are presented as willing partners, as part of our family, as equals from whom we have so much to learn, and their display is coded as art, as education, and as conservation.

Ironically, this emphasis on conservation has backfired. Some animal rights groups protest against the capture, training, and display of animals for profit. Theme parks like Sea World have had to turn increasingly to captive breeding programs so they can reproduce the raw material, that is, whale bodies, from which their shows are built. The emphasis on breeding as a sure sign of animal happiness, of the correct reproduction of the natural conditions of life so that animals will breed in captivity, covers over the monetary necessity of such breeding programs. The celebration of Baby Shamu in this show and of the other calves born at Sea World since 1985 presents breeding as a natural family discourse, or a discourse of naturalized familiality, and structures the show around this baldest of financial necessities while completely hiding them.

This discourse of the familial is also carried out in the park's exhibits through animal-human analogs. A new promotion during the summer of 1991, for instance, gave children special maps to travel the park in search of all sorts of animal babies. The unstated assumption, of course, is that the animal offspring and human children have much in common. This notion of similarity is emphasized throughout the show at the bodily level as well when mimicry posits animal body parts as parallel to human ones, as flippers wave and whale "faces" nod yes or no.

The oscillation between physical and social similarity and difference can be traced right through the formulaic construction of the show. Although the shows vary from day to day, each follows a specific formula in the ordering of its ingredients. In these generic segments we can see alternating conceptions of the whales as stand-ins for wild nature and whales as part of the human family. The same sequence is followed for the killer whale show and for the dolphin show. The formula consists of six segments: (1) introduction, (2) meet an audience member, (3) whale ballet, (4) educational segment, (5) training segment, and (6) high-energy ending segment, as I have described above.

First we see the whales without verbal framing (with the exception of the "all friends in the sea" overture). Our visual perception of them, their size and speed, is emphasized. Then these behemoths are named, personalized (in the introduction phase). Next, they are shown as obedient and safe, and possibly humorous (meet the audience). They are idealized as equal partners during the ballet, where their size and strength are harnessed into a duet with the trainer, culminating in the spyhop, in which they perform together the most spectacular move of the day. The education segment emphasizes their cognitive abilities rather than their expressive or physical ones. But size and power take over again in playtime, where the whales splash us with gigantic sweeps of their tails. And, finally, acrobatic ability, trainability, cooperativeness, precision, and body mass are all emphasized together in the huge unison somersaults at the end.

The "bodyness" of the orcas is at times highlighted, at times down-played, but ultimately underwritten by the intelligence and trainability of these animals. Our consumption of radical bodily difference, played upon in the opening speed runs, without narration, and highlighted throughout the show, is ultimately a safe consumption tempered by similarity. Their bodies may be different, indeed must be spectacularly different, as their feats demonstrate. But they still hunger for hugs as well as fish, for fun as well as food, and for companionship rather than freedom, or so it seems.

Like huge pets, they embody the difference between human and other, between wild and tame, and between danger and safety. But ulti-mately, their mental capacity, their mammalness, and their tractability render their difference easily consumable. The orca "mind" makes the orca "body" safe and knowable. The mind/body binary that underlies the culture/nature division is overcome again in this framing as the whales are given the attributes of reason and emotion. An orca, the most powerful predator in the ocean, is simultaneously the cute and cuddly Shamu. The simultaneity is what sells so well at Sea World because it demonstrates the drawing of borders and their transcendence at the same time. This simultaneity operates through a discourse of natural behaviors and their extensions.

Training, Naturalism, and Performance

In the earlier discussion of the bird, tiger, and whale shows at Marine World Africa, I began to tease apart the web of assumptions that links notions of the natural and its presentation, prohibition, or "improve-ment" in the context of a performance. "Bad" natural behaviors, like fighting, are prohibited. Even "good" or desirable natural behaviors, like breeding, are tightly controlled. "Natural" can refer to behaviors occurring in a natural versus man-made setting, that is, in the wild, or it can refer to behaviors occurring in man-made settings but without in-struction from humans, such as leaping, swimming, and so on. The term is also used to refer to behaviors that are directly contradictory to "instinct" but which still involve an action that occurs in the wild. For example, the tiger can be taught to leap (natural) through a burning ring of fire (the instinct would be to move away from fire, not toward it).

Using this range of conceptual flexibility, which emerges in the shows' discourse of natural behavior, it is difficult to think of anything that an animal could possibly do that could *not* in some sense be con-sidered, and presented as, natural. If Shamu could be taught to speak English, that would be unnatural, since orcas don't speak English to one

another, but even that could be framed as an extension of a natural vocalizing ability, an inborn ability that would be necessary for any sound
making at all.

The natural is both cultivated and disciplined in the training process.
Animals are trained through operant conditioning. Behaviors are isolated, shaped, and linked into sequences with rewards, caresses or food,
given for proper performance. Punishment for incorrect behavior or for
noncooperation is the withdrawal of the trainer from the interaction.
Shaping, as the word implies, involves the gradual refinement of a behavior, like developing height in a jump or making the pathway of a
body rotation in the air perfectly round. For example, teaching an animal to jump over a rope suspended above the water requires first training it to swim over, not under, the rope in the pool, then over the rope
floating on the water's surface, then to jump over the rope as it is gradually raised higher and higher into the air.

The notion of extending natural behaviors codes several processes in
constructing a performative style. First, it involves performing something on cue and for the purpose of receiving a reward rather than for
any other instrumental purpose, such as hunting. Second, it takes a
generic activity, like breaching or flipping in the air, and makes it more
aesthetically pleasing and links it in a series. This can be done by codifying a specific pathway through space (a perfect circle in the air rather
than an oblong one, or a repeating sequence of leaps done in a certain
part of the pool), and/or by setting a timing that is in unison with the
movements of another animal or with a human. Space and time are regulated and codified with respect to the animal's body, so that its usage of
space and time is not only correct but predictable. Movement is disciplined, as is nature.

It is not so much an *extension* of behaviors that is going on as it is the
choreographing of complex and precisely articulated movements
which the animal is *capable* of performing because the biomechanics of
the movements are within the realm of possibility for that body. The
movements of a highly skilled ballet dancer, for example, could be said
to be based on the natural movements of the human skeleton—walking,
jumping, and extending limbs. But few people would consider the 180-
degree leg split of a Balanchine dancer's arabesque to be natural. Consider that a whale rolls over in the water. This movement then becomes
choreographed so that its meaning is entirely rewritten. The rolling is repeated in a sequence in the whale ballet, with the trainer riding the spi-
raling whale around the pool like a spinning log. The biomechanics of
the rolling may be roughly the same, although repeated and performed

at a regularized pace. But the meaning of the roll in the Shamu stadium, with a trainer running on top, bears no relation to the meaning of the roll in the open sea. "Extension" is as much a reference to the ideological content of the act as it is to any notion of natural behavior.

Within the industry, however, the rationale for new behaviors is presented not only in terms of developing new performance material for the shows but also in terms of satisfying the whales' psychological needs for stimulation. The familial discourse emerges here, too, with the whales positioned as children and the trainers as parents or teachers. For instance, Sea World's show supervisor, John Spafford, notes that new behaviors sometimes emerge from "play sessions" between the trainer and a whale. He likens trainers' work to that of play school teachers who must always offer a variety of activities and diversions for children with short attention spans and a lot of energy. Both he and Nancy Hotchiss, educational director of the AAZPA, stressed the animals' need for a complex and stimulating environment, which includes learning extended natural behaviors. So within the marine mammal industry, this cultivation and discipline is posed as a benefit for the whales. It may or may not be so, but the familial discourse of playful stimulation smooths over the fact that ultimately the extending of behaviors is done to benefit Sea World, both by providing new performance material and by cultivating whale tractability.

What the current shows' emphasis on natural abilities does seem to refer to is, in fact, a move away from presenting the animals as characters in a narrative. Such narrative/non-narrative configurations are rarely absolute, however. We saw that, even in the non-narrative tiger show at Marine World Africa, "Lucy" was the star character. Also, during the bird show, the flying behaviors were framed within a loose narrative, which was left behind at specific moments, especially at the end of the show, when a plea was made to the audience to take an active part in the environmental movement and in the protection of endangered species.

In the rhetorical construction of most shows, the emphasis on natural abilities now has a corollary emphasis on the display of the natural body. The whales, birds, tigers, and dolphins are all shown unadorned, whether they are framed in loose narratives or tight narratives or as personalities (like Shamu, Namu, and Baby Shamu). But at least in one instance, in the early shows developed by Karen Pryor at Sea Life Park in Honolulu, one of the star porpoises appeared in costume. "Lei," wore a flower lei around her "neck" as she did the "hula," a wiggling tail walk with a group of other hula-ing porpoises.[22]

Even without the aid of costumes, a heavily narrativized format can cloak the natural body in an overlay of meaning that redefines the parts of the body, their movements, and its meaning in the same ways a costume can direct our perception of a human actor's body. The most obvious example of this is with the anthropomorphized behaviors that are named as such, like moving a flipper back and forth upon the command to "wave good-bye."[23] For example, at Sea World the sea lions "clap" for their own excellent performances during the "Pirates of Pinniped" show by repeatedly placing front flippers together. Here the joke effect is doubled by having them "clap" and by having them clap for their own behavior, self-congratulatorily.

Another category of behaviors in the whale show consists of the animals' mimicking human behavior in a sort of follow-the-leader style. For example, during the ballet duet, the trainer might duck down, shooting her legs straight up in the air and wiggle them. The whale will imitate by diving and waving his or her tail back and forth above the water, too. In these mimicking actions the analogous nature of the bodies is highlighted; head, "arms," middle body, and "legs" can function in similar ways.

But ultimately the meaning of the action ("look, he's waving to us") and its fascination for the audience depend on the dissimilarity between the animal and ourselves. With apes, this mimicry can extend farther (as the appearance of the orangutan Jolyn in red satin running shorts during the "Magic of Animals" show at Marine World Africa reminds us). But with the whales, part of the pleasure of this type of activity is, I think, generated precisely by the acknowledgment of the difference between the whales and ourselves, in terms of body construction and dimension, and the simultaneous closing of that gap momentarily through the performance of anthropomorphically framed behaviors. The whale doesn't have legs, but uses its tail as if it were legs. The as-if of the construction is the linkage that gives the action its specific intelligibility within the show and also produces the specific pleasure, the laugh of recognition for example, that the action evokes. The as-if-ness also puts the actions into a performance category that separates natural behavior from its extensions, in this case an extension of the meaning of the behavior.

This is balanced by an opposing emphasis on the whales' nonanthropomorphic behaviors, the spectacular display of their strength and mass, which far exceed our own yet which appear harnessed to our uses (pleasure) by their apparently willing cooperation as the performers. However, there have been telling moments of disruption in this willing-partner discourse. A few years ago a couple of bad accidents tarnished Sea World's image, endangered its staff and animals, and caused a re-vamping of training style and attitude at Sea World.

In 1988, serious injuries resulted when whales turned on two train-ers, and in the following year two performing whales collided and began fighting.[24] One bled to death after the fight.[25] The incidents received not only regional but national press attention as well. Since then, Spafford notes, the trainers work with more restrictive rules for their in-teractions with the animals. The trainers, he asserts, had gone too far: "We thought they [the whales] loved us. We believed our own P.R." It seems the trainers, too, were beginning to think of the whales as cute, lovable people in whale suits. But the whales can become aggressive when they don't get what they want or expect or become confused. Now the operant-conditioning training proceeds in more clearly defined steps. Safety commands take precedence over all others. For instance, the signal to return to the central stage area and station, or hover in place, is always heavily rewarded. This way the whales can be recalled if their behavior in the pool grows threatening. Professionals now feel that the public does not have adequate respect for the animal-ness of the whales, as perhaps the trainers did not a few years ago. Apparently, the culturalization of nature had gone too far and threatens the very dialec-tic on which the marine mammal industry is based.

These two incidents blow the willing partner and familial discourses wide open and reveal the hierarchies of force and domination that such ideologies naturalize. The whales exhibited natural behavior in fighting after an accidental collision, which bore hallmarks of aggression. How-ever, this was forbidden natural behavior, as it threatened the economic stability of the park. The investment in the two animals was huge, as was their earning power. The aggression also contravened the familial discourse of peaceful unity among animals and particularly between humans and animals.

When directed against the trainer, this aggression exposed the crux of the shows—absolute obedience to trainer commands presented as pleasurable for the whales. This loss of control was obscene, as obscene as the sight of pristine azure pools polluted with blood. The problematic of the natural as that which is ultimately subordinate to human cultural practice became insupportable in those moments. They threatened the stability of the Sea World conglomerate built on such a problematic, and required a great deal of "spin control" from the public relations office, which isolated these events as accidents not symptoms.

Ultimately this subtext of danger is necessary to the successful functioning of Sea World, but it must not be allowed to erupt into visibility. Awesome strength, power, and mass must be coded as acrobatic ability, kinesthetic thrills, or grace and beauty, then tempered with "intelligence," and redirected through a relational discourse of emotional attachment to the trainers. The choreography constructs and presents this ideological process, staging bodily actions as symbolic practice. Combining awe, potential terror, beauty, grace, and power with massive scale, Sea World packages a controllable sublime.

Past and Future: Staging the Natural

The history of the shows preceding "Baby Shamu Celebration" and the plans for future shows all reveal varying strategies for staging particular relationships between the natural and the cultural. In each case, various performative configurations construct the dialectic slightly differently, but the components remain the same. Notions of freedom and wildness must be retained, while the fact of the imprisonment of the whales must be papered over. Transferring attention to the human-animal relationship is the primary way of accomplishing this. Early shows relied heavily on comedy and anthropomorphism to frame this relationship, and plans for future shows indicate a move toward increasingly sophisticated visual technology to construct this bond. A concomitant shift from narrative to spectacle, from the pleasures of comedy to the pleasures of the sublime, mark the history of the shows.

The American public's exposure to cetaceans began over a century ago. One of the first displays in North America was in the Boston Aquarial Gardens in the early 1860s, when a white whale (beluga) and a porpoise were exhibited.[26] Dolphin training began at Marine Life Studios in Florida in the 1930s. It was followed by the opening of Marineland in California and the Seaquarium in Florida. These were commercial oceanariums which also combined some animal behavior research with their displays and shows. In the early 1960s the training and display of marine mammals took a significant step forward with the opening of parks such as Sea World in San Diego, and Sea Life Park outside Honolulu. The latter is where Karen Pryor pioneered the performance-training techniques that still form the basis of the training today.[27] The popularity of the 1960s television show *Flipper,* featuring a dolphin's relationship with a human family, whom he saved from disaster every week, added to the public affection for marine mammals during this time.[28] Whereas the other oceanariums featured performing porpoises (also referred to interchangeably as dolphins), Sea World was the first marine park to feature killer whales, starting with the Shamu show in

1968.[29] The trend has spread rapidly. Killer whales are now on display at marine zoological parks in Japan, China, Australia, South America, Canada, and Europe, as well as the United States.[30]

What Flipper and the dolphin shows did for porpoises—garnering public interest and affection for the animals that has helped win support for protective legislation (such as tuna fishing net requirements)— Shamu has done for whales. The shows have increased public awareness of whales but have also ultimately contributed to their own destabilization by building affection for the animals and providing fuel for animal rights activists, who now protest performing animal parks.[31] John Spafford estimates that half of the park staff's energy is now devoted to countering the activists' protests and negative publicity.

Narrative and Earlier Shamu Shows

The first killer whale show at Sea World San Diego was called "Doctor Doolittle." Opening in 1968, it was based on the premise of an encounter between a hapless human and a patient, all-enduring whale. Like a bungling circus clown, the trainer as Doctor Doolittle stupidly sticks his head into the jaws of this man-eating beast, dares to ride him, and so forth. Shamu plays the straight man in this comedy. The potential for danger is there, but Shamu's positive personality overcomes it.

In the early 1970s a new show, "Shamu Runs for Mayor," cast Shamu in the role of the comedian and the trainer in the role of the straight man. San Diego was in the midst of a mayoral election, and the timely show rests on the implausible plot of running Shamu for mayor. Shamu does all the things good politicians do to get elected like tossing his hat into the ring (literally) and kissing babies. The trainer plays the protagonist, the antagonist is drawn from the audience, and Shamu rights the world. Meanwhile, the trainer does death-defying tricks with the whale, but the charge of danger is negated by the comedic casting of Shamu as the anthropomorphized mayor.

In 1977 a shift in the shows takes place. The show remains heavily narrativized, but the emphasis is now on changing the public perception of killer whales. In "Shamu Goes to College," Shamu plays himself (and is so credited when the parts and actors are acknowledged in a voiceover at the end of the show).[32] Shamu is no longer presented as dangerous, or as a mindless fish, or merely as a character played for laughs. Instead he is presented as a boy's best friend, intelligent, capable, fun, and worthy of respect.

This twenty-minute show was staged in one of the older, smaller pools, with a complete stage set featuring a white clapboard house and a backdrop of college buildings for Ocean University. It involved four human characters and one volunteer from the audience. The proportion of "educational" to "story line" writing in this performance is completely different than in the current shows, which eschew story line and pack in the information.

The plot is as follows. Davy Jones and Shamu have applied to Ocean University to be part of an innovative program in interspecies oceanography. They are accepted, but, when they arrive at the school, Dean Goodfellow, in academic gown, tells them that the board of trustees has had second thoughts about the safety of admitting killer whales to the college. Bigmouth Joe College makes fun of Shamu, but bright-eyed Davy, the ingenu, shows him and the dean how wonderful, smart, and cooperative killer whales are. Eventually the dean relents, Davy and Joe become friends, and Davy and Shamu enroll in Ocean University. The show ends with Davy and Shamu promenading around the tank to the strains of the college song.

Shamu functions as a character in the story, with "lines" that he speaks by vocalizing on cue or performing gestures. For instance, Shamu shakes his head yes when Davy asks him: "You wouldn't do anything funny to Joe, would you?" And there are actions performed in relation to the other actors that demonstrate character relationships. Personified as a savvy practical joker, Shamu takes off with the hapless Joe lying on top of the whale's back, clutching the vinyl bridle in one hand, and wrapping his legs around the vertical dorsal fin. Shamu skims around the tank at top speed, scalloping into and out of the water like a rollercoaster ride. Joe hangs on and waves, chagrined, with each airborne leap, like a novice riding a bucking bronco.

There is also a type of verbal humor and of physical comedy that is no longer seen in today's shows, because it positions the whale as the butt of the joke. For example, Joe calls Shamu "you big guppy." And, as Davy and Shamu set off for college, Davy sits on top of the whale, which swims on his back, belly to the sky, while Davy "rows" him like a boat, using his two side flippers as oars. This type of demotion of whale to object, a staple of Chaplinesque physical comedy, where an object is transformed through the way it is used, is not seen in the later shows. The humor here is at the whale's expense, although it is also dependent on his cooperation and scripted role as "friend."

While for most of the narrative, Shamu's "wildness" is retained within its framework, there is one point at the end where he breaks free and whale-as-character is replaced by whale-as-physical-essence. "He'll dive deep into his books, just as he dives thirty-two feet down for this jump," runs the script. Shamu explodes from the water just as the music reaches its highest notes. His nose touches a target suspended twenty feet in the air. "THIS IS SHAMU!!" At this moment, Shamu is barely contained by the narrative. The physicality of the spectacular maneuver, and its non-human-ness, exceed the boundaries of the play. Neither can this leap be read as an expression of joy or exuberance, the way some of the earlier leaps were narrativized. (Could anyone be so overjoyed at the thought of diving into the books?) Here is the excess of spectacle, the spectacle which will dominate in the later shows, when the frame of education replaces the narrative frame that created the character of Shamu in these early shows.

But the power of the last jump is tempered by the final action of the show. Shamu returns to the school, and Davy hops on. As the Ocean University song plays, Davy and Shamu coast serenely around the tank. Davy stands on Shamu's back, waving expansively, like a beauty queen on a parade float. Shamu is once again tamed and contained, dominated while being celebrated.

Even with its differences from the current shows, it is still easy to see the beginnings of the dominant frames that structure "Baby Shamu Celebration." There is the willing partner discourse, the trope of family, the emphasis on cross-species bonding and mutuality, and a utopian yearning for a world where the divide between land and sea, culture and nature, is easily crossed, at least by the whales, which come into our world to study theirs at Ocean University. The place of spectacle is also beginning to be highlighted, as improved training methods for the whales produce ever-more stunning actions.

In the shows that have followed, Shamu is increasingly acknowledged as a killer whale rather than as a character, but the emphasis on the relationship between human and animal continues to be foregrounded. The next show, "This Is Shamu," in the early 1980s, is described by Spafford as "a crazy mishmash of previous shows, including singers and dancers." The shift away from narrative and toward spectacle seems to be under way, but has not yet been yoked with the conservation/education theme. The variety show format persists to some extent in the prescribed segments that structure the shows now. It was in these early 1980s shows that the whale ballet segment was first introduced and the current forms of the shows began to take shape, leading to the "New Friends" and then "Baby Shamu Celebration" shows.

The current show evidences the shift to a combined format of education and spectacle, with the former underwriting the latter as something more than "mere entertainment" and thereby justifying the captivity of the whales and their training.[33] The potentially uninteresting increase in information reportage ("education") has been balanced by increasing spectacle. The actions in the show have become more acrobatic, more complex, and involve longer chains of behavior. Where Shamu was once a character in a play, he/she is now an athlete, even an artist, as well as an inter-species interlocutor.

The shift from a narrative, anthropomorphizing formula to an education/spectacle is influenced by animal rights activists, among other things. But, interestingly, this shift applies only to the whales and dolphins. At Sea World, the sea lion, walrus, and sea otter show called "The Pirates of Pinniped" is fully narrativized, with the animals playing the parts of sailors and pirates along with two human performers who also play characters.[34] It follows the format of a musical, with moments of narratively framed spectacle (a sailor's test for entrance into the pirates, for instance, consists of a series of ball-retrieving maneuvers for one of the sea lions), interspersed with narrative development in the plot.[35] This seems to reflect an interesting hierarchy in the public importance and respect accorded these categories of marine mammals, which are clearly hierarchized by size and perceived intelligence.

The drive to produce new and ever-more spectacular shows by developing new animal behaviors has apparently approached its limit. "Baby Shamu Celebration" is representative of what has been going on for the last decade or so. Although during this time show designers have used different costumes and different sets, the shows all use the same building blocks of animal activity as safely as they can. With the current emphasis on grand spectacle, as opposed to the earlier narrative shows, show supervisor Spafford personally feels that they are now "pressing the envelope" in terms of the optimal capabilities of the animals and the safety of the humans. Nonetheless, there is constant pressure to come up with new behaviors and activities. (The Association of Marine Mammal Trainers, for example, has a yearly contest for the best new behavior.) But just how much farther can they go?

The Look of the Future: Technology, Vision, Bodies

The move in the future will be not toward the development of ever more and more spectacular behaviors but, rather, toward a more visually complex presentation of what there already is. New shows using the Sony Jumbotron video projection screen represent this philosophy. This is not so much a philosophy about animals as about marketing. Spafford remarked that the show needs a "new hook" to continue bringing in and even increasing its audience. Since the limit has just about been reached in terms of what they can train the whales to do safely, it is the packaging of those behaviors and of the animals themselves that is open to revision.[36] This increased technological mediation will probably increase the tension between our perception of the whales as the embodiment of physical difference and of the abstraction and emblematization of that difference into graphic or schematic form.

In the production booth, I watched a whole team of technical experts preparing a new show, rehearsing camera angles and cuts for the thirty-foot-high Sony Jumbotron video screen. Standing at the back center of the pool by the staging area, it will show images from several different cameras. A director will select the images live during the show, just as major sports events are called live for television broadcast. Cameras in the stadium will be able to zoom in on trainers for close-ups, or on audience members, showing their individual reactions, especially during the splashing sequences.

The video supplies the illusion that we get closer to the animals and the action while at the same time presenting the movements in a more complexly mediated, fragmented, and rearranged version that rearticulates "real" relations of physical scale and temporal sequence. The instant replays, for instance, show isolated images larger than life. Only the punctum of a sequence is shown, fetishizing extreme moments of exertion. In the "Baby Shamu Celebration" show, the instructions to the audience to photograph the spyhop when it is repeated is a sort of manual version of this repetitive, technological fetishization.

Even as the spectacle element is heightened further by video enhancement, the ultimate draw of Sea World remains the physical presence of Shamu. Her real body is essential to our perception of scale, mass, power, and danger that produce the consumable sublime. It is the truth guarantor that the control of the power that we are seeing is really there, dependent on unique interactions between specific humans and specific whales. The surrogacy of our own interaction with the natural through Shamu's interactions with trainers and audience volunteers is also an essential part of this sublime. It provides the transcendent mechanism with a vigor that contemplation of a noninteractive visual representation cannot match. The statues of Shamu, the myriad of photographs of Shamu on publicity materials, and the stuffed Shamu toys in the souvenir shops cannot substitute for the capacity of the living body to essentialize the concept of nature as a living force. All of these simulacra elaborate the concept of Shamu, but they are ultimately dependent on the anchorage of that concept in the physical existence of the killer whales, one of which must be personified as Shamu.

Without the audience's encounter with the living Shamu, without its visual perception and investigation of that body, without the physical and temporal coexistence of the audience and the whale, the entire Sea World structure as it now exists would collapse of its own conceptual weight.[37] While the shows may ultimately contain the power of the whale, they cannot continue without her physical presence. Whatever meanings are attached to the display of such presence, the living evidence of such bodily difference as a synecdoche of the natural, and not merely its visual or rhetorical representation, is absolutely necessary.

Family, Discourse, Americanism

The combined emphasis on whale bodies and family discourse yields an intriguing subdiscourse of gender. In the early shows "Shamu Goes to College" and "Shamu Runs for Mayor," Shamu is referred to as "he." In the "Baby Shamu Celebration" that I saw, Shamu is referred to as "she," as is Baby Shamu. What is most important in all of this is not the pronominal designation of the whale, but the fact that, in the current shows at least, the use of a gendered pronoun is exaggeratedly avoided. Shamu is almost always referred to as "Shamu." This was the case during the show, in the souvenir videos, and on several Sea World documentaries that appeared on television within the last few years. It is true for all of the publicity releases and promotional material for the shows.

On the surface, this would seem to facilitate the substitution of one Shamu for another as time passes and a new whale is needed. But such a pronominal avoidance accomplishes much more than that. Obviously, the whales can't be referred to as "it," because although that would avoid the issue of the biological sex of the animal, it would undercut the all-important personification. We've also seen that a lack of sexual dimorphism is no impediment to the imposition of a sex-linked gendered discourse, as was the case at the Monterey Bay Aquarium.[38] The avoidance of gendered reference is not for any practical reasons, but for ideological ones.

The competing conceptions of the natural and the cultural as wild and tame, and their transcendent unity in the figure of Shamu, is the key to this rhetorical practice. The traits of power, size, strength which encode the natural as a force are still associated with males in our culture. Personableness, affection, huggability, playfulness, grace, and beauty are still associated with females. Yet Shamu must embody all of these traits. Above all, the whale must not exhibit aggression, the most strongly sex-linked trait of all. Shamu must not be too male, or the willing partner discourse is disrupted. On the other hand, she/he must not be too feminized through cute and cuddly behaviors, or the awe-inspiring components will be lost. The choreographic demonstration of all these properties together produces the culturalization of the natural and the utopian fantasy of crossing the border between the two. The lack of sexual dimorphism in whales facilitates this performative hermaphroditism.

A similar degendering happens with the trainers. Although half are women and half men, all participate equally in the shows; there is no gender-linked apportionment of behaviors. Wetsuits do reveal bodily shape, and gender is never in question, but at the same time the unisex mode of dress and behavior tends to neutralize the trainers into "human" surrogates for ourselves, male or female, in the audience.[39] This transposition of the individual (male or female) into the supraindividual symbol of "human" is part of the equation of animal plus human united equals utopian family.[40]

However, the family trope, no matter how abstracted and utopianized, contains within it the social matrix of heterosexuality. It is in fact one of the constituent institutions of heterosexuality. But in one important sense I believe this matrix is transcended. For the individual spectator, the de-genderedness of the trainers and the bi-gendered attributes of Shamu may offer a freeing mobility of spectator identification that crosses gender lines and produces through that freedom a sense of the utopian.[41] This process parallels the border crossing of the nature/culture binary. The crossing is facilitated by a constitution of the border as unstable, ever shifting as the various meanings of "the natural" as including or excluding humans are invoked.

In another sense, though, the imposition of the family discourse, especially with the emphasis on babies (children being the defining factor of families, which reproduce the social structure as they reproduce themselves), results in a liberal, not radical, vision of utopia. The songs that accompany the show are revealing. For instance, the 1989 "New Friends" show theme song has these lyrics: "Seen with children's eyes, there are miracles revealed, fantasies so real for us to see, forever free . . . when we take the time [to look]." Children represent idealized, uncorrupted viewers, closer to nature, willing to accept the reality of fantasies. The voiceover at the end of the show connects the concept of family with history. The announcer says: "The Sea World Experience allows us to remember the past, treasure the present, and dream of the future. . . ." The past presumably was an Edenic one where humans and animals lived in harmony, the present is the time where at Sea World we can learn to recapture that lost past, and the future, which belongs to our children, represents an extension of that idealized state of harmony beyond the borders of Sea World into the culture at large.[42]

The widest implications of this "nostalgic" future are revealed in the words of the whale ballet song, used in both the "New Friends" and "Baby Shamu Celebration" shows. The gentle but soaring female voice sings: "Black and white, simple and bright, the colors of the friends of ours against the deep blue sea . . . black and white is the power, strength, and might, the never ending mystery. . . . " The unity of opposites is captured in the phrase "black and white," and linked to the whale's body, which is so different from ours yet made similar through mimicry. Our "friends" can be expanded further still to imply a unity of social opposites, an overcoming of racial and cultural differences ("black and white . . . the colors of . . . friends"). At Sea World, notes Davis, "difference is carefully arranged—against a field of white, so to speak—so that, unthreatening, it can be incorporated."[43] This is a utopian vision of America as one family, united in "power, strength, and might," and devoted to a political model of international parenthood, the United States itself as a benevolent patriarch.

The celebration of the natural that Sea World sells is simultaneously a celebration of certain visions of the cultural and the fantasies that they encapsulate. This vision is ultimately a liberal one, which through its emphasis on the heterosexual family, individuation, and unproblematic "harmony" and universalism, serves conservative political interests. It is consonant with the beliefs and desires of both the corporate backers of Sea World and the predominantly white middle-and upper-middle-class consumers who form its audience base. The culturalization of nature (its simultaneous production as that which is beyond/outside culture and as a model of social organization—of culture—itself) naturalizes this vision of a world in harmony, attaching it to the authenticating physicality of Shamu, which represents both the force of nature and its transcendence through personification. The resulting vision of an Edenic world community, simultaneously nostalgic and utopianly futuristic, depends, just as the Shamu show does, on making invisible the lines of force that produce it as natural.

Bodies and Tourism

All that kissing at Germaine's Luau and my great desire to kiss the killer whale at Marine World Africa (foiled by the lucky little kid who got to do so) are related. The parallel structure of the shows is telling: both involve a kissing of "strangers," a crossing of borders, and moments of literal, physical contact. Herein lies the heart of these industries of cultural tourism and animal tourism: each represents a vision of a world in harmony, a vision that is at once nostalgic, utopian, and futuristic—a vision of Edenic pasts as prototypical futures. To erect this vision, each industry rests on the physical display of bodies perceived as fundamentally, radically, different from those of the majority of the audience who pays to see them.

The live presence of the performers is crucial to this economy of pleasure, for it provides the guarantee of authenticity on which such commodification rests. This physical foundationalism, the implicit framing of the body as that which is "really real," is the shared heart of these epistemologies of difference, whether they be dubbed "culture" or "nature." In this concluding chapter, I want to consider further what is really at stake in these industries and speculate on what future alternatives might look like.

In this book, I have placed bodies and physicality at the center of tourism research. Through detailed readings of zoo exhibits, of early mainland hula shows, the Shamu show, Germaine's Luau, the Monterey Bay Aquarium kelp forest, and so on, I have attempted to dissect the deployment of these assumptions about a more natural world and to demonstrate how, at the most concrete levels of staging, choreography, aquarium design, and so forth, such assumptions signify utopian

251

realms outside the everyday lives of the white U.S. middle-class consumers who form the base for these industries.

I have proposed that in both cultural and animal tourism, bodies legitimate, specify, present, and represent that which is being displayed (Hawaiian culture, animal life), and they do so through explicit or implicit discourses of naturalism. Thus, animals must be presented as exhibiting natural behaviors even when performing circus acts like jumping through a ring of fire or dancing with a human partner in a watery pas de deux. On the human side, complexities of genealogical backgrounds, of shifting historical ideals of beauty (of the hapa-haole hula girl, for example) and of contemporary political debate (like sovereignty issues) must all be banished from the presentation of "heritage" in paradise.[1] The seeming prediscursive qualities of physical presence enable these maskings, declaring them irrelevant to the "facticity" of naturalized bodies.

This does not imply that the meanings attached to various bodies are historically unchanging. As Donna Haraway reminds us, "Bodies as objects of knowledge are material-semiotic generative nodes. Their boundaries materialize in social interaction [and] are drawn by mapping practices; 'objects' do not pre- exist as such. . . . What boundaries provisionally contain remains generative, productive of meanings and bodies."[2] While poststructuralism has usefully disseminated this understanding that "objects" do not exist as such before their evocation in discourse, my point here, of course, has been that they often function epistemologically as if they do and in doing so become vehicles for certain ideological formulations.

PLACING THE BODY CENTER STAGE

To understand better how these shows work, I have tried to extend the concept of "the tourist gaze" to include other senses of perception, especially to propose a more fully developed kinesthetic analysis both of the performers and of the audiences. With regard to the performers, this emphasis on embodied action has translated into an analysis of the relationship between bodily display and bodily actions (who does what, how, with whom, and why). The analysis of the interspecies duet in the Shamu whale ballet exemplifies this approach.

The audience too has a wider kinesthetic experience than the concept of the gaze would imply. They are not only static viewers; they are literal and metaphoric actants in these tourist consumptions. Tourist advertisements acknowledge and invite this self-conception. For example, a colorful brochure for the Waimea Falls Park in Hawai'i pictures active tourists involved in a number of activities. Verbs in big print invite us to "touch," "explore," "hold," "hear," "tour," "learn," "see," "sway," "play," "meet," and "wander."[3] In previous chapters, I have noted the kisses, the tourist hula lesson, the splash zone at Sea World, the sneaking up on massive elephant seals, craning our necks to get the best view at the San Diego Zoo's Gorilla Tropics exhibit, shifting our eyes from deep focus to near to watch sardines swirl in a clear cylinder at the Monterey Bay Aquarium, or dressing up in a "grass" skirt for a commemorative photo at the Kodak Hula Show—these are all moments of embodied practice which simultaneously stage the audience as an individual and collective subject (one who is, sees, hears, feels, knows) and stage a politics of knowledge, a way of knowing dependent on vision, proximity, and kinesthetic response.[4]

Another deeper level of embodiment operates more in the realm of the imaginary. This has less to do with our literal, physical experience than with the implied experiences the shows provide—the invitation to "Come to Life in Hawai'i," for example, mentally calls forth a rejuvenating rush of blood, enlivening us, giving us a sense of awakening or rebirth. Other examples include: our imagined experience (also pulse pounding) of a charge by the elephant seals, narrated as always a potential danger by the park ranger/tour guide, or our feeling of physical discontinuity between ourselves and the diaphanous pulsings of the jellyfish's white tendrils against the black backdrop, or imagining the feel of a kiss on the cheek from the huge mouth (no lips!) of the whale when she busses the audience member standing in for ourselves.

Issues of embodiment take on still another aspect in these analyses. These audiences, like the performers, are always already socially constituted. They exist in relation to preexisting categories of social difference—of race, of class, of age, of gender, of nationality and so forth, some of which, like race and gender, are anchored in physical difference. Demographic information for all of the audiences of all of the shows I've discussed in this book is not available. The Hawaiian Tourist Bureau, for example, breaks down its survey data by income, region, gender, and national residence, but does not sort its statistics by race. Neither have I seen statistics on zoo attendance that do so. San Diego's Sea World does provide some statistics but only divides its client base into "Anglo" and "non-Anglo" categories.[5] Additional research would be needed, site by site, to track these dimensions more closely.

Still, on the basis of the archival and fieldwork research that I've done, and extrapolating from recent audience research reports, it is plausible to propose that the sites investigated here all attract a predominantly white, middle-class audience (including upper and lower divisions of that vast category in the United States). Those from the working classes and the most elite economic rungs also participate, as do members of all ethnic and racial groups, but probably not in direct proportion to their representation in the mainland population at large. Hawai'i's distance from the mainland means that while it is accessible to working-class vacationers, especially those traveling on cheaper package tours, it is an "easier" purchase for those in the middle class, who may go more often or more casually. This concentration of middle-class consumers also translates into a predilection for cultural attractions since "Hawai'i ranks second only to the nation's capital for the share of its domestic [U.S.] visitors who take in a historical or cultural activity."[6] A similar concern with the environment and hence the natural world (i.e., preservation, salvation) appears to be "most marked amongst those with non-manual occupations, and especially those doing profession-managerial work," reinforcing the class dimension.[7]

What does this audience profile tell us when considered in relation to the commodification of the natural that the sites purvey? What are they buying, and why do they want it? In what ways does the constitution of these groups as audience contribute to their social positioning as white and middle class in the United States? And how can a focus on physical foundationalism tell us something about the answer to that question that we couldn't otherwise know?

To answer these questions, we must consider the links between consumers and a dominant tourist industry discourse which frames their perceptions—the "salvage paradigm." This belief assumes that that which is most natural is vanishing and is in need of saving, whether the object of that salvation be cultural heritage or nature itself.[8] Ultimately this is a liberal attitude with potentially conservative outcomes. While seeming to celebrate cultural difference or the natural world, this paradigm dehistoricizes certain people, practices, geographic regions, and their animal inhabitants, setting them up as avatars of unchanging innocence and authenticity, as origin and as ideal.[9] Such people and places then are recast as the patrimony of humankind or as sources of salvation (cancer cures and as-yet-undiscovered species lurking in the rain forest) or rejuvenation ("Come to Life in Hawai'i"). For tourists, nostalgia replaces history.[10]

In marketing a trip to Hawai'i as a momentary return to a preindustrial past, to harmony with nature (wearing flowers and leaves, using gourds), and to happiness (exemplified by the smiling, lei-greeting employee of the big tour companies, who meet planeloads of mainlanders everyday), it is obviously essential that Honolulu's traffic-jammed H-1 highway, its own growing big-city troubles with gangs, homeless people, and other domestic ills be erased from the tourist's experience, just as Capt. Bob's silly jokes on the bus ride out to Germaine's Luau created a tourist bubble which distracted us from the industrial developments and multilane highway between Waikiki and the beach site. This conception of a nonhybrid, "essential" culture is necessary to the selling of Hawai'i and to its consumption as a transformational place.

The natural, represented by this essential culture and constituted through a century of mainlander representations since organized tourism began, emerges as something lost by white middle-class tourists and briefly rediscovered through invigorating contact with representatives of that culture. While desirable, such a world is ultimately incommensurate with and unincorporable into the ongoing "now" of the tourist's lives and is available only as nostalgia for a time past. (In tourist brochures, we never see Native Hawaiians represented as lawyers, doctors, or businesspeople, for example, only as dancers, lei makers, or storytellers. These occupations, which may be venerated on the islands, represent preindustrial labor, that is, "the past," for mainlanders.) Or the natural may represent a longing for a time in the future when the balance of the world will be righted again so that urban, contemporary ennui can be replaced with the invigorating, embodied pleasures of song, dance, and kissing strangers.

A related salvage paradigm yields a similar encounter, with similar constitutive effects, at the animal sites I've discussed here. The international Species Survival Plan is now shared by zoos around the world as a basis for cross-matching breeding possibilities for endangered species. Only a tiny fraction of all species can be saved this way, even in the test tube, let alone in the zoos themselves, where space is money, yet this fiction of conservation is the dominant public relations and marketing approach for zoos these days.[11] What was once proudly displayed as imperialist "booty" at the turn of the last century is now presented as the last hope for conservation and education. "Baby" nurseries, a popular part of new zoo displays, are exhibits where hand-fed animals held in loving human arms can be seen through large glass windows, staging humans as the nurturing mothers of the natural world. In animal shows like the "Baby Shamu Celebration" (more babies!) bodily difference—the sense that these animals live in a different world—is highlighted and then contrasted with moments through which we can enter their worlds as our vision and occasionally our whole bodies cross the permeable and ever- shifting nature/culture border. This melding is typified by the interspecies ballet between whales and humans at Sea World. At these moments, different worlds merge, and a sublime harmony reigns ("black and white, all friends . . . living in harmony," to quote from the Shamu show lyrics).

This is the ultimate fantasy, that which would both remove for the white middle class the fears associated with contestatory social eruptions by nonwhite, non-middle-class populations and simultaneously provide the reinvigoration associated with the greater naturalism and natural expressivity (i.e., a fuller embodiment) ascribed by whites to these others and to the natural world as a model for cultural organization. This vision of a harmonious world is one in which white, middle-class values remain normative while becoming more inclusive.

The rapidly growing tourist industries indicate that this desired confirmation is increasingly attractive. The expansion of Hawaiian tourism in the 1960s is usually attributed to the development of passenger jet service that cut travel time and costs and thus made such a trip more affordable, expanding the target range beyond the upper classes. But we should note also that since the civil rights movements of the 1960s, there has been vociferous public debate about the "appropriate" place of women, nonwhites, nonheterosexuals, and, yes, even animals in the national polity. Along with these debates have come legal and economic changes which have begun to shift power. The perceived need for realms of experience *outside* these contestations has grown apace with the explosion of Hawaiian tourism and attendance at zoos and aquariums. A trip to Sea World or to Waikiki can provide the confirmation that things are still as they were or "should" be.

The microcosm of the heterosexual family provides a minimodel (a small version of the nation state) of a natural system where power is traditionally apportioned along lines of biological difference. As we have seen throughout these pages, both Waikiki tourist shows and zoos offer a heavy dose of confirmation for the rightness and naturalness of this arrangement. Indeed, it becomes something to be celebrated.

One of Hawai'i's main market segments is honeymooning couples and those celebrating anniversaries. Hosts at the big tourist shows always single out celebrants, touting the number of years of wedded bliss while the entire audience applauds this achievement. The feminization of Hawai'i, alluring yet unthreatening and encapsulated by the figure of the gracious hula dancer, promises to release sensuous heterosexual desires as we "Come to Life in Hawai'i."[12] Thus the notion of a "honeymoon in paradise" collapses into "a honeymoon (heterosexual wedded bliss) is paradise," the highest attainable goal. The underlying transposition of sensuosness into sexual passion under the permissive rubric of the honeymoon makes clear the implicit link between Hawaiian tourism and the reinforcement of the heterosexual family discourse.

A highly ironic counterpoint to this "honeymoon capital of the world" story is currently unfolding. Owing to a very successful legal campaign, Hawai'i may soon become the first state to approve gay and lesbian marriages. Soon planeloads of gay honeymooners may descend on Waikiki, shaking up the MC routines at lū'au shows.

In the natural world on display at zoos and animal theme parks, we find a similar reinforcement of heterosexuality and the heterosexual family as a model of social organization. Babies are everywhere, and everywhere celebrated as evidence of successful conservation and of "happy" captive animals. Mating and reproduction are presented as necessary and natural events, even when accomplished with test-tube assistance. Furthermore, relations of domination between humans and animals are masked, cast as mutual friendships of loving consent.[13] In the case of the Shamu show, for instance, the fact that the whales are in captivity and forced to "work" for a living is rewritten in a narrative stressing how much the whales enjoy and benefit from the psychological stimulation of training and from their close emotional bonds with their trainers.[14] Similarly, in the cultural shows, the global conditions of economic and political inequities that structure the demographics of international travel (from "first" world to "third" as tourists, from "third" to "first" as legal or illegal immigrants in search of work) are never brought to mind. By naturalizing such relations of dominance structured along lines of biological difference, these sites can be seen as endorsing traditional relationships between men and women, and ultimately between whites and nonwhites as well.

The utopian fantasy of crossing boundaries while simultaneously reinscribing them is central to these meanings in both animal and cultural shows. While the tourist experience may ultimately reinforce notions of whiteness and biological rightness, it does so in a way that incorporates to some degree difference which might be threatening. A utopian future built on images of an Edenic past is one in which all people and all animals coexist peacefully. When naturalized, hierarchies might be maintained without contestation. They might become invisible, just "the way things are." Part of this naturalization depends on rewriting hierarchies while not substantially altering the material and epistemological structures which support them. Conservation and cultural celebration are two of the most powerful discourses to accomplish this. These are ultimately gestures of inclusivity, not of fundamental change.

It is likely that the types of cultural tourism and animal tourism investigated in this book will continue to be hugely popular and profitable in the foreseeable future. While U.S. demographic forecasts indicate that the percentage of whites relative to the whole population is on the decline, that very decline may spur a more intensive desire for this consumption which constitutes white, middle-class heterosexuality as normative. In these dehistoricized moments of transformational sublimity, the audience themselves becomes guilt-free "soft primitives," reembodied, one with nature, happy, in social harmony.[15] The incommensurability of these utopian moments with the daily lives of the tourists ensures that they must be purchased again and again, the essence of commodity capitalism.

FURTHER RESEARCH

Further research is needed to understand related habits of touristic consumption by nonmajority consumers. Breakdowns by class, by race, and within each by gender will tell us more about what presumptions are widely shared and which are rejected in comparison with those I've sketched here. Since those data are not generally available from the industries themselves, outside studies must be funded.[16]

In addition, we need further audience research that tells us more explicitly how tourists interpret their own experience. While the effects of consumption may conform to the broad outlines I have sketched above, such a streamlined model cannot account for the varieties of meaning that tourists make. Such experiences are always cross-cut with ironies and ambivalences, the complexity of which I can only indicate but not document fully here. Some scholars, like Susan Davis, Richard Handler and Eric Gable, and Geoff White have made important contributions to the study of tourist consumption through their fieldwork studies of tourist sites, but many times researchers have to rely on audience survey data supplied by the industries.[17] Such surveys are revealing as documents themselves in that they indicate how the industry conceives of its product, but they are subject to the limitations described above and are designed mostly to aid the industries in developing cost-effective strategies for attracting tourists and making sure they leave satisfied enough to return again. The level of detail in these surveys rarely provides more than a thumbs up or thumbs down indication of how the tourist perceives certain aspects of her or his experience.

To answer some of the questions posed in this book better, and to test more fully its provisional answers, future work that emphasizes audience response will be very useful. Throughout the book, my closest readings have been of the structure of the shows and the nature of the performances. I have supplemented these with analyses of historical context and, when available, with information on the attitudes of performers, management, and tourists. When I have written about the pleasures tourists take in these activities, I have relied on my contemporary observation of tourists' reactions and behaviors or on written reports from earlier times, and I have extrapolated from what seems to be being sold (analyzed through the rhetorical structure of advertisements, performances, and so on). But while I am occasionally able to document explicitly what the tourists themselves say by drawing on survey data conducted by the industries, I have not made this a focus of my study. It is the necessary next component in extending these analyses.

By talking directly with consumers about what they think they are consuming, we can at least know what conscious meanings they are crafting of the experience. That is not all that is going on, of course, and the difficulties of interpreting self-reporting are well known to anthropologists. But at the very least we would know something more about the conscious frameworks and acts of interpretation that tourists engage in. For historical studies, documents like travel writing, letters to the editor, and personal letters and diaries may offer clues, although they offer limited possibilities for comparing reactions among varying members of a group. Still, with all these limitations, understanding the meanings people make of their experiences from their own points of view is a crucial component of larger analyses that include investigations of the rhetorical, visual, and corporate/economic structures that undergird specific tourist industries. And, because contemporary tourisms grow out of specific historical relations which shape their current contours, historical tracking, such as I've tried to do in the extended case study of Waikiki through archival research, is necessary and illuminating.

All together, the elements of such an approach require a blending of analytical tools drawn from both the humanities and social sciences. The former contributes highly developed strategies for dissecting the rhetorical structures of texts, while the latter excels in analysis of social structures and historical evidence. Revealing the intricate linkages between performance texts and the social structures they articulate and sustain, as I have endeavored to do throughout this book, calls for a melding of both types of analysis.

ALTERNATIVE VISIONS?

One of the payoffs of extended work on specific tourist practices of consumption is that it will help us imagine other ways these practices might unfold. If, as I've argued above, most of today's tourist shows are ultimately conservative, even when masquerading as liberal (and hence individual rather than systemic in their vision of a better future), is a truly alternative tourist practice possible? If so, what would it look like? Can we imagine alternative tourist shows, or are live encounters so impossibly mired in physical foundationalism that we should just give up on them?

The answers lie not in a banishment of visual/bodily encounters, but in repositioning them not as moments of utopian transcendence that write out history but as encounters which reveal histories and our own situation in their legacies. This is a more Brechtian approach, a sort of alienation effect, but it too offers pleasures, just of a different kind. For we must remember that tourisms are voluntary actions taken for pleasure. So—how could different pleasures be supplied, ones that unsettle rather than confirm a status quo?

In part 1, I briefly discussed two examples of contemporary Hawaiian shows that successfully walk this fine line of giving the tourist what she expects while making her think about why she expects it, and then substituting a new vision of a similar offering, now reframed as the result of past historical moments. In Frank Kawaikapuokalani Hewett's lū'au on Kaua'i, past styles of hula, including the Hawaiian wedding song, and the popular sexy cellophane skirts of the thirties, reappear, but framed as examples of how Hollywood popularized hula on the mainland. Suddenly, hula has a history for tourists, who become self-reflexively aware of their own historical moment, continuing the history of tourism.

A related strategy undergirds the performance of the Cazimero Brothers at the Bishop Museum discussed in chapter 1. By relating songs to their own experiences growing up as Native Hawaiians on the islands, Roland and Robert Cazimero engage the audience in the particularity of experience, not a generalized, idealized trope to fulfill a destination image. References to contemporary politics frame the dancing and lyrics too. Narrativizing the spectacle in this way forces tourists to recognize their co-evalness with performers and their own limited knowledge about island complexities.

In the Cazimero shows, the images of idealized hula performers (slender, young, native females) are rewritten as well when *kumu hula*

Leinaʻalā Kalama Heine takes center stage, her powerful, large frame dominating the space. A contemporary of the middle-aged Cazimero brothers, she rewrites our perception of the young performers who precede her in the show. While matching the physical stereotype of young, slender, attractive dancers, they also become representatives of an early stage in life, a stage to be passed through as one ages, but one whose passing does not mean the end of dancing or of the beauty, grace, and power of hula. The linkage of hula to sexual allure, with which most tourists arrive, is replaced with a more complicated image of powerful subjectivity and expressivity. Sexuality, as allure for outsiders, is replaced with a fuller sense of sensuality in which both performer and spectators take physical pleasure in dancing.

In moments like these, the potential of cultural tourism becomes clear. Commodification is not somehow magically banished; the tourists still buy tickets, and the Cazimeros make their living in large part from such shows. But "what" is commodified changes slightly. Bodily presence becomes not just the ultimate guarantor of cultural authenticity, the physical foundationalism that I dissected in operation throughout this book. Instead, the *physical co-presence* of tourist and of resident becomes the precondition of an encounter, with the potential to illuminate, even if just momentarily, the history of relations between the two groups. Within tourism exists the possibility of acknowledging and self-reflexively staging that history and its contemporary legacies.

Ultimately, imperialisms are structures of relationships, unequal relationships to be sure, but relationships nonetheless. Tracking and articulating the mutually defining characteristics of this history can both acknowledge it and acknowledge that the effects of this relationship have gone both ways. The mainland craze for Hawaiian music in the teens, the influence of Hawaiian music on the country and western sound of the slide guitar, the role that early tourism played in sustaining performing careers for Hawaiian musicians and dancers, the role of the radio show *Hawaiʻi Calls* in shaping the musical tastes of an entire mainland generation, the influence of mainland political movements of the 1960s on the development of the 1970s Hawaiian renaissance of Native Hawaiian cultural practices, and so on can all be traced in song and dance and could provide the basis of a type of tourist show anchored in history while still providing the visual, aural, and kinesthetic pleasures of spectacle.

As long as tourism remains a for-profit industry (and I see no signs of this changing), there will be political limitations on what can be said and how, and the hardest facts of past inequities and their contemporary legacies may remain "unspeakable" because both the audiences and the corporations that lead the industries are linked to those pasts. Therefore, some may argue that tourism should just be abandoned. But that too is a utopian view, one which writes out the history and power of capitalism all at once. Tourism, poised to be the largest industry in the world in the early years of the twenty-first century, will not just go away. Such a massive presence calls for intensive work by academics, residents, policy-makers, and activists in shaping what gets sold and how.

At root lies the question "Can politically progressive 'products' sell, and will they provide the pleasure which forms the basis of leisure industries?" Or, Can the aesthetic pleasures (sight, sound, movement) sell when their ideological framework is rewritten? I think so, at least to a limited extent. The Cazimero shows already provide evidence of such success. But major industry players will only change when pressured by local groups and when they see it as to their advantage. The Sheraton Waikiki poolside shows are a good example. The Sheraton's ultimate motivation may be to develop good working relations with the local community and to get some low-cost shows for free entertainment for their guests. But the result are hula shows which feature tiny tots, grandmothers, and references to sovereignty, all of which rewrite the idealized look of the hula girl. No tourist, lounging by the pool at 5 p.m. and casually encountering such shows, can help enlarging his or her notion of Hawaiian cultural practices and complexities. These types of shows, all staged by Native Hawaiian *kumu hulas*, begin a process of redesigning the "product" of cultural consumption.

A related issue is the ownership of the means of production. In the example above, the Sheraton organization has ultimate approval over both the script used in the shows and the selection of hula troupes that perform. A different example of indigenous tourist performance provides a more radical approach. In 1995 I traveled to the north of Finland with a group of academics who were participating in an international cultural studies conference. The highlight of that trip for most of us was a visit to a reindeer farm above the Arctic Circle. Saami families, members of the indigenous population, have special rights over these arctic grazing lands, and their rights are protected by the state. To supplement their income from reindeer herding, one family decided to open their farm to tourist groups, accommodating no more than fifty people at a time. They provided a number of activities: the opportunity to see and pet reindeer that came to a circle in the woods when called, instruction in traditional Saami skills like reindeer lasooing, a taste of Saami tea and cookies, a visit to a one-room museum displaying family artifacts like household goods and clothing gathered over several generations, and a brief performance consisting of songs and storytelling.

Clearly these displays of performative and material culture, along with a narration explaining their meaning, are the familiar stuff of cultural tourism. So is the participation segment of rope-throwing lessons, which parallels the "teaching the tourist to dance" motif in Hawai'i. But the effect here was entirely different from that of Germaine's Luau. The political sophistication and contemporaneity of the hosts, along with their considered choices of what to show and how, were not masked but came through loud and clear. The youngest member of the family, a daughter, was host for the visit, discussing contemporary youth, her own bilingualism, what it was like being one of few women ever to attend the community college reindeer-husbandry course, and the family's choice to don "costumes" (fancy traditional dress with bright embroidery and curved-tipped shoes) for our visit. A question and answer session at the end provided further interaction.

Here the mythic reindeer (which elicited squeals of delight from all of us who had grown up with Christmas stories of St. Nick) and the essentializing presumptions about traditional culture that we may have brought with us were both met, challenged, and reformulated. The reindeer we petted were, in fact, looking pretty mangy, since it was their molting season, thus undercutting their mythic status. The traditional costumes, far from indicating a more traditional people caught in a time warp, were clearly not worn all the time, but just for tourists and just for Saami parties, when people felt like getting dressed up. Storytelling revealed a sharp sense of humor and positioned one of our group, a willing volunteer, as the butt of the joke about a hapless suitor, but a joke shared by tellers and listeners alike and one which, by incorporating the tourist into the Saami narrative, emphasized co-contemporaneity. Neither were the economics of the exchange masked. Our hosts made it clear that their choice to start this tourism business was a way to bring in extra income.

One might object that a tour group of cultural studies scholars is fundamentally different from other tourists—more sophisticated about cultural issues, more politically aware, and so on. But I don't think other tour groups visiting this farm react that differently to the experience. This is an engaging, warm, funny, and entertaining experience made up of sights, sounds, actions, songs, dances, and so on. But it is in no way merely a celebratory or utopian view—on either side. At no time were notions of Saami culture reified into something unchanging and always wonderful. The socially limiting gendered prescriptions of tradition, undercut by a female reindeer herder, were brought to the fore. Difficulties for Saami youth in getting higher education without having to leave their homelands made the tough choices of their contemporary situation clear. And the active and selective nourishing of cultural practices, like when to don traditional dress, was put up front.

This business was possible because the host family has land-use rights supported by the state. Similar shifts in Hawai'i, not unthinkable in the future as a result of the sovereignty movement, may mean that more and more Hawaiians can stage tourist encounters on their own terms and in their own facilities.[18] It is foreseeable that the big lū'aus like Germaine's will become increasingly passé. They may be replaced by smaller (but more numerous) shows along the lines of the Cazimeros' or experiences like the Saami reindeer farm, which provide a historicized encounter along with the spectacle of difference. In these cases, the function of the body as anchor and guarantor of cultural difference would recede, replaced by histories of cultural practices.

But if there are some models of alternative modes of cultural tourism, what of animal tourism? After all, unlike humans, who can potentially reorganize the tourist encounter, animals can take no such initiative. Perhaps it would be better to work toward the abolition of zoos and aquariums, now that film and computers can provide so much visual and factual information about different species.[19] Is the physical encounter still necessary, or should zoos be banished and replaced by video "safaris"?

Tourists go to zoos and animal theme parks not just to find out more about animals but also to coexist in the same place and time with them. This pleasure is irreplicable. Film images do not provide it, and that is one reason that zoos and animal theme parks, despite increasing pressure by animal rights activists, will be unlikely to disappear. In fact, such appetites are now embracing ever-wider ranges of species. The increasing popularity of aquariums relative to zoos may indicate that the desire for difference is being reformulated away from the colonial booty of elephants, lions, and tigers and toward nonmammalian bodies ever more different from humans. Now the diaphanous jelly fish competes with the elephant as a big audience pleaser. Rather than an attenuation of our appetite for physical difference between humans and animals, we are seeing its extension and elaboration into ever-more diversified realms of habitat.

The pleasures produced by these experiences are based on our calibration of relative size, scale, body structure, and function between the animal and ourselves—all ways of experiencing the simultaneous sense of similarity and difference I've discussed in part 2 of this book. But behind this calibration lies the fantasy of species boundary crossing, of an encounter which produces an interaction of some sort. For this to occur, the human and animal must be in the same place at the same time.

When animals respond to humans, or seem to, this fantasy is momentarily fulfilled, producing pleasure. This is the secret to the appeal of the watery duet between trainer and Shamu, of the lion-show chorus line of synchronized leaps directed by a trainer. It is why children sometimes harass animals in the zoo, throwing peanuts, shouting, and banging on cages—all to get the animals to "do" something, not just to see the kinesthetic display of difference but to have the animals react to them: in short, to communicate across the species barrier. In this process of communicating, we experience both the crossing of a barrier and its simultaneous reassertion. Experiences of ourselves as "not them" invoke a sense of collective human identity while making communication across this chasm of difference seem remarkable and transcendent.

The history of this desire is documentable.[20] Just as cultural tourism offers the possibility of historicizing relations between tourist populations and residents, it is possible to present a historicized view of humans relations with animals or, better, of specific human populations' relationship to specific species. For example, the shift from a bars-and-shackles mode of display to today's zoo habitats exemplifies not just a change in zoo design but new conceptions of the relationship between animals and humans. Some zoos, like Chicago's Lincoln Park, leave one of the old cages intact so visitors can see what they looked like. However, this is usually presented as a mute testament to the past, unexplored in its implications. For most visitors, I suspect the response is "Oh, aren't things better for the animals now," an implicit endorsement of enlightened progress. The historical questions of why and how such things changed are not engaged, but they could be.[21]

Tourism is double-edged. The simultaneous emphasis on and experience of difference (physical, cultural, species) help the tourist define him- or herself as part of a different collectivity from that on display. And the fantasy of peaceful, harmonious, coexistence envisions a merging with all that is different. That this happens in an ahistorical bubble both makes the fantasy seem realizable and reduces its most insidious aspects to play without apparent social cost. The cost, of course, is the continued inequalities of power and control that determine the flow of visitors and visited, and the gain is the confirmation of collective differences (arranged in hierarchies of power) through their naturalization.

This naturalization is ultimately produced by transmuting history to spectacle and anchoring it in the display of that most natural of all entities, the body. Only by historicizing these encounters and thus disrupting the physical foundationalism on which they rest can we envision a future of tourism as more than its past.

The implications of this study extend beyond the confines of tourism. Despite thirty years of social constructivism as the leading edge of thought in the social sciences and humanities, I believe that we have yet to grasp fully the profoundly intractable role bodily difference plays in structuring our paradigms of social classification. The discourses of naturalism, embodiment, salvation, and self-transformation that intertwine throughout these pages and, I have argued, form the basis of hugely profitable industries emerge as well in tightly braided formulations in realms as disparate as avant-garde art practice, public policy debates, contemporary critical theory, and the hard sciences. They underpin some of our current formulations of performativity,[22] a great deal of public discourse about multiculturalism,[23] and even huge, federally sponsored initiatives, like the proposed Human Genome Diversity Project.[24]

In a period of academic discourse that celebrates "posts" (postmodernism, postcolonialism, postnationalism) and a new sense of hybrid positionalities and fluidity of categories, it is imperative that we give adequate weight to the intransigence of physical evidence in systems of social differentiation and track these operations in public discourse. Tracking that trace is the only way potentially to disrupt it and to reconfigure the possible meanings of bodily presence.

Notes

1. I do not mean to imply that this physical foundationalism has exerted a similar structuring function in all times, places, and societies. Rather I am making claims about its centrality in European-dominated societies, particularly the United States, at least during the last two centuries, and most intensely during the period which I am investigating in this study, roughly the last hundred years.

2. "Whiteness" of course is not a unitary category either. Differences of class, national origin, generation, and region also need to be considered. John Urry, for example, argues that intra-European travel by Europeans (predominantly white) is an important aspect of forging an identity as part of a newly unified "Europe," one which depends just as much on the manufacture or maintenance of cultural distinctiveness, and a belief in the right of all citizens of Europe to consume it, for a new claim to cosmopolitanism. See Urry, *Consuming Places,* chap. 11.

3. MacCannell, *Empty Meeting Grounds,* p. 1.

4. John Urry reports the world trade figure in his book *The Tourist Gaze,* p. 47. The U.S. figure is noted in *Travel and Leisure* magazine, January 1997, p. 46, "Future Flash" section.

5. See Roig, "Flights," p. B-8. Animal attractions figures from "Animal Attractions," p. D-1.

6. See, e.g., Harriet Ritvo's excellent *Animal Estate: The English and Other Creatures in the Victorian Age.* Ritvo examines English attitudes toward pets, zoos, and big-game hunting, among other examples, as they intersected with anxieties about social discipline, England's imperial role, and discourses of humanitarianism. See also Jennifer Ham and Mathew Senior, *Animal Acts: Configuring the Human in Western History.*

7. I can only suggest a small segment of the full range of this literature here. See, e.g., Smith, *Hosts and Guests;* Culler, "Semiotics of Tourism"; Stewart, *On Longing;* Jules-Rosette, *The Messages of Tourist Art;* Frow, "Tourism and the Semiotics of Nostalgia"; Baker, *Picturing the Beast;* Spurr, *The Rhetoric of Empire;* Pratt, *Under Imperial Eyes;* Norton et al., eds., *Ethics on the Ark;* Masson and McCarthy, *When Elephants*

Weep; Pearce, *The Social Psychology of Tourist Behaviour;* and Timberlake, "Animal Behavior: A Continuing Synthesis." Engerman's "Research Agenda for the History of Tourism" also provides an extensive bibliography of works relevant to research on tourism.

8. See MacCannell, *The Tourist,* p. 156. He extends many of these considerations in his later *Empty Meeting Grounds.* In that book he introduces the concept of "reconstructed ethnicities," which imply a "generalized 'other' within a white cultural frame. . . .

Reconstructed ethnicity is fully dependent on the earlier stages in the construction of ethnicity. But it represents an end point in dialogue, a final freezing of ethnic imagery which is artificial and deterministic, even, or especially, when it is based on a drive for authenticity. . . . Under these conditions, ethnicities can begin to use former colorful ways both as commodities to be bought and sold, and as rhetorical weaponry in their dealings with one another . . . a symbolic expression with a purpose or an exchange value in a larger system" (p.168).

9. *Lincoln Park Zooreview,* "The Lions of India," p. 19.

10. Kirshenblatt-Gimblett, "Objects of Ethnography," p. 414. See also her new book *Destination Culture,* which appeared while this book was in press. While Kirshenblatt-Gimblett's emphases and objects of analyses are somewhat different from mine, her arguments about museums, heritage, and exhibitionary practices are very relevant to these discussions. Leah Dilworth also writes about the intersection of cultural exhibition and live performance in her fine, historically situated study of the Hopi snake dance, which drew an overwhelming number of white tourists in the teens and twenties. See her book *Imagining Indians in the Southwest,* esp. chap. 1, "Representing the Hopi Snake Dance."

11. David Whisnant's excellent *All That Is Native and Fine* provides a historical account of the production of Appalachia as an idealized yet "primitive" site that attracted the attentions of middle-and upper-class whites before World War II. My emphasis on the ways in which tourist encounters construct an "us" while displaying a "them" echoes his investigations into the popularity of mountain crafts and music but places a different emphasis on bodily display.

12. Culler, quoted in Urry, *The Tourist Gaze,* p. 3.

13. Urry, *The Tourist Gaze,* pp. 45–46. In his later book, *Consuming Places,* Urry offers a number of other types of "tourist gazes," too (such as the spectatorial, environmental, and anthropological), relevant to the consumption of the environment and notes that these may occur in combination, varying in accordance with variations in the temporal, spatial, and institutional forms of tourism involved, and in the populations employing them. See *Consuming Places,* pp. 187–92.

14. Urry, *The Tourist Gaze,* pp. 11–12; emphasis added.

15. As John Urry notes, tourism usually involves the suspension or inversion of everyday obligations: "There is licence for permissive and playful 'non-serious' behaviour and the encouragement of a relatively unconstrained 'communitas' or social togetherness." *The Tourist Gaze,* p. 10.

16. For a sampling of some of these works, see MacCannell, *The Tourist,* and his more recent *Empty Meeting Grounds;* Culler, "Semiotics of Tourism"; Frow, "Tourism and the Semiotics of Nostalgia"; Kirschenblatt-Gimblett, "Objects of

Ethnography," in *Exhibiting Cultures;* Urry, *The Tourist Gaze.* An extensive sociological literature also exists.

A sampling of relevant works on theorizing "the body" and conceptualizing social structures includes: Martin, *The Woman in the Body;* Haraway, *Simians, Cyborgs, and Women;* Clifford and Marcus, *Writing Culture;* Foster, *Corporealities;* Desmond, *Meaning in Motion;* Anderson, *Imagined Communities;* Hobsbawm and Ranger, *The Invention of Tradition;* Pollock, *Vision and Difference;* and Karp and Levine, *Exhibiting Cultures.*

17. These ideas of naturalism and primitivism certainly have longer histories as part of European and Euro-American imaginaries, but in the United States the late nineteenth century saw an intensification of these ideas and the public institutions that supported them, like world expositions. The turn of the century also marks the beginnings of organized tourism to Hawai'i.

INTRODUCTION TO PART ONE

1. A possible exception is Spain's female flamenco dancer, but that sign is particularly relevant for the Andalusian region. In general, the image of the male bullfighter, also an image figuring a dramatic performative act of public entertainment, is a more dominant symbol. Many contemporary tourist advertisements do feature dancing figures as a symbol of female spectacle to be encountered in an "exotic" realm (see, e.g., advertisements for Mexico and Thailand), but these figures do not have the iconic weight of the "hula girl."

2. See Smith, *European Vision and the South Pacific.* In the specific case of Hawai'i, the notion of graciousness draws on the Native Hawaiian concept of "aloha," or the "ties of man to fellow man . . . strengthened in mutual regard and love," which was and is highly valued among Native Hawaiians (see Pukui, Haertig, and Lee, *Nama I Ke Kumu: Look to the Source,* p. 3). Some tourist businesses are currently instituting "aloha training" for their employees. This indicates both the perception that aloha has been lost and that its promotion benefits the tourist industry. For a full discussion of concepts of aloha and its contemporary mobilization in commercial and political contexts, see Kanahele, *"Ku Kanaka" Stand Tall,* chap. 12.

3. See Lears, *No Place of Grace;* and Torgovnick, *Gone Primitive.*

4. Torgovnick, *Gone Primitive,* p. 156.

5. Williamson, "Woman Is an Island," p. 106.

6. Ibid., p. 107.

7. Chon, "The Role of Destination Image in Tourism."

8. While visual, verbal, and performative renditions all contributed to the mainland image of Hawai'i, it was only after the appearance of Hawaiian musicians at the 1915 Pan Pacific Exposition in San Francisco spawned a national craze for Hawaiian music that live performances proliferated. I will discuss these in the next chapter, along with a couple of exceptions, such as the performance of Native Hawaiian dancers at the 1893 Columbian World's Exposition in Chicago.

9. Twain spent four months in Honolulu in 1866, writing a series of dispatches for the California newspaper the *Sacramento Union.* He later drew on his experiences for numerous other poems, stories, and articles. Stevenson also wrote journalistic pieces, publishing a series of letters about Hawai'i in the *New York Sun* in

1891, as well as several stories, such as "The Bottle Imp," which became well known. See Twain, *Mark Twain in Hawaii*, p. xxxiii; and Stevenson, *Travels in Hawaii*.

10. This development must be seen in relation to the shifting visibility of hula from the nineteenth to the twentieth centuries. Missionaries, arriving in the 1820s, denigrated the hula as lascivious. Many Native Hawaiians who converted to Christianity shared the view that hula was suspect. Until the reign of King Kalākaua (1874–91) in the late nineteenth century, hula largely went underground. Public performances were regulated by laws, including licensing requirements and fees for permission to stage performances. Noncompliance was punishable by very heavy fines or jail time. Large public performances at Kalākaua's coronation (1883) and his fiftieth birthday jubilee (1886) helped restore hula to public respectability. However, debates continued to rage regarding the morality of hula dancing, and it wasn't until the teens and twenties that many *kumu hula*s and their *halau*s reemerged more publicly. At least part of that increased visibility was due to the incorporation of hula into the tourist industry. For a discussion of some of these issues, see Barrere, Pukui, and Kelly, *Hula*, esp. pt. I, "The Hula in Retrospect," by Barrere.

11. Using U.S. Census data, Michael Haas reports the 1910 population as: 20 percent Hawaiian (and part-Hawaiian); 23 percent white; 11 percent Chinese; 42 percent Japanese; and 3 percent Puerto Rican. Haas, *Institutional Racism*, p. 5.

CHAPTER ONE

1. The term "hula girl" was popularized on the mainland and connotes a sexually attractive young woman. When used throughout this book, it refers to that mainland usage in contradistinction to the term "hula dancer." Hula dancers (male and female) were highly respected participants in precontact Native Hawaiian society, and dances and chants had important religious, social, and political functions. With the coming of the missionaries in the early nineteenth century, hula was censured. As Native Hawaiians converted to Christianity, many turned away from hula, and took on missionary attitudes that regarded it as lascivious and immoral. In the twentieth century hula has regained its popularity in the islands.

2. The long history of colonialism in Hawai'i (including the role of missionaries in banning the hula as lewd) and its impact on tourism are central to an understanding of the current situation in Hawai'i, but cannot be related in detail here. For key analyses of Hawaiian history, see Kame'eleihiwa, *Native Land and Foreign Desires*; Stannard, *Before the Horror*; Sahlins, *Islands of History*; and Kuykendall, *The Hawaiian Kingdom*.

3. Kamahele, "Hula as Resistance," p. 42.

4. Smith, *European Vision and the South Pacific*; Barrere, Pukui, and Kelly, *Hula*. See also Kaeppler, *Hula Pahu*, and her "Visible and Invisible in Hawaiian Dance," pp. 31–43; Buck, *Paradise Remade*; and Tatar, *Strains of Change*.

5. Torgovnick, *Gone Primitive*, esp. chaps. 1, 4, and 5.

6. Smith, *European Vision and the South Pacific*, esp. chap. 1.

7. Torgovnick, *Gone Primitive*, p. 17.

8. Trask, *From a Native Daughter*, p. 180.

9. Chon, "The Role of Destination Image in Tourism."

10. Not only is the hula girl figure used to sell Hawai'i to visitors before they arrive, but it is also replicated upon arrival in numerous ways, beckoning from the cover of ubiquitous visitors guides, like *This Week Oahu,* that are available free all over Waikiki.

11. See Goss's excellent "Placing the Market and Marketing Place" for a detailed consideration of advertising campaigns and how they work. Goss emphasizes the ways in which advertisements situate Hawai'i as an "Other" from the United States, but a safe Other: "Tourists are promised a profound intersubjective experience, a meeting with the Other and the sharing of its culture . . . through participating in [native's] everyday cultural activities, and through learning foreign languages and customs" (p. 672).

12. Even the currently popular U.S. "multicultural" categories can be obviated by concepts of Hawaiian-ness, since the Pacific usually falls outside these categories in U.S. mainland public discourse.

13. Obviously, not all U.S. tourists from the mainland are of Euro-American descent, but this group vastly predominates. African-American tourists are in evidence, but not in large numbers. This may be due in part to negative attitudes toward African Americans reported by some locals. The primary African-American presence in Hawai'i is in U.S. military personnel. While soldiers stationed in Hawai'i do take advantage of Honolulu's leisure options, they also have their own entertainments. For example, the military stages a biweekly lū'au at a Honolulu site which is closed to outsiders. Military personnel experience Hawai'i somewhat differently than tourists, and their experiences are not a part of this study.

The Hawai'i Visitors Bureau records of visitor characteristics that I have seen do not give breakdowns of data by race for visitors from the United States. Males and females are almost exactly equal in their numbers. Age ranges are categorized as from twenty years old to over sixty, with the majority being between thirty and fifty years old. Three-fourths are traveling for pleasure, with smaller numbers coming for conventions or visits with friends or relatives. Breakdown by income is not available, but occupations are noted. The largest groups are reported as follows: 10 percent characterize themselves as senior management, another ten percent as middle management, and 21 percent as professional. Technical, trade, clerical, labor, and military service together total approximately 24 percent, with another 4 percent being students, 8 percent being self-employed, and 13 percent being retired. Exactly what is meant by terms like "professional" or "middle management" cannot be determined. See the Hawai'i Visitors Bureau Market Research Department's 1992 *Annual Research Report.*

14. There is some evidence that Japanese tourists may be more drawn to the spectacular Las Vegas–style reviews in Waikiki, perhaps consuming them more as markers of "America" than of "Hawai'i." Terry Fowler, general manager of the Waikiki Beachcomber hotel, notes that Don Ho's island-oriented show has more pull with the U.S. visitors, while "Boylesque," a Las Vegas–style female-impersonator show is more geared to the "Oriental market." See Glauberman, "Viva Waikiki!" On the other hand, hula is very popular in Japan, especially among middle-aged women, who flock to Japanese *halaus.* The consumption of Hawaiiana by Japanese visitors deserves its own detailed study.

15. The majority of all U.S. tourists to Hawai'i are repeat visitors (65 percent, as reported in the 1992 *Annual Research Report* of the Hawai'i Visitors Bureau Market Research Department, p. 13), indicating that they liked what they saw the first time and that their expectations from the destination image were met or exceeded upon arrival. Tourism research indicates that visitor satisfaction is highest when the promises of a destination image, no matter how stimulating or pedestrian to begin with, are met or exceeded once the tourist arrives. The least satisfaction results from inflated images and pedestrian results, even when the resulting experience was described as adequate. Hence, the relationship between the destination image and the experience that the tourist industry provides on site is key. See Chon, "The Role of Destination Image in Tourism."

16. Roig, "Flights Help Big Island Hotels."

17. John Goss calls this "the consistent representation of Hawai'i as relatively uninhabited, a romantic tropical paradise ready for personal discovery by readers-become-tourists." See his "Placing the Market and Marketing Place," p. 676.

18. Ross, *Chicago Gangster Theory of Life*, p. 85.

19. The Hawai'i Visitors Bureau promotes just this concept of culture and excitement when it notes in its monthly members' newsletter that today's vacationers want not just relaxation but excitement. Recent research, they note, indicates that "excitement . . . means a real adventure in a must-see destination that offers a unique culture and sightseeing opportunities." *Hawaiian Beat*, Nov. 1994, p. 2.

20. "Local" is an important designation in Hawai'i. It indicates someone of non-Caucasian descent and may refer to any combination of mixed genealogical inheritances. Sometimes the term "local haole" is used to refer to a Caucasian (haole) from the islands, usually with several generations of family ties there. The category "local" is used in opposition not only to haole but also in contradistinction to outsiders and to *malihini,* or newcomers, a term which may indicate a tourist or someone whose family has not lived in the islands for a long time. For discussions of the meanings of "local," see Imada, "The Local That Is Never *Pau*: Contemporary Local Literature of Hawaii"; and Okamura, "Why There Are No Asian Americans in Hawaii," pp. 161–78.

21. MacCannell, *Empty Meeting Grounds*, p. 168.

22. The "Keep It Hawai'i" campaign was initiated in 1990. In 1996, when a new convention center opened, the HVB changed its name to the Hawai'i Visitors and Convention Bureau. I use HVB to refer to actions by this organization before 1996, and HVCB for post-1996 references.

23. "Keep It Hawai'i," 1992 brochure prepared by HVB.

24. The award is cited in the cruise line's promotional materials. As this one example illustrates, and as will become clear in the following chapters, the tourist industry has provided employment for some of Hawai'i's most highly regarded musicians and dancers and thus has helped sustain these practices. Owner Cody Engle purchased the cruise line in the mid-1990s and retained professionals from the Bishop Museum's staff to oversee the installation of a 3,366 square foot mini-imuseum. On-board activities include hula, lei making, and ukulele classes, performances by award-winning *halaus*, and a traditional Hawaiian church service on Sundays. Although describing himself as a "steely-eyed capitalist," Cody says the

cruise line's objective "is to present the real Hawai'i to our passengers. We believe in and are committed to this concept. Passengers will board our ships as tourists and leave as *kama'aina* [residents]" (Tsutsumi, "Cruising Hawaiian-Style aboard the SS *Independence*," pp. 22 and 25).

The cover of the glossy brochure advertising the 1997 Hawaiian cruises reveals, however, how often these presentations are framed as part of the soft primitivism imaginary, a nostalgic evocation of the past. Leaning against a curving palm tree and surrounded by flowers, a Polynesian-looking woman dreamily strums a ukulele on the beach in the foreground as a huge ocean liner pulls into port against a mountain backdrop. The graphic design style of the cover recalls the thirties, and the pictorial elements—lone woman with ukulele and palms in the foreground, ship, blue sea, and mountain behind—can be found on tourist advertisements as early as 1916.

25. *Honolulu Star Bulletin*, "Magnificent Royal Hotel Opened amid Riot of Color and Song," p. 3.

26. Interview with B. J. Hughes, Director of Public Relations, Sheraton Waikiki Hotel, Honolulu, August 1, 1994. The *halau* is Na Mea Hula o Kahikinaokalalani, with *kumu hula* Karla Akiona. See also Glauberman, "Sheraton Waikiki Hosts Entertainers," p. C-1. The Sheraton spends about $18,000 per week on entertainment, which includes musicians and dancers in styles ranging from Hawaiian to jazz.

27. "Ala Moana Hotel Unveils New Hawaiiana Program," and "Maui Inter-Continental Delves into Hawaiiana," *Aloha Magazine*, pp. 11 and 12.

28. See Glauberman, "Viva Waikiki!" p. C-1. This figure includes all types of Waikiki shows. A breakdown specifically for Hawaiian entertainment is not available.

29. HVB 1992 *Annual Research Report*, p. 3.

30. For an extensive consideration of the Polynesian Cultural Center (PCC), see Ross, "Cultural Preservation in the Polynesia of the Latter-Day Saints," in his *Chicago Gangster Theory of Life*. Ross considers, among other topics, the relationship between cultural conservation movements in the Pacific and tourism.

31. Personal interview with Christina Kemmer, then-president of the Waikiki Improvement Association, Honolulu, August 8, 1994.

32. See works by Imada and by Okamura, for a discussion of "local" as a contemporary identity category in the islands.

33. This particular, very popular commercial lū'au presents the boldest playing out of the main themes I develop in this chapter. Paradise Cove Luau, the main competitor, is a little different. It employs respected *kumu hula* O'Brien Eselu as MC, but his background is never mentioned during the show, and an unknowledgeable mainlander audience may interpret his very large size and joking manner as that of just another jolly comedian. His show doesn't feature all the kissing described below, nor do his dancers wear coconut bra tops, but the themes of escape, indulgence, and sexuality are the same. The Paradise Cove dancers appear to be better trained than those at Germaine's, exhibiting a greater degree of unison in performance, and some of the work seen at that lū'au might also be deemed appropriate for nontourist audiences and shown in a venue like the Merrie Monarch Hula competition. *Kumu hula* Vicky Holt Takamine, who directed the show before Eselu, felt that it was possible to negotiate with the management to present a show that was entertaining to

tourists but nonoffensive to her dancers and herself. She refused, for example, to have her dancers wear the coconut bra tops (personal communication, summer 1994). This indicates that there is some flexibility even within the most commercialized practices, but the key themes and visuals must remain the same.

34. Personal interviews with Kimo Alama Keaulana, July 6, 1995, and with Vicky Holt Takamine, July 27, 1994, and phone interview with Dovie Borges, July 13, 1995, all in Honolulu. In the 1990s the hapa-haole look is also being joined, in some tourist advertisements or on postcards, by depictions of women of Filipino background.

35. The specific frames of these racialized categories, and the resulting "Hawaiian" look, are revealed by the preceding discussion of casting practices. The historical development of this perception will be investigated in the next chapters.

36. See Stillman, "Hawaiian Hula Competitions," p. 358.

37. Stillman emphasizes that "participation in hula performance is multiethnic" and states that "the fact of displaying the hula as a Hawaiian cultural tradition is evidently separable from the ethnic makeup of its presenters" (ibid., pp. 360–61). Stillman also notes that "cultural performances held by the [Native Hawaiian] community contrast greatly with Hawaiian entertainment presented in the tourism industry" (p. 360).

38. The term "Oriental" is often used in the islands to indicate someone not of mixed local heritage, but of an unmixed Chinese or Japanese background.

39. Stillman, "Hawaiian Hula Competitions," p. 360.

40. This is not to say that all population groups are represented in *halaus* proportionally with their numbers in the population at large, but that members of all groups participate in hula. The selection of hapa-haole-looking professional dancers from this wider population of dancers in the islands represents the commercial touristic promotion of an idealized vision of what the hula girl and, to a much lesser extent, a male dancer, is supposed to look like.

41. Kamahele, "Hula as Resistance," p. 45.

42. This is not to say that there are no tensions within the hula world regarding these issues of who does what. A 1993 panel discussion at Windward Community College among hula experts who were discussing foreign *halaus* revealed differences of opinion. Some believed that knowledge of the hula should be shared with all who are seriously interested in learning, that the aloha spirit requires sharing. Others felt that foreigners could never really come to understand hula at a deep level. The basis for that belief seemed not so much that foreigners weren't Native Hawaiian but rather that they did not live in the islands. The importance of a sense of place, especially given the emphasis in hula songs and chants on delineating specific places or the physical beauty of the islands (e.g., gestures show many different kinds of rain), meant that such knowledge could not be grasped without substantial firsthand experience.

On the other hand, there were some grumblings when in 1995 a *halau* from Japan won an award at the King Kalākaua Hula Competition, the second most important competition. This was the first time a foreign *halau* had competed head to head with local *halaus* and beaten most of them. A somewhat similar ambivalence exists regarding competition between island *halaus* and those on the mainland, especially the West Coast. A complicated point-scoring system and a team of judges means that the accomplishments of the Japanese *halau* were documented and the win was uncontestable, whether or not all members in the audience were enthusiastic about it.

43. Domínguez, "The Marketing of Heritage."

44. Kamahele, "Hula as Resistance," discusses these meanings of hula.

45. Barbara Kirshenblatt-Gimblett, "Objects of Ethnography," p. 388.

46. Throughout this chapter, as I will throughout the book, I have used the terms "Native Hawaiian" to refer to persons who claim genealogical lineage back to pre-contact populations and "native" to refer to the European imaginary of such populations. For a discussion of the issues of time and history with regard to tourism, see Fabian, *Time and the Other*; MacCannell, *The Tourist*; Frow, "Tourism and the Semiotics of Nostalgia; Brown, *Hawaii Recalls*; and Urry, *The Tourist Gaze*.

47. Buck, *Paradise Remade*, p. 191.

48. Hewett's show was one of 18 companies or individuals honored in 13 award categories from a field of 262 entries. Criterion for judging included: "authenticity, uniqueness to Hawai'i, historical value, educational value and utilization or preservation of Hawaiian cultural expressions and traditions." See Pochereva, "The Kahili Awards," p. 4.

49. As a way of competing with the lū'aus, the museum offered the option of a preshow Hawaiian dinner served in a souvenir box woven from palm fronds. The entertainment portion of the evening took place afterward, in one of the halls of the museum, which featured, among other artifacts, early colonial renditions of European visions of Native Hawaiians.

50. I discuss the range of these positions in "Invoking the 'Native': Body Politics in Contemporary Hawaiian Tourist Shows." Issues of citizenship and the defining categories for who will count as Hawaiian and as Native Hawaiian are complex and hotly debated. Suggested requirements range from blood quantum to cultural knowledge to length of residency.

51. Office of Hawaiian Affairs, '*Onipa'a*.

52. I thank David Forman for bringing this information to my attention. My quotation of Sonny Ching's statement and description of the coalition are adapted from his unpublished paper "The Perpetuation of Native Hawaiian Sovereignty through Legal Customs." Sonny Ching is *kumu hula* of the dance group Halau Na Mamo O Pu'uanahulu. See also Enomoto, "Kumu Hula."

53. This indirect approach may be more in keeping with hula aesthetics. As Adrienne Kaeppler has argued, indirectness is "one of the most important traditional values in Hawaiian communication." *Kaona*, or hidden meanings, are an important dimension of hula song and dance. This may militate against direct political statements for some *kumu hula*s. See Kaeppler, "Visible and Invisible in Hawaiian Dance," p. 31.

54. *Honolulu Advertiser*, "Hawaiian Vote: A Signal for Caution."

55. *Hawaiian Beat*, "Sovereignty Media Packets Distributed."

56. Belknap, "Hawaiian Culture and Tourism," p. 1. See also Kennedy, "Hotel Management, Hawaiian-Style." This article discusses the work of George Kanahele, a well-respected expert on Hawaiian music, who serves as a consultant to the

tourist industry, promoting hotel management according the Native Hawaiian values.

57. U.S. Congress, *The Apology to Native Hawaiians on behalf of the United States for the Overthrow of the Kingdom of Hawaii.*

58. Data and quotations are taken from Hawai'i Visitors Bureau's Market Research Department's 1990 *Visitor Satisfaction Report,* which for the first time included a new section on life-style analysis, pp. 69–71. Results are based on multivariate analysis of more than 6,000 questionnaires, allowing for the analysis of key factors and activities to be separated out, such as the impact of lū'au attendance on satisfaction.

Although there is no direct breakdown by income, two bits of data are suggestive. Lū'au attendees planned their trips several more months in advance than nonattendees, and although 8 percent said they were likely to revisit Hawai'i within the next five years, of those who would not, significantly more lū'au attendees than nonattendees cited personal finances as a barrier for not revisiting. This may indicate that financial concerns are more pressing for this group than for some others, thus placing a majority in the lower-middle to middle-middle class rather than the upper-middle and above. No breakdown by race was available. There are, however, elite lū'aus which advertise themselves as authentic and cater to the more upscale tourist than the big commercial lū'aus discussed here.

CHAPTER TWO

1. The dancer's name appears only inside the front cover, enhancing the iconicity of the picture.

2. For a discussion of the geopolitical forces that set the context for annexation, see Kent, *Hawaii,* pp. 56–69. See also the discussion of annexation in Dudley and Agard, *A Call for Hawaiian Sovereignty.* A petition of 29,000 signatures by Native Hawaiians protesting the annexation had been delivered to the U.S. Congress in 1897.

3. For a discussion of the "great *mahele,*" or land division, and its devastating effects on Native Hawaiians, see Kame'eleihiwa, *Native Land and Foreign Desires.* See also Trask, *From a Native Daughter,* pp. 87–110, for a discussion of contemporary land-rights politics.

4. Such an organization has been in existence ever since. The Hawaiian Promotion Committee was renamed the Hawai'i Tourist Bureau in 1919, the Hawaiian Travel Bureau in 1944, and the Hawaiian Visitors Bureau in 1945. Schmitt, *Historical Statistics of Hawaii,* p. 281. In 1996 it changed names again, to the current Hawai'i Visitors and Convention Bureau.

The melding of tourism possibilities with U.S. annexation is brought out clearly in the 1893 visit of James Thurston to the mainland. While making arrangements for a Hawaiian exhibit at the Columbian Exposition, designed to publicize the islands to potential visitors, he also stopped in Washington, D.C., to discuss annexation possibilities. (See Kuykendall, *Hawaiian Kingdom,* pp. 110–12 and 534.)

As soon as the Promotion Committee was formed, an on-site visitors bureau was opened in Honolulu's Young Hotel. A photograph surviving from that period shows a large room offering brochures, timetables, and reference books. Assistance in arranging activities was offered.

5. *Pacific Commercial Advertiser,* October 20, 1891; quoted in Kuykendall, *Hawaiian Kingdom,* p. 10.

6. See *Life,* May 5, 1904.

7. *Life,* Sept. 24, 1903, and repeated throughout the year.

8. *Life,* Dec. 24, 1908.

9. *Life,* Nov. 19, 1903, and Dec. 4, 1903.

10. In addition to the steamship companies and the Hawaiian Promotional Committee, railroads like the Union Pacific (*Life,* Jan. 5, 1911) also touted Honolulu as a winter getaway. Competing advertisements of the time invited wealthy vacationers to Cuba, "the Riviera of America" (*Life,* Dec. 24, 1903), the West Indies, and the Bahamas.

Hawai'i was part of a mainland Pacific imaginary long before the Hawaii Promotion Committee decided to turn that fixation to profit. During the second half of the nineteenth century, popular stories and newspaper reports by Jack London, Mark Twain, and Robert Louis Stevenson added to the islands' allure, building on a long history of explorers', adventurers', and missionaries' depictions ever since ongoing European contact was first initiated in 1778 with the voyages of Captain James Cook. For an excellent source, see Smith, *European Vision and the South Pacific.* Smith discusses European ideas, descriptions, and visual depictions of native inhabitants in many Pacific Island groups, covering the period from Captain Cook's voyages through approximately 1850.

11. *Pacific Commercial Advertiser,* "Moana Hotel Opened Last Evening with Glitter and Good Cheer," p. 2.

12. In 1910 there were still nine secular and three religious Hawaiian-language newspapers, although they were on the decline following the passage of an 1896 law that banned the use of Hawaiian in the schools. See Schutz, *The Voices of Eden,* esp. pp. 353 and 363.

13. Translations by Amy K. Stillman, of lines 7–10 from "Kupaa Oiaio Me Ka Lahui," printed in *Buke Mele Lahui,* (1895): "Kui aku e ka lono lohe o Maleka,/ Eia Hawaii i ka ehuehu,/ Aia i ka luna o Daimana Hila,/ Ke aloha aina e hoolulu nei, . . . " Stillman, "History Reinterpreted in Song"; quotation on pp. 10–11.

14. Waikiki had been developing as a recreational center during the last decades of the nineteenth century. It had been an important recreational site for the upper class *ali'i,* and haoles later filtered in, first as day-tripping bathers, then as residents. Improved transportation, including the construction of a road between Honolulu and Waikiki in the 1860s, and an omnibus and then tram line (1889), set the stage for further development. Early efforts to attract tourists began as the sugar industry went into a decline in the 1880s. An article in the *Daily Bulletin* (Feb. 18, 1888) argued that "the use of all legitimate means to induce people to come and see us is wise policy and promotive of our own material interests" (quoted in Kuykendall, *Hawaiian Kingdom,* p. 10). A few years later the *Pacific Commercial Advertiser* argued that tourism would provide a period of prosperity despite the falling sugar prices: "The tourist travel to these Islands is capable of an almost indefinite expansion. It might yield an income of several millions a year" (Oct. 20, 1891; quoted in Kuykendall, *Hawaiian Kingdom*).

Early efforts to attract visitors included the publication of tourist guides like

Henry M. Whitney's *Hawaiian Guide Book, for Travelers* (1875) in an edition of 4,000 copies, and his more elaborate *Tourists' Guide through the Hawaiian Islands*, issued fifteen years later. In 1887 James J. Williams, best known as a photographer, published a miniature *Tourists' Guide for the Hawaiian Islands,* and in January of 1888 he began publishing a monthly journal devoted to Hawaiian tourist interests called *Paradise of the Pacific,* which later developed into a slick periodical depicting Hawai'i's scenic resources and history. These were also distributed on the mainland to increase interest. By 1888 travel agencies in the United States began to sell Hawaii, with agents visiting the islands themselves (Kuykendall, *Hawaiian Kingdom,* pp. 112–13). Scenic beauty and the power of volcano Kilauea on the Big Island were emphasized, the latter having been promoted through a cyclorama at the 1893 Hawai'i exhibit at the World's Columbian Exposition in Chicago. The linkage between Caucasian businessmen's drive for annexation and their desire to develop the tourism market is exemplified by Lorrin A. Thurston, a leader in the secret Annexation Club, which sent him to Washington in 1892 to lobby for annexation. On the same trip he went to Chicago to make arrangements for the Hawaiian exhibit at the Columbian Exposition (ibid., p. 534).

15. As Torgovnick notes in *Gone Primitive,* European-derived discourses of the primitive are developed through a series of tropes that are infinitely malleable. Such malleability allows for the application of similar tropes not only to external Others but also to internal Others (e.g., nondominant races, classes, and women): "In each case, the needs of the present determine the value and nature of the primitive. The primitive does what we ask it to do. Voiceless, it lets us speak for it. It is our ventriloquist's dummy—or so we like to think" (p. 9; see also p. 8). Regarding the historical specificity of the contours and values associated with European tropes of "the primitive," Torgovnick argues: "When versions of the primitive show specific historical and cultural variations, they expose different aspects of the West itself. Primitivism is thus not a 'subtopic' of modernism or postmodernism: to study primitivism's manifold presence is to recontextualize modernity" (p. 193). Tropes of the primitive were found not only in the nascent tourist industry but also in modern art, literature, and the emerging social sciences.

16. During the period from about 1890 to 1910, the social sciences were established as disciplines in U.S. colleges and universities, and professional journals proliferated (Stocking, *Race, Culture, and Evolution,* p. 122).

17. As Fatimah Tobing Rony has argued, analysis of the body was central to the rise of ethnography and to the depiction of difference through visual technologies. Scientific illustrations, early ethnographic films, the display of humans at world expositions, the "scientific" charting of physical and moral "deviance" in terms of physical markers, all proposed linkages between vision, bodily difference, and systems of knowledge. See *The Third Eye,* esp. chap. 1.

18. Fabian, *Time and the Other.*

19. Stocking, *Race, Culture, and Evolution,* p. 119.

20. Ibid., p. 120.

21. I use "cultural tourism" in quotes because it is somewhat anachronistic. It was not until the teens that the influence of Franz Boas and his students reoriented the use of the term "culture" to mean a whole way of life. Previous usages had de-

pended on a Germanic origin, referring to the development of arts and letters, practices associated with the attainment of civilization. Boas and his followers were influential in introducing ideas of what today might be termed "cultural relativism."

22. Lears, *No Place of Grace.*

23. Church, *Picturesque Cuba, Porto Rico, Hawaii, and the Philippines*, p. 43.

24. Quotes taken from Matson Navigation Co. and Hawai'i Tourist Bureau advertisements appearing in vol. 50 (Jul.–Dec. 1926) of *National Geographic.*

25. Beard, quoted in Trachtenberg, *The Incorporation of America*, p. 47. I also draw on Trachtenberg's characterization of class relations.

26. While not all vacationers were wealthy, a Hawaiian vacation required days of steamship travel each way. Most tourists came for several weeks. Such extended leisure required a lot of disposable income and the freedom to determine one's work schedule. At the turn of the century, new hotels like the Moana (1901) and the Alexander Young Hotel, built at a cost of $2 million in 1902, catered to this elite set.

27. A related version of this decontemporaneity exists in tourist advertising today. Native Hawaiians are almost without exception portrayed only as engaged in crafts or activities (like hula or lei making) which are strongly identified with Native Hawaiian culture. Usually these activities are de-urbanized, i.e., shown without context or by a beach. Native Hawaiians are never portrayed in tourist brochures as professionals involved in law, medicine, education, or politics who live in a major metropolitan area. Since nontouristic discourses rarely include such images either, mainlander encounter a very limited set of depictions of Hawai'i and of Native Hawaiians.

28. Neil Harris discusses the development of half-tone reproduction, issues of perceived truthfulness, and fears about the potential for misuse of photographs as inaccurate illustrations that would be taken to be true, in his essay "Iconography and Intellectual History: The Halftone Effect," in *Cultural Excursions*, pp. 304–17.

29. While it is not possible to date precisely specific images, records from the Keystone Stereoscope Company, housed in the California Museum of Photography at the University of California, Riverside, indicate that shots of Hawaiian hula dancers were included in several different sets of cards, including "South Sea Islands and Hawaii," the "Canadian Set," and "World Tour."

30. Stereoscopic viewing was remarkably popular both in the United States and in Europe. Judith Babbitts estimates that five to seven million different images were produced by American publishers. The first major producer of stereoviews, the London Stereoscopic Company, was established in 1854, but the bulk of the production had shifted to the United States by the late nineteenth century, with the last American company closing in the late 1930s. Babbitts has argued that stereoscope views of the world worked to forge a new identity of "American," one that unified burgeoning immigrant populations while instructing them in American values of industrious entrepreneurialism. A key device in this formulation was found in the text and photos purveyed by the companies and most eagerly purchased by their subscribers from door-to-door salesmen in the form of boxed sets, "world tours" which were seen as offering proof "of the superiority of the white race over 'less advanced' peoples." "Made in America," p. 46.

31. Holmes, "The Stereoscope and the Stereograph," reprinted in Trachtenberg, *Classic Essays on Photography*, pp. 74 and 79.

32. Photo no. 1985.53, a stereoscopic photo by Davy, from the Bishop Museum archives, pre-1900. Although there is no date on the stereocard, by the mid-1860s most island photographers were selling stereoviews. See Davis, *Na Pa'i Ki'i: The Photographers in the Hawaiian Islands, 1845–1900*, p. 22. Davis also notes that cartes de visites were popular, and shots of the King of Hawai'i were available. Photography galleries actively pursued the tourist trade, offering souvenir photographs of Hawaiian sites (p. 35).

33. The caption continues: "The hula-kui has been another dance popular with athletes. It is really a revival of a more ancient dance, in which those joining tried to outdo each other in vigorous postures and graceful gestures. It looks to the outsider like a boxing match in which the blows always fall harmlessly. In some ways it is somewhat like the 'cakewalk' of the South." The reference to the cakewalk dance, which originated among African Americans, ties the Hawaiian native with the southern ex-slave population, racializing the image further and underlining the "uncivilized" dismissal. References to the South will appear again in mainland debates over Hawaiian statehood. Some southern legislators opposed the admission of more "colored" populations.

34. Individual images are very hard to trace owing to the vast numbers produced and the buying of one company by another, with transferral of stock. Stock cards from the Keystone ledgers at the California Museum of Photography do identify specific images of Hawaiian hula dancers, although I have not been able to find production information on the shot of dancers performing for the audience (Keystone view no. 1044; caption: "Hawaiian Hula Girls in a Characteristic Ancient Native Dance"). However, another hula dancer stereoscope is listed not only as part of the "South Sea Islands and Hawaii" set but also of three different "World Tour" sets, indicating something of the popularity of the subject.

35. The combination of spectacle, nationalism, and exotica implicit in the heyday of the postcard is foreshadowed by its association with the world's fairs and expositions during the latter half of the nineteenth century. The 1893 World's Columbian Exposition in Chicago marked the debut of the first U.S. picture postcards. Schor, "*Cartes Postales.*"

36. Lantern slide shows were also another popular genre. The most prolific photographer of Hawai'i, Ray Jerome Baker, many of whose pictures were turned into postcards, also gave lantern slide shows on the mainland as part of the Chatauqua circuits, popular cultural tent shows, in the teens. Making explicit the connection between this "educational" genre and tourism, Baker takes credit for "[bringing] a number of visitors to the islands" through his shows. Baker, "Promoting Hawaii on the Chautauqua Circuits."

37. Stewart, *On Longing*. See esp. chap. 5, "Objects of Desire."

38. Ibid., pp. 137–38.

39. These hand-tinted cards usually rendered skin tone as a light brown. Generalizations must be made with caution given the way inks can fade, but the originals and reproductions of postcards that I've seen from this era indicate that hula dancers were usually presented with light skin, from light brown to a rosy cream

color. Pictures of men fishing or "ethnographic" postcards of Native Hawaiian families eating tend to feature darker brown skin tones, supporting my argument that the hula dancer image presented an ideal for Euro-Americans who valued lighter skin over darker. This is borne out also in the "races of Man" categorizations that I discuss later in this chapter.

40. The reprinting and recropping of images was common practice in postcard manufacturing. Shots of buildings, beach scenes, and streets were also reissued, sometimes enlarged, recropped, or with drawn-in details.

41. A note in the Bishop Museum archive where I found this postcard indicates that these women have recently been tentatively identified by a *kumu hula* as court dancers of King Kalākaua, who reigned from 1874 to 1891.

42. Missionary intervention had resulted in the covering of most women's breasts early in the nineteenth century. This particular staging of a bare-breasted native thus not only assured sexual commodification but staged a fiction of the present in the images of the past. Pictures of bare-breasted women were also a staple in educational and scientific publications, as the next section discusses. The *National Geographic* magazine, which incorporated photographs in the teens, became a primary disseminator of photos of bare-breasted women from Asia, Africa, and the Pacific. For a superb analysis of photography and the construction of cultural difference through the union of "science and pleasure" that the *National Geographic* represented, see Lutz and Collins, *Reading National Geographic.*

43. Without further information about the production and consumption of these images it is hard to tell exactly which images were considered pornographic and which were considered ethnographic. The larger point is that both categories allowed for a type of voyeurism, a pleasure in the visual consumption of difference. I have no information on whether photographs of hula dancers considered pornographic circulated primarily among outsiders like sailors and tourists or if there was a similar demand among island residents and, if so, what the demographic breakdown of that consumption might be.

44. Davis, *Na Pa'i Ki'i*, p. 47, n. 6.

45. See Davis, *Na Pa'i Ki'i.*

46. Ibid., p. 37.

47. The term "hula girl" was popular on the mainland. I use it to refer to the mainlander conception of a hula dancer, with connotations of sexual allure. Ukeke's troupe appeared during King Kalākaua's 1883 coronation ceremonies. A report in the *Daily Pacific Advertiser* (Feb. 27, 1883) described him thus: "Our dandy is an artist, and the hands that can pack coal or handle the sugar bags can handle most deftly the common jews harp [the "ukeke," a stringed instrument]. . . . He has moved . . . the sympathies and dollars of Royalty. . . . He accompanied [the dancers'] gyrations with his tremulous-toned instrument." Quoted in Kanahele, *Hawaiian Music and Musicians* p. 394.

48. Hula itself should not be presumed to present a simple, authentic counter-discourse to the tourist industry representations of it. Despite hula's return to the public sphere, many Native Hawaiians as well as other residents still regarded it with suspicion, some finding it inappropriate for Christians. For good historical discussions of hula styles and practices, consult the following: Stillman, *Sacred*

Hula; Kaeppler, *Hula Pahu;* Barrere, Pukui, and Kelly, *Hula: Historical Perspectives;* and Takamine, "The Hula 'Ala'apapa."

49. The location of the sailors, on shore leave in the islands, would seem to give permission to interracial recreational sex, even when many states had antimiscegenation laws on the books. The card does not imply long-term liaisons, however, and any evidence of interracial sex (i.e., children) would have no impact on the sailors, who, presumably, would be long gone.

50. The presence of the sailors may indicate something of a class dimension in perceptions, with lower-class viewers generalizing from "brown" to "black," but much more evidence would be needed to support such a generalization.

51. For example, this "brownness" is declared on Keystone Stereoscope 10156 T, no. 315, "Native Hula Girls in Characteristic Attire near Honolulu," which states "Hawaiians belong to the brown race," and is evidenced in the light skin tones of hand-tinted postcards.

52. One variation on this hula girl iconography occurs in a *Life* magazine (Dec. 2, 1915). An advertisement for a trip to Honolulu on the SS *Great Northern,* requiring only four-and-a-half days sail from the mainland to the Islands (first class $65 and up, tourist class $45 and up, $35 for steerage), uses the palm tree, beach, and woman symbols, but the woman is large, matronly and wearing a mu'umu'u, not a hula skirt. Weaving a mat, she is still primitivized by the setting and activity of unmechanized labor. It may be that the hula girl image circulated more freely in photos and postcards than in business advertisements during this early period— perhaps not being perceived as "classy" enough, given the high cost of the trip and the elite status of travelers targeted.

53. Bryan, *Our Islands and Their People,* pp. 5–6; quoted in Womacks, "Estudiarlos, Juzgarlos ye Gobernarlos," p. 6 n. 9.

54. Womacks puts forth this argument about feminization in "Estudiarlos, Juzgarlos y Governarlos."

55. Ibid., p. 8; my translation.

56. This is precisely the split that is found in the *Pictorial History of America's New Possessions,* noted in the text . Along with pictures of Hawai'i's pineapple and sugarcane plantations, four pictures of Native Hawaiians are included. One shows a male in an outrigger canoe, and another is a picture of Princess Kaiulani at a royal residence. The last two photographs are paired on one page, literally representing Womacks' point (and reproduced here). In one, a hapa-haole-looking young woman, "a Hawaiian school girl in native decorations," wears a straw hat, a striped, highnecked, puff-sleeved blouse, and a garland of maile leaves, while the other features "Hawaiian Hula Dancers in Native Costumes," three very young, barebreasted women posed with hula implements, wearing only white cloth skirts and leis—clear evidence that bare-breasted shots circulated in pornographic, touristic, and educational texts. Again, no indication is given that women no longer went bare breasted, following eighty years of missionary intervention. The same shot was also made into a hand-tinted postcard.

In addition, this book features long excerpts from the diaries of Captain Cook and those of other early European explorers, recirculating stories a century after they were written, adding to the process of decontemporizing discussed earlier.

57. See Mullins, *Hawaiian Journey,* pp. 32–33.

58. Womacks, "Estudiarlos, Juzgarlos y Gubernarlos," p. 11.

59. A caption by Bryan from *Our Islands and their People,* quoted on p. 5 in the brochure for the exhibit "Archipielago Imperial: Imagenes de Cuba, Puerto Rico, Hawai'i ye Filipinas bajo el Dominio Estadounidense, 1898–1914," curated by Lanny Thompson Womacks for the Museo de la Historia de Ponce, Oct. 11–Dec. 11, 1995, Ponce, Puerto Rico.

60. Cuba and Puerto Rico could not be easily nativized because they no longer had a native population. Native Americans had been virtually wiped out by Spanish colonists, although some educational books of the time attempted to present remnant populations. Although the Spanish were regarded negatively, as Europeans they could be presented more positively than residents of African origin. The Philippines presented a different situation to U.S. analysts. While not a slaveholding site, they did have a native population, which was often portrayed as "bad" primitives, nearly naked and carrying spears. Spanish-origin populations fared better in these representations, but they were still the enemy. I thank Ralph Cintron for suggesting some of these issues.

61. Browne, *The New America and the Far East,* p. 22; quoted by Womacks in "Archipielago Imperial" exhibit brochure, p. 9.

62. Leah Dilworth makes this argument in her discussion of Chief Geronimo's appearance at the 1904 Louisiana Purchase Exposition in St. Louis. As she notes, Geronimo, then a prisoner of war, sat in a booth in the Indian Building, positioned between a woman grinding corn and a Pueblo potter. See Dilworth's *Imagining Indians in the Southwest,* p. 49.

63. Bush and Mitchell, *The Photograph and the American Indian,* p. xxii.

64. Despite these differences, the development of cultural tourism as a fledgling industry in the Southwest no doubt prepared the way for the rise of a tourist industry in Hawai'i, both through its demonstration of profitability and in its inculcation of the idea of safe cross-cultural encounter for whites with nonwhite indigenous populations. For excellent studies of Southwest tourism, see Weigle and Babcock, *The Great Southwest of the Fred Harvey Company and the Santa Fe Railway.* Barbara Babcock's "First Families: Gender, Reproduction, and the Mythic Southwest" (pp. 207–17) in that book is especially relevant in its analysis of white depictions of indigenous women.

65. Winchell, *Preadamites,* p. 172.

66. See, e.g., Winchell, chap. 11, "Racial Distinctions."

67. Winchell's work is a striking example of what Stephen Jay Gould has called "scientific racism," that is, the turn-of-the century union of evolutionary theory with quantification in a new, "unholy alliance." Gould, *The Mismeasure of Man* p. 74.

68. Winchell, *Preadamites,* p. 181.

69. Ibid., p. 252.

70. Ibid., p. 317, fig. 12.

71. Wells, *New Physiognomy.*

72. In a gruesome but telling aside Wells begs American explorers, sea captains, and others to "render essential service to science by procuring crania in all parts of

the world for ethnological study" so that more complete comparisons can be made. Wells, *New Physiognomy,* p. 470.

73. Ibid., pp. 470–71. Unnoted in this section is the fact that by the latter half of the nineteenth century there already was significant intermarriage between Native Hawaiians and Euro-American settlers.

74. Domínguez, "Exporting U.S. Concepts of Race," p. 6. References to skin color appear in Hawaiian-language newspapers as early as the 1850s, but it is important to remember that the vast majority of such publications up until the 1860s were written and edited by Anglo-Americans. The early use of the term "haole" meant foreigner (*ha ole,* or "without breath," that is, without an understanding of the Hawaiian culture), not "white." See Domínguez, "Life With and Without Race," p. 19. Despite these importations, race has never been as important or as relevant a category in the islands as on the mainland, as the continuing significance of the category "local" indicates.

75. Kamehele, in Viotti, "A Look back at Prince Lot," pp. D-1+.

76. Cartoon by Fred Morgan in the *Philadelphia Inquirer,* reproduced in Johnson, *Latin America in Caricature,* p. 163. I thank Sylvia Hilton for bringing this cartoon to my attention. Other cartoons of the time also portrayed Queen Liliʻuokalani as a "pickaninny." For such cartoons, see the video *Act of War,* by Puhipau and Lander. In that video, historian Jon Osorio notes that pro and con annexation arguments in the U.S. Congress were often couched in racist terms.

77. The census made distinctions between native-born and foreign-born residents. The former were categorized as Hawaiian, Part Hawaiian, Caucasian, Portuguese, Negroes, South Sea Islanders, Japanese, and Chinese. See Domínguez, "Life With and Without Race." The slippage between national origin and racial categories, and the translation of the former into the latter, reflect the growing power of racial definition. Such a consolidation ever more deeply binds the association of bodily difference with cultural difference.

78. Ridpath, *Great Races of Mankind,* p. 392.

79. Ibid., p. 396.

80. Ibid., p. 401.

81. Ibid., pp. 401–4.

82. Brown, *The New America and the Far East,* p.163; quoted in exhibit brochure by Womacks, "Archipelago Imperial," p. 6.

83. Bryan, *Our Islands and Their People,* p. 690; quoted in exhibit brochure by Womacks, p. 11.

84. Bhabha, "Of Mimicry and Man," pp. 125–33.

85. Bryan, *Our Islands and Their People,* p. 431; quoted in exhibit brochure by Womacks, p. 13.

86. Using U.S. Census data, Michael Haas reports the 1910 population as 20 percent Hawaiian (and part-Hawaiian), 23 percent white, 11 percent Chinese, 42 percent Japanese, and 3 percent Puerto Rican. Haas, *Institutional Racism,* p. 5.

87. Barthes, *Camera Lucida.*

88. In 1910 there were still nine secular and three religious Hawaiian-language newspapers, although they were on the decline following the passage of an 1896 law that banned the use of the Hawaiian language in the schools. See Schutz, *The Voices of Eden,* esp. pp. 353 and 363.

89. The allusion to counterdiscourses can only hint at the complexity of responses by Native Hawaiians and other island residents. An extended history of photography in the islands would offer additional insights, as would a detailed accounting of Native Hawaiian reactions to the early moves toward commercialization of Hawaiian cultural practices by the tourist industry. With the growing resurgence of the Hawaiian language, it will soon be possible for scholars to track more closely relevant public discourse from this early period in the many Hawaiian-language newspapers. Given the varieties of positions among Native Hawaiians and the many other populations in Hawai'i at the turn of the century, we should expect this discourse to be complex. No simple presumptions of oppositionality can capture the views of populations complexly demarcated by class status, by religion, by attitudes toward the continuance of Native Hawaiian cultural practices like hula, by national origin, and by degree of intermarriage with Euro-Americans.

CHAPTER THREE

1. For a discussion of the flow of influences between the islands and the mainland, see Tatar, *Strains of Change: The Impact of Tourism on Hawaiian Music.*

2. Two sources mention this poster: Hopkins, *The Hula,* pp. 44, 45; Sereno, *Images of the Hula Dancer and "Hula Girl": 1778–1960,* p. 161.

3. The pre-1900 history of hula in the islands far exceeds the limits of my study here yet remains an important component of how tourist performances and their interpretations developed. See Barrere, "The Hula in Retrospect," pp. 48–56; and works by Stillman, Takamine, and Kaeppler. See also Costa, "Dance in the Society and Hawaiian Islands as Presented by the Early Writers, 1767–1842"; and Emerson, *Unwritten Literature of Hawaii.*

4. Quoted in Barrere, "The Hula in Retrospect," p. 49; translation by Mary Pukui.

5. Born in 1872, Wilson was soon *hānai'*ed, or adopted out to be raised as a foster child, by Kapahu Kula-O-Kamamalu, a chanter and friend of Queen Kapi'olani. She joined King Kalākaua's troupe of court dancers at age sixteen.

6. Sereno, pp. 155–58, 165–68.

7. Audiotaped interview by Jean Charlot with Jennie Wilson (1872–1962), February 4, 1961. Charlot Tape no. 008, Special Collections, Hawaiian Collection, University of Hawai'i at Manoa. All information on Wilson taken from this tape unless otherwise noted.

8. The casual linkage to animals indicates the ties to zoo displays, which similarly allowed visitors to stroll through vast geographical stretches, each represented by specimens "in the flesh." "Through the Looking Glass," *Chicago Tribune,* November, 1, 1893, p. 9; quoted in Rydell, *All the World's a Fair* p. 65; see also pp. 38–71.

9. Wilson and her troupe of musicians and dancers also toured abroad, appearing in Munich, Berlin, Cologne, and for three months at the Folies-Bergères in Paris, followed by a two-month tour of England during 1894 (Kanahele, *Hawaiian Music and Musicians,* p. 172).

10. Odell, *Annals of the New York Stage,* p. 739.

11. *Oxford Companion to American Theatre,* p. 81.

12. Entry on Laurette Taylor, by Colby Kullman, in Barranger, Roberts, and Robinson, *Notable Women in the American Theatre,* pp. 857–61.

13. These quotes from *New York Times* reviews, Jan. 14, 1912, VII:5:1, and Jan. 9, 1912, VIII:8:4.

14. A slight countermeasure to the predictability of this story comes from Luana's royal position. A subplot focuses on white businessmen's plans for annexation, and Luana is asked to be ruler. She refuses. According to one reviewer, the reason is that ascension to the throne will require a move to Honolulu, where there will be more women hoping "to lure her white husband from her." *New York Times,* Jan. 14, 1912, V11:5:1.

15. Ibid.

16. Native Hawaiians were not the only ones so portrayed, but the specificity of their portrayal in this way will have long-lasting effects on the tourist industry, as I will argue later. African Americans and others received similar treatment in popular entertainments before and since. In the case of blackface minstrelsy, however, "beauty" was not the prime attached signifier.

17. Rydell, *All the World's a Fair,* p. 209.

18. Kanahele, *Hawaiian Music and Musicians,* pp. 291–92.

19. Ibid., pp. 388–89.

20. Lott, *Love and Theft;* Kortiz, "Dancing the Orient for England."

21. Thomas, *Colonialism's Culture.*

22. Mizejewski, *Ziegfeld Girl.*

23. In *Steppin' Out,* Erenberg notes: "Black entertainers were perceived as natural, uncivilized, uninhibited performers, naturally smiling, because they had what whites lacked: joy in life" (p. 255). By contrast, star performer Doraldina, lauded for refining the native hula, represented the natives while not quite becoming one, despite her exotic looks. She never had to fear the "uncivilized" label, both because of her own status as non-Native and because of the good-native status accorded Hawaiians.

24. Mizejewski, *Ziegfeld Girl.*

25. Koritz, "Dancing the Orient for England."

26. Quoted in Erenberg, *Steppin' Out.*

27. "Doraldina Tells of the Hula," *New York Sun,* July 2, 1916, p. 3.

28. Obituary for Doraldina, *New York World Telegram,* Feb. 14, 1936, from the Doraldina clipping file, New York Public Library Dance Collection (n.p.). In addition to her Broadway performances, Doraldina was featured at the Montmartre supper club, where, their advertisements assure us, "exclusive New York meets after midnight." And she was not the only supper-club hula star. Playing at the exact same time in New York was "Veronica, the Dancing Venus of Maui on her first appearance in America," in "marvelous native dances," accompanied by Clark's Royal Hawaiian Serenaders. Veronica appeared at the Hawaiian Room of Reisenweber's on Columbus Circle, in two shows a night. (Advertisements for these shows appeared in the *New York Times,* e.g., on July 9, 10, and 13, 1916.)

29. Quoted in Erenberg, *Steppin' Out,* pp. 219 and 225. See also his chap. 7, "Broadway Babies: Gloryfying the American Girl, 1915–1922."

30. Entry on Doraldina, by Cohen-Stratyner, *Biographical Dictionary of Dance,* p. 270.

31. In discussing the popularity of similar performances at "lobster palaces," up-

scale supper clubs, Lewis Erenberg has contended that for couples this entertainment craze formed part of a new sense of intimacy in relationships between the sexes. Cabaret shows catered to middle-and upper-class male patrons with their wives and girlfriends, even daughters, so that sexuality had to be presented as fun, young, wholesome, athletic, not as torrid or threatening to either the men or the women in the audience. This is the same type of sensuality, not sexuality, that sells in the tourist industry today, and most shows attract men and women in couples.

The "whitening" process that Doraldina was praised for was part of this transposition of what was perceived as a more primitive sexuality into an acceptable artistic sensuality. A related move was afoot in the emergent modern dance world, where performers like Ted Shawn and Ruth St. Denis, among others, created a series of highly popular dances based on a variety of foreign or archaic "types." I discuss this process in "Dancing Out the Difference." In fact, Shawn choreographed the "South Sea Ballet of Hawaii" in 1915, presenting it with the Denishawn dancers at Los Angeles's Mason Opera House, October 4, 1915, anticipating the Broadway Hawaiian craze of 1917. (A picture of this production survives in the photo file, New York Public Library Dance Collection.)

32. Mizejewski, *Ziegfeld Girl*, p. 120.

33. Kitchen, *Evening World*, Friday, 31, 1930 (n.p.).

34. Tatar, *Strains of Change*, p. 5.

35. Ibid., p. 7.

36. Ibid., p.11.

37. Quoted in ibid., p. 12.

38. Stratyner, *Ned Wayburn and the Dance Routine*, pp. 48–49.

39. Bohemian fantasy clubs in New York in the 1920s also provided a type of three-dimensional tourist advertisement. As Erenberg notes, the clubs not only presented themed shows but now recreated exotic locales, as well. Architecture and decor became part of the show, the experience of fantasy leisure. Generalized South Sea Islands, gypsy camps, and pirates' coves were favorite settings. When Gilda Gray headlined at the Rendezvous on Broadway in a program of South Sea Island dances, it was transformed into an island atmosphere. Reisenweber's club had pioneered this style by changing one of its rooms into "Doraldina's Hawaiian Island" in 1916, naming it after its star performer. These architectural re-creations stood as three-dimensional advertisements for Hawaiian tourism, enticing patrons with the sense of what it might be like to really "be there."

40. Stratyner, *Ned Wayburn*, p. 35.

41. Ibid., p. 50.

42. Byrne MacFadden, "Dance of the South Seas." The article is presented as a backstage interview with Gray.

43. The defining work on Orientalism remains Said's book.

44. I discuss the facilitating framing of such Orientalism in "Dancing out the Difference."

45. Gray, quoted in MacFadden, "Dance of the South Seas," p. 11.

46. MacFadden, "Dance of the South Seas," p. 72.

47. Gray, quoted in ibid., p. 12.

48. Ibid., p. 72.

49. See Kaeppler, *Hula Pahu.*

50. Gray, quoted in MacFadden, "Dance of the South Seas," p. 72.

51. See Erenberg, *Steppin' Out,* pp. 250–51, for a brief narration of Gray's career. He notes: "The sources of dances like the charleston and the black bottom lay in black culture, and they found wide introduction in New York after the popularity of *Shuffle Along,* a black musical of 1921–1922" (p. 251).

52. See Mizejewski *Ziegfeld Girl,* esp. her excellent chapter "Racialized, Glorified American Girls."

53. Eric Lott also provides a very fine discussion of desire and disgust in cross-racial representation in the white, antebellum minstrel shows in *Love and Theft.* This prior history of racial representation is relevant to the theatrical traditions which informed these 1920s revues, as are the vaudeville routines which stereotyped new immigrants. All may be seen as part of the process of negotiating power and change in the public imaginary, and as specific renditions of race as "sexed" and vice versa. However, the contemporary meanings of each of these renditions is dependent not only on the available theatrical traditions but also on the wider social habitus within which they are mobilized at any historical moment. Therefore, my goal is to locate the hula craze both within the larger practice of representing others and with specific regard to which others, when, and how. Primitivisms, like colonialisms, may share specific contours but are always particular as well.

54. Mizejewski notes in reference to the Ziegfeld performers' use of cafe-au-lait makeup in some numbers that "imitation was permissible precisely because it was identifiable as disguise" (p.131). The situation of Toots Parka was different. Her claims to be Hawaiian underwrote her self-presentation as authentic and seems to have been a key to her success. She never made a name for herself as other than a Hawaiian performer, however, unlike Gilda Gray and Doraldina, who rode a series of dance styles to fame. Different still will be the wild success of the Hawaiian rooms that arise in many urban centers during the 1930s and feature entertainers from the islands rather than mainland entertainers' renditions of Hawaiiana.

55. Mizejewski, *Ziegfeld Girl,* p. 122.

56. Gray, quoted in MacFadden, "Dance of the South Seas," p. 12.

57. Erenberg (*Steppin' Out,* p. 249) notes that this name transformation was in part suggested by Sophie Tucker, a well-known Jewish performer of the period. See also Erenberg's discussion, in his chap. 6, of the ambiguous presence of Jews on the stage as both the same as and different from other whites.

CHAPTER FOUR

1. Los Angeles Steamship Co. advertisement, *Life* magazine, Oct. 13, 1927, p. 35.

2. Hawaii Tourist Bureau advertisement, *Life* magazine, Sept. 16, 1926, n.p.

3. Nash and Jeffrey, *The American People,* p. 775.

4. Los Angeles Steamship Co. advertisement in *Life* magazine, April 5, 1928, p. 44.

5. The shifting ambivalence about natives as native or as nativized Caucasians is continued today in the casting of hapa-haole dancers in tourist shows as well as the opportunities to dress up and "go native" for a commemorative photo. Such photo practices are part of the tourist itinerary today at places like the Kodak Hula Show and the Polynesian Cultural Center.

6. The postcard is available in the Hawaiian collection at the Bishop Museum. Baker produced a similar series of advertising photos in 1921, all featuring Heather in similar garb, perched on a palm, kneeling in a grass house, and gesturing in hula style. For these and other Baker photographs, see Van Dyke, *Hawaiian Yesterdays*.

7. The lower-class associations of hula with the midway that began with Jennie Wilson's 1893 appearances persisted well into the twentieth century. A surviving photo in the Bishop archives shows a 1937 performance of hula dancers and musicians as part of the Ringling Brothers and Barnum and Bailey Circus Side Show. The dancers, dressed in glittering cellophane skirts, look mostly hapa-haole. Even later, in a surviving postcard (also in the Bishop archives) showing the Cole Brothers Circus (the largest touring tent circus in the country at that time) in Louisville, Kentucky, in 1946, the sideshow posters advertise Joe Carvello's Royal Hawaiians as "Beautiful—Sensational." The dancers appear alongside a minstrel jubilee, a female snake trainer, an armless boy, the world's smallest midget, and Chinese jugglers.

8. *Honolulu: Tourist Guide and Handbook*, p. 41.

9. Some postcards offer an exception to this and show family units, but not the advertisements. Presumably such postcards functioned more as "ethnological evidence" of how natives lived than as iconographic symbol for Hawaii as a whole.

10. Hawaii Tourist Bureau advertisement in *Life* magazine, April 7, 1927, n.p.

11. Nash and Jeffrey, *The American People*, p. 769.

12. Hawaii Tourist Bureau advertisement, *Life* magazine, Dec. 27, 1929 .

13. Ibid., May 20, 1926.

14. See Matson Navigation Co. and Hawaii Tourist Bureau advertisements that appear in July–Dec. 1926 issues of *National Geographic*.

15. *National Geographic*, Feb. 1924, special issue on Hawai'i.

16. The volcanoes on the Big Island had been heavily hyped on the mainland as part of tourist promotion. Photographer Jerome Baker, for instance, included lantern slides and a short film of the brimming molten lava of Kilauea volcano in his tour of Midwest chautauquas during 1918 (Baker, "Promoting Hawaii on the Chautauqua Circuits," pp. 21–23), and earlier a cyclorama of Kilauea had been exhibited at the 1893 Chicago fair (Kuykendall, *Hawaiian Kingdom*, p. 115).

17. Grosvenor, " Hawaiian Islands," p. 115.

18. Ibid., p. 120.

19. Ibid., p. 159.

20. This photo had been taken ten years previously by Jerome Baker (see Van Dyke, *Hawaiian Yesterdays*). A nearly identical image of his circulated during the teens as a postcard. The caption on the front (not reproduced in *National Geographic*) said: "Shark Bait on the Beach at Waikiki, Honolulu" (available in Bishop Museum Archive Hawaiian collection). Similar references to African-American children as "alligator bait" were on cartoon postcards produced on the mainland.

21. Grosvenor, "Hawaiian Islands," p. 139.

22. Ibid., p. 177.

23. Cohen, *Pink Palace*, p. 18.

24. Ibid., p. 24.

25. *Honolulu Star Bulletin*, "Royal Hotel to Capacity by March 15."

26. This information taken from photographs in Cohen, *Pink Palace*.

27. *Honolulu Star Bulletin*, Jan. 31, 1927.

28. *Honolulu Star Bulletin*, "All the Glamour and Glory of Old Hawaii Remain."

29. *Honolulu Star Bulletin*, "Tourists Come to Islands by the Thousands."

30. Ibid, p. 31. Also, "Hawaii People Absorbing Study in Race Mixture."

32. Cohen, *Pink Palace*, p. 42.

33. *Honolulu Star Bulletin*, "Diving Boys on Waterfront to Be 'Gentlemen.'"

34. Blanding, "Perfection in Every Detail," p. 3.

35. Ibid.

36. This wasn't the first staging of such a pageant. In 1910 a similar pageant had been staged beside the Seaside Hotel, as part of a celebration started in 1906, which eventually became known in 1916 as the King Kamehameha Day Parade. That first pageant included hula dancing as well, but the hula dancers and those playing the parts of warriors all had to wear brown-dyed union suits fully covering their bodies in deference to religious complaints that it was "immoral to show your bare skin on the beach at Waikiki (see Van Dyke, *Hawaiian Yesterdays*, p. 87). By 1914 the whole event was rechristened the "Mid-Pacific Carnival" and held over a ten-day period, with the hopes of increasing tourism.

37. *Honolulu Star Bulletin*, "Brilliant Touches of Old Hawaii."

38. *Honolulu Star Bulletin*, "Ancient Pageantry, Music and Dancing to feature Opening." The women's names are given in Cohen, *Pink Palace*, p. 44.

39. Blanding, "Old and New Meet amid Waves of Color," p. 3.

40. This pageant was part of a similar mainland taste for pageants at the time, many of which offered idealized visions of national unity and assimilation. See Prevots, *American Pageantry*. Here the context is slightly different, affirming a past of difference as a backdrop for a Caucasian future.

41. The hotel also arranged for deep-sea fishing trips, scenic drives, Hawaiian surfing both in canoes and on boards, ti-leaf sliding, riding, tennis, golf, lū'aus and hulas, and Chinese and Japanese luncheons and dinners. Lest the hotel guests be forced to mix with unwanted locals, the hotel controlled all surfing in front of its property and furnished selected local/native crews for outrigger canoes and surfboard rides. See *Honolulu Star Bulletin*, "Hotel Guests to Get Complete Recreation."

42. *Honolulu Star Bulletin*, "Hotel Social Center."

43. *Honolulu Star Bulletin*, "Hula Makes Big Hit in 'Prince of Hawaii' at San Francisco."

44. Photo in Sheraton Waikiki Hotel archives, no. 835, blue binder, "Old Pictures of Guests of the Royal Hawaiian."

45. Reproduced in Brown, *Hawaii Recalls*, p. 14.

46. Reproduced in *Hawaiian Memories*.

47. Photo no. 874, blue binder, "Old Pictures of Guests of the Royal Hawaiian Hotel," in Sheraton Waikiki Hotel archives.

CHAPTER FIVE

1. Visitor counts rose from approximately 8,000 visitors per year in 1920 to 22,190 visitors in 1929. These numbers may seem small today, when Honolulu alone has a population of roughly three-quarters of a million inhabitants, but in 1929 the whole territory of all the islands only had a population of approximately

300 thousand. During that year, tourists added $11 million to the economy. Steven J. Friesen cites these figures, from the HTB estimates, in "The Origins of Lei Day."

2. *Life* magazine, April 10, 1931.

3. *Life* magazine, Dec. [n.d.], 1931.

4. This is one of the first times that HTB ads use a large image of a hula dancer, as opposed to those found earlier on steamship company advertisements or song-sheets or calendars. Aeko Sereno, "Images of the Hula Dancer and 'Hula Girl': 1778–1960," argues that the HTB was wary of the salacious image of the hula on the mainland and did not use it in early advertisements. In the 1930s the HTB begins a new campaign, refiguring the image as graceful and elegant, as the advertisement discussed above indicates.

5. I do not mean to imply that performers were heretofore unpaid. Dancers at King Kalākaua's court were supported by the royal family, for instance, and danced for guests. What changed was the ability of tourists to purchase this experience for themselves easily. Hula becomes an exchange commodity.

6. A full account of this resurgence remains to be written. It involves a complicated set of changes in public discourse by island haoles as well as Native Hawaiian and local residents during the decades following King Kalākaua's reign. See Kaeppler's *Hula Pahu*, which discusses the 1930s revival of *hula pahu*, a particular type of hula thought to be related to precontact religious rituals.

7. The recycling of this photograph over at least a fifteen-year period and probably longer is typical of the decontemporizing processes of representation that I discuss in chapter 2.

8. Spreckels, "Hawaii for Tourists," p. 662.

9. Langton, "Give the Tourists More Variety," p. 15.

10. Ibid.

11. *Waikiki, 1900–1985: Oral Histories,* p. 1630.

12. Ibid., p. 1629.

13. Ibid., pp. 1628–29 and 1631.

14. Lears, *Fables of Abundance,* pp. 325 and 327.

15. This advertisement appeared in *National Geographic,* July, 1934. Some professional dancers wore bobbed hair in the 1930s, departing slightly from the long-haired look of previous decades and introducing a visual tension between modernity and timeless tradition. Cellophane skirts had a similar effect.

16. This was part of a general trend toward the increased use of photography in advertisement. Jackson Lears argues that this trend was "part of a broader attempt to restore an emotionally charged vision of 'real life' to national advertising" (*Fables of Abundance,* p. 328). He cites a catalogue for a 1930 advertising photography exhibition at the N. W. Ayer Gallery which saluted photography's ability to combine "sincerity in displaying [the] product and drama in portraying its virtues" (quoted on p. 324). A few years later, the Ayer company hired Steichen.

17. Steer, quoted in an interview by Krauss, "Hula Star Recalls Days of Glory at the Royal Hawaiian."

18. DeSoto Brown notes that more than 125,000 of the Eugene Savage menus had been given away or sold at small cost to ship passengers by 1951. The pictures, which were adapted from murals painted between 1938 and 1940, were not used

commercially until the late 1940s. Reproductions of the work of both MacIntosh and Savage are popular today, gracing notecards and even fabric. Pictures of work by Savage, MacIntosh, and Blasingame appear in Brown's book *Hawaii Recalls*. In the thirties aloha shirts also became popular, featuring scenes of Hawaiiana like surfers, dancers, and Diamond Head. Like the menus and souvenir photographs, these visual products returned to the mainland, where they further enforced the iconography of the destination image.

19. The employers, not the greeters, furnished these elaborate flower leis to complete the picture, indicating the importance of the iconography. "You ought to see what I used to wear, the kind of leis I used to wear, to go meet those planes," recalls Steer. "*Pikake*, sometimes; *'ilima*, sometimes. . . . And then, when I go to the Royal [Hotel], they always had a nice lei for me. . . . It was really a nice experience" (*Waikiki, 1900–1985*, p. 1632).

20. The extended circuitry of these predominantly female images is hardly paltry. A decade ago an article saluting the fiftieth anniversary of the show noted that the bleachers seat 3,000, with at least one-third of the audience having cameras. An estimated 12,000 photos are taken at each show. In 1987, only Disney World and Disneyland sold more film than the Kodak show (Krauss, "After 50 Years, Hula Show Still Clicks"; and Taylor, "Celebrating 50 Years of Snapshots"). By 1997 an estimated 10 million people had seen the show (Ryan, "Kodak Hula Show Celebrates 60 Years of Aloha").

21. The Kodak Hula Show wasn't Steer's first dancing job. She began dancing professionally at the Royal Hawaiian in 1929, when she was only fourteen, and by 1936 she was a featured performer there, along with such dancers as Winona Love, Aggie Auld, and Beverly Noa, each of whom crafted her own special performance style. Steer recalls Winona Love doing a sweet hapa-haole hula and that "all the men liked her. Aggie was theatrical. She did the kind of dance the Hawaiians didn't call the hula. Very scintillating." Bevery Noa, she notes, emphasized a more dynamic style. Steer describes her own signature hula, "Mi Nei," or "How About Me?" as having a hidden meaning (*kaona*) without being vulgar. Even in these brief descriptions, something of the range of performance styles emerges, including the danger zone of vulgarity and Native Hawaiians' mixed attitudes toward what was and wasn't publicly appropriate. Krauss, "Hula Star Recalls Days of Glory at the Royal Hawaiian."

22. Auntie Louise Akeo was the founder, leader, and manager of the Royal Hawaiian Girls' Glee Club. Originally based at the YWCA, it became a major source of entertainers for the Matson hotels. Akeo started the modern hula blouse, with wide straps over the shoulders and extending just below the waist, to be tucked under a hula skirt. Before that, the blouse "had long sleeves and reached way down to the knees." Steer also remembers that Akeo used short green hula pants under the skirts, whereas before they went to the knee. These dress changes gave a more modern look and simultaneously exposed more of the body to view.

23. Krauss, "Hula Star Recalls Days of Glory at the Royal Hawaiian."

24. High pay could, of course, indicate other things as well, including the notion that it was hard to get women to do this work or that few good dancers were available—issues relating to supply and demand. However, neither Steer nor Reiplinger

indicates a distaste for the work that would have to be overcome by high pay. As far as availability goes, it does appear that a relatively few dancers were employed consistently by the Royal Hawaiian Hotel and that some of the dancers, like Steer, were in high demand for other jobs as well, like the Kodak Hula Show. Since parks and recreation shows during the period indicate that the number of people publicly performing hula was growing (and, of course, had never died out despite missionary censure and lingering denigration by some), I am assuming that there was an adequate supply of dancers and that those hired in the highest-paying jobs best fit the employers' requirements in terms of looks, dance ability, and, since there was considerable client contact, personality.

25. These figures taken from Beechert, *Working in Hawaii,* pp. 251, 253, 254. Plantation wages are hard to calculate because they varied from site to site and between different racial groups. Federal assistance during the Depression, which was dependent on compliance with standardized practices of record-keeping, and successful, if bloody, labor strikes during the twenties and thirties helped raise wages. The minimum wage cited above was decreed by the Agricultural Adjustment Administration. It stipulated that the women's minimum wage be not less than 75% percent of men's wages.

26. Krauss, "Hula Dancer Recalls Days of Glory." This may indicate the degree to which hula dancers were regarded as a necessary part of any party. It also underlines the appeal of hula performance to the local populace, including women, not just males and not just visitors.

27. Lila Reiplinger was born in Honolulu in 1923, and started studying hula at a young age. She danced in Waikiki hotels as a child, working at the Moana Hotel, then the Royal Hawaiian Hotel, and then in 1938–40, ages fifteen to seventeen, at the Halekulani Hotel. She was an original member of the Royal Hawaiian Girls' Glee Club and the Honolulu Girls' Glee club, and one of the original dancers in the Kodak Hula Show (see *Waikiki, 1900–1985,* pp. 1325–73). During this period of the mid-to-late 1930s, the famous Clara Inter ("Hilo Hattie") and 'Iolani Luahine also performed in the hotels.

28. Ibid., p. 1343.

29. Ibid., pp. 1330–31.

30. Clark, *Hawaii with Sydney Clark,* pp. 205–6.

31. Forms more closely allied with precontact times, such as *hula pahu,* which were performed to chants in the Hawaiian language, and accompanied not by ukeleles but by the sonorous tones of the large *pahu* drum, were performed at the Royal Hawaiian Hotel by the Royal Hawaiian Girls' Glee Club from the late 1930s through the 1950s, when the hotel changed owners. See Kaeppler, *Hula Pahu,* p. 47.

32. Leila Reiplinger remembers performers mingling with tourists at the Royal Hawaiian Hotel performances: "Lots of people [performers] had friends you know, that would call them over and sit down and talk with them. You could do that." Although most performers were women and teenage girls, the Halekulani included two men's groups. (See *Waikiki, 1900–1985,* pp. 1342, 1372.) In addition to the big hotels, Waikiki nightspots like Don the Beachcomber's, the Niumalu Night Club, and the Queen's Surf also offered top entertainment (Kaeppler, *Hula Pahu,* p. 109).

33. *Waikiki, 1900–1985,* pp. 1370–71.

34. Personal communication, June 9, 1994.

35. Anecdotal evidence indicates that part-Hawaiian dancers who looked "too" white (had very light hair, for instance) also had a hard time getting hired even if they were extremely skilled performers. One dancer recalled a brief time in the 1970s when blondes were included in Polynesian shows that included both hula and jazz dancing, but the blondes wore dark wigs for the hula segments, reproducing the hapa-haole image.

36. Schmitt, *Hawaii in the Movies, 1898–1959*, p. 5.

37. Delores Del Rio is cast as a Hawaiian princess in the 1932 film version of the 1912 play *Bird of Paradise* and Argentinian Mona Maris was featured in *White Heat* (1934). Betty Compton plays the daughter of a wealthy haole planter and his Hawaiian wife in the 1923 film *The White Flower,* following in the footsteps of Doraldina, who played Regina, a Hawaiian beauty and hula expert, in the 1921 silent film *Passion Fruit.*

38. There were some exceptions. The locally produced *Aloha Hawaii* (1930) featured hulas by well-known dancer Winona Love (Schmitt, *Hawaii in the Movies,* p. 32).

39. *Variety Film Reviews.*

40. Sereno, "Images of the Hula Dancer and 'Hula Girl,'" p. 187.

41. Some island performers like Hilo Hattie and Duke Kahanamoku did have limited film careers, but never as romantic leads.

42. Nugent, "Waikiki Wedding."

43. Quoted in Schmitt, *Hawaii at the Movies,* p. 41.

44. Interestingly, none of these shorts features hula, although there is plenty of Hawaiian steel guitar and ukulele music. Shots of Honolulu buildings, hotel scenes, and agricultural plantations are peppered with views of beautiful beaches, mountains, volcanoes, and gardens. When Native Hawaiians are filmed, they are shown fishing or surfing. Other local residents, male and female, are shown working on the plantations or in canneries, providing the sugar and pineapples that grace mainland tables. Nonwhites appear only in manual labor pursuits or at play, surfing. These shorts are somewhat different from then-current advertisements, which never portrayed non-Hawaiian, non-Caucasian populations that worked on plantations.

45. A later film by the same name, but with a different narrative, was released in 1942 by Twentieth Century Fox, starring Betty Grable, with Hilo Hattie in a comic role. That story takes place on a fictitious island called "Ami-Ami Oni-Oni." My discussion of the HTB film is based on a public screening of the restored film by Bishop Museum archivist DeSoto Brown at Queen Emma's Summer Palace, Honolulu, sponsored by the Daughters of Hawai'i, on July 20, 1995.

46. One person involved in the filming has noted that producers did not cast George Mossman as Pualani's father in the film because, they said, he looked too haole. This may possibly indicate a difference in the types of looks deemed acceptable for men and for women by those devising tourist advertising.

47. Allen, "Hulas of Old Hawaii Being Revived Here."

48. Spaeth, "Hawaii Likes Music," p. 424. The incorporation of mainland styles into Hawaiian music was common, as Betty Tatar has noted in *Strains of Change.*

49. Statements by Pualani Mossman introducing a showing of *Song of the Islands,* July 20, 1995, Honolulu. At that showing, several elderly women, most appearing

to be Euro-American, got up and danced the hulas they had learned as young women at Lalani Village in the 1930s. That they remembered the dances after all these years is a testament to the seriousness of the teaching.

50. *Honolulu Star Bulletin,* "Hula Contest Finals Near"; "Hula Festival Will Be Offered July 20 at Academy of Arts"; *Honolulu Advertiser,* "4,000 See Hula Trials."

51. Hula still retained its suspect reputation in some circles. As a front page Associated Press story in the *Honolulu Star Bulletin* ("Hula Ruled 'Out' in Capital") reported, Speaker Byrns, U.S. congressman from Tennessee, stopped a hula performance in the U.S. Capitol arranged by Sam King of Hawai'i as part of Hawaiian night for the secretaries of congressmen. Only music, no dancing, was permitted, and King delivered an address on Hawaiian life and customs.

52. Allen, "Hula Vogue Is Current, Says Teacher Here," p. 1.

53. Excerpted from "Priscilla Poses," by W. S., in Taylor, "The Real Hawaiian Hula."

54. *Honolulu Star Bulletin,* "Popularity of Hawaiian Dances on the Increase."

55. Beach, "Teaching Hula Dancing Becomes a Big Business in Hawaii."

56. Those who studied seriously obviously also gained a greater understanding of Native Hawaiian culture, especially when the context of the classes was something like Lalani Village. But even for serious students, when they returned home to display their skills, mainland neighbors may have perceived the dancing as more titillating than educational.

57. MacDonald, "Our Envoys of the Hula."

58. Ibid.

59. Following her New York appearances, Holt went to New Orleans for a three-month run at the opening of the new Hawaiian room in the Hotel Roosevelt. Other well-known dancers also appeared on the mainland, including comedienne Clara Inter ("Hilo Hattie"), known for her comic hulas, Lily Padeken, and Kahala and Odetta Bray, along with musicians like Ray Kinney.

60. Macdonald, "Our Envoys of the Hula."

61. Kanehele, *Hawaiian Music and Musicians,* pp. 120–21.

62. The live show included dancing at the hotel. After ending in the 1970s, the radio show has recently been started up again on a smaller scale.

63. Pascoe, "Miscegenation Law, Court Cases, and Ideologies of 'Race' in Twentieth Century America."

64. Ibid., p. 48.

65. For instance, Pascoe (p. 54) cites Daniel Folkmar's *Dictionary of Races and Peoples,* compiled in 1911 for the U.S. Immigration Commission, which lists forty-five different races or peoples among U.S. immigrants.

66. Rodgers, "The Native Hawaiian," p. 232.

67. Ibid., pp. 234, 236.

68. Ibid., p. 235.

69. Krauss, "Eyes of the Pacific," p. 218. A fellow of the Royal Academy of Sciences in Stockholm, Krauss spent the late 1930s studying "biological and social phenomena of race crossing" in Hawai'i.

70. Quoted in Nash and Jeffrey, *The American People,* p. 809. The designation "Indian" did not include Native Hawaiians.

71. Quoted in Pascoe, "Miscegenation Law, Court Cases, and Ideologies of 'Race'

in Twentieth Century America," p. 55. *The Races of Mankind* was published in Washington, D.C., in 1943.

72. Domínguez, "A Taste for 'the Other.'"

73. Ideologies of primitivism intersected in complicated ways with emerging discourses of anthropology (the earliest studies of which described nonindustrial and non-European people, often in Oceania), and of a new wave of American nativism, a xenophobic and pro-WASP movement of U.S. nationalism during the post-Depression decade. Primitivism could be recast as authenticity and traditional ways of life in certain circumstances, as Whisnant's work reveals.

74. See Mullin, "The Patronage of Difference: Making Indian Art 'Art, Not Ethnology'"; and Whisnant, *All That Is Native and Fine.* Members of the Frankfurt school made related claims about how mass production could result in ersatz culture, decimating both the authentic folk cultures and elite art production.

75. See Melosh, *Engendering Culture.* Melosh argues that women were consistently portrayed as mothers and wives in these murals, which is, of course, the opposite of the hula girl image. But what is striking is the way that many murals idealized rural life, producing a nostalgia for the preindustrial that emerges even in depictions of technology and mass production. These, Melosh argues, embodied "the nostalgia for an imagined past of individual dignity lost in the modern world of rationalized work and impersonal bureaucracy" (p. 92). Advertisements for Hawai'i, although hardly aimed at the working class, promised elite businessmen a similar pastoral antidote to the deadening demands of bureaucracy, a rejuvenating return to their individual selves. I thank John Raeburn for bringing Melosh's work to my attention.

CHAPTER SIX

1. The term "beachboy" is misleading and paternalistic. These workers were not necessarily boys or adolescents. They ranged in age from young adult to middle-aged and older. Although visual depictions usually portray attractive men with athletic physiques, not all of the men working the beach matched that depiction.

2. Immigration legislation was passed in 1921, 1924, and 1927, limiting the numbers of southern and eastern European immigrants (including Jews), as well as virtually banning all Asian immigrants, many of whom had already been denied access through the Chinese Exclusion Act of 1882, which severely limited legal immigration. As Pascoe contends, in "Miscegenation Law, Court Cases, and Ideologies of 'Race' in Twentieth-Century America," antimiscegenation laws usually resulted in freeing white men from social and economic responsibilities to non-Caucasian women and the children of their unions.

3. Ibid., p. 49.

4. The sole exception to the one-drop rule was an allowable one-sixteenth of American Indian blood for those categorized as "white," as Pascoe notes (ibid., p. 59). For an extended discussion of legal cases relating to the historical construction of categories of "white" and "colored," see Domínguez, *White by Definition.*

5. Emerson, p. 23; quoted in Timmons, *Waikiki Beachboy,* p. 25.

6. See Banner, *American Beauty,* for a discussion of the 1920s tanning vogue and the shifting attitudes toward sports, esp. pp. 242–43 and 276–77. On surfing and

beachboys, see Timmons, *Waikiki Beachboy,* the only book I am aware of devoted to that subject. Timmons notes that in 1907 Chicago entrepreneur Alexander Hume Ford began a campaign to restore the "sport of kings" and, leasing land adjoining the Moana Hotel, founded the Outrigger Canoe Club, with an almost exclusively Caucasian membership. In 1911 a rival club, composed mainly of Native Hawaiians and part-Hawaiians, was founded, called Hui Nalu, or "Club of the Waves," including among its members Duke Kahanamoku, who in 1912 won fame with his gold medals in Olympic swimming. Members of this club became the first beachboys, assisting tourists in learning surfing and canoeing.

7. Other famous guests in the 1930s included Charlie Chaplin, George Bernard Shaw, Paulette Goddard, Babe Ruth, Shirley Temple, Mary Pickford, Carole Lombard, Groucho Marx, Bing Crosby, Peter Lawford, and William Powell. Publicity about the stars helped spread a feeling of glamour about Waikiki. See Hibbard and Franzen, *The View from Diamond Head,* for more on the history of Waikiki.

8. Advertisement from *National Geographic,* Jan.–June, 1929.

9. By the mid-1930s, surfing was so strongly associated with Hawai'i that a thirteen-page *National Geographic* article on Amelia Earhart's visit to Honolulu devotes eight full pages to surfing and canoe-riding photos, although the article mentions these watersports not at all! (See Earhart, "My Flight from Hawaii.")

10. Pay rates as of 1939 were $2.50 to $3.00 an hour for surfing lessons and $3.00 per half-hour for canoe rides. Cited in Clark, *Hawaii with Sydney A. Clark,* p. 154. Just like the hula dancers' incomes discussed earlier, these represented excellent wages. By way of comparison with other service industry jobs, note that men working in the islands' restaurant businesses in 1939 averaged $12.80 per week. Reported in Beechert, *Working in Hawaii,* p. 250.

11. Gessler, *Isles of Enchantment,* p. 148.

12. This Dec. 15, 1938, *Vogue* picture was by female photographer Toni Frisell, the same one who rejected Tootsie Notsley Steer as a model because of her Polynesian looks. Given the magazine, we can safely assume the targeted audience was upper-class females.

13. Quoted in Timmons, *Waikiki Beachboy,* p. 138.

14. Ibid., pp. 139–40.

15. Ibid., pp. 137 and 140.

16. Clark, *Hawaii with Sydney A. Clark,* p. 55. J. Walter McSpadden, also writing in 1939, makes a very similar observation, digressing from a long paean to surfing to consider the male surfers' bodies: "The racial origin of these people is one thing that is still puzzling the ethnologists. It is not Negroid. To style it Polynesian is still begging the question. There is a kinship both to the Malay and the Mongolian. The typical Hawaiians have large mouths and thick lips, rather flat noses, but otherwise their features are regular and comely; the hair black and straight; the complexion that of a quadroon. They walk with the pantherlike grace of men who have disdained regular work for generations, living the untrammeled life of the open. But, back from ethnology to surfboarding . . . Why not try it?" McSpadden, *Beautiful Hawaii,* p. 40. Female tourists may well have been consciously aware of this public discourse of classification.

17. Quoted in Timmons, *Waikiki Beachboy,* p. 140.

18. These tensions were revealed in a deadly way in the early 1930s, when Honolulu was wracked by a rape case that made national headlines. In 1931 Thalia Massie, wife of a navy lieutenant, reported being raped on a beach near Waikiki. Five youths were charged with the crime and then acquitted. One of these was later murdered by Massie's family and some other navy men. In a 1932 article published in the *Honolulu Star-Bulletin* Hollywood actress Dorothy Mackaill said such an incident had been waiting to happen owing to the romances between beachboys and rich American women. "What can we expect of these people when they see Kanakas openly receiving the attentions of American white women?" she asked. Noting that the five men accused are of "mixed breed," she said, "It is a tribute to the real Hawaiian people that none of the men accused of attacking Mrs. Massie was a Kanaka [Hawaiian]"; quoted in Timmons, *Waikiki Beachboy*, p. 33.

Here the tension between perceptions of Hawaiians as "not white" and as "good natives" come into focus. While the "mixed breeds" may be dangerous, the Hawaiian men are all right, merely responding to the invitations of white women. Tensions were high on the beach after this incident, and, in response, the Waikiki Beach Patrol was formed under the auspices of the Outrigger Canoe Club to unite individual entrepreneurs into a single concession. By the time little Shirley Temple was named honorary captain of the Waikiki Beach Patrol in 1935, the professional image was set.

19. Beachboys sometimes took a proprietary attitude toward their clients. George "Airedale" McPherson described his role this way: "Nobody touches these people. They are in our protective custody, they are our guests." Snobs and poor tippers could pay a price, though. Chick Daniels, famous beach captain at the Royal Hawaiian Hotel had a system. Those he liked got the good chairs on the beach, while others were sent to "Siberia," a remote stretch of beach far off in the corner. Timmons, *Waikiki Beachboy*, pp. 107, 154.

20. White men were less likely than white women to be pictured learning to surf with Hawaiian beachboys, although both men and women went for outrigger canoe rides paddled by Native Hawaiian men. However, an unusual 1940 ad for Canadian Club Whiskey features a large picture of a beachboy standing and a white man lying down on a surfboard as the *malihini* (newcomer) makes his first surfing run and then tries his first drink of Canadian Club, both apparently equally thrilling. In the series of vignettes portrayed in the ad a white friend drapes a lei on the newcomer (unusual in itself, since most lei greetings were portrayed as given by a woman) and then dares him to try surfing. The native man thus serves as a conduit to adventure, introducing zest and life, as a gift from one white man to another—a feminized conduit role. This advertisement appeared in *Life* magazine, Nov. 15, 1940.

21. Levine, "American Culture and the Great Depression."

22. McEvoy, "The Land of the Lei," p. 8.

23. Levine, "American Culture and the Great Depression."

24. Rydell, *World of Fairs* chap. 6.

CONCLUSION TO PART ONE

1. Quoted in Flanagan, "Servicemen in Hawaii," pp. 79, 83. This study also reveals that not all servicemen were enamored of Hawaii and its multiracial popula-

tions. Beth Bailey and David Farber cite this article and the huts and hula girls quotes, noting that "a great many [servicemen] had taken the films at face value." See their *The First Strange Place,* p. 39. They also discuss the prostitution industry on Hotel Street. Most women working as prostitutes were Caucasian mainlanders, although some were local (pp.107, 237). The photo businesses were right next door to the brothels, as were tattoo parlors, where hula girl figures were a popular choice. The spatial proximity of these experiences, and their linkage in the soldier's repertoire of entertainment, melded the idea of illicit sex with hula girls, even if the three-minute sexual experience in the brothels was with a white woman.

2. Taylor, "Correspondence: A Dancer in Wartime Hawaii," p. 68.

3. *Life,* "Speaking of Pictures."

4. I thank DeSoto Brown, of the Bishop Museum Archives in Honolulu, for this information about servicemen's photo albums.

5. *Life,* "Classic Hula."

6. Beamer, quoted in Small, "Seven Young Ladies with 242 Old Hulas."

7. See Schmitt, *Hawai'i in the Movies.* For a good discussion of one of the most popular movies, *South Pacific* (1958), see Jolly, "From Point Venus to Bali Ha'i," in Manderson and Jolly, *Sites of Desire, Economies of Pleasure,* pp. 99–122.

8. Woodside, the sister of highly respected *kumu hula* Mae Loebenstein, began dancing with the Waikiki Girls at the Royal Hawaiian Hotel, under the direction of Lena Guerrero, just after the war, at age twenty-one. See Silva and Suemori, *Nana I Na Loea Hula: Look to the Hula Resources,* p. 143.

9. Magazine advertisement for Aloha Week, Oct. 13–18, 1952; in Kent Ghirard's scrapbooks, Bishop Museum Archives (magazine source not noted).

10. "Tahiti Torso Twisters Take over Waikiki"; in Kent Ghirard's scrapbooks, Bishop Museum Archives.

11. Today the mass tourist spectacles like Germaine's Luau continue this Polynesian smorgasbord approach, and even the more conservative Kodak Hula Show includes a Tahitian number in its offerings. For the tourists, although the Tahitian origins of the dances may be noted, they become part of the exotica of Hawai'i.

12. For a discussion of the musical aspect of the renaissance, see Kasher and Burlingame, *Da Kine Sound.*

13. The Kodak Hula Show had long been known for the precision of its line of hula dancers, but not all shows emphasized such discipline. Even today the big commercial lū'aus rarely exhibit the absolute unison demanded of groups dancing in competitions.

14. Since then tallies have ranged from four to nearly five million. See Hawai'i Visitors Bureau 1992 *Annual Research Report,* p. 12. In the 1980s the population of Japanese tourists really started s to play a significant role, topping one million per year in 1984 and 2.5 million in 1992.

15. I thank Amy Stillman for bringing this to my attention.

16. The reasons for these shifts can be complex and indirect, reflecting change in a different sphere altogether. In the tourist industry, for instance, the available pool of dancers might shift depending on how the local economy is doing and whether dancing is regarded as a well-paying or not so well-paying job. Members of new im-

migrant populations, if they are less well established, may be more willing to take jobs that pay poorly, for example.

17. There have been exceptions to the long-hair requirement. Some dancers in the forties and early fifties in the Kodak Hula Show wore bobbed hair in styles that were fashionable on the mainland at the time. There have also been some exceptions to the skin-tone "requirements." At least one Polynesian show in the 1970s cast dancers with skin tones of a darker hue, hiring some dancers who had been unsuccessful in finding work in other shows.

18. These statistics are from Hawai'i Visitors Bureau 1992 *Annual Research Report*, p. 36.

19. Ibid., p. 15. Although these statistics vary somewhat from year to year, the overall contours stay the same; thus these data can be used to profile tourists in the 1990s generally. Remember that Japanese tourists are not included in these numbers, which would account for the filling of more middle-and upper-range rooms.

20. These figures are unsatisfactory for several reasons. The divisions between middle and senior management remain undefined, as does the term "professional." Similarly, some proportions of those working in technical and trade professions (especially union workers) may earn higher salaries than some middle managers. Income alone cannot be an accurate indicator of social class.

21. Hawai'i Visitors Bureau 1990 *Visitor Satisfaction Report*; all quotations from pp. 28–29.

22. Ibid., p. 29.

23. See Wright, "Bias against Blacks Cited Here." African Americans make up just 2% of the population of the islands, compared with approximately 14% of the U.S. population as a whole.

24. "Asian American" can also include references to Pacific Islander, as it does in some federal documents, but I believe a majority of white mainlanders, unless they live in an area of large Pacific Islander settlements, are unlikely to think of Pacific Islanders when they hear the term "Asian American."

25. As I mentioned in chapter 1, the experiences of the large segment of the visitor industry that comes from Japan will be different, too, and deserves its own analysis. The Hawai'i Visitors Bureau provides data on Japanese travelers, who have a somewhat different profile from that of the Americans in age, spending habits, patterns of consumption, and so on. For many of them Hawai'i represents America, too, but in a different way than for U.S. mainlanders.

26. The complexity of sexualities in the islands, including the presence of *mahu*, or males who may take on some "feminine" characteristics, including dress, goes undetected. See Robertson, "The Ethnomusicologist as Midwife."

INTRODUCTION TO PART TWO

1. Souza, "Extend Aquarium to Natatorium."

2. Rydell, *All the World's a Fair*, p. 150.

3. Ibid., pp. 145–49. Similar attitudes toward the display of people and animals are documented in Rydell's discussion of another exposition three decades later, the 1931 Exposition Coloniale Internationale in Paris. See chap. 3, "Coloniale Moderne," of his *World of Fairs*.

4. The animalization of the racial/cultural other is common and dramatically

foregrounded in documents like war propaganda, where the enemy may be pictured in animal form. In addition, stories of mixed animal-human offspring offer a continual reworking of crossed boundaries akin to species miscegenation. Children's stories like "Beauty and the Beast" or Disney's recent animated film *The Little Mermaid* put a positive spin on cross-species intimacies while tabloid reports like "Dolphin Grows Human Arms" combine fascination with horror (e.g., Stone, "Captured Dolphin Has Human Arms!" a lead story in the *Weekly World News*).

5. Concepts of animals will reveal sociopolitical underpinnings. It is plausible, for instance, to see the animal rights movement as related not only to increased environmentalism but also to an extension of the claim to civil rights by minority or subordinated populations in the United States during the late 1950s and 1960s. Peter Singer's book *Animal Liberation*, first published in 1975 and in print continuously since, sounded the call for the animal rights movement and put the argument for animal liberation in just such a way (Singer, *Animal Liberation*). Donna Haraway makes a related point about the politics of representing animals when she notes, with reference to primates, how "scientific stories were also shaped materially by contemporary political struggles" (*Simians, Cyborgs, and Women*, p. 108).

6. As Raymond Williams has noted, the word "nature is perhaps the most complex word in the [English] language." Williams distinguishes three primary areas of meaning. "Nature" can refer to: "(i) the essential quality and character *of* something; (ii) the inherent force which directs either the world or human beings or both; (iii) the material world itself, taken as including or not including human beings." Williams emphasizes that "precise meanings are variable and at times even opposed [and] all three senses . . . are still active and widespread in contemporary usage." Williams, *Keywords*, p. 219.

Throughout these meanings we can trace a striking ambivalence regarding the position of humans. They may be positioned inside or outside the discourse of the natural. Humans may be described as subject to or outside the inherent forces of nature, and as included or not included in the material world itself. In certain usages "nature" is said to be or to possess rational laws, and in others rationality is reserved for humans and opposed to chaos or instinct.

The intertwining histories of the concept of culture with that of nature is revealed in the earliest usages of the word. Developing from the Latin *colere, cultura* took on the primary meaning of husbandry, "the tending of natural growth." From the early sixteenth century onward, this idea of tending was extended by metaphor to a process of human development. Not only fields but minds could be cultivated. It was not until the late eighteenth century, Williams notes, that "culture as an independent noun, an abstract process or the product of such a process" became important. Such usage was not widespread until even later, the middle of the nineteenth century.

As with his investigation of the concept of nature, Williams notes three broad and active categories of meaning for "culture" in modern usage. The first describes a "general process of intellectual, spiritual and aesthetic development." The second "indicates a particular way of life, whether of a period or a group." And a third sense "describes the works and practices of intellectual and especially artistic activity." This reference to the arts of literature, painting, theater and so on is the most common usage today, but all three meanings coexist. See Williams's entry "Culture," in *Keywords*, pp. 87–93.

If humans slip back and forth across the nature/culture distinctions, sometimes being considered part of the animal "kingdom," sometimes outside, beyond, or above it, there is one way that animals too can cross the divide and that is through the discourse of anthropomorphism. As the next three chapters will show, this is one of the dominant tropes in animal tourism, even when it is complexly attenuated by discourses of scientific objectivity which emphasize animals as distinct from humans.

7. I noted earlier how nature and culture related to ideas of the primitive as inherently good (following the laws of nature, which were equated with order) or as in need of the redemptive powers of civilization. Or the terms can be reversed. Civilization can be seen as corrupt and artificial, with nature (or by extension "primitive/natural" societies) posed as the ideal. Since the late eighteenth century, Williams argues, the sense of nature as inherent goodness and innocence has been one of the most dominant.

8. See Williams, "Ideas of Nature," pp. 67–85.

9. Ibid., p. 81.

10. Berger, "Why Look at Animals?"

11. Ibid., p. 13.

12. Stuffed animals for children continue to be extremely popular today, of course, but there is also a new twist on this idea of "stuffed" representations that further blurs the line between real animals and their representations. In the 1990s there is an increasing demand for freeze-dried pets, that is, freeze-dried corpses of deceased household pets, especially cats. The remarkably lifelike animal can then be displayed in its favorite spot in the home, on the hearth, say, or on top of the television. The dried body then becomes a simulacrum of the living animal as well as a beautiful fluffy object of decor. The documentary television program *Cats* produced by the British Broadcasting Corporation and aired May 8, 1993, on the Lifetime cable channel notes this practice.

13. Berger, "Why Look at Animals?" p. 19.

14. Haraway discusses taxidermy in "Teddy Bear Patriarchy"; quotation on p. 243. Although I emphasize the differences between taxidermy and live animal display here, zoos and taxidermy share a common mystification. Just as taxidermy requires the animal's death so it can be resurrected in everlasting lifelikeness, so too do zoo displays require (or did before zoo breeding programs) the capture of the animal and its transport from the wild. Both zoos and taxidermy mask the act of acquisition in favor of the visual power of the now—the co-presence of the animal and viewer in shared space and time.

15. Even in the wild, animals spend large portions of their time resting, but in zoos the irony is that many behaviors like hunting are forbidden or useless; therefore our desire to see them do something is escalated in proportion to the lessening of the allowable range of behaviors in the zoo.

16. Wilson, *The Culture of Nature*, p. 246.

CHAPTER SEVEN

1. Nelson, "Going Wild."

2. Figures cited in "Animal Attractions." The graphic offers a breakdown by venue: 28 percent of adults who visited an animal attraction in the past year went to

zoos, 17 percent to aquariums, and 10 percent to wild animal parks. While 40 percent of all adults attended one of the three venues, the figures for those aged eighteen to twenty-four was even higher, with 53 percent of that age group attending. No breakdown by race or gender was provided.

3. There is a related, but separate, category of animal sport, like greyhound races, horse races, and blood "sports," like cock fighting. But my concern is not with these latter activities, where the emphasis is on animals competing against one another. Rather, it is on the large range of places and ways in which we go to see the animals themselves, not to see them win.

4. Conway, "Zoo Conservation and Ethical Paradoxes," p. 2.

5. Phone conversation with Nancy Hotchiss, director of education, the American Association of Zoological Parks and Aquariums (AAZPA), March 19, 1992.

6. These figures taken from the souvenir book, *The San Diego Zoo,* pp. 2–4.

7. Admission to the San Diego Zoo in 1992 was $12 for adults, but only $4 for children.

8. See Luoma, *Crowded Ark,* p. 5.

9. Of course, this is not to say that the meaning of the act is the same or even similar for all people or communities of people. Animals in general and selected categories of animals in particular are differentially regarded, valued, and treated by different communities and in different historical eras. And different types of animal viewing are more expensive than others. Going out on a whale-watch boat can be very expensive, around $30 a person for a three-hour ride. Admission to the Circus Vargas, a one-ring traveling circus I attended in California in 1992, was a minimum of $8.50 for adults, and $4.00 for children. But my observation at zoos, aquariums, and marine theme parks suggests that even when the activities are moderately expensive, they are engaged in by people of varying incomes. For some families, the trip may be a special outing, for others a more casual expense.

10. See Nelson, "Going Wild," for information about marine facilities.

11. Luoma, *Crowded Ark,* pp. 5–7. See Luoma's chap. 1 for a summary of zoo history.

12. The "Species Survival Plan" was developed in 1978 by the American Association of Zoological Parks and Aquariums to coordinate zoo-breeding programs of endangered species. Under this program, conservation is the primary goal of member zoos. Most of the species targeted for conservation are large mammals like the snow leopard, Asian elephant, Siberian tiger, and the gorilla. Luoma, *Crowded Ark,* pp. 38–39, and 68.

13. *The San Diego Zoo,* p. 6.

14. Quoted in Luoma, *Crowded Ark,* p. 9.

15. Ibid., pp. 8–9.

16. Ibid., p. 11.

17. The development of zoos in Asia, Africa, South America, and other areas may well have a somewhat different history. It may be that menageries similarly represented domination of exotic others, but these would certainly be *other* others, and the particularities of those relationships and the animal metonyms that encoded them deserve their own investigations.

18. Page, *Zoo,* p. 18.

19. There has been some move away from this, not to replace the African mammals, but to include less exotic species. In the late 1960s, Bronx Zoo director William Conway "challenged his colleagues to consider the feasibility of building a spectacularly successful exhibit around the most unlikely and mundane of creatures: the run-of-the-mill bullfrog," to demonstrate that all animals are meaningful in a biological sense (Luoma, *Crowded Ark,* p. 170). Although he had second thoughts in 1982, when asked to reprise his speech for the AAZPA, some newer exhibits today do concentrate on the mundane. The Minnesota Zoo features a working beaver pond in a land where there are many. The Cincinnati Zoo spent more than $1 million building Insect World, which has become a popular draw (Luoma, *Crowded Ark,* pp. 172–74).

20. See ibid., pp. 13–14.

21. Harriet Ritvo offers an insightful reading of big game hunting in her superb study of animals and the meanings humans made of and through them in nineteenth-century England *(Animal Estate)*. In the following discussion of English zoos of the nineteenth century, I draw on her book, esp. chap. 5, "Exotic Captives."

22. Ritvo, *Animal Estate,* p. 214.

23. Ibid., p. 207.

24. Quoted in ibid., p. 215.

25. Ibid., pp. 205, 217, 230.

26. Koebner, *Zoo Book,* esp. chap. 3, "Travelling Shows to Immersion Exhibits"; quotation on p. 67.

27. Quoted in Haraway, "Teddy Bear Patriarchy," p. 281. Haraway's article is an outstanding examination of these issues and emphasizes the importance of realism as a visual technology during the period from the turn of the century to the 1930s, as the museum refined its display techniques, mounted a massive number of collecting safaris, and sponsored early nature films.

28. *The San Diego Zoo,* pp. 7–9.

29. Luoma, *Crowded Ark,* p. 152.

30. Going to the zoo or to an animal theme park is still a very social activity; few people go alone. The emphasis is on families, as revealed by the steep differences between adult and child ticket prices at the San Diego Zoo. But the viewing structures of the exhibits have changed to promote an emphasis on looking at the animals.

31. Luoma, *Crowded Ark,* p. 152.

32. In fact, this enforced closeness was quite a shock the first time I walked into the building. Being used to the open vistas of habitat exhibits, I was simultaneously disconcerted and electrified to be within two feet of a huge hippopotamus, which yawned widely, exposing a huge, gaping mouth half the size of my body. Seeing the size and the body detail so close up was an amazing experience, one typical of this era of display and atypical of today's habitats, but it also brought powerfully home the element of captivity and the force required to produce this experience of safe proximity. In contrast, the elements of force and captivity are very muted, indeed nearly invisible, in the lush habitat displays of the newest zoos, where we are supposed to be visitors in "their" world. The politics of such ownership and coercive display are harder to feel in the new zoos and, as such, more insidious.

33. Luoma, *Crowded Ark,* pp. 153–54.

34. Quoted in ibid., p. 14.

35. Rothfells is completing a book-length study of Hagenbeck and the historical interpretations of his career. I thank him for sharing portions of his unpublished manuscript with me.

36. Reproduced on p. 9 of *The San Diego Zoo*.

37. Nigel Rothfells documents Hagenbeck's animal training career, and I draw on his description of the show, reconstructed from programs for the Columbian Exposition.

38. Although there is an increasing emphasis on education at zoos and animal theme parks, that does not necessarily detract from the visual display as the primary activity of the park. Most people read very little at such places. The emphasis is increasingly on activities to get people to absorb information not readily visible, like how an animal's eyesight or hearing works. Exhibits, especially for children, involve physical participation, like "touch tanks," where starfish and rays can be touched, or vision goggles that show us what an animal sees with its night vision, compared with ours. It is interesting that exhibits which are based on bodily display are often then extended intellectually through the use of the human body. A close history of animal exhibition would reveal changing historical attitudes about the acquisition of knowledge through vision and the structuring of relationships between viewer and viewed as constitutive of a theory of the relation between the natural and the cultural. One part of the cultural is the construction of the natural and our interaction with it. See Foucault, *Order of Things*, esp. chap. 5, "Classifying," for a discussion of the complex epistemological shifts in the history of European thinking about plants and animals and their relationship to humans.

39. Hagenbeck, quoted by Rothfells.

40. Wilson, *Culture of Nature*, p. 251.

41. Luoma, *Crowded Ark*, p. 15.

42. See the recommendations on exhibit design in Norton et al., *Ethics on the Ark*, p. 320.

43. Luoma, *Crowded Ark*, p. 156.

44. Even in the newest types of displays, where species are shown together, such as the San Diego Wild Animal Park, where exhibit spaces cover several acres and often show whole herds rather than single animals, predator and prey are never displayed together.

45. Wilson, *Culture of Nature*, p. 252.

46. Hackney, "N.C. Zoo Offers Spectacular Gardens."

47. Wilson, *Culture of Nature*, p. 253.

48. Quotes from *The San Diego Zoo*, p. 102.

49. Quoted in Rubenstein, "The Jellies Will Leave You Quivering."

50. An exception is local history museums or regional or ethnic museums, which often assume that a majority, but not all, of their audience will come to see "themselves" represented.

51. The in-fake-situ category is the best and most complicated example of the mix of presentation and representation. As noted above, real North American plants, for example, are presented to represent African tropical plants that they look like. The construction of a realistic habitat that functions both as itself and as a rep-

resentation of a naturally occurring habitat in another part of the world is typical. Like actors playing a part, these organic environments are both what they are and what they are not for the duration of our viewing.

52. This changing history of realism in display does seem to create an increasing emphasis on the subjectivity of the inhabitant of the display, but it also reflects and is part of the drive toward ever more realistic representations in much of our technology, from the still camera, to the moving camera, to holograms and television. The realisms of these devices, far from being absolute, are examples of the changing standards for realism, and each carries with it a particular mode of reading practice which interprets the visual codes as representative of the real. But the technological drive has been toward ever-more detailed information in each representation, now marked by the imminent release of high-definition television. The growth in ecotourism marks a similar expanding desire for the really real, the in-situ, a privilege once afforded only a few members of expeditions and travelers but now increasingly available to tourists of humans and other species.

53. Information obtained in conversation with several workers/performers at the PCC, July 1991.

54. Quoted in Luoma, *Crowded Ark*, p. 165.

55. Luoma describes this exhibit, p. 21.

CHAPTER EIGHT

1. This seems to be a trend in aquarium/oceanarium architecture. The Chicago Oceanarium, opened in 1991 on the site of and connected to the Shedd Aquarium, features a performance pool for dolphins backed by a two-story-high glass wall looking out over Lake Michigan. From the viewing bleachers, the dolphins seem to be jumping in the sea.

2. *Monterey Bay Aquarium* (souvenir book), p. 36.

3. Quoted in Ratner, "Monterey Bay Aquarium to Reveal Unfamiliar Worlds."

4. *Monterey Bay Aquarium*, p. 2.

5. The growing popularity of shark-encounter exhibits at animal theme parks pushes this dynamic to its extreme. Visitors walk under shark-filled waters through an acrylic tube.

6. The Monterey Bay Aquarium often uses a graphic image of an irresistible otter lolling on its back in its publications to overcome this "personality" deficit. I thank Kathleen Newman for pointing out this irony. The otter exhibit is a minor part of the aquarium's offerings.

7. Connor and Baxter, *Kelp Forests*, pp. 26–28.

8. Haraway, *Simians, Cyborgs and Women*, pp. 11–12.

9. Le Boeuf, *Elephant Seals*, p. 1.

10. For example, a video series put out by Time Life Videos and sold on the Discovery Channel in 1992 promises a titillating conjunction of sex and violence in the animal world. The remarkable and distasteful advertisement for this series, which resulted in a viewer's letter of protest in *TV Guide*, shows shot after shot of animals chasing, attacking, and eating each other and mating shots of a variety of species. Each of the tapes features a specific category of animal behavior, such as "predators and prey," or "reproduction." The graphic footage and quick editing end with a

close-up of a roaring bear. "Find out why we call them ANIMALS," sneers the male voiceover. These are animalistic animals, rapacious and dangerous, and without the civilizing effects of culture to hold such instincts in check. They are, this advertisement implies, what we are when we act like animals, or what we would still be without civilization. These shows are related to "reality TV" shows like *Cops*, which also offer "real" violence and danger.

11. Le Boeuf, *Elephant Seals;* and Howe, *Mirounga.*

12. Marine World Africa USA souvenir booklet and park guide, front flap. This free, ninety-three page booklet is like a souvenir playbill from a Broadway show, complete with advertisements from major corporations like Chevrolet and Kodak. The advertisements almost all feature some sort of natural setting or animals. There is extensive copy on all aspects of the park, including staff and animals, and it is profusely illustrated with color photos. In the following discussions, quotations are from the 1991–92 edition. Every visitor receives a copy upon entry to the park, along with a schedule of the day's shows.

13. The research projects concentrate on communication in dolphins, which are learning to control elements in their environment by selecting a series of visual symbols, and on language acquisition and usage among whales. This second project has found that whales living in different pods, or groups, speak different "dialects" and that these can be learned. Vigga, the younger of the killer whales, from the North Atlantic, "spoke" a different dialect than Yaka, which is from the North Pacific but was able to learn Vigga's completely different vocalizations and dialect of calls.

14. Steve Nagle, trainer of the orangutan Jolyn, noted that realistic representations of habitats are unnecessary to the animals' well-being. Jolyn, for example, would be happy with a little grass and something to climb on. Fake trees are expensive, and real trees would be destroyed by animals that would eat the foliage. Places like the San Diego Wild Animal park deal with this by using a combination of real and fake trees, protecting the real trees with wire mesh or plastic tubing around their bases and providing feeding stands of hanging foliage on poles to stand in for real trees.

15. Visitor's park guide and souvenir booklet, p. 1.

16. Disabled animals, twice rendered different from ourselves, are especially potent at activating our care-taking empathies. The San Diego Zoo features a blind seal in one of its educational shows, and Scholastic publishing has even put out a book that tells the story of Corky and her retraining after becoming blind. Like a suddenly disabled human, Corky had to learn to negotiate life without sight so that she could still continue as a professional performer. See Irvine, *True Story of Corky the Blind Seal* .

17. The parallel in human terms would be with organizations like the American Field Service or the Peace Corps, which promote world peace through one-to-one contact.

18. Wilson, *Culture of Nature,* pp. 154–55.

19. The shark exhibit at the Monterey Bay Aquarium, which let us "see" as a shark sees, is not the same thing as dressing up as an animal, for it emphasizes a fractured approach to the senses, not a chance imaginatively to become a shark, fully embodied.

20. This pickpocket ploy may be a standard bird-show joke, for it was also featured at the San Diego Wild Animal Park.

21. A new bird show, started at Sea World in San Diego in 1992, also uses a narrative format. "You'll enjoy the hilarious antics of investigative reporter Tippy Hitchcock and wacky Dr. William Wingspan as they try to unravel the mystery at hand," runs the description for the new show in the season-pass-holders' newsletter, *Pass Times* (spring 1992).

22. Not only is nature improved, so, it is claimed, are the animals' individual lives through the stimulation that training provides.

23. This is precisely the icon used to advertise the Circus Vargas that I attended in California in 1992. During the tiger act at the circus, however, red electric lights rimmed the hoop with simulated fire. Ron Whitfield uses real fire.

24. During the question-and-answer period that follows, the trainer notes that house cats have the same intelligence as the tigers and are capable of learning any of the same behaviors. (Of course, the effect would be quite different and would hardly attract the same number of paying customers.) Interestingly, a terribly hokey "how-to" videotape on loan from my veterinarian, called "Bring Out the Ham in Your Cat," does feature some similar tricks, including getting a group of house cats to sit up on their hind legs in unison, just as the tigers did. The element of controlled danger is missing from such a display, however, and the final effect is just silly, not spectacular.

25. The gray whale, e.g., which is seen in migrating groups off the Pacific and Atlantic coasts of the United States, can reach a length of fifty feet and a maximum weight of 56,000 pounds. Compare that with the maximum length of thirty-two feet and maximum weight of 16,000 pounds for the killer whales (*Zoobooks: Whales*). The blue whale is almost inconceivably big. This largest of all whales may attain a length of 102 feet and a weight of 392,000 pounds.

26. Compare the orcas with the great white shark, for example. In the movie *Jaws III*, a shark attacks a marine mammal park, and uncontrollable nature contaminates controllable nature, with resulting mayhem.

27. The trainers are allowed to improvise to some extent while keeping within the outlines of the planned script. In Sea World, this would be especially true during the whale ballet segment, where the trainer will determine the exact sequence of behaviors during each show.

28. The concept of creativity in these animals is an interesting one. They do contribute to the development of new behavioral material through play sessions with the trainers. And one trainer, Karen Pryor at Sea Life Park in Hawai'i, wrote about a dolphin, Malia, that was trained to produce creative behaviors; i.e., the dolphin was rewarded only for showing the trainer something "new." See Pryor, *Lads before the Wind*, pp. 234–53.

29. Information from Nancy Hotchiss, education director, American Association of Zoological Parks and Aquariums, phone interview, March 19, 1992.

30. The trainability of marine mammals has not been lost on researchers outside the animal performance field, of course, especially regarding communication and "language," or symbolic comprehension studies. But there are other things that these animals are being trained to do, too. In Santa Cruz, California, sea lions are in

training to "spy on whales" as part of a scientific research project. The sea lions, named Beaver, Hoover, Sake, and Sushi, will wear lightweight, seagoing video camcorders as they swim along with migrating gray whales, "to record the whales' behavior with an intimacy of detail no human could possibly capture." See Perlman, "Sea Lions Rigged to Tell Secrets." Former "Flipper" dolphin trainer Richard O'Barry alleges that far more sinister training is underway by the U.S. Navy. He accuses the navy of training dolphins to attack enemy ships, fitting them with explosive devices that will detonate on impact when the dolphins ram the ship. The animals will be killed in the process. Another plan, the "swimmer nullification program," involves placing a long, hollow hypodermic needle over the dolphin's snout and having it ram enemy frogmen, injecting pressurized CO_2 into them to cause death. He charges that the navy has been involved in war training with dolphins since the 1960s and continued at least until 1989, when O'Barry published his book written with Keith Coulbourn, *Behind the Dolphin Smile* (see pp. 301–9). The navy maintains more than 130 dolphins and other marine mammals at bases in Hawai'i, San Diego, and Key West, notes O'Barry. This context brings a whole new meaning to the phrase "performing animals."

CHAPTER NINE

1. For a comparison, see Waldman and Turner, "Park Wars." They note that, as Disney World has proven, billions can be made from having a marketable character.

2. Kraul, "Anheuser-Busch to Buy Sea Worlds for $1.1 Billion."

3. This figure is the estimate reported by the Alliance of Marine Mammal Parks and Aquariums, which represents the seaquariums. See Miller, "Almost Home," p. 56.

4. The Busch conglomerate now owns seven theme parks, including Sea Worlds in Cleveland, Orlando, and San Antonio. Other theme parks include Busch Gardens in Williamsburg, Virginia, Busch Gardens in Tampa, and Cypress Gardens and Adventure Island in Tampa, Florida. By comparison, Marine World Africa USA is a small operation. However, their killer whale show is clearly modeled after the successful Shamu operation, but placed in a different context. At Marine World, marine mammals are only one of the big draws, along with the tiger show and the people shows, like the "Magic of Animals," or the Shanghai Acrobats. But at Sea World, the marine environment is all.

5. The information on thirty years of attendance, the annual number of paying customers, and schools broadcasts is found in Davis, "Touch the Magic." Davis expands this work in her book *Spectacular Nature*. Davis's book appeared after this chapter was completed, so I draw mainly on her previous article here. While our work proceeded independently, we have arrived at similar conclusions regarding certain aspects of Sea World, and her book, which emphasizes the corporate dimensions of Sea World and the discourses of research and scientism, offers a very complementary investigation to my emphases here, which focus on the live performance of Shamu, the ways the whale body takes on meaning, and the oscillation of the "nature/culture" divide.

See also my "Performing 'Nature,'" in Case, Brett, and Foster, *Cruising the Performative*.

6. Davis, "Touch the Magic," p. 207.

7. Davis identifies this self-selecting and notes that in this respect Sea World is different from other Southern California theme parks like Disneyland, which costs roughly the same or slightly more and which has a stronger rate of participation by minority groups. See Davis, "Touch the Magic," p. 508 n. 32.

8. Sea World of California park guide, a brochure/map provided free to all visitors.

9. Davis, "Touch the Magic," p. 508 n. 32. Davis also discusses this relation of education to ideas of childhood; see p. 213.

10. By way of comparison, note that the December 1991 price for admission to Disneyland was $27.50 per ticket, to the San Francisco Forty-Niners' football games, was approximately $35.00, to the Monterey Bay Aquarium was $9.75, to the San Francisco Symphony was between $20.00 and $48.00, and for baseball's Oakland A's, between $4.00 and $16.00 (Whiting, "Take Me Out to the Ballgame but First Let's Hit the ATM").

11. Phone conversation with Nancy Hotchiss, March 19, 1992.

12. So noted in Busch brochure describing all of their entertainment parks.

13. See Dyer, Stars, for a discussion of star personas.

14. My viewings of the "Baby Shamu Celebration" show took place in March 1992.

15. "Sea World Shows: Little Whales, Big Whales, Pirates and Parrots," publicity release supplied by the public relations office, dated February 1992, p. 1.

16. Noted in "Sea World of California Fact Sheet," provided by the public relations office, dated February 1992.

17. The immense size, the deep blue of the water, and the clear sides of the pool, which allow us to see the animals underwater when they are by the rim, mean this "stage" is much more striking than the smaller version at Marine World Africa USA and help to spectacularize the orcas.

18. See Goffman, Presentation of the Self in Everyday Life, esp. chap. 3, for a discussion of frontstage and backstage visual access. Viewing backstage is facilitated by glassed-in walkways along both sides of the huge holding tanks, where the visitors can watch the whales training or swimming around before and after the shows. A piped-in voice describes the scene, with facts about the whales, but this was barely audible above the crowd noise when I walked through. Looking overtook fact-based instruction in words.

19. At Disney World, e.g., entrance via boat or monorail transports you to the heart of the theme park, which is set off from the surrounding area.

20. Davis, "Touch the Magic," p. 215.

21. Such a breaching is thought to help the whale survey its above-water surroundings in the wild, hence the name.

22. Pryor, Lads before the Wind, p. 114.

23. Like the caption of a photograph or the written copy for a visual advertisement, these linguistic frames anchor the meaning of the visual display and guide the audience's reading of the polysemic movements and postures. See Barthes, "Rhetoric of the Image," in his Image, Music, Text, for a discussion of this anchoring process.

24. See articles by Robert Reinhold, "At Sea World, Stress Tests Whale and Man," in the New York Times, April 4, 1988. p. 13 (N), A 19 (L), col. 3., and in the Los

Angeles Times, June 11, 1988), p. 24, col. 1, "Trainers Allowed Back in Water with Sea World's Killer Whales" (no author given).

25. See Reza, "Whales Collide," and the follow-up article by Reza and Johnson, "Killer Whale Bled to Death after Breaking Jaw in Fight." This was considered of national, not merely regional, importance, and the *New York Times* also covered the story. See "Performing Whale Dies in Collision with Another."

26. Reeves and Leatherwood, *Sea World Book of Dolphins* , p. 80.

27. For a description of those early days and Karen Pryor's development of her training techniques from 1963 to 1971, see her *Lads before the Wind.* Part of the pathos of this book lies in its revealing the harm done to some animals while their human trainers figured out how to communicate with them and what the animals' biological and social needs were.

28. Flipper's trainer is now actively involved in protesting the capture and training of dolphins and has appeared on several nature shows on PBS to do so.

29. Technically, the killer whales are really the largest of the dolphins, but throughout this writing I have used the common term "whale" to describe them, both because that is how they are most often referred to and because the connotation of "whale," with its huge size and power, is part of their allure.

30. Reeves and Leatherwood, *Sea World Book of Dolphins,* p. 85.

31. The popular 1993 movie, *Free Willy,* and its sequels, built on this ecoactivism, celebrating the friendship of a boy and a whale, which he eventually frees from a seaquarium, helping him return to the ocean. Ten million people saw the movie. Keiko, the whale that played "Willy," had been working in a Mexican theme park and was eventually purchased and transported to a special recuperation facility built for him in Oregon. In 1998, he was relocated to Iceland, his home area, with the ultimate goal of retraining him for survival outside of captivity. There are currently about fifty orcas in captivity. See Miller, "Almost Home."

32. I am grateful to John Spafford, the entertainment division, and to Dan LeBlanc and the staff of the public relations office at Sea World for providing me with a videotape of this show and of the later "Shamu Celebration."

33. Animal rights activists protest such captivity, arguing that animals should not be imprisoned for profit. Marine mammal parks argue that displaying the animals ultimately benefits them by raising public awareness and respect for the animals. Both sides of the debate have merit. Sea World discourse covers up the bald fact of imprisonment for profit. And such shows have increased public awareness of the animals, influencing protective legislation. In his preface to the revised 1990 edition of his 1975 book *Animal Liberation,* Peter Singer acknowledges the growth of this movement, stating that now thousands and perhaps even millions of people are involved in the animal liberation movement (p. viii). A call for action sponsored by the groups Defense of Animals and Action for Animals (May 1992) put the call this way, in an announcement of an upcoming rally: "Rally to Save Marine Mammals in Captivity, Saturday May 30 (1992). Freedom Rally at Marine World Africa. 3 of its 5 orcas are now dead and 32 of its 49 dolphins as well." On the evening of May 30, 3,000 representatives from the tourism industry were being bused there. "Let's meet them and let them know that tourism based on animal suffering and deprivation must end." Other performing animal sites like circuses are also targeted for demon-

stration by groups such as the Washington, D.C., based People for the Ethical Treatment of Animals. For a report on attitudes toward whale capture, see Freed's article in the *Los Angeles Times,* "Killer Whale Capture Plan Assailed."

34. The title alludes to the operetta *The Pirates of Penzance,* and since it is set on the HMS *Pinniped,* also recalls the operetta *HMS Pinafore.* A pinniped is the class of animal to which sea lions and walruses belong.

35. See Altman, *Genre: The Musical.*

36. John Spafford, personal interview at Sea World of San Diego, March 26, 1992.

37. Nancy Hotchiss, education director for the AAZPA, notes the importance of the live presence of the animals when she says that "TV doesn't do it; there's no eye to eye contact" (phone conversation, March 19, 1992). She is speaking about nature films but touches on the importance of people and animals being in the same space at the same time. The same fundamental reliance on the coexistence in place and time of tourist and "native" populations is essential to the concept of tourist performances, which are also built on the presence of the authentic, living body to both perform and represent cultural difference.

38. The primary visible difference between the sexes is size, but since whales are so big, this is relative and only perceptible in a comparative situation.

39. Davis notes the increased presence of female trainers and female voiceovers, sometimes granting them more authority than the male trainers. Davis suggests that this correlates with a view by the park of their audience as "dominantly female and the average Sea World customer as a woman with children" (*Spectacular Nature,* p. 224).

40. Davis suggests that Sea World and the Shamu show "[create] a set of overlapping parallels between human families, whale families, and corporate 'families'" (*Spectacular Nature,* p. 219). I agree with this analysis but here place more emphasis on the matrix of heterosexuality and its link to white normativity.

41. I am not arguing that such crossings do not occur even when the performative is tightly structured along clearly gendered lines, but that the fluidity that is always present is here accentuated, facilitated rather than constrained.

42. See Davis for a discussion of the particular, corporate-friendly vision of nature that Sea World purveys. Sea World, she writes, "advances a vision of nature's future that is consonant with the interests of corporate America [which] makes democratic pressures for environmental preservation, safety, and health invisible" ("Touch the Magic," p. 215). Davis also emphasizes the long history of Euro-American uses of nature education to "model a hierarchical social order" and notes that at Sea World "the orcas are always discussed in terms of social organization, intelligence, and especially reproduction," paralleling humanity (p. 214). My emphasis here is related in that it invokes the process of "making invisible" competing political forces and embedded paradigms of social relations.

43. Davis shares my concerns about the racial subtext of the Shamu show. She notes that "although race and gender find little explicit place in the rest of the theme park, in fact can barely be detected there, they are central to the meanings Sea World constructs around the whale." She develops this argument in part with reference to Shamu's linkage to indigenous people (noted in some shows), and to Sea World's incorporatist notion of multiculturalism (*Spectacular Nature,* p. 226).

CONCLUSION

1. John Urry makes a distinction between history and heritage in his discussion of heritage tourism in Britain. "This nostalgia," he notes, "is for an idealised past, for a sanitised version not of history but of heritage." *Consuming Places* , p. 218.

2. Haraway, *Simians, Cyborgs, and Women*, p. 201.

3. 1993 brochure, "Waimea Valley, Home of Waimea Falls Park: Preserving Hawaii's Heritage and Beauty." The park is a tourist attraction that combines nature tourism and cultural tourism through botanical and zoological displays and live performances representing Native Hawaiian life before European contact.

4. There are, of course, varieties of viewing sophistication, of degrees of ironic distance, that individuals might take as part of an audience. But given the wide variety of other entertainments available, and the cost of attending these shows, I'll assume that a majority of the audience members take pleasure in what they see and are, if not "ideal" viewers, then at least not antipathetic ones. Many who would actively contest these shows tend to avoid them. For example, when I attended the Kodak Hula Show with a group of college students from the University of Hawai'i, a majority of whom were of Native Hawaiian ancestry and some of whom expressed strong antitourism sentiments, most had never attended the show before, and did so then as part of a music class assignment.

5. Susan Davis noted this in her article "Touch the Magic."

6. Garcia, "History, Culture Lure Isle Visitors."

7. Urry, *Consuming Places*, p. 224. He is discussing attitudes in Western Europe. Some variation may exist in the U.S. case.

8. The concept of a salvage paradigm is elaborated by Clifford, Domínguez, and Minh-ha in "Of Other Peoples." The idea of "salvaging" indigenous cultures has a parallel in saving endangered animals too, which are thought to be indigenous also, both in the sense of being historically unique and in danger of dying out and in having been "here" since before the arrival of Caucasians.

9. Donna Haraway, discussing the American Museum of Natural History, posits a similar belief system behind its displays: "By saving the beginnings, the end can be achieved and the present can be transcended." "Teddybear Patriarchy," p. 239.

10. Proactive movements of cultural nationalism or animal rights groups can also mobilize concepts of nostalgia and utopian views of the past, but these usually coexist with deep outrage about past abuses. In these cases utopian visions are promulgated to change the future, not to maintain the present.

11. Cherfas, *Zoo 2000*, esp. chap. 4, "Better Breeding." Cherfas estimates that no more than 10 percent of the world's known species could be saved in zoos and that saving species requires judicial killing of individual animals when required.

The flip side of nostalgic loss is the joy of discovery. A front-page Associated Press science news brief in my local paper heralded the "discovery" in Vietnam of "deerlike animal with tiny antlers and a doglike bark," identified by tissue samples as "a previously unknown species," the muntjac. An international expedition is planned, hoping for "live sightings." The last sentence declares, deadpan: "The animal is widely hunted for its meat." Apparently many other people had long ago "sighted" this animal and found other uses for its "tissue samples." "Barking Deer Identified in Vietnamese Jungles."

12. The tourist shows' emphasis on the lyrical '*auana,* or modern, style hula performed to melodious music reinforces this nonthreatening vision the feminine. The more powerful and percussive *kahiko,* or ancient, style dances—performed to drumming and chanting and very popular at big competitions—provide a much more vigorous and assertive sense of the feminine, but these are seen less frequently in tourist shows.

13. Certain ecotourism programs offer the ultimate version of this fantasy of contact through mutual choice. For example, tours promising visitors the opportunity to "swim with the dolphins" in Costa Rica emphasize that they cannot be sure how many dolphins will show up for the encounter. Of course, since the tours take tourists to places that dolphins already frequent, the element of choice on the dolphin's part is not so simple. In presenting this information, WildQuest Tours (Santa Fe, NM) write in their 1998 brochure: "Of course, because they are in the wild, we cannot guarantee what will happen on each trip. We feel it is an honor to be among the first to explore the human-dolphin connection with these particular pods." Such a statement offers the additional inducement of "first contact" to the experience. Past WildQuest participants write: "Thank you for a week of truth," and "none of us were ready to break the bond of magic" when it was time to go home.

14. This notion of animals working is implicitly revealed in the park's schedule for displaying birds. The bird collection, mostly flamingos, parrots, and other eye-catching birds with bright plumage, goes on rotating display, one day on, the next off, hidden from the public's view. Being on display is stressful to the animals, hard work in a sense, even when, unlike the acrobatic maneuvers required of the large mammals, all the birds have to do is stand around and look beautiful (performing themselves) in a picturesque setting (information from a 1992 behind-the scenes tour of the facilities offered to park guests).

15. I thank Kathleen Newman for suggesting this formulation of the tourist as the new soft primitive.

16. Also, additional research on the staging of cultural practices within specific communities for those communities is needed and will shed further light not only on those events but also, contrapuntally, on the large-scale tourist attractions I've discussed here. I indicate something of this possibility in chapter 1's discussion of hula practices outside the tourist realm. Amy Ku'uleialoha Stillman has begun this work with her consideration of tradition and innovation in the hula community through a look at the history of the Merrie Monarch Hula Competition. See her "Hawaiian Hula Competitions: Event, Repertoire, Performance, Tradition."

In addition, studies stressing what those involved in tourist performance experience as performers are needed. For example, many of those involved in tourism work that I talked to stressed that this was, for them, a good job that provided enough income for them to put their children through college. Some emphasized that they liked connecting with those tourists who genuinely seemed to appreciate their performances. Some Native Hawaiians, like George Kanahele, who serves as a consultant to various hotels and sets up training programs for employees to increase their understanding of Hawaiian culture, are actively working in the tourist industry to "Hawaiianize" it. These views contrast sharply with the excoriating criticism by some Native Hawaiians, like scholar and activist Haunani-Kay Trask, who likens tourist industries to prostitution of Native culture (*From a Native Daughter*).

17. See Davis, *Spectacular Nature*; Handler and Gable, *The New History in an Old Museum*; and White, "Moving History." White's piece is part of a larger project using fieldwork and textual analysis to explore the production and consumption of national memory at Pearl Harbor.

18. The current initiative to encourage aloha training for tourism employees and management, led by Native Hawaiians who want to Hawaiianize the industry, moves in this direction but does not, to my knowledge, fundamentally challenge the ownership of tourist infrastructure.

19. Doing this research has led me to examine my own profoundly ambivalent feelings about animal captivity for human pleasure. While I cannot endorse it, I must at the same time acknowledge how much pleasure I take in seeing animals. Despite my feelings that these are guilty pleasures and such displays should not exist, their abolition in the near future seems incredibly unlikely.

20. Ecotourism is the latest version of this desire, now emphasizing an even more heightened desire to merge worlds, this time without disturbing the animal world or the animals. In aquariums, new display designs that allow visitors to walk through glass tunnels while sharks swim undisturbed overheard also encapsulate this ecotourism fantasy.

21. However, this would mean confronting, at bottom, the fact that captive animals live their lives for human pleasure, even when that pleasure is coded as conservation. On some level, human performers choose to perform, even if the larger structures of capitalism render this a "choice" more in principle than in fact. But this possibility of choosing or not choosing to participate is not even a theoretical possibility for animals. This makes it harder to conceive of a historically reflexive show of captive animals that could explicate the past without implicating itself in the history of domination, except by using a discourse of progressive enlightenment, scientific value, or salvation, like those of education and conservation that predominate in animal theme parks today.

22. I develop these arguments further in my "Invoking the 'Native': Body Politics and Contemporary Hawaiian Tourist Shows."

23. While acknowledging some political effectiveness for a discourse like multiculturalism, some scholars are now investigating its essentializing potential, noting that multicultural categories often merely recode racial divisions into cultural ones without fundamentally changing the balance of political power. Virginia Domínguez discusses the relationship of "culturalism" to ethnicity in her "Invoking Culture." Peggy Phelan's *Unmarked* cautions against conflating identity politics with "visibility politics," or political power with (textual) representation, especially in artistic productions; see esp. chap. 1, "Broken Symmetries." See also Stratton and Ang, "Critical Multiculturalism," for an illuminating comparison of the Australian and U.S. versions of multiculturalism.

24. The Human Genome Diversity Project is a proposed federally funded

sampling program intellectually, if not directly, related to the massive Human Genome Project to map all known genes. Highest priority in the HGDP will be given to "sampling" groups defined as "unique" or "in danger of dying out." See Roberts, "Anthropologists Climb (Gingerly) on Board." Donna Haraway offers a brief but cogent consideration of the HGDP in her *Modest Witness@Second Millennium.*

References Cited

Act of War: The Overthrow of the Hawaiian Nation. Videocassette. Produced by Puhipau and Joan Lander. Na Maka o ka ʻAina, 1993.

Allen, Gwenfread. "Hulas of Old Hawaii Being Revived Here," *Honolulu Star Bulletin,* Feb. 23, 1934, p. 12A.

———. "Hula Vogue Is Current, Says Teacher Here," *Honolulu Star Bulletin,* March 26, 1932, p. 3-1+.

Allen, Robert C. *Horrible Prettiness: Burlesque and American Culture.* Chapel Hill: University of North Carolina Press, 1991.

Aloha Magazine. "Ala Moana Hotel Unveils New Hawaiiana Program," 18, no. 5 (Oct. 1995): 11–12.

———. "Maui Intercontinental Delves into Hawaiiana," 18, no. 5 (Oct. 1995): 12.

Althusser, Louis. "Ideology and Ideological State Apparatuses," in *Lenin and Philosophy.* London: New Left, 1971, pp. 127–86.

Altman, Rick, ed. *Genre: The Musical.* London: Routledge and Kegan Paul, 1981.

Anderson, Benedict. *Imagined Communities: Reflections on the Origin and Spread of Nationalism.* Rev. ed. London: Verso, 1991.

Babbitts, Judith. "Made in America: A Stereoscopic View of the United States," in *American Photographs in Europe,* David E. Nye and Mick Gidley, eds. Amsterdam: V. U. University Press, 1994, pp. 41–56.

Bailey, Beth, and David Farber. *The First Strange Place: The Alchemy of Race and Sex in World War II Hawaiʻi.* New York: Free Press, 1992.

Baker, Ray Jerome. "Promoting Hawaii on the Chautauqua Circuits." *Paradise of the Pacific* 67 (1955 annual ed.): 21–23.

Baker, Steve. *Picturing the Beast: Animals, Identity, and Representation.* Manchester: Manchester University Press, 1993.

Banner, Lois W. *American Beauty.* New York: Alfred A. Knopf, 1983.

Barrere, Dorothy B., Mary Kawena Pukui, and Marion Kelly. *Hula: Historical Perspectives.* Pacific Anthropological Records no. 30. Honolulu: Bishop Museum, 1980.

Barringer, Milly S., Vera Mowry Roberts, and Alice M. Robinson, eds. *Notable Women in the American Theatre: A Biographical Dictionary.* New York: Greenwood Press, 1989.

Barthes, Roland. "The Rhetoric of the Image," in *Image—Music—Text*. New York: Hill and Wang, 1977, pp. 32–51.

———. *"Camera Lucida": Reflections on Photography*. Trans. Richard Howard. New York: Hill and Wang, 1986.

Beach, Bonnie. "Teaching Hula Dancing Becomes a Big Business in Hawaii," *Honolulu Star Bulletin*, July 24, 1937, p. 3-1.

Beechert, Edward D. *Working in Hawai'i: A Labor History*. Honolulu: University of Hawai'i Press, 1985.

Belknap, Jodi Parry. "Hawaiian Culture and Tourism." *Hawaiian Beat: The Monthly Membership Publication of Hawai'i Visitors Bureau* 10, no. 1 (1993): 1–2.

Berger, John. "Why Look at Animals?" in *About Looking*. New York: Pantheon, 1980, pp. 1–26.

Bhabha, Homi. "Of Mimicry and Man: The Ambivalence of Colonial Discourse." *October* 28 (Spring 1984): 125–33.

Blanding, Don. "Old and New Meet amid Waves of Color," *Honolulu Star Bulletin*, Feb. 2, 1927, p. 1–3.

———. "Perfection in Every Detail," *Honolulu Star Bulletin*, Feb. 2, 1927, p. 3.

Bordman, Gerald, ed. *Oxford Companion to American Theatre*. 2d ed. New York: Oxford University Press, 1992.

Bourdieu, Pierre. *Outline of a Theory of Practice*. Cambridge: Cambridge University Press, 1977.

———. *Distinction: A Social Critique of the Judgment of Taste*. Cambridge, MA: Harvard University Press, 1984.

Boyce, William. *United States Colonies and Dependencies*. Chicago: Rand McNally, 1914.

Brown, DeSoto. *Hawaii Recalls: Selling Romance to America—Nostalgic Images of the Hawaiian Islands, 1910–1950*. Honolulu: Editions Limited, 1982.

Browne, G. Waldo, ed. *The New America and the Far East: A Picturesque and Historic Description of These Lands and Peoples*. Boston: Marshall Jones, 1907.

Bryan, William S., ed. *Our Islands and Their People, As Seen with Camera and Pencil*. 2 vols. St. Louis: Thompson, 1899.

Buck, Elizabeth. *Paradise Remade: The Politics of Culture and History in Hawaii*. Philadelphia: Temple University Press, 1993.

Bush, Alfred L., and Lee Clark Mitchell. *The Photograph and the American Indian*. Princeton, NJ: Princeton University Press, 1994.

Butler, Judith. *Gender Trouble: Feminism and the Subversion of Identity*. New York: Routledge, 1990.

———. *Bodies That Matter: On the Discursive Limits of "Sex."* New York: Routledge, 1993.

Cats. [BBC television documentary.] Aired on Lifetime channel, May 8, 1993.

Charlot, Jean. Interview. Charlot tape no. 008: Jennie Wilson (1872–1962). Special Collections, Hawaiian, University of Hawai'i at Manoa, Honolulu.

Cherfas, Jeremy. *Zoo 2000: A Look beyond the Bars*. London: British Broadcasting Corporation, 1984.

Chon, Kye-Sung. "The Role of Destination Image in Tourism: A Review and Discussion." *Tourist Review*, no. 2 (1990): 2–9.

Church, A. M., ed. *Picturesque Cuba, Porto Rico, Hawaii, and the Philippines.* Springfield, OH: Mast, Crowell, and Kirkpatrick (Farm and Fireside Library), 1899.

Clark, Sydney A. *Hawaii with Sydney Clark.* New York: Prentice-Hall, 1939.

Clifford, James, and George Marcus, eds. *Writing Culture: The Poetics and Politics of Ethnography.* Berkeley: University of California Press, 1986.

Clifford, James, Virginia Domínguez, and Trinh T. Minh-ha. "Of Other Peoples: Beyond the 'Salvage' Paradigm," in *Discussions in Contemporary Culture No. 1,* Hal Foster, ed. Seattle: Bay Press, 1987, pp. 121–50.

Cohen, Stan. *The Pink Palace: The Royal Hawaiian Hotel—A Sheraton Hotel in Hawaii.* Missoula, MT: Pictorial Histories, 1986.

Connor, Judith, and Charles Baxter. *Kelp Forests.* Monterey, CA: Monterey Bay Aquarium Foundation, 1989.

Conway, William, "Zoo Conservation and Ethical Paradoxes," in *Ethics on the Ark: Zoos, Animal Welfare, and Wildlife Conservation,* Bryan G. Norton, Michael Hutchins, Elizabeth F. Stevens, and Terry L. Maple, eds. Washington, DC: Smithsonian Institution Press, 1995, pp. 1–9.

Cook, Captain James, and Captain James King. *A Voyage to the Pacific Ocean . . . in His Majesty's Ships Resolution and Discovery.* 3 vols. Dublin: H. Camberlaine et al., 1784.

Costa, Mazeppa King. "Dance in the Society and Hawaiian Islands as Presented by the Early Writers, 1767–1842." MA thesis, University of Hawai'i at Manoa, Honolulu, 1951.

Culler, Jonathan. "Semiotics of Tourism." *American Journal of Semiotics* 1 (1981): 127–40.

Davis, Lynn. *Na Pa'i Ki'i: The Photographers in the Hawaiian Islands, 1845–1900.* Bishop Museum Special Publication no. 69. Honolulu: Bishop Museum Press, 1980.

Davis, Susan G. "Touch the Magic," in *Uncommon Ground: Toward Reinventing Nature,* William Cronen, ed. New York: W. W. Norton, 1995, pp. 205–17.

———. *Spectacular Nature: Corporate Culture and the Sea World Experience.* Berkeley: University of California Press, 1997.

Desmond, Jane. "Dancing Out the Difference: Cultural Imperialism and Ruth St. Denis' 'Radha' of 1906." *Signs: Journal of Women in Culture and Society* 17, no. 1: 28–48.

———. "Invoking the 'Native': Body Politics in Contemporary Hawaiian Tourist Shows." *TDR: The Drama Review—A Journal of Performance Studies* 41, no. 4 (1998): 83–109.

———, ed. *Meaning in Motion: New Cultural Studies of Dance.* Durham, NC: Duke University Press, 1997.

———. "Performing Nature: Shamu at Sea World," in *Cruising the Performative: Interventions into the Representations of Ethnicity, Nationality, and Sexuality,* Sue-Ellen Case, Philip Brett, and Susan Foster, eds. Bloomington: Indiana University Press, 1995, pp. 217–36.

Dilworth, Leah. *Imagining Indians in the Southwest: Persistent Visions of a Primitive Past.* Washington, DC: Smithsonian Institution Press, 1995.

Domínguez, Virginia. "A Taste for 'the Other': Intellectual Complicity in Racializing Practices." *Current Anthropology* 35, no. 4 (Aug.–Oct.): 333–38.

———. *White by Definition: Social Classification in Creole Louisiana.* New Brunswick, NJ: Rutgers University Press, 1986.

———. "The Marketing of Heritage." *American Ethnologist* 13, no. 3 (Aug. 1986): 546–55.

———. "Invoking Culture: The Messy Side of 'Cultural Politics,'" in *Eloquent Obsessions: Writing Cultural Criticism,* Marianna Torgovnick, ed. Durham, NC: Duke University Press, 1994, pp. 237–59.

———. "Life with and without Race." The Lewis Henry Morgan Lectures in Anthropology, University of Rochester, 1995.

———. "Exporting U.S. Concepts of Race: Are There Limits to the US Model?" *Social Research* 65, no. 2 (Summer 1998): 369–99.

Dudley, Michael Kioni, and Keoni Kealoha Agard. *A Call for Hawaiian Sovereignty.* Honolulu: Na Kane O Ka Malo Press, 1993.

Dyer, Richard. *Stars.* London: British Film Institute, 1986.

Earhart, Amelia. "My Flight from Hawaii." *National Geographic* 67, no. 5 (May 1935): 593–610.

Emerson, Nathaniel. "Causes of the Decline on Ancient Hawaiian Sports." *The Friend* (Aug. 1892): 23.

———. *Unwritten Literature of Hawaii: The Sacred Songs of the Hula.* Bureau of American Ethnology Bulletin no. 38. Washington, DC: Government Printing Office. [Rpt. Rutland, VT: Charles E. Tuttle, (1909) 1965.]

Enomoto, Catherine Kekoa. "Kumu Hula: Taking a Stand in Hawai'i Politics," *Honolulu Star-Bulletin,* April, 16, 1998, pp. A-1, A-16.

Engerman, David, "Research Agenda for the History of Tourism: Towards an International Social History." *American Studies International* 32, no. 2 (October 1994): 3–31.

Erenberg, Lewis A. *Steppin' Out: New York Nightlife and the Transformation of American Culture, 1890–1930.* Chicago: University of Chicago Press, 1981.

Fabian, Johannes. *Time and the Other: How Anthropology Makes Its Object.* New York: Columbia University Press, 1983.

Flanagan, Cabell V. "Servicemen in Hawai'i—Some Impressions and Attitudes toward Hawai'i." *Social Processes in Hawai'i* 9–10 (July 1945): 75–85.

Forman, David. "The Perpetuation of Native Hawaiian Sovereignty through Legal Customs." Unpublished manuscript, University of Hawai'i School of Law, 1998.

Foster, Susan Leigh, ed. *Corporealities: Dancing Knowledge, Culture, and Power.* New York: Routledge, 1996.

Foucault, Michel. *The Order of Things: An Archaeology of the Human Sciences.* New York: Vintage Books, 1973.

Freed, David. "Killer Whale Capture Plan Assailed: Some Lawmakers Join in Opposing Sea World Proposal," *Los Angeles Times,* Aug. 17, 1983, p. I-25.

Friesen, Steven J. "The Origins of Lei Day: Festivity and the Construction of Ethnicity in the Territory of Hawaii." *History and Anthropology* 10, no. 1 (1996): 1–36.

Frow, John. "Tourism and the Semiotics of Nostalgia." *October,* no. 57 (Summer 1991): 123–51.

Garcia, Joseph. "History, Culture Lure Isle Visitors," *Honolulu Advertiser,* Aug. 8, 1997, p. B-4.

Gates, Henry Louis, Jr., ed. *"Race," Writing, and Difference.* Chicago: University of Chicago Press, 1986.

Gessler, Clifford. *Isles of Enchantment.* New York: Appleton-Century, 1937.

Gilman, Sander. "Black Bodies, White Bodies: Toward an Iconography of Female Sexuality in Late Nineteenth-Century Art, Medicine, and Literature," in *"Race," Writing, and Difference,* Henry Louis Gates Jr., ed. Chicago: University of Chicago Press, 1986, pp. 223–61.

Glauberman, Stu. "Sheraton Waikiki Hosts Entertainers," *Honolulu Advertiser,* June 26, 1995, p. C-1.

———. "Viva Waikiki!" *Honolulu Advertiser,* June 26, 1995, pp. C1–C2.

Gleason, Philip. "American Identity and Americanization," in *Concepts of Ethnicity,* William Petersen, Michael Novak, and Phillip Gleason, eds. Cambridge, MA: Harvard University Press, 1982, pp. 57–143.

Goffman, Erving. *The Presentation of the Self in Everyday Life.* New York: Doubleday, 1959.

Goss, John. "Placing the Market and Marketing Place: Tourist Advertising of the Hawaiian Islands, 1972–1992." *Environment and Society D: Society and Space* 11 (1993): 663–88.

Gould, Stephen Jay. *The Mismeasure of Man.* New York: W. W. Norton, 1981.

Grosvenor, Gilbert. "The Hawaiian Islands: America's Strongest Outpost of Defense—The Volcanic and Floral Wonderland of the World." *National Geographic* (Feb. 1924).

Haas, Michael. *Institutional Racism: The Case of Hawaii.* Westport, CT: Praeger, 1992.

Hackney, Rod. "N. C. Zoo Offers Spectacular Gardens," in *Friends of the Zoo Newsletter* (May/June 1992). Ashboro: North Carolina Zoological Society.

Halstead, Murat. *Pictorial History of America's New Possessions.* Chicago: Dominion, 1899.

Handler, Richard. "Consuming Culture (Genuine and Spurious) as Style." *Cultural Anthropology* 5, no. 3 (Aug. 1990): 346–57.

Handler, Richard, and Eric Gable. *The New History in an Old Museum: Creating the Past of Colonial Williamsburg.* Durham, NC: Duke University Press, 1997.

Haraway, Donna. *Modest Witness@Second Millennium. FemaleMan Meets OncoMouse: Feminism and Technoscience.* New York: Routledge, 1997.

———. *Simians, Cyborgs, and Women: The Reinvention of Nature.* New York: Routledge, 1991.

———. "Teddy Bear Patriarchy: Taxidermy in the Garden of Eden, New York City, 1908–1936," in *Cultures of United States Imperialism,* Amy Kaplan and Donald Pease, eds. Durham, NC: Duke University Press, 1993, pp. 237–91.

Harris, Neil. "Iconography and Intellectual History: The Halftone Effect," in *Cultural Excursions: Marketing Appetites and Cultural Tastes in Modern America.* Chicago: University of Chicago Press, 1990, 304–17.

Ham, Jennifer, and Mathew Senior, eds. *Animal Acts: Configuring the Human in Western History.* New York: Routledge, 1997.

Hawai'i Visitors Bureau, "Keep It Hawai'i." [Brochure.] Honolulu, HI, 1992.

Hawaiian Beat: The Monthly Membership Publication of Hawai'i Visitors Bureau. "Sovereignty Media Packets" (Feb. 1993): 7.

Hawaiian Memories: Postcard Book. Honolulu: Mutual, 1989.

Hawai'i Visitors Bureau. *Market Research Department Annual Research Report.* Honolulu: HVB, 1992.

———. *Visitor Satisfaction Report.* Honolulu: HVB, 1990.

———. *Visitor Satisfaction Report.* Honolulu: HVB, 1992.

Hibbard, Don, and David Franzen. *The View from Diamond Head: Royal Residence to Urban Resort.* Honolulu: Editions Limited, 1986.

Hinsley, Curtis M. "The World as Marketplace: Commodification of the Exotic at the World's Columbian Exposition, Chicago, 1893," in *Exhibiting Cultures: The Poetics and Politics of Museum Display,* Ivan Karp and Steven D. Lavine, eds. Washington, DC: Smithsonian Institution Press, 1991, pp. 344–67.

Hobsbawm, Eric, and Terence Ranger. *The Invention of Tradition.* Cambridge: Cambridge University Press, 1983.

Holmes, Oliver Wendell. "The Stereoscope and the Stereograph," rpt. in Trachtenberg, *Classic Essays on Photography.*

Honolulu Advertiser. "4,000 See Hula Trials," June 3, 1939, p. I-4.

———. "Who's Who in a Hawaiian Nation," Sep. 5, 1993, p. A-4.

———. "Hawaiian Vote: A Signal for Caution." Editorial. Sep. 12, 1996, p. A-12.

Honolulu Star Bulletin. "All the Glamour and Glory of Old Hawaii Remain," Jan. 31, 1927, p. 1–8.

———. "Ancient Pageantry, Music and Dancing to Feature Opening," Jan. 31, 1927, 1st ed., p. 8.

———. "Diving Boys on Waterfront to Be 'Gentlemen,'" Jan. 31, 1927, p. 1.

———. "Hawaii People Absorbing Study in Race Mixture," Jan. 31, 1927, p. 11–15.

———. "Hotel Guests to Get Complete Recreation," Jan. 31, 1927, p. I-8.

———. "Hotel Social Center," Jan. 31, 1927, p. I-8.

———. "Tourists Come to Islands by the Thousands," Jan. 31, 1927, p. 15.

———. "Royal Hotel to Capacity by March 15," Feb. 1, 1927.

———. "Magnificent Royal Hotel Opened amid Riot of Color and Song," Feb. 2, 1927, p. 3.

———. "Hula Makes Big Hit in 'Prince of Hawai'i' at San Francisco," Feb. 3, 1927, 1st ed., p. 10.

———. "Hula Ruled 'Out' in Capital," Mar. 6, 1935, p. 1.

———. "Hula Contest Finals Near," Sep. 10, 1938, p. 3.

———. "Popularity of Hawaiian Dances on the Increase," Feb. 10, 1938, p. 3.

———. "Hula Festival Will Be Offered July 20 at Academy of Arts," July 17, 1939, p. 6.

———. "Brilliant Touches of Old Hawaii," Feb. 2, 1927, p. 3 [features sec.].

Honolulu Sunday Star Bulletin and Advertiser. "Who Is 'Hawaiian' Today?" Feb. 14, 1993, p. B-3.

Honolulu: Tourist Guide and Handbook. Honolulu: Mid-Pacific Folder Distributing, 1925.

Hopkins, Jerry. *The Hula.* Hong Kong: Apa, 1982.

Howe, Sheri. *Mirounga: A Guide to Elephant Seals.* Davenport, CA: Frank S. Balthis, 1986.

Imada, Adria. "The Local That Is Never Pau: Contemporary Local Literature of Hawai'i." Unpublished manuscript, Yale University, 1993.

International People's Tribunal. *Interim Report*. Honolulu: International People's Tribunal, 1993.

Iowa City Press Citizen, "Barking Deer Identified in Vietnamese Jungles," Aug. 22, 1997, p. A-1.

Irvine, Georgeanne. *The True Story of Corky the Blind Seal*. New York: Scholastic, 1987.

Johnson, John J. *Latin America in Caricature*. Austin: University of Texas Press, 1980.

Jolly, Margaret, "From Point Venus to Bali Ha'i: Eroticism and Exoticism in Representations of the Pacific," in *Sites of Desire, Economies of Pleasure: Sexualities in Asia and the Pacific*, Lenore Manderson and Margaret Jolly, eds. Chicago: University of Chicago Press, 1997, pp. 99–122.

Jules-Rosette, Bennetta. *The Messages of Tourist Art: An African Semiotic System in Comparative Perspective*. New York: Plenum, 1984.

Kaeppler, Adrienne. "The Polynesian Dance as 'Airport Art,'" in *Asian and Pacific Dance: Selected Papers from the 1974 C.O.R.D.-S.E.M. Conference*, Adrienne Kaeppler, Judy Van Zile, and Carl Wolz, eds. *Dance Research Annual* 8 (1977): 71–84.

———. *Polynesian Dance, with a Selection for Contemporary Performances*. Hawai'i: Alpha Delta Kappa, 1983.

———. *Hula Pahu: Hawaiian Drum Dances*. Honolulu: Bishop Museum Press, 1993.

———. "Visible and Invisible in Hawaiian Dance," in *Human Action Signs in Cultural Context: The Visible and the Invisible in Movement and Dance*, Brenda Farnell, ed. Metuchen, NJ: Scarecrow Press, 1995.

Ka Lāhui Hawai'i. "Constitution." [Ka Lāhui Sovereignty Education Materials.] Honolulu, n.p., n.d.

Kamahele, Momi. "Hula as Resistance." *Forward Motion* 2, no. 3 (1992): 40–46.

Kamakau, S. M. *Ruling Chiefs of Hawaii*. Rev. ed. Honolulu: Kamehameha Schools Press, 1992.

Kame'eleihiwa, Lilikalā. *Native Land and Foreign Desires*. Honolulu: Bishop Museum Press, 1992.

Kanahele, George. *Ku Kanaka "Stand Tall": A Search for Hawaiian Values*. Honolulu: University of Hawai'i Press, 1992.

———, ed. *Hawaiian Music and Musicians*. Honolulu: University Press of Hawai'i, 1979.

Karp, Ivan, and Steven Lavine, eds. *Exhibiting Cultures: The Poetics and Politics of Museum Display*. Washington, DC: Smithsonian Institution Press, 1991.

Kasher, Robert Kamohalu, and Burl Burlingame. *Da Kine Sound: Conversations with the People Who Create Hawaiian Music*. Honolulu: Press Pacifica, 1978.

Kennedy, Ed. "Hotel Management Hawaiian-Style," *Honolulu Advertiser*, June 22, 1997, p. G1–G2.

Kent, Noel J. *Hawaii: Islands under the Influence*. New York: Monthly Review Press, 1983.

Kirshenblatt-Gimblett, Barbara. "Objects of Ethnography," in *Exhibiting Cultures: The Poetics and Politics of Museum Display*, Ivan Karp and Steven D. Lavine, eds. Washington, DC: Smithsonian Institution Press, 1991, pp. 386–443.

———. *Destination Culture: Tourism, Museums and Heritage*. Berkeley: University of California Press, 1998.

Kitchen, Karl. [Newspaper article in *The Evening World*, clipping file at Sheraton Waikiki Hotel]. 1930, n.p.

Koebner, Linda. *Zoo Book: The Evolution of Wildlife Conservation Centers.* New York: Forge Press, 1994.

Koritz, Amy. "Dancing the Orient for England: Maud Allan's 'The Vision of Salome,'" in *Meaning in Motion: New Cultural Studies of Dance,* Jane Desmond, ed. Durham, NC: Duke University Press, 1997, pp. 133–52.

Kraul, Chris. "Anheuser-Busch to Buy Sea World for $1.1 Billion," *Los Angeles Times,* Sept. 29, 1989, p. I-1.

Krauss, Bob. "After 50 Years, Hula Show Still Clicks," *Honolulu Advertiser,* March 7, 1987, p. A-3.

————. "Hula Star Recalls Days of Glory at the Royal Hawaiian," *Sunday Star Bulletin and Advertiser* (Honolulu), Oct. 13, 1991, p. A-3.

Krauss, William. "Eyes of the Pacific." *Asia Magazine* 42 (April 1942): 218–69.

Kuykendall, Ralph S. *The Hawaiian Kingdom.* Vol. 3: *1874–1893.* Honolulu: University of Hawai'i Press, 1967.

Langton, Elinor A. "Give the Tourists More Variety." *Paradise of the Pacific* 18, no. 3 (March 1, 1905): 15.

Lears, T. J. Jackson. *Fables of Abundance: A Cultural History of Advertising in America.* New York: Basic Books, 1994.

————. *No Place of Grace: Antimodernism and the Transformation of American Culture, 1880–1920.* Chicago: University of Chicago Press, [1981] 1994.

Le Boeuf, Burney J. *Elephant Seals.* Pacific Grove, CA: Boxwood Press, 1985.

Legare, Evelyn. "Canadian Multiculturalism and Aboriginal People: Negotiating a Place in the Nation." *Identities: Global Studies in Culture and Power* 1, no. 4 (April 1995): 347–66.

Levine, Lawrence W. "American Culture and the Great Depression." *Yale Review* 74 (1985): 198–223.

Lévi-Strauss, Claude. *The Savage Mind.* Chicago: University of Chicago Press, 1966.

Life. "Speaking of Pictures: Sailors Like to Pose in Hawaii with Hula Girls," Dec. 28, 1942, pp. 4–5.

————. "The Classic Hula: American Girls Are Now Learning Ancient Native Dance of Hawaii," March 6, 1944, pp. 47–48+.

Lincoln Park Zooreview. "The Lions of India," (Winter 1995): 19.

Linnekin, Jocelyn. *Sacred Queens and Women of Consequence: Rank, Gender and Colonialism in the Hawaiian Islands.* Ann Arbor: University of Michigan Press, 1990.

Los Angeles Times. "Trainers Allowed back in Water with Sea World's Killer Whales," June 11, 1988, p. 24.

Lott, Eric. *Love and Theft: Blackface Minstrelsy and the American Working Class.* Oxford: Oxford University Press, 1993.

Luoma, Jon R. *A Crowded Ark: The Role of Zoos in Wildlife Conservation.* Boston: Houghton Mifflin, 1987.

Lutz, Catherine A., and Jane L. Collins. *Reading National Geographic.* Chicago: University of Chicago Press, 1993.

MacCannell, Dean. *The Tourist: A New Theory of the Leisure Class.* New York: Schocken, [1976] 1989.

————. *Empty Meeting Grounds: The Tourist Papers.* New York: Routledge, 1992.

MacDonald, Betty. "Our Envoys of the Hula," *Honolulu Star Bulletin,* September 30, 1939, p. 3-1.

McEvoy, J. P. "The Land of the Lei," *Saturday Evening Post,* June 6, 1936, pp. 8–9+.

MacFadden, Byrne. "The Dance of the South Seas." *Dance Lovers Magazine: Magazine of Stage and Screen,* Oct. 1924, pp. 10–12 and 72.

McSpadden, J. Walter. *Beautiful Hawaii.* New York: Thomas Y. Cowell, 1939.

Marine World Africa USA. "Marine World Africa USA." [Souvenir booklet.] N.p.: Pali Arts Communications, 1991.

Martin, Emily. *The Woman in the Body: A Cultural Analysis of Reproduction.* Boston: Beacon Press, 1987.

Masson, Jeffrey Moussaieff, and Susan McCarthy. *When Elephants Weep: The Emotional Lives of Animals.* New York: Delacourt Press, 1995.

Maugham, W. Somerset. "Honolulu," rpt. in *A Hawaiian Reader,* A. Grove Day and Carl Stroven, eds. Honolulu: Mutual, 1984, 218–44.

Melosh, Barbara. *Engendering Culture: Manhood and Womanhood in New Deal Public Art and Theater.* Washington, DC: Smithsonian Institution Press, 1991.

Miller, Kenneth, "Almost Home." *Life,* March 1996, pp. 54–57.

Minh-ha, Trinh T. *Woman, Native, Other: Writing Postcoloniality and Feminism.* Bloomington: Indiana University Press, 1989.

Mizejewski, Linda. *Ziegfeld Girl: Image and Icon in Culture and Cinema.* Durham, NC: Duke University Press, 1999.

Moanalua Gardens Foundation. "Fourteenth Prince Lot Hula Festival." [Program.] Honolulu: Moanalua Garden Foundation, July 20, 1991.

Monterey Bay Aquarium. *Monterey Bay Aquarium.* N.p.: Monterey Bay Aquarium and Blake Printing and Publishing, 1985.

Mullin, Molly M. "The Patronage of Difference: Making Indian Art 'Art, Not Ethnology.'" *Cultural Anthropology* 7, no. 4: 395–424.

Mullins, Joseph G. *Hawaiian Journey.* Honolulu: Mutual, 1978.

Mulvey, Laura. "Visual Pleasure and Narrative Cinema." *Screen* 16, no. 3 (1975): 6–18.

National Geographic Magazine. [Special issue on Hawai'i.] 45, no. 2 (Feb. 1924).

Nash, Gary, and Julie Roy Jeffrey. *The American People: Creating a Nation and a Society,* vol. 2. New York: Harper and Row, 1986.

Nelson, Andrew J. "Going Wild." *American Demographics* 12, no. 2 (Feb. 1990): 34.

Ness, Sally Ann. "Festival Tourism in the Philippines: From the Manila Carnival to the Marcos Era Ethnic Festivals." Paper presented at the Conference on Southeast Asia, University of California at Berkeley, February 16, 1991.

New York Sun, "Doraldina Tells of the Hula," July 2, 1916, p. 3.

New York World Telegram. "Obituary of Doraldina," Feb. 14. 1936, n.p.

New York Times. "Performing Whale Dies in Collision with Another," Aug. 23, 1989, p. A-12.

Norton, Bryan G., Michael Hutchins, Elizabeth F. Stevens, and Terry L. Maple, eds. *Ethics on the Ark: Zoos, Animal Welfare, and Wildlife Conservation.* Washington, DC: Smithsonian Institution Press, 1995.

Nugent, Frank S. "*Waikiki Wedding*," March 26, 1937, in *N.Y. Times Film Reviews*, p. 1377.

O'Barry, Richard, and Keith Coulbourn. *Behind the Dolphin Smile*. New York: Berkley, 1989.

Odell, George C. D. *Annals of the New York Stage*. Vol. 15: *1891–1894*. New York: Columbia University Press, 1949.

Office of Hawaiian Affairs. *'Onipa'a, Five Days in the History of the Hawaiian Nation: Centennial Observance of the Overthrow of the Hawaiian Monarchy*. Honolulu: Office of Hawaiian Affairs, 1994.

Okamura, Jonathan. "Why There Are No Asian Americans in Hawaii: The Continuing Significance of Local Identity." *Social Process in Hawaii* 35 (1994): 161–78.

Pacific Commercial Advertiser. "Moana Hotel Opened Last Evening with Glitter and Good Cheer," March 12, 1901, p. 2.

Page, Jake. *Zoo: The Modern Ark*. New York: Facts on File Press, 1990.

Pascoe, Peggy. "Miscegenation Law, Court Cases, and Ideologies of 'Race' in Twentieth Century America." *Journal of American History* 83, no. 1 (June 1996): 44–69.

Pass Times. [Newsletter.] San Diego: Sea World, 1992.

Pearce, Philip L. *The Social Psychology of Tourist Behavior*. Oxford: Pergamon Press, 1982.

Perlman, David. "Sea Lions Rigged to Tell Secrets," *San Francisco Chronicle*, June 1, 1992, p. A-13.

Phelan, Peggy. *Unmarked: The Politics of Performance*. New York: Routledge, 1993.

Pochereva, Mele. "The Kahili Awards." *Hawaiian Beat: The Monthly Membership Publication of Hawai'i Visitors Bureau* 7, no. 10 (1993): 4–5.

Pollock, Griselda. *Vision and Difference: Femininity, Feminism and the Histories of Art*. London: Routledge, 1988.

Pratt, Mary Louise. *Under Imperial Eyes: Travel Writing and Transculturalism*. New York: Routledge, 1992.

Prevots, Naima. *American Pageantry: A Movement for Art and Democracy*. Ann Arbor: UMI Research Press, 1990.

Pryor, Karen. *Lads before the Wind: Diary of a Dolphin Trainer*. North Bend, WA: Sunshine, 1975.

Puhipau, and Joan Lander. *Act of War: The Overthrow of the Hawaiian Nation*. [Video.] 1993.

Pukui, Mary Kawena, E. W. Haertig, and Catherine A. Lee. *Nama I Ke Kumu: Look to the Source*, vol. 1. Honolulu: Hui Hana, Queen Lili'uokalani Children's Center, 1983.

Ratner, David. "Monterey Bay Aquarium to Reveal Unfamiliar Worlds," *Capitola Courier*, 2, no. 1 (June 1992), 10.

Reeves, Randall R., and Stephen Leatherwood. *The Sea World Book of Dolphins*. New York: Harcourt, Brace, Jovanovich, 1987.

Reinhold, Robert. "At Sea World, Stress Tests Whale and Man," *New York Times*, April 4, 1988, pp. N-13, A-19.

Reza, H. G. "Whales Collide, 1 Fatally Injured in Sea World Tank," *Los Angeles Times*, Aug. 22, 1989, p. I-3.

Reza, H. G., and Greg Johnson. "Killer Whale Bled to Death after Breaking Jaw in Fight," *Los Angeles Times*, Aug. 23, 1989, p. I-3.

Ridpath, John Clark. *Great Races of Mankind: An Account of the Ethnic Origin, Primitive Estate, Early Migrations, Social Evolution, and Present Conditions and Promise of the Principal Families of Men.* Cincinnati: Jones Brothers, 1893.

Ritvo, Harriet. *The Animal Estate: The English and Other Creatures in the Victorian Age.* Cambridge, MA: Harvard University Press, 1987.

Roberts, Leslie. "Anthropologists Climb (Gingerly) on Board." *Science* 258 (1992): 1300–1301.

Robertson, Carol, "The Ethnomusicologist as Midwife," in *Musicology and Difference: Gender and Sexuality in Music Scholarship,* Ruth Solie, ed. Berkeley: University of California Press, 1993.

Rodgers, C. A. "The Native Hawaiian." *Mid-Pacific Magazine* 24, no. 3 (Sept. 1922): 232–36.

Roig, Suzanne. "Flights Help Big Island Hotels," *Honolulu Advertiser,* June 26, 1997, p. B-8.

Rony, Fatimah Tobing. *The Third Eye: Race, Cinema, and Ethnographic Spectacle.* Durham, NC: Duke University Press, 1996.

Ross, Andrew. "Cultural Preservation in the Polynesia of the Latter Day Saints," in *The Chicago Gangster Theory of Life: Nature's Debt to Society.* London: Verso, 1994, pp. 21–98.

Rothfells, Nigel. "Paradise." Unpublished manuscript, 1998.

Rubenstein, Steve. "The Jellies Will Leave You Quivering," *San Francisco Chronicle,* April 1992, p. E-12.

Ryan, Tim. "Kodak Hula Show Celebrates 60 Years of Aloha," *Honolulu Star-Bulletin,* March 10, 1997, p. B-1.

Rydell, Robert W. *All the World's a Fair: Visions of Empire at American International Expositions, 1876–1916.* Chicago: University of Chicago Press, 1984.

———. *World of Fairs: The Century-of-Progress Expositions.* Chicago: University of Chicago Press, 1993.

Sahlins, Marshall. *Historical Metaphors and Mythical Realities: Structure in the Early History of the Sandwich Islands Kingdom,* Association of Social Anthropology in Oceania, Special Publication no. 1. Ann Arbor: University of Michigan Press, 1981.

Sahlins, Marshall. *Islands of History.* Chicago: University of Chicago Press, 1985.

Said, Edward. *Orientalism.* New York: Pantheon, 1978.

The San Diego Zoo. San Diego: Zoological Society of San Diego, 1991.

Scarry, Elaine. *The Body in Pain: The Making and Unmaking of the World.* New York: Oxford University Press, 1985.

Schechner, Richard. *Performance Theory.* Rev. ed. New York: Routledge, 1988.

Schmitt, Robert C. *Historical Statistics of Hawaii.* Honolulu: University of Hawai'i Press, 1977.

———. *Hawaii in the Movies, 1898–1959.* Honolulu: Hawaiian Historical Society, 1988.

Schor, Naomi, "Cartes Postales: Representing Paris, 1900." *Critical Inquiry* 18 (Winter 1992): 188–241.

Schutz, Albert J. *The Voices of Eden: A History of Hawaiian Language Studies.* Honolulu: University of Hawaii Press, 1994.

Sea World. "Sea World of California." [Press packet.] San Diego: Sea World, 1992.

———. "Sea World of California Fact Sheet." [Publicity release.] San Diego: Sea World, Feb. 1992.

———. "Sea World of California: Park Guide." San Diego: Sea World, 1992.

———. "Sea World Shows: Little Whales, Big Whales, Pirates and Parrots." [Publicity release.] San Diego: Sea World, Feb. 1992.

Sereno, Aeko. "Images of the Hula Dancer and 'Hula Girl': 1778–1960." Ph.D. diss., University of Hawai'i, 1990.

Silva, Wendell, and Alan Suemori, eds. *Nānā I Na Loea Hula: Look to the Hula Resources.* Honolulu: Kalihi-Palama Culture and Arts Society, 1984.

Singer, Peter. *Animal Liberation.* 2d ed. New York: Avon, 1990.

———, ed. *In Defense of Animals.* Oxford: Blackwell, 1985.

Slyomovics, Susan. "Cross-Cultural Dress and Tourist Performance in Egypt." *Performing Arts Journal* 11, no. 3 (1989): 139–48.

Small, Ellen, "Seven Young Ladies with 242 Old Hulas," *San Francisco Chronicle,* Nov. 7, 1948, p. 25.

Smith, Bernard. *European Vision and the South Pacific.* 2d ed. New Haven: Yale University Press, 1985.

Smith, Valene. *Hosts and Guests: The Anthropology of Tourism.* Philadelphia: University of Pennsylvania Press, 1989.

Souza, Pomaika'i R. "Extend Aquarium to Natatorium." [Letter to the editor.] *Honolulu Advertiser,* June 4, 1997, p. A-9.

Spaeth, Sigmund. "Hawaii Likes Music." *Harper's* 176 (Mar. 1938): 423–27.

Spreckels, John D. "Hawaii for Tourists." *Overland Monthly* 25 (June 1895): 660–62.

Spurr, David. *The Rhetoric of Empire: Colonial Discourse in Journalism, Travel Writing, and Imperial Administration.* Durham, NC: Duke University Press, 1993.

Stannard, David. *Before the Horror: The Population of Hawai'i on the Eve of Western Contact.* Honolulu: Social Science Research Institute, University of Hawai'i, 1989.

Stevenson, Robert Louis. *Travels in Hawaii.* A. Grove Day, ed. Honolulu: University of Hawai'i Press, 1973.

Stewart, Susan. *On Longing: Narratives of the Miniature, the Gigantic, the Souvenir, the Collection.* Durham, NC: Duke University Press, 1993.

Stillman, Amy Ku'uleialoha. "History Reinterpreted in Song." *Hawaiian Journal of History* 23 (1989): 1–30.

———. "Hawaiian Hula Competitions: Event, Repertoire, Performance, Tradition." *Journal of American Folklore* 109, no. 434: 357–80.

———. *Sacred Hula: The Historical Hula 'Āla'apapa.* Bishop Museum Bulletin in Anthropology no. 8. Honolulu: Bishop Museum Press, 1998.

Stocking, George W., Jr. *Race, Culture, and Evolution: Essays in the History of Anthropology.* Chicago: University of Chicago Press, 1982.

Stone, Kent. "Captured Dolphin has Human Arms!" *Weekly World News,* March 17, 1992, p. 27.

Stratton, Jon, and Ien Ang. "Critical Multiculturalism." *Continuum: The Australian Journal of Media and Culture,* 8, no. 2 (1994): 124–58.

Stratyner, Barbara Cohen. "Entry on Doraldina," in *Biographical Dictionary of Dance.* New York: Schirmer, 1982.

———. *Ned Wayburn and the Dance Routine: From Vaudeville to the Ziegfeld Follies.* Studies in Dance History no. 13. N.p.: Society for Dance History Scholars, 1996.

Takamine, Vicky Holt. "The Hula 'Āla'apapa: An Analysis of Selected Dances and a Comparison with Hula Pahu." M.A. thesis, University of Hawai'i, 1994.

Tatar, Elizabeth. *Strains of Change: The Impact of Tourism on Hawaiian Music.* Bishop Museum Special Publication no. 78. Honolulu: Bishop Museum Press, 1987.

Taylor, Albert Pierce. "The Real Hawaiian Hula." *Paradise of the Pacific* 40, no. 8 (Aug. 1927): 31–32.

Taylor, Josephine, "Correspondence: A Dancer in Wartime Hawaii." *Dance Observer* (June–July 1943): 68.

Taylor, Lois. "Celebrating 50 Years of Snapshots," *Honolulu Star and Advertiser,* Mar. 1, 1987, p. E-1.

Therborn, Goran. *The Ideology of Power and the Power of Ideology.* London: Verso, 1982.

Thomas, Nicholas. *Colonialism's Culture: Anthropology, Travel and Government.* Princeton, NJ: Princeton University Press, 1994.

This Week Oahu. "This Week Oahu." [Tourist pamphlet.] July 15, 1991.

Timberlake, William. "Animal Behavior: A Continuing Synthesis." *Annual Review of Psychology* 44 (1993): 675–708.

Timmons, Grady. *Waikiki Beachboy.* Honolulu: Editions Limited, 1989.

Torgovnick, Marianna. *Gone Primitive: Savage Intellects, Modern Lives.* Chicago: University of Chicago Press, 1990.

Trachtenberg, Alan. *The Incorporation of America: Culture and Society in the Gilded Age.* New York: Hill and Wang, 1982.

————, ed. *Classic Essays on Photography.* New Haven, CT: Leete's Island, 1980.

Trask, Haunani-Kay. *From a Native Daughter: Colonialism and Sovereignty in Hawai'i.* Monroe, ME: Common Courage Press, 1993.

Travel and Leisure. "Future Flash." Jan. 1997, p. 46.

Tsutsumi, Cheryl Chee. "Cruising Hawaiian-Style Aboard the S.S. *Independence.*" *Aloha Magazine* (May/June 1995): 20–24.

Twain, Mark. *Mark Twain in Hawaii.* Honolulu: Mutual, 1990.

Urry, John. *The Tourist Gaze: Leisure and Travel in Contemporary Societies.* London: Sage, 1990.

————. *Consuming Places.* London: Routledge, 1995.

USA Today. "Animal Attractions." [Snapshot graphic.] May 23, 1997, p. D-1.

U. S. Congress. *The Apology to Native Hawaiians on Behalf of the United States for the Overthrow of the Kingdom of Hawaii.* Rpt. Kapolei, HI: Ka'imi Pono Press, 1994.

Van Dyke, Robert E., ed. *Hawaiian Yesterdays: Historical Photographs by Ray Jerome Baker.* Honolulu: Mutual, 1982.

Variety Film Reviews. "Bird of Paradise" [September 13, 1932], in *Variety Film Reviews.* New York: Garland, 1983.

Viotti, Vicki. "A Look Back at Prince Lot," *Honolulu Advertiser,* July 18, 1997, p. D-1+.

Waikiki Beach Press. "Tahiti Torso Twisters Take over Waikiki," Nov. 15–21, 1995, p. 1.

Waikiki 1900–1985: Oral Histories, vol. 4. Oral History Project, Social Science Research Institute, University of Hawai'i at Manoa, June 1985.

Waldman, Peter, and Richard Turner. "Park Wars: Shamu is the Big Prize Buyer of Sea World Will Get for its Money," *Wall Street Journal,* Aug. 28, 1989, p. A-1.

Weekly World News, "Dolphin Grows Human Arms!" March 17, 1992, p. 27.

Weigle, Marta, and Barbara Babcock, eds. *The Great Southwest of the Fred Harvey Company and the Santa Fe Railway.* Phoenix: Heard Museum, 1996.

Wells, Samuel R. *New Physiognomy, or, Signs of Character, as Manifested Through Temperament and External Forms, and Especially in "The Human Face Divine."* New York: Fowler and Wells, 1883.

Whisnant, David E. *All That Is Native and Fine: The Politics of Culture in an American Region.* Chapel Hill: University of North Carolina Press, 1983.

White, Geoff, "Moving History: The Pearl Harbor Films." *Positions: East Asia Cultures Critique* 5, no. 3 (Winter 1997): 709–44.

White, Trumbull. *Our New Possessions.* Boston: Adams, 1898.

Whiting, Sam. "Take Me Out to the Ballgame but First Let's Hit the ATM: How Not to Go Broke at the Ballpark," *San Francisco Chronicle,* May 28, 1992, p. 3, sec. D-1.

Whitney, Henry M. *The Tourists' Guide through the Hawaiian Islands Descriptive of Their Scenes and Scenery.* 2d ed. Honolulu: n.p., 1895.

Williams, Raymond. "Ideas of Nature," in *Problems in Materialism and Culture: Selected Essays.* London: Verso, 1980, pp. 67–85.

———. *Keywords: A Vocabulary of Culture and Society.* Rev. ed. New York: Oxford University Press, 1983.

Williamson, Judith. "Woman Is an Island: Femininity and Colonization," in *Studies in Entertainment: Critical Approaches to Mass Culture,* Tania Modleski, ed. Bloomington: Indiana University Press, 1986, pp. 99–118.

Wilson, Alexander. *The Culture of Nature: North American Landscape from Disney to the Exxon Valdez.* Cambridge, MA: Blackwell, 1992.

Winchell, Alexander. *Preadamites; or a demonstration of the Existence of men Before Adam; together with A Study of Their condition, Antiquity, Racial Affinities, and Progressive dispersion over the Earth.* Chicago: S.C. Griggs, 1881.

Womacks, Lanny Thompson. "'Estudiarlos, Juzgarlos ye Gobernarlos': Conocimiento y poder en el Archipielago Imperial Estadounidense." Paper presented at the Congreso Internacional "La Nacion Sonada: Cuba, Puerto Rico y Filipinas antes el '98," April 24–28, 1995, Aranjuez, Spain.

Wright, Walter, "Bias against Blacks Cited Here: Pastor Says 'Melting Pot Fails Many.'" *Honolulu Advertiser,* Jan. 19, 1993, p. A-3.

Zoobooks: Whales. San Diego: Wildlife Foundation, 1987.

Index

African-American women: supposed hyperbolic sexuality of, 68–69, 76–77
Akeo, Louise, 292n22
aloha, 269n2
American Indians: Native Hawaiians compared to, 51–52, 88
American Southwest: tourism in, 52, 283n64
animal conservation, 55, 147–48
animal parks and shows: compared to zoos, 150–52; economics of, 153–54, 302n2; present bodies in motion, 150–51; selection of performances, 173–74. *See also* zoos
animal rights activists, 235–36, 243, 246, 301n5, 311n32
animal tourism, 258, 303n9; extensions of natural behaviors, 174–75, 177, 223, 237–40; future potential of, 264; gradation of venues in, 166, 168–69, 174; history of, 154–60; linkage to cultural tourism, 144–45, 149, 152, 190, 251; live performance in, xv, 212–16; nature and naturalism in, 147–49, 190–91, 237–38, 250; photography in, 183; public display of bodies in, 149–50, 174–75
animal-human relationship: future potential of, 265; at Marine World Africa, 194–97, 200–1; at Sea World, 217, 226–30, 242, 245; sexual subtext of, 198
animals: anthropomorphization of, 15–16, 191–92, 194–96, 198, 200–2, 204–7,
209–10, 226, 240, 246; authenticity of, 156–57; in blood sports, 156–57, 218, 303n3; disabled, 196, 307n16; as representative of nature, 147; sex and violence among, 191–92, 306n10; as social beings, 198–99; as stuffed toys, 148–49, 302n12; trained to exhibit unnatural behaviors, 204–7. *See also* mammals
Año Nuevo State Park (California), 193; as ecotourism, 186, 188–90, 192; elephant seal mating at, 187–89, 191–92; in-situ venue at, 176–77, 186–92; photography at, 189
anthropomorphization: of animals, 191–92, 194–96, 198, 200–2, 204–7, 209–10, 215–16, 226, 240, 246
antimiscegenation laws, 123
audiences: demographics of, 253–54
authenticity: of animals, 156–57; in commercial luʻaus, xix–xx, 17, 95; live performance and, 16–17; naturalism as, xiv, xix–xx, xvi, 22, 149, 178, 190, 204, 251; and public display of bodies, xxii

beachboys, 296n1; earnings as, 125–26, 297n10; as Hawaiian icon, 129; physical interaction with female tourists, 122, 124, 126–28; relationship with male tourists, 128–29
Beamer, Nona, 132
Benedict, Ruth, 118–19
Bird of Paradise (play and film), 65–66, 110

331

Boas, Franz, 118
bodies, public display of: in animal tourism, 149–50, 174–75; and authenticity, xxii; in cultural tourism, 131; and identity categories, xiii–xiv, 9; in motion, 150–51; and naturalism, 239–40, 251–52; and subjectivity, xiii
bodily difference: as basis of tourism, xiii–xiv, xvi, xxi–xxiii, 135–36, 145, 183; commodification of, 166; as defining characteristic, 202, 231, 237, 240, 248, 255, 257
body: and race, 38–39, 87–88; as sign of itself, xx, 28
books, travel and educational: and feminized image of U.S. colonies, 49–50, 57, 59, 282n56, 283n60
Broadway: hula performances on, 65–66, 69, 116

California gold rush: Native Hawaiians in, 40, 61
Cazimero brothers: offer alternative luʻau, 29–31, 260–62
Chicago World's Fair (1893): hula performances at, 62–64, 66, 69
chorus girls, 70–71
colonialism: effect on popular entertainment, 61–68; and nationalism, 69
colonies, U.S.: feminized image of, 49–50, 57, 59, 68
conservation: as theme at Sea World, 235–36, 243
cultural tourism, xv, 39, 43, 258, 268n10, 278n21; future potential of, 260–62, 262; linkage to animal tourism, 144–45, 149, 152, 190, 251; public display of bodies in, 131
culture: and race, xiv, xx, xxiii, 7, 12, 30, 118–19, 124; scientific concepts of, 117–21

Del Rio, Dolores, 109–10, 117
"diving boys," 91–92
Dollywood (Tennessee), xvi
dolphins: military uses of, 308n30
Doraldina, 68, 70–71, 82, 109, 115, 286n28, 286n31

ecotourism, 169–70, 176–78, 183, 186, 188–90, 192, 314n13, 315n20

elephant seals, 186–92
ethnography: in tourism, 37–38
Europe: tourism in, xvi, 267n2

family: as theme at Sea World, 217–18, 220, 225, 234–36, 239, 241, 249
family, heterosexual: as the norm, 256
feminism: and naturalism, 5, 48
films: as advertising for Hawaiʻi, 132–33; Hawaiian culture as presented in, 109–12, 114, 133
Finland: cultural tourism in, 262–64
flamenco dancers, 269n1
Flipper, 242–43
Free Willy, 311n31

Germaine's Luau, 174, 251, 273n33; operations, 20–25; racial labeling in, 23–24
Gray, Gilda, 68, 71, 73–74, 76–78, 82, 109

Hagenbeck, Carl, 162–64
hapa-haole: as ideal Hawaiian native, xxii
hapa-haole look: as standard of beauty, 23, 48, 50, 62, 66–67, 69, 71, 77, 93, 103–4, 108, 111, 116, 132, 134–35, 274n40, 294n35
Hawaiʻi: as alternative authentic lifestyle, 129–30; ethnic diversity and immigration in, 7–8, 23, 26–28, 58, 84, 87–88, 91, 140, 296n2; Euro-American tourism in, 12–13, 271n13, 277n10, 279n26; feminized image of, 68, 81, 256, 296n75; "hula girl" as icon of, xx, xxii, 10–11, 30, 47–48; Japanese tourism in, 12–13, 271n14; military personnel in, 271n13; sovereignty movement, 30–33; surge in tourism to, 134–35, 256; Twain on, 6, 269n9; U.S. hegemony established in, 35
Hawaii Calls, 2, 11, 116–17, 261
Hawaii Five-O, 11
Hawaiian culture: mainland ignorance of, 108–9; as presented in films, 109–12, 114; tourist industry commodifies, 3, 8, 14–17, 19, 84–85, 94–96, 99–101, 114, 116–17, 121, 139, 285n89
Hawaiian men: in advertisements, 125, 127; as beachboys and surfers, 122, 124–29; racial interpretation of, 127–28. *See also* Hawaiian natives; Hawaiian women

Hawaiian monarchy: U.S. overthrows, 31–33, 35–36, 50

Hawaiian music and dance: mainland craze for, 67–74, 76–78, 79, 82, 100–1, 160, 261, 287n39; renaissance in, 134–35

Hawaiian natives, 275n46, 298n18; in advertising, 82–84, 279n27; in California gold rush, 40, 61; compared to American Indians, 51–52, 88; as ideal natives, 4–8, 30, 49–51, 53, 56–58, 60, 78, 255; racial interpretation of, 7, 50–51, 54–58, 60–61, 63, 87–88, 117–19, 127–28, 130, 297n16; *See also* Hawaiian men; Hawaiian women

Hawaiian Renaissance, 134–35, 261

Hawaiian Tourist Bureau, 79–80, 82, 90–91, 93, 98, 253; produces films, 111–12, 294n44; promotes surfing, 125

Hawaiian tourist industry: advertising by, 10–12, 14, 79–85, 90–91, 101–3, 296n75; and changing demographics among visitors, 134–41, 272n15, 276n58; commodifies Hawaiian culture, 3, 8, 14–17, 19, 84–85, 94–96, 99–101, 114, 116–17, 121, 139, 285n89; economics of, 13–14, 79, 98, 106, 290n1; entices local residents, 19, 99, 272n20; establishment and evolution of, 4–7, 35–37, 78, 79–81, 84–85, 88–90, 131, 276n4; hotels promote "Hawaiianness" in, 15–17, 89, 99, 262; ignores Asia ethnic groups, 58; live performance in, 3–4, 6–7; projects hula girl image, 3, 6–7, 10–12, 14, 34, 41–45, 94–96, 98–99; promotes "Hawaiianness," 14–15; racial minorities underrepresented in, 139–40; and sexual conservatism, 141; and sovereignty movement, 32–33; targets middle class visitors, 133–34; in World War II, 131–32

Hawaiian Visitors Bureau, 10, 12, 15–16; "Lifestyle" profiles, 137–39

Hawaiian women, 296n75; idealized beauty and eroticism of, 24–25, 34–35, 44, 47, 50, 54, 68–69, 77–78, 116. *See also* Hawaiian men; Hawaiian natives

Hewett, Frank: offers alternative lu'au, 29–31, 260

Ho, Don, 2

hula, 275n53; costumes, 74; instruction in, 2–3, 75–76, 113–14; missionary suppression of, 61–62, 270n1, 270n10, 281n42; modified for Western sensitivities, 70–71, 75–76; Polynesian style, 24–25, 133–34; role in Hawaiian society, 26–28, 61–62, 97, 107, 260, 274n42, 281n48; sexual interpretation of, 62–64, 82, 110, 115, 261, 286n31, 314n12

hula, live performances, xvii, 97, 314n16; on Broadway, 65–66, 69, 116; at Chicago World's Fair, 62–64, 66, 69; on the mainland, 59, 60, 94, 99, 115–17, 289n7; in New York curio museum, 64; at Panama-Pacific Exposition, 59, 61, 66; selection of performances, 174; at USO shows, 132

"hula girls" and hula dancers, 270n1, 281n47; early photographs and postcards of, 6, 41–48; and early pornography, 46, 281n43; earnings as professionals, 106, 292n24; as Hawaiian icon, xx, xxii, 10–11, 30, 47–48, 94–96, 98, 105, 109, 129, 256; as ideal feminine, 11–12, 43, 57; image in advertising, 80–83, 95–96, 98–99, 282n52; image in commercial lu'aus, 22–25, 30, 101; physical requirements for, 134, 300n17; postwar demand for, 133–34; racial interpretation of, 47–48, 135–36; as tourist-greeters, 94–95, 102, 105

hula shows, commercial, 18–20, 100–1

identity categories: public display of bodies and, xiii–xiv, 9

imperialism: zoos as symbols of, 149, 157, 264

Japanese tourism: in Hawai'i, 12–13, 271n14

jellyfish, 167–68

Kaiulani (princess), 50

Kalākaua (king): revives hula, 32, 44, 47, 59, 62–63, 270n10

Kamehameha I (king), 92

Kamehele, Momi: on hula girl image, 10–11

"Keep It Hawai'i" campaign, 15–16, 29

killer whales, 146, 210–16; creativity among, 214, 308n28; subjectivity among, 212–14. *See also* Shamu

Kodak Hula Show, 18, 95, 102, 105–6, 174, 199
kumu hulas, 26–27, 31–32

Lalani Village, 99, 112; offers hula instruction, 113–14
Langton, Elinor, 100–2
live performance: in animal tourism, xv, 212–16; in Hawaiian tourism, 3–4, 6–7; hula as, xvii, 59, 60–61; in tourism, 268n10, xiii
live performances: and authenticity, 16–17
looking: museum mode of, 180–83; theatrical mode of, 188–89; "tourist gaze," xx–xxi, 37–38, 252–53, 268n13, 313n4
lu'aus, commercial, 14, 49, 100–1, 141; alternative shows, 29–30; authenticity in, xix–xx, 17, 95; economics of, 18; history of, 17; promote ohana, 20–21; sexual subtext of, 20–22, 25, 28

mainland: craze for Hawaiian music and dance on, 67–74, 76–78, 79, 82, 100–1, 160, 261, 287n39; live hula performances on, 59, 60, 94, 115–17, 289n7; racialized exotic entertainment on, 67–68
mammals: bodily similarity to humans, 166. See also animals
mammals, marine: human identification with, 168
Marine World Africa USA (California), xix, 176, 237, 251; animal-human relationship at, 194–97, 200–1; bird show at, 201–3, 239; elephant rides at, 194, 196; killer whale and dolphin show at, 146, 210–16, 225; lion and tiger show at, 203–7, 239, 308n24; magic act at, 208–9; Magic of Animals show at, 207–10, 240; non-animal performances at, 194; nonprofit research at, 193, 307n13; out-of-situ venue at, 190, 192–216; souvenirs at, 199–200; as theme park, 193
Merrie Monarch Hula Festival, 26, 31, 34, 135
Minnesota Zoological Park, 172–74
minstrel shows, 68, 288n53
missionaries: suppress hula and surfing, 61–62, 124, 270n1, 270n10, 281n42
Monterey Bay Aquarium (California), 170, 172, 176, 193, 206, 248; design and construction of, 177–79; as ecotourism, 177–78, 183; in-fake-situ venue at, 177–86, 190; jellyfish exhibit at, 167–68; kelp forest exhibit, 177–81; photography at, 182–83; reproductive behavior at, 184–86
Mossman, Pualani, 111–13
museums, 169–70

National Geographic: perpetuates stereotypes, 85–88, 113
nationalism: and colonialism, 69
Native Hawaiian, as distinguished from "Hawaiian native," 5
native, ideal: image of, xxii, 4–8, 40, 43–44, 48–50
nativization: of Caucasian women, 80–82
nature and naturalism, 269n17, 301n6; in animal tourism, 147–49, 190–91, 237–38, 250; as authenticity, xiv, xvi, xix–xx, 22, 149, 178, 190, 204, 251; commodification of, 148–49, 220–22, 235, 254; and feminism, 5, 48; and public display of bodies, 239–40, 251–52
nostalgia: in tourism, 199, 254, 313n11

ohana, 20–21
Our Islands and Their People, as Seen with Camera and Pencil (1899), 49–50, 69

Paka, Toots, 67, 70–71, 115, 288n54
Panama-Pacific Exposition (1915): hula performances at, 59, 61, 66, 160
Pan-American Exposition (1901): animal and cultural displays at, 144–45; hula performances at, 144
Paradise Cove Luau, 273n33
Paradise of the Pacific, 100, 104
people tourism. See cultural tourism
photography: in animal tourism, 183; and presentation of primitivism, 40–43, 47, 49–50, 59; in tourism, 37, 41, 48, 100, 102–5, 279n30, 280n36, 291n18
physical foundationalism, 266, 267n1, xiv
picture postcards: as tourist trophies, 43–44, 47–48, 59, 280n39
Polynesian Cultural Center (Hawai'i), 171, 174, 199
Polynesian look, 104
primitivism, 269n17, 278n15, 296n73; photographic presentation on, 40–43, 47,

49–50; regenerative powers of, 4–5, 7–8, 11–12, 39, 80, 302n7; in Social Darwinism, 38–40, 63; "soft," 11–12, 50, 68, 84–85, 97, 258

race: and body, 38–39, 87–88; and culture, 7, 12, 30, 118–19, 124, xiv, xx, xxiii
racism, scientific, 53–56, 63, 117–19
reconstructed ethnicity, 268n8
reindeer herding, 262–63
Reiplinger, Leila, 107–8, 293n27
Ridpath, John Clark, 55–56
Royal Hawaiian Girls Glee Club, 16, 106–7, 292n22
Royal Hawaiian Hotel (Waikiki), 88–94, 99, 107, 109

San Diego Zoo, 154–55, 159–60, 162; Gorilla Tropics exhibit, 164–65, 170–71
Sea World (San Diego), xxiii–xxiv, 172, 176, 242, 309n4; accidents and injuries at, 241; aesthetics of display at, 218, 223–24, 227, 230–31; animal-human relationship at, 217, 226–30, 242, 245; audience participation at, 226; Baby Shamu Celebration show, 224–34, 245–47, 256–57; conservation as theme at, 235–36, 243; corporate sponsorship at, 221–22; economics of, 219, 221; educational and entertainment goals of, 168–69, 231, 233, 245–46, 312n42; family as theme at, 217–18, 220, 225, 234–36, 239, 241, 249, 312n40; history of shows at, 242–45; necessity of breeding program at, 235–36; new show development, 246–48; nonprofit research at, 221, 231–32; Penguin Encounter, 219, 221; Pirates of Pinniped show, 240, 246; species borders at, 234–35, 237; subtext of danger at, 241–42; trainer-whale communication at, 228–30, 232–33; training methods at, 238–39, 241; visitor demographics at, 220; "Whale Ballet," 227–31, 255
Seaside Hotel (Waikiki): pageant at, 290n36
Shamu, xxiii–xxiv, 216, 237; commodification of, 222–23, 247; and gender avoid-
ance, 248–49, 312n43; as star performer, 217, 219, 223, 247; as symbol of whale conservation, 243; See also killer whales
shimmy, 72, 74
Social Darwinism: primitivism in, 38–40, 63
soldiers: as tourists, 131–32
Song of the Islands (film), 111–12
spectacle: function of, xvi
"staged authenticity," xix
Steer, Doveline "Tootsie" Notley, 102–6, 109, 117, 292n21
Steichen, Edward, 102–3
subjectivity: public display of bodies and, xiii
surfing, 122, 297n9, 298n20; missionary suppression of, 124

tourism: action and movement in, 252–53; in American Southwest, 52, 283n64; bodily difference as basis of, xiii–xiv, xvi, xxi–xxiii, 135–36, 183; economics of, xvii; ethnography in, 37–38; in Europe, xvi; live performance in, xiii, xv; nostalgia in, 199, 254, 313n11; photography in, 37, 41, 48, 100, 102–5, 279n30, 280n36, 291n18; research methods in, 258–59, xvii–xxiv; as search for the "natural," 145. See also animal tourism; cultural tourism
Twain, Mark: on Hawai'i, 6, 269n9

Ukeke, Ioane, 46–47
United States: overthrows Hawaiian monarchy, 31–33, 35–36, 50

venues: gradation of in animal tourism, 166, 168–69, 174; in-fake-situ, 177–86, 190, 305n51; in-situ, 186–92; out-of-situ, 190, 192–216, 235
viewing. See looking

Waikiki: as center of Hawaiian tourism, 13–14, 40, 88–89, 277n14
Wayburn, Ned, 72–73
Wild Animal Park (San Diego), 171–72
Wilson, Jennie, 62–64, 66, 69, 82, 144
Winchell, Alexander: and scientific racism, 53–54
World War II: Hawaiian tourist industry in, 131–32

Ziegfeld showgirls, 69, 77, 288n54
zoo design, 306n52; bars and shackles
    model, 160–61; evolution of, 150, 158,
    265; habitat model, 163–65; landscape
    immersion model, 164–65; naturalist
    model, 162–63; theatricalization in,
    161–62, 304n32
zoos: animal movement and behavior in,
    172–73, 305n38; authentic specimens
in, xix; compared to animal shows,
    150–52; criticism of, 155–56; estab-
    lishment of, 148–49; history of, 154–
    55, 157–60; as imperialist symbols,
    149, 157, 264; international breeding
    programs in, 255, 303n12, 313n11;
    social function of, xxiii, 264. See also
    animal parks and shows